2000 SUP

CORPORATE CONTROLLER'S
HANDBOOK OF
FINANCIAL MANAGEMENT

SECOND EDITION

Joel G. Siegel, Ph.D., CPA
Jae K. Shim, Ph.D.
Nicky A. Dauber, MS, CPA

PRENTICE HALL

Library of Congress Cataloging-in-Publication Data

(Revised for Suppl.)
Shim, Jae K.
    Corporate controller's handbook of financial management / Jae K.
    Shim, Joel G. Siegel, Nicky A. Dauber.—2nd ed.
       p.   cm.
    Siegel's name appears first on the earlier edition.
    Includes Index.
    1. Corporations—Finance.   2. Managerial accounting.   I. Siegel,
    Joel G.   II. Dauber, Nicky A.   III. Title.
    HG4026.S486   1997   97-17048
    658.15—dc21   CIP
    ISBN 0-13-021241-5

© 2000 by Prentice Hall, Inc.

Printed in the United States of America

10 9 8 7 6 5 4 3 2 1

This publication is designed to provide accurate and authoritative information in regard to the subject matter covered. It is sold with the understanding that the publisher is not engaged in rendering legal, accounting, or other professional service. If legal advice or other expert assistance is required, the services of a competent professional person should be sought.
—From the Declaration of Principles jointly adopted by a Committee of the American Bar Association and a Committee of Publishers and Associations

ISBN 0-13-021241-5

PRENTICE HALL
Paramus, NJ 07652

On the World Wide Web at http://www.phdirect.com

WHAT THIS SUPPLEMENT WILL DO FOR YOU

This supplement updates the main volume of *Corporate Controller's Handbook of Financial Management, Second Edition.* It includes current developments in financial management, accounting, and taxes. These developments take the form of recent trends in finance, new technology or software applications, and new authoritative accounting requirements. The following are some of the areas which have been updated:

- New pronouncements of the Financial Accounting Standards Board in the areas of earnings per share, segmental reporting, stock compensation plans, impairment of assets including loans, asset transfers, capital structure, and comprehensive income.
- Updates to leases, pensions, accounting for income taxes, and divestitures.
- Environmental reporting and disclosures.
- Updates for new tax laws affecting business decisions.
- Expansion of various tax areas such as corporate liquidation.
- Electronic funds transfer.

The following are new chapters which take into account recent developments and/or provide for more comprehensive coverage of corporate finance:

- Information Security and Data Protection
- What Financial Managers Must Know About Artificial Intelligence, Expert Systems, and Neural Networks
- Business Law
- Accounting for Multinational Operations
- Total Quality Management (TQM) and Quality Costs

- Risk Management and Analysis
- Reengineering and Outsourcing the Business
- Forecasting and Financial Planning
- Financial and Earnings Forecasting
- Cash Flow Forecasting
- Interest Rate Forecasting
- Forecasting Foreign Exchange Rates
- Evaluation of Forecasts
- Forecasting Tools and Software
- The Use of Computer Software in Managerial Accounting
- Corporate Valuations
- Management Analysis of Operations
- Economic Indicators
- Legal and Regulatory Environment of the Firm
- Financial Derivative Products and Financial Reengineering
- Going Public—About an Initial Public Offering (IPO)
- Venture Capital Financing

Like the main volume, the contents of this supplement are clear, concise and to the point. Use the cumulative Index at the back of this work to locate topics covered in this work or the main volume. Use the two works as your handy "how to" reference tool.

SUPPLEMENT CONTENTS

INFORMATION SECURITY AND DATA PROTECTION*

MANAGING COMPUTER SECURITY

Security concerns have heightened in recent years including computer-related data errors, thefts, burglaries, fires, and sabotage. The increased use of networked computers, including the Internet, intranets, and the extranets, has had a profound effect on computer security. The nature of the computing environment has changed significantly. The greatest advantage of remote access via networks is convenience. This convenience, however, makes the system more vulnerable to loss. As the number of points from which the computer can be accessed increases, so does the threat of attack. More caution is clearly needed to counter such threats.

The first step in managing computer security is to identify the resources that need to be protected. For example, the resource to be protected might be CPU cycles or computer time. This is unlikely to be the objective of most attackers or hackers. Frequently, hackers are interested in obtaining access to private or confidential information. Sometime, the organization may not even consider the information to be "valuable" to anyone else and may not be willing to take security precautions. This is a serious mistake. Hackers often steal or destroy data or information simply because it is there! Other hackers may delete or destroy files in an attempt to cover their illegal

---

*This chapter was authored by Anique Qureshi, Ph.D., CPA, CIA, Associate Professor of Accounting and Information Systems at Queens College.

activity. This leads to just one conclusion. A casual attitude towards computer security is never justified.

The second step in managing computer security is to determine against whom you want to protect your system? The security needs of a military computer system are likely to be significantly different from the security needs of a corporation. Are you trying to protect your computer system from teenagers "playing around" or corporate spies or industrial espionage?

The third step in managing computer security is balancing the costs and benefits of various security safeguards. In other words, how much are you willing to spend on security? Clearly, it is prudent to spend more on protecting resources that are of greater value to the organization. The cost of security safeguards include not only the direct cost of the safeguards, such as equipment and installation costs, but also indirect costs such as employee morale and productivity. It is important to recognize that increasing security typically results in reduced convenience. Employees for example, may resent the inconvenience that results from implementing security safeguards. Too much security can be just as detrimental as too little security; a balance must be maintained.

The last step in managing computer security is contingency planning. Assuming that security is violated, how do you recover? What are the data backup policies? What are the legal consequences? What will be the financial impact? A risk analysis should be performed in planning computer security policies and financial support. Computer security risks fall into one of three major categories: destruction, modification, and disclosure. Each of these may be further classified into intentional, unintentional and environmental attacks. The threat comes from computer criminals and disgruntled employees who intend to defraud, sabotage, and "hack". It also comes from computer users who are careless or negligent. Lastly, the threat comes from the environment; an organization must protect itself from disasters such as fire, flood, and earthquakes. An effective security plan must consider all three types of threats: intentional attacks, unintentional attacks, and environmental attacks. What is the company's degree of risk exposure? Insurance policies should be taken out to cover such risks as theft, fraud, intentional destruction, and forgery. Business interruption insurance covers lost profits during downtime.

COMPUTER SYSTEM FAILURES

A computer system can fail for several reasons, including:

- operator mistakes
- user mistakes

- malicious acts
- hardware malfunction
- software bugs
- environmental factors, such as lightning, fire, earthquake, or power outage

When discussing computer reliability, it is useful to distinguish between *errors, failures* and *faults* in a computer system. An error occurs when there is a deviation from expectations. Some errors are acceptable because they can be overcome, others are not. An unacceptable error is a failure. If the failure can have serious consequences, it is considered a critical failure. A fault is a condition that results in a failure.

System reliability is distinct from system security. Security is designed to protect against intentional misuse and does not consider malfunction. Improving one factor often enhances the other factor. Both factors need to be considered in managing risk.

ESTABLISHING A SECURITY POLICY

Every organization should have a security policy that defines the limits of acceptable behavior and the organization's response to violations of such behavior. Its purpose is to assign accountability and delegate authority across the organization. The security policy will naturally differ from organization to organization, based on its own unique needs. For example:

- There may be an edict barring the playing of computer games on corporate computers.
- There may be a policy against visiting adult web sites on the Internet using corporate Internet accounts or computers.
- Some organizations may wish to restrict the use of a specific protocol because it cannot be administered securely.
- Employees may be prohibited from taking copies of certain corporate data out of office premises.
- There may be a policy prohibiting use of pirated software.

The security policy should not only define acceptable behavior, but it should also contain the organization's response to violations. How will the violators be reprimanded? Will the organization reprimand violators inside the organization differently from violators outside the organization? What type of civil or criminal actions might be taken against violators?

The security policy should be a broad statement that guides individuals and departments in achieving certain goals. The specific actions needed to realize the goals are contained in supporting standards rather than in the policy document. The security policy should be concise and to the point, generally not exceeding ten pages. It should be easy to understand. Its focus should be on emphasizing the role of individuals and departments in achieving the objectives. It is not the purpose of the security policy to educate or train individuals. Such an objective is better served through training seminars.

The background for developing a security policy should be discussed. It should explain the purpose of security, including why data integrity must be maintained. The importance of maintaining confidentiality and privacy of information resources should be emphasized. The continuous availability of information is important for the organization and any interruption can have serious financial consequences.

Employees should understand computer security is everyone's responsibility. The scope of the computer security policy should encompass all locations of the company and all of its subsidiaries. Security is only as strong as its weakest link and therefore the same set of standards should be used throughout the organization. This means that the standards should be flexible enough so they can be used in a wide variety of circumstances and conditions, yet they should provide consistency and quality across the organization.

The security policies apply to all computer facilities and the data they contain, including standalone computers, Internet and intranet sites, local area networks (LANS), and wide area networks (WANS). All forms of electronic communication, including email and fax and data transmissions are covered by the security policy. Other printed material, such as documentation and technical specifications, should be included in the security policy.

Computer security should be viewed as a means to an end and not an end itself. Computer security is an integral component of an organization's overall risk management strategy. The responsibilities of various departments and individuals should be identified in the security policy. The policy established should be evaluated on a periodic basis to incorporate changes in technology or circumstances. The authority for issuing and amending the security policy should rest with a committee such as the Information Technology Management Committee. This committee should be responsible for determining when circumstances justify departure from the policy; all exemptions and exceptions should be approved by the committee.

Active participation by individuals and departments is needed for a security policy to succeed. It is well established that individuals are more likely to accept the security policy if they have had input during its creation. The real benefit of participation is that employees or departments will make a positive contribution to the policy by imparting their knowledge. Senior management's support and cooperation is critical in implementing the policy.

The relationship between the computer security policy and other corporate policies should be described. For example, the computer security policy should be used in conjunction with the firm's policies for:

- the internal control structure
- contingency plans, including business resumption planning
- privacy and confidentiality
- compliance with local and federal laws and regulations

A process should be in place to ensure compliance with laws and regulations. Privacy and confidentiality issues have a serious effect on computer security. Increased governmental regulation should be expected in the future. The legal department should assist department heads in complying with laws and regulations.

The Information Systems department's and its security personnel's responsibilities should be defined in the security policy document. These responsibilities include:

- ensuring that security personnel have the training and skill needed to perform duties required by the security policy
- provide computer security assistance to other departments
- be responsible for all computer networks and communications
- providing systems development methodology for security needs
- be responsible for all cryptographic methods and keys
- provide and manage virus detection software for networked and stand-alone computers
- be responsible for acquiring hardware or operating systems that are not currently part of the organization's architecture
- authorizing the use of the network, including the Internet and Intranet
- review, evaluate and approve all contracts with third parties concerning information systems

For personal computer systems, additional precautions are needed and should be addressed in the security policy. Some points to consider include:

- all original data should be backed up on a periodic basis
- personal computers connected to a network may be a source of viruses; virus detection software should always be used, especially before copying data or programs on to the network

- confidentiality and privacy of data may be compromised
- certain types of confidential or important data should never be stored on a local hard drive; instead such data should be stored on the network, or on floppy or compact disks or removable hard drive so that it may be removed and stored in a secure place
- standards should be established for remote access
- personal computers should not be directly connected to the Internet since the Internet is a source of virus infections and hackers may be able to gain access through it; Internet access should be only through the company's Internet server which is capable of protecting itself

PHYSICAL SECURITY AND DATA SECURITY

Physical and data security considerations are equally important. An effective security system should prevent a security breach. However, if in spite of proper protection, a system is successfully attacked, the system should create an audit trail to allow prompt investigation.

Unauthorized access to the computer facilities should be restricted and sensing and surveillance devices should be installed. Computer environment, including heating, cooling, dehumidifying, ventilating, lighting, and power should be protected. Appropriate care must be taken to protect the plant from harm and accidents and disasters such as fire and floods. Adequate emergency lighting should be available for safe evacuation in case of fire or other disaster. Consideration must be given to loss or damage to computer equipment and peripherals. Media, such as disks, tapes, and output should be protected. User manuals for equipment and software must be protected to maintain continuity of proper operations. Surge protectors should be used to protect the computer system against power line disturbances. Of course, the organization must consider loss of or injury to its personnel.

The layout of computer facilities is important in planning for computer security as well as achieving cost savings. As computers become smaller, they can be housed in smaller areas and this changes the way facilities are designed and planned. For example, it is no longer necessary to have raised floors in the computer room. If wiring is a concern, cables can generally be along the walls. If flooding is a concern, aluminum channels or I-beams can be used to raise components and cabinets. Cabling costs can be saved by placing the network equipment inside, next to the processing equipment. Smaller components may be stacked vertically to conserve floor space and reduce cable costs.

The computer facilities should be housed in a building's core area near wire distribution centers. Care should be taken to avoid a location where water or steam pipes cross either vertically or horizontally. The room should be sealed to keep out smoke and dust.

Only one door should be used for access into a secured area. The door should be self-closing and it should not have a hold-open feature. A combination or programmable lock may be sufficient. An alarm system should be installed. There should not be any direct access from public places.

WIRES AND CABLES

With the increase in distributed computing, it is even more essential to protect the wiring system. Wires and cables are generally made of either copper or optical fiber. Fiber optics offer significant performance and security advantages. However, they cost more to install. Still, if considerable data needs to be transferred, the cost disadvantage of fiber optics rapidly diminishes.

Cables and wires are fragile. They can be easily damaged. It is not possible to repair damaged wires; they must be replaced. The electrical properties of cables may also be affected and the data may become unreliable. Alternate paths should be provided for cables linking important or critical paths.

Fiber optics offer better security protection. It is relatively easy for someone to wire tap copper lines if they can obtain access anywhere along its length. Such wiretaps are very difficult to detect. In contrast, it is difficult and expensive to wire tap fiber optics. Moreover, normal operations are disturbed in a fiber optics tap and can therefore be detected more easily. Even with fiber optics, it is possible that a skilled individual with proper equipment can tap the system undetected. Fiber optics provide a deterrent, but should not be viewed as being perfectly secure. Of course, the best way to protect sensitive data is to use some type of encryption.

Fiber optics are not affected by electrical or magnetic interference. Copper wires have to be shielded with cabling and grounded metal conduits have to be provided.

The ends of all fiber optic cables must be microscopically smooth. They have to be exactly aligned and positioned. This requires the use of expensive special equipment and highly trained personnel.

Data wiring should be certified by a knowledgeable and experienced individual. Such an individual should

- perform a visual inspection
- check that each cable is connected correctly
- check that there are no crossed pairs
- use a reflectometer to detect if there are any constrictions, bad terminations, or external interference

Purchase orders for any wiring should specify:

- who will certify the wiring

- what equipment will be used to test the wiring
- what standards will be followed

DESTROYING DATA

Once data is no longer needed, it must be properly destroyed. Information on magnetic media is typically "destroyed" by over-writing on it. While the information appears to have been destroyed, there are many subtleties to consider. For example, if the new file is shorter than the old file, information may remain on the magnetic media beyond the new file's end-of-file marker. Any information beyond the end-of-file can be easily retrieved. A safe method is to overwrite the entire media. However, overwriting the entire media is time consuming and other methods, such as degaussing should be used. Degaussers are essentially bulk erasure devices that when used within their specification provide adequate protection.

Formatting a disk does not safely destroy all information. It is important to note that magnet media may retain a latent image of the preceding bit value after the write insertion of a new bit value. This occurs due to the inability to completely saturate the magnetization. While normal read/write operations are not affected by this limitation, it does pose a security threat and anyone with sophisticated equipment could exploit it.

For papers and other soft materials, such as microfiche and floppy disks, it is possible to shred them. Some shredders cut in straight lines or strips. Others offer cross-cutting and particle producing. Some shredders disintegrate by repeatedly cutting and passing the material through a fine screen. Shredders may also grind the material and make pulp out of it.

Burning is still another way to destroy sensitive data that is no longer needed. As with shredding, burning means that the storage media can no longer be reused. Even when burning, one needs to exercise caution. It is possible, for example, to retrieve printed information using special techniques from intact paper ashes, even though the information may no longer be visible to the human eye.

ENVIRONMENTAL CONSIDERATIONS

Computer facilities are susceptible to damage from environmental factors. Fire security is especially important and is discussed in detail in a separate section. Other important factors include heat, water, humidity, dust, and power failure.

- *Heat* and high temperature can cause electronic components to fail. Air conditioning is generally essential for reliable operation. Simple precautions should be taken to ensure that air vents are not blocked and that the air is allowed to circulate freely. Backup power should be available for air conditioning if the computer system will be used even if the primary power fails.

- *Water* is an obvious enemy of computer hardware. Floods, rain, sprinkler system, burst pipes, etc. could do significant damage. Attention should be given to the design of routing water pipes and the location of the computer facilities. Instead of a traditional sprinkler system, consider using an alternate fire-extinguishing agent that will not damage the hardware.

- *Humidity* at either extreme is harmful to the hardware. High humidity is likely to lead to condensation which can corrode metal contacts or cause electrical shorts. Low humidity is likely to permit the buildup of static electricity. Computer facilities should either be housed on bare floors or floors covered with anti-static carpeting. Humidity should be continuously monitored and kept at acceptable levels.

- *Dust,* dirt, and other foreign particles can ruin computer hardware. For example, dust can interfere with proper reading and writing on magnetic media. Personnel should not be permitted to eat or drink near the computer facilities. Air should be filtered and filters replaced at appropriate intervals.

- *Power failure* can render all equipment useless. Brownouts and black-outs are the most visible sign of power failure. However, voltage spikes are much more common and can cause serious damage. Spikes may be produced by lightening and such spikes may either damage equipment or randomly alter or destroy the data. A drop in line voltage can also lead to malfunction of computer equipment and peripherals. Voltage regulators and line conditioners should be used if electrical fluctuations occur. Use of uninterruptible power supplies should be considered.

MAINTENANCE AND PREVENTIVE CARE

Facilities should be protected against adverse effects of the weather and other environmental factors. Regular maintenance can help prevent unexpected downtime. Diagnostic programs should be run as part of regular maintenance. Maintenance logs should be kept. Recurring problems can be quickly identified by scanning the logs. The maintenance log should include, at a minimum, the following information:

- Description of equipment serviced
- Company Identification number of equipment serviced
- Date of service

- Services performed, including the results of diagnostic tests
- A note indicating whether the service was scheduled or unexpected

Computer areas should be properly cleaned and dusted. Eating, drinking, and smoking should be prohibited in computer areas. Personnel should be trained in proper handling of computer equipment and peripherals. Personnel should be trained in proper handling of magnetic media and CD-ROMS. For example, magnetic media should not be placed on top of or near telephones, radios, and other electric equipment. Or, labels should be prepared prior to placing them on disk; many untrained personnel will affix the label to the disk and then write on the label using a ball point pen.

Computers and peripheral equipment should be cleaned on a regular basis using cleaning products recommended by the manufacturer. Electrical equipment should never be sprayed directly with cleaning liquids. Keyboard surfaces should be cleaned with a damp cloth and vacuumed using special computer vacuums.

Magnetic media devices, especially the read/write heads and transport rollers, should be cleaned using commercially available cleaning products for such purpose. Dust, smoke, finger prints, and grease can build up on recording surfaces and lead to crashes or permanent damage to the equipment and magnetic media. Printers may need to be cleaned to remove fibers, dust particles and lint.

Simple precautions, such as using static-resistant dust covers protect the computer equipment and peripherals. Such covers should only be used when the equipment is not in use. Otherwise, the equipment may overheat and be damaged.

WATER ALERT SYSTEMS

Water alert systems should be installed in locations where water might damage computer equipment. Generally, water alert systems should be installed in the basement or in floors above the computer systems. Water sensing systems are especially useful in protecting electrical cables under the floor. Water sensors should be installed within suspended ceilings and inside water cooled computer cabinets and process cooling equipment. The water sensors should activate an alarm as well as some type of a drainage pump.

STATIC ELECTRICITY

Static electricity results from an excess or deficiency of electrons. An individual could easily become charged to several thousands of volts. While the current from electrostatic discharges is too low to harm humans, electronic equipment could easily be damaged.

Protective measures against electrostatic discharges include grounding, shielding, filtering and limiting voltage. Vinyl flooring is generally better than carpeting to avoid a build up of static electricity. Simple precautions can minimize the dangers from static electricity; these include:

- using anti-static spray
- grounding computer equipment
- using anti-static floor and table mats
- maintaining the proper level of humidity

HUMIDITY CONTROL

Humidity should be tightly controlled and maintained at an optimal level. When the air is too dry, static electricity is generated. When humidity is too high, generally at levels above 80% relative humidity, there may be problems with electric connections, as a process similar to electroplating starts to occur. Silver particles start to migrate from connectors on to copper circuits, thus destroying electrical efficiency. A similar process affects the gold particles used to bond chips to circuit boards. Generally, an optimal relative humidity level is about 40 to 60 percent.

FIRE PROTECTION

According to insurance companies, fire is the most frequent cause of damage to computer centers. No combustible material should be allowed in the computer room. This means special care should be taken in selecting office furniture. Waste receptacles should not be in the computer room. Instead, waste receptacles should be located nearby, just outside the computer room.

Fire detectors should be installed in appropriate locations and connected to an automatic fire alarm system. Fire detectors sense either changes in temperature or thermal combustion and its byproducts. Fire detectors may be actuated by smoke, heat, or flame.

Smoke actuated devices provide early warning for slowly developing fires. Smoke detectors should be installed in air conditioning and ventilating systems. Smoke detectors typically rely upon either *photoelectric* devices or *radioactive* devices.

- *Photoelectric Smoke Detectors:* Variations in the intensity of light cause changes in electric current in the photoelectric cell. Photoelectric smoke detectors are generally of three types:
    - *Area-sampling* photoelectric devices draw in air from the area to be protected, and if smoke is present in the sampled air, the light reflections on the photoelectric cell will trigger the alarm.

- *Beam* photoelectric devices focus a beam of light on to a photo-electric cell from across the protected area. The smoke causes an obstruction in the light and activates the alarm.
- *Spot* photoelectric devices, unlike beam photoelectric devices, contain the light source and the receiver in one unit. Light is not projected across the protected area. Instead, smoke entering the detector causes the light to reflect onto the photoelectric cell hence activating the alarm.

- *Radioactive Smoke Detectors:* These smoke detectors contain a minute amount of radioactive material in a special housing. Smoke interacts with the radioactive material and changes its ionization which activates the alarm. Radioactive detectors are most commonly the *spot* type. The response time for radioactive smoke detectors is affected by several variables, including the stratification of air currents and the nature of products of combustion. Generally, the heavier the particles resulting from combustion, the longer it takes for them to reach the ceiling where the smoke detectors are usually attached and the longer the response time of the unit. Incidentally, the danger from radiation from such detectors is minimal and all detectors must meet or exceed government standards.

Heat actuated detectors can be of two types. The first type will activate the alarm when the temperature reaches a fixed predetermined value. The second type of detector senses the rate of change in temperature. Typically when the rate of rise in temperature exceeds 15° to 20° F, the alarm is activated.

For highly combustible areas, the rate of rise temperature detectors are recommended due to their faster response time. However, fixed temperature detectors tend to be more reliable and are not as prone to false alarms. Some heat actuated detectors contain both types of sensors.

Heat actuated detectors are available in *line* or *spot* coverage styles. Line type detectors usually rely upon heat sensitive cables or a pneumatic tube. Spot type detectors are placed at fixed intervals in each zone.

Flame actuated detectors are of two types: Flame-Radiation-Frequency and Flame-Energy. Radiation-frequency detectors sense the flame related flicker caused by combustion. These sensors tend to be expensive and are therefore suitable under limited circumstances. Flame-energy detectors sense the infrared energy of the flame. These are also expensive and tend to be suitable for protecting expensive equipment. The principal advantage of flame-energy detectors is their super-fast detection of infrared energy of flame. These detectors are also capable of producing enough voltage to trigger the release of an extinguishing agent.

Different types of fires require different types of extinguishing agents. Using the wrong extinguishing agent can do more harm than good.

- Fires involving ordinary *combustible materials,* such as wood, paper, plastics, and fabric can be safely extinguished using water or tri-class (ABC) dry chemical.
- Fires involving *flammable liquids and gases,* such as oil, grease, gasoline, and paint can generally be safely extinguished using tri-class (ABC) and dry chemical, Halon, FM-200, and carbon dioxide.
- Fires involving live electrical equipment should be extinguished using a non-conducting extinguishing agent, such as tri-class (ABC), regular dry chemical, Halon, or carbon dioxide.

Most computer room fires will be electrical, caused by overheating of wire insulation or other components. Smoke from an electrical fire may be toxic and it should be avoided in even small quantities. Generally electrical fires cannot be extinguished till the heat source is eliminated.

A power panel with circuit breakers for the major pieces of equipment should be placed at an easily accessible location, preferably inside the computer room. The circuits should be clearly labeled so equipment can be shut down quickly in an emergency. Redundant devices should be on separate circuits. There should be one emergency switch to shut down everything in the event of a fire.

In the event of a major fire or explosion, the only concern should be the safety of human life. Computer equipment and wiring is likely to be destroyed by the intense heat. Backup copies of disks and data should always be kept at off-site locations. Not only will this help when attempting to recover from a fire, but it can also help during the fire since the personnel will not attempt to save backup data by risking their lives.

Halon has the potential of depleting the ozone layer. While Halon is still in use, an international agreement was reached to stop its manufacture as of January 1, 1994. FM-200 is now available as a Halon substitute. Both Halon and FM-200 systems tend to be expensive and governmental approval is often required. These systems are also not very effective against electrical fires. In an electrical fire, it is essential that the power be shut off because a fire extinguishing system will only suppress the fire till power is stopped.

Water sprinkler systems are simple and a relatively inexpensive protection against fire. Most new buildings are required by code to have a sprinkler system. Accidental activation of the sprinkler system can cause substantial damage and it may take a long time before normal operations are resumed. In an electrical fire, water may even intensify the fire and cause greater damage. Sensors should be installed to cut off electrical power before sprinklers are turned on. It should be possible to activate sprinkler heads individually to prevent damage to a wide area. There should be a shut-off valve inside the computer room so that water can be shut off when it is no longer needed. This will minimize damage in the event of accidental activation.

Carbon dioxide, Halon, and FM-200 extinguishers do not require any clean-up after discharge. However, carbon dioxide discharge can suffocate humans. Foam or dry chemicals can be hard to remove. Hand-held fire extinguishers should be mounted on walls. Self-contained breathing apparatus should also be mounted on the wall.

Quick removal of smoke should be a priority. Special fans and blowers should automatically be activated by the smoke or fire alarm.

If computer equipment starts smoking, the first step should be to cut off the equipment's electrical power. This is frequently sufficient and the fire will probably extinguish by itself. If there are visible signs of fire, or if you can feel the heat, an appropriate fire extinguisher should be used. Carbon dioxide extinguishers are often recommended for microcomputer related fires. When using a carbon dioxide extinguisher, do not spray the extinguishing agent directly onto the surface glass surface of the CRT, since it will lead to a sudden drop in temperature and shatter the glass.

Personnel should be trained for fire emergency. Company policy should state exactly what action should be taken in the event of a fire or smoke alarm. Personnel should be strictly forbidden from risking injury or loss of life to protect data or equipment.

The following steps can reduce the damage caused by fire, and in the process, reduce insurance premiums:

- Safes for storage of documents should have a minimum four-hour fire rating.

- Walls, floors, and ceilings of computer facilities should have a minimum two-hour fire rating.

- Fire alarm should ring simultaneously at the computer facility and the nearest fire department. In addition, fire alarm signals should be located where prompt response is assured.

- Vaults used for storing backup tapes and records should be located in a separate building at a sufficient distance.

- Smoke and ionization detection systems should be installed throughout the ceiling of the computer facilities. Water detection systems should be installed under the floor of computer facilities.

- Halon, FM-200 or a similar fire extinguishing system should be installed throughout the computer facilities. Automatic sprinkler systems can be used in the supply and support areas. In case of destruction, there should be a disaster recovery plan.

- Building code and fire marshal regulations must be adhered to strictly.

CONTROLLING ACCESS

Access controls guard against improper use of equipment, data files, and software. The oldest method of restricting physical access is by using some type of lock. Locks may be classified into two types: preset locks and programmable locks.

With preset locks, it is not possible to change the access requirements short of physically modifying the locking mechanism. Programmable locks may be either mechanical or electronic. The combination on the programmable locks can be more easily changed as security needs change. A basic problem with such locks is that the entry codes are frequently easy to obtain by an observer. Some types of electronic locks overcome this problem by using a touch screen that randomly varies the digit locations for each user and by restricting directional visibility to basically perpendicular angle.

Security guards and security dogs are another way to restrict access in a wide variety of situations. The physical presence of guards and dogs serve as a deterrent. In the event of a problem, the guard is able to respond appropriately. Preemployment screening and bonding are essential when hiring security guards. Certain states, such as New York, have mandatory training requirements for guards.

Limitations with such methods are well known. Guards can become easily bored with the routine work and may not fulfill their duties as expected. It is easy for someone to forge identification and be let in by a guard. Another limitation of guards is that they may not be informed and through procedural error allow unauthorized individuals access to restricted areas.

Guard dogs are also very useful and act as deterrents. Dogs have excellent hearing and a keen sense of smell. Guard dogs can be trained to "hold" intruders till security personnel arrive. One disadvantage of security dogs is that additional liability insurance must be purchased. Training and maintaining dogs is expensive. Finally, guard dogs generally cannot differentiate between authorized and unauthorized visitors.

Still, security is enhanced if guards and/or dogs patrol the facilities frequently and at random intervals. The use of guards and dogs contribute to psychological deterrence. It lets a potential attacker or intruder know that he might be caught. A determined attacker, of course, is unlikely to be deterred by psychological deterrents and security should always be supplemented through other means.

Something as simple as lights greatly enhances security. Lights improve the ability of security personnel to carry out surveillance. Lights also deter intruders from entering the facilities. Lights may either be left on all the time, on timer control, on ambient control, activated by motion detectors, or manually operated.

Computer and terminal access controls include:

- *Automatic Shut-Off:* The system signs off the user if the user fails to sign off after the transmission is completed.
- *Call Back:* A phone call is made to the terminal site to verify the user's identity before access is granted to the system.
- *Time Lock:* Access is denied to the system during specified hours, such as after normal business hours.

Within the plant, areas containing sensitive data should be accessible only to authorized personnel. These areas, including the computer room should have only a single entry door which can be operated by an appropriate encoded magnetic-strip ID card. Physical controls include having a librarian keeping a log. A lockout should occur with repeated errors. Logs should automatically be kept of the ID number, time of access, and function performed. Further, data dictionary software provides an automated log of access to software and file information. Intrusion detection devices such as cameras and motion detectors should be used to monitor sensitive and high-risk areas against unauthorized individuals.

Are controls being diligently followed over processing, maintaining records, and file or software modification? Each individual function (e.g., accounts receivable, payroll) may have its own password so that users have access to limited areas of their authorization. The computer can keep an internal record of the date and time each file was last updated. This internal record should be compared against the log. The hours to access "key" microcomputer files should be limited. This prevents unauthorized access after normal working hours. Files should be expressed in terms of different levels of confidentiality and security such as top secret, confidential, internal use only, and unrestricted. Confidential information should not be displayed on the screen. To control access to sensitive data, there should be a mapping of access requirements to the system components. Access rights should be based on job function, and there should exist an appropriate segregation of duties. Temporary employees should be restricted to a specific project, activity, system, and time period.

HARDWARE SECURITY

Computer hardware has improved in reliability and speed tremendously. These technological advances have not always had a beneficial impact on computer security and data integrity. Most integrated circuit chips on hardware equipment appear to be inscrutable to a lay person. There are hundreds of thousands of transistors on a small semi-conductor. Still, it is possible for a bug to be planted into electronic equipment and it may be very difficult to detect. Several techniques may be used to seal the hardware against tampering.

Records should always be kept of hardware failure and computer down times. Regular maintenance should be performed on periodic intervals and records should be maintained. If computer equipment frequently requires servicing, personnel might be tempted to bypass controls and take shortcuts. The possibility of human errors therefore increases considerably. Records should be analyzed to determine if an unfavorable trend is observed for the downtime or if the equipment frequently requires unscheduled service.

Records should be kept of all computer equipment and peripherals. The hardware inventory logs should contain at least the following information:

- a description of the hardware
- manufacturer's name
- model number
- serial number
- company identification number
- date of purchase
- name, address and phone number of stores from where the item was purchased
- date warranty expires
- the department or location where the hardware equipment will be used
- the name and title of responsible individual
- the department name
- the signature of the responsible individual or department head
- if the equipment is taken off premises, the date and time the equipment is checked out, and the date and time the equipment is returned, along with the signature of the authorized individual

The hardware inventory logs should be stored in a secure location. A copy of the logs should also be stored in an off-site location. All hardware equipment should be etched or engraved with the company name, address, telephone number, manufacturer's serial number, and company's identification number. To prevent theft, locking devices should be used to secure computer equipment and peripherals to desktops, etc.

SOFTWARE SECURITY

Segregation of duties is essential in protecting computer programs during the development and modification stages. When software is developed and maintained internally, changes are frequently made to meet changing requirements. The source code is generally stored in the source library, while the compiled and executable version of the program is stored in the production library. The source library is under the control of the programmer, whereas the production library should be under the control of computer operations or a similar entity that does not have programming responsibilities.

All programs and data files should have date and time stamps, including both production and test versions. Date and time stamps make it possible to determine the current version of the program in the event of an error or malfunction.

The transfer from test status to production status of programs should be accompanied by authorization by management. The quality assurance department should do a formal review before releasing the final production version.

Whenever modification to a program are required, the reasons and requirement must be documented to prevent fraudulent modification. Requests for modification should include at least the following information:

- description of change
- why is the change needed
- how will the change benefit the department or organization
- name, title, and department of individual requesting the change
- approval of department head or another authorized individual
- date of request
- date of desired completion (time by which modifications should be made)

Once the Information Systems department receives the request to modify a program, it should determine:

- the priority of modification and the estimated date of completion
- the cost to make the modifications and the charge to the user department

The user department should be notified of the budgeted cost and the estimated completion time. The user department should approve the estimated completion time and budgeted cost.

A control sequence number should be assigned to the modification. Change requests should be tracked from the time they are initially submitted to the time the changes are completed. A programmer or analyst should be assigned the primary responsibility for making the changes. A determination should be made as to how the modified program will be tested. This generally requires the cooperation of the user department.

Small changes or emergency modifications should be possible without going through the full formal control procedure. Such changes should be carefully monitored. At a minimum, the following information about the modification should be documented:

- description of modification
- approval of the user department
- review of source code changes by a supervisor

PASSWORD SECURITY

Passwords are subject to attack using several techniques. One technique, which relies on brute force, was frequently used in the past. All possible combinations were tried till the attacker was successful. To prevent such unauthorized access, the number of unsuccessful tries should be limited. Moreover, unsuccessful login attempts should be audited.

A hacker is often able to guess the correct password because many individuals select words or strings of characters that have a logical association with the individual under attack. For example, individuals often select the following easily guessable words:

- spouse's or girlfriend's/boyfriend's name
- children's name
- pet's name
- social security number
- phone number
- own birthday, or a loved one's birthday
- words like "password" or "code"

It is best to select a password that does not appear in a dictionary. It is also a good idea to include numbers or characters, such as a question mark or a percentage or a dollar sign in the password.

It is sometimes possible for a hacker to edit the password file and insert bogus user names and passwords. To protect against such an attack, the password file should be properly protected against unauthorized writing.

The passwords should always be kept in an encrypted format. Otherwise, it is easy for someone to scan for commands that are followed by passwords, such as logins, to capture passwords either from storage, or as they are being typed or routed in transit.

A serious design flaw can sometimes result in the creation of a "universal password." Such a password satisfies the requirements of the login program without the hacker actually knowing the true and correct password. In one case, for example, a hacker could enter an overly long password. The overly long password would end up overwriting the actual password, thus allowing the hacker unauthorized access.

AUDIT TRAIL

Audit trails contain adequate information regarding any additions, deletions or modifications to the system. They provide evidence concerning transactions. An effective audit trail allows the data to be retrieved and certified. Audit trails will give information regarding the date and time of the transaction, who processed it, and at which terminal.

Computer-related risks affect the company's internal control structure and thereby affect the company's audibility. Electronic Data Interchange (EDI) systems are on-line systems where computers automatically perform transactions such as order processing and generating invoices. Although this can reduce costs, it can adversely affect a company's audibility because of the lessened audit trail.

The AICPA has issued control techniques to ensure the integrity of an EDI system. The AICPA recommends controls over accuracy and completeness at the application level of an EDI system to include: checks on performance to determine compliance with industry standards, checks on sequence numbering for transactions, reporting irregularities on a timely basis, verifying adequacy of audit trails, and checking of embedded headers and trailers at interchange, functional group and transaction set level. Control techniques at the environmental level include: review quality assurance of vendor software, segregation of duties, ensuring that software is virus-free, procuring an audit report from the vendor's auditors, and evidence of testing. To ensure that all the EDI transactions are authorized, the AICPA provides these authorization controls: operator identification code, operator profile, trading partner identifier, maintenance of user access variables, and regular changing of passwords.

NETWORK SECURITY

Computer networks play a dominant role in transmitting information within and between firms. A network is simply a set of computers (or terminals) interconnected by transmission paths. These paths usually take the form of telephone lines; however, other media, such as wireless and infrared transmission, radio waves, and satellite are possible. The network serves one purpose: exchange of data between the computers and/or terminals. The considerations in selecting a network medium are:

- Technical reliability
- Type of business involved
- The number of individuals who will need to access or update accounting data simultaneously
- Physical layout of existing equipment
- The frequency of updating
- Number of micros involved
- Compatibility
- Cost
- Geographic dispersion
- Type of network operating software available and support
- Availability of application software
- Expandability in adding additional workstations
- Restriction to PCs (or can cheaper terminals be used?)
- Ease of access in sharing equipment and data
- Need to access disparate equipment like other networks and main frames
- Processing needs
- Speed
- Data storage ability
- Maintenance
- Noise
- Connectivity mechanism
- Capability of network to conduct tasks without corrupting data moving through it

Backup capability is an especially important feature of networks. For instance, if one computer fails, another computer in the network can take over the load. This might be critical in certain industries such as financial institutions.

Data flows between computers in a network use one of three methods.

- Simplex transmission is in one direction only. An example of simplex transmission is radio or television transmission. Simplex transmission is rare in computer networks due to the one-way nature of data transmission.
- Half-duplex transmission is found in many systems. In a half-duplex system, information can flow in both directions. However, it is not possible for the information to flow in both directions simultaneously. In

other words, once a query is transmitted from one device, it must wait for a response to come back.

- A full-duplex system can transmit information in both directions simultaneously; it does not have the intervening stop-and-wait aspect of half-duplex systems. For high throughput and fast response time, full-duplex transmission is frequently used in computer applications.

Data switching equipment is used to route data through the network to its final destinations. For instance, data switching equipment is used to route data around failed or busy devices or channels.

THE SECURITY ADMINISTRATOR

The size and needs of the company will dictate the size of the security administration department. This department is responsible for the planning and execution of a computer security system. They make sure that the information system's data is reliable and accurate. The security administrator should possess a high level of computer technical knowledge as well as having management skills and a general understanding of the organization's internal control structure.

A security administrator should interact with other departments to learn of the organization's changing needs and be able to maintain and update the security system efficiently. The security administrator is responsible for enacting and customizing policies and standards for the organization based on specific needs. Checks on performance and monitoring of staff should be done to ensure that these policies and standards are being complied with. In developing these policies and procedures, as well as the overall information computer security system, the security administrator must perform a risk assessment.

CONTINGENCY PLANNING

Many man-made and natural disasters can strike a company. A disaster may be defined as anything that will create a significant disruption in an organization's ongoing activities for a considerable period of time. Proper contingency planning can help minimize the loss of human life, data, and capital. Preparedness is the key to recovering from disaster.

The primary focus of computer security should always be to take preventive action, not corrective action. Nonetheless, it is impossible to prevent every security breach. It is virtually impossible to anticipate every problem and even if a problem can be anticipated, the cost/benefit criterion may not justify taking any preventive action. Sometimes the precautionary measures may prove to be ineffective because of human or other error. Productivity and efficiency may also be sacrificed if precautionary measures are taken too far.

Emergency procedures should be established for the each type of disaster that may occur. For each type of disaster, a determination should be made about the effect of the disaster on data processing and business operations. In other words, how long will the service be interrupted and at what level would the company be able to operate.

LEGAL ISSUES

Legal issues are important in considering computer security. Substantial liability may be incurred by a company for violating legal requirements. Sometimes management may even be held personally liable.

Privacy and other personal rights may be violated due to lack of computer security. The public is very concerned about privacy and this is reflected in the ever increasing legal requirements and regulations.

The general rule at the federal level is that all government files are open to the public unless there is a specific reason, enacted by the legislature, to keep the information secret. The Freedom of Information Act makes it possible for citizens and organizations to obtain access to most government records.

The federal government has passed legislation to protect private information. The Financial Privacy Act of 1978 was one step in this direction. The 1987 Computer Security Act showed further commitment toward computer security. This act states that, "improving the security and privacy of sensitive information in the federal computer systems is in the public interest." This by no means should be limited to the federal government. The private sector also has to play their part in ensuring that private information is kept private. The public is very concerned about information getting into the wrong hands, and is concerned when asked to provide sensitive information.

With the 1987 Computer Security Act, the *National Institute Of Standards and Technology* (NIST) was assigned the responsibility to develop cost-effective standards and guidelines to protect sensitive information in the federal databases. The Act also created a twelve-member panel to help NIST in performing their role. The private sector and the corporate world as a whole should not rely entirely on the government to take the steps towards improving security. To ensure that the individual privacy is protected, the following needs to be considered.

- Classification of Information
- Accuracy
- Protection of Sensitive Information

Once the information is determined to be sensitive, it should be verified for accuracy before being put into a database. Such information should be afforded the necessary protection to keep it confidential and adequately protected.

The Federal Privacy Act applies to records maintained by certain branches of the federal government. When contracting with agencies subject to the Federal Privacy Act, the act applies to the contract. The contractor and its employees are subject to the same requirements. Agency and criminal penalties may result from failure to comply.

Most states have Public Records Acts similar to the federal Freedom of Information Act. Several states have also enacted Fair Information Practices Acts which regulate the information state agencies, and those contracting with the state agencies, may maintain about individuals.

At the international level, especially in Europe, there are laws covering both governmental and private records. Computerized data banks must be licensed and certain laws apply only to them. Rules concerning disclosure are generally strict. There are frequently prohibitions against transferring information across national boundaries.

Email communications may be a source of claims of privacy violations. The organization should have a clearly stated policy about using computer systems for personal communications. For example, the organization may want to clearly state that the organization has the right to read all email communications. Courts have generally held that the employer has the right to view employee email; still it is prudent to have a written policy on this issue.

The Computer Fraud and Abuse Act is a federal law making it a crime for any unauthorized use (copying, damaging, obtaining database information, etc.) of computer hardware or software across state lines. Offenders can be sentenced to up to 20 years in prison and fined up to $100,000.

The Foreign Corrupt Practices Act (FCPA) of 1977 applies to all companies whose securities are registered or filed under the Securities Exchange Act of 1934. This Act requires the companies to keep accurate accounting records and to maintain a system of internal control. In other words, this Act mandates that these companies maintain appropriate computer security of its accounting records. Criminal prosecution can result from willful violations.

Computer security related legal liability may be incurred in a variety of situations, ranging from programming errors to civil or criminal violations. A company is expected to exercise due care and violation of the due care standard could result in liability. Consider a computer program that was originally designed properly, bug-free and operating effectively. However, due to lack of appropriate security, an attacker is able to place a logic bomb that causes the system to crash at a specified time in the future. The organization and its senior management may be held personally liable for any damages arising from the crash of the program. Such damages may include, for example, loss in market price of stock shares. Human life might also be affected if the program that crashed performed critical functions, such as a medical diagnosis system.

Consider another scenario where the attacker is able to modify the database of a construction company. Assume the database contains information about the strength of various types of steel that will be used to construct an office building. Engineers may rely upon the modified database and use steel that is not strong enough. The building eventually collapses and human life is lost. The liability that may result in such circumstances is likely to be astronomical, especially if it is proven that appropriate security could have prevented modification of the database.

The National Institute of Standards and Technology (NIST) has published several national standards in the area of computer security. Some of the standards include:

- password usage
- physical security and risk management
- data encryption standards
- user authentication techniques
- contingency planning
- electrical power for computer facilities
- key management
- automated password generators
- digital signature standard

The Department of Defense (DOD) also publishes booklets known as the Rainbow Series to help developers, evaluators and users of trusted systems. It includes information on networks, databases, and other problems with distributed computer systems. Similar guidelines are issued by other countries. The governments of Britain, Netherlands, France, and Germany have jointly issued detailed Information Technology Security Evaluation Criteria (ITSEC).

It is prudent to consider using these standards in managing computer security. In a lawsuit alleging breach of security, failure to follow these standards may be used by plaintiffs to prove negligence, even if your organization was not required to follow these standards.

WHAT FINANCIAL MANAGERS MUST KNOW ABOUT ARTIFICIAL INTELLIGENCE, EXPERT SYSTEMS AND NEURAL NETWORKS*

The corporate financial manager must have an understanding of artificial intelligence (AI) applications, including expert systems and neural networks, that are used by companies to properly conduct his/her accounting, audit, and tax services. The purpose of this chapter is to aid the corporate accountant's understanding of artificial intelligence software and to make practical use of it.

HOW ARTIFICIAL INTELLIGENCE AND EXPERT SYSTEMS WORK

Artificial intelligence (AI) applies human reasoning techniques to computers. The software and hardware simulate the human mind. Expert systems and neural networks are an application of artificial intelligence. Expert systems are computer programs reflecting the behavior characteristics of the

---

*This chapter was coauthored by Anique Qureshi, Ph.D., CPA, CIA, Associate Professor of Accounting and Information Systems at Queens College, CUNY.

hired experts (specialists) in the field. The computer software is designed to emulate how the experts would solve clearly defined problems and make decisions. Expert systems provide advice using its "knowledge and experience base," and are designed to ask for additional information in a reasoning process to help solve a business problem such as how to reduce a specific cost (e.g., manufacturing cost, service cost), improve productivity, and improve quality. It is also appropriate for unstructured situations and tasks, is interactive, and uses judgment.

Expert systems may be used by production and service managers to analyze and solve their "narrowly" defined, specific problems. The expert system interacts with users in formulating optimal decisions. The expert system continually asks users for sufficient facts until it is ready to make the decision and will also provide the user with its logic in making that decision. The expert system continues to learn more and more as it receives additional input information and answers to its questions so it is able to make better decisions for the CPA. There are six key components in an expert system consisting of:

1. Knowledge data base of rules, cases, and criteria in making decisions. Examples are auditing rules issued by the AICPA, FASB financial accounting requirements, SEC releases, tax laws, and industry standards.

2. Domain database of appropriate information in the specific area of study.

3. Database management system to control the input and management of the above two databases.

4. Inference engine (processing system) comprising of the interface strategies and controls used by experts in using and manipulating the first two databases. It is the brain of the expert system. It receives the request from the user interface and conducts reasoning in the knowledge base. The inference engine aids in problem solving such as by processing and scheduling rules. It asks for additional data from the user, makes assumptions about the information, and formulates conclusions and recommendations. The inference engine may also determine the extent to which a recommendation is qualified and, in the case of multiple solutions, rank them. The inference engine can aid in many "key" decisions such as financial accounting approaches, and asset and debt management.

5. User interface are the explanatory features, on-line help, debugging tools, etc. aiding the user in understanding and properly using the expert system.

6. Knowledge acquisition facility enables interactive processing between the user and the system, and enables the system to obtain the relevant knowledge and experience of the human expert.

Table 1 lists commercially available artificial intelligence software products, describes their major features, gives their prices, and provides developers' names, addresses, and telephone numbers.

AVAILABLE EXPERT SYSTEM SHELLS AND PRODUCTS

A "shell" is a collection of software packages and tools used to design, develop, implement, and maintain expert systems for a company. There are different forms of shells including generic ones (already prepared off-the-shelf ones in final form) or customized ones (requiring special preparation). The user enters the relevant information and parameters, and the expert system generates the solution to the problem or situation.

Expert system development tools are also available to simplify, facilitate, and quicken the establishment or enhancement of an expert system. The development aids include if-then rules, interfaces with data bases, tools to better make use of spreadsheets and programming languages, and tools to generate the interface engine.

The user is asked a series of logical sequential questions by the expert system. Follow-up questions are based on the answers to the prior questions. After all queries have been asked and answered, conclusions are drawn by the expert system.

Practical Business Applications

Expert systems are being used by many companies in transaction processing, determining adequacy of expense provisions and revenue sources, scheduling, routing, financial analysis, competitive analysis, report preparation and analysis, accounting, auditing, risk evaluation, appraisal of internal controls, credit authorization, claim authorization and processing, strategic planning, strategic marketing, configuration and organizing, manufacturing and capacity planning, repairs and maintenance, resource planning, data communications, and security.

Applications in Accounting

Expert systems can consistently apply standards in preparing accounts and conducting audits. Expert systems are ideal for internal accounting systems such as in the areas of appraising cash flows, accounts receivable, and accounts payable. Expert systems provide decision models for planning and control. It may also be used to schedule production and do inventory analysis.

In accounting, expert systems can aid in maintaining ledger accounts, analyzing revenue (by price, volume, mix of product/service), payroll

Table 1   Artifical Intelligence Software (In alphabetical order by developer's name)

Vendor	Product and Descriptions
1. AI Ware 3659 Green Road Beachwood, Ohio 44122 Tel: (216) 514-9700 Fax: (216) 514-9030 e-mail: ai-sales@aiware.com	a. BUSINESS ADVISOR is a complete business forecasting and optimization decision support system providing solutions to business problems. It utilizes neural networks and fuzzy logic in modeling. The software tells the businessperson how to achieve his objectives for any one or combination of outputs. It identifies the values of the inputs or outputs to achieve an optimized condition based upon the established constraints and priorities. Relationship patterns are uncovered between business and operating strategies. Business models relate to how you perform your tasks, procedures, policies, and operating conditions and uncovers their effects on profitability and operating strategies. The business models enable you to anticipate problems so you can make more efficient use of resources and time. It aids in selecting financial opportunities and lowering risk. It improves decision making by simulating decision choices and appraising each one based on your goals and constraints. Sensitivity analysis identifies relative effects of varying inputs. There are multi-objective features and import/export capabilities with Microsoft Office. BUSINESS ADVISOR has many business applications including fraud detection, risk management, forecasting revenue and costs (including by area or product), budgeting, bankruptcy prediction, valuing securities, estimating production yields, maximizing rate of return on investments, resource requirement planning, lost sales evaluation, demographic appraisal, fault detection in machinery and products, quality appraisal and improvement, site selection, optimizing product/service mix, analyzing survey responses, predicting personnel staffing levels, and pinpoints sales prospects. *Price: $9,995* b. PROCESS ADVISOR is a process monitoring and optimization system. It develops process models considering such factors as manufacturing costs, age of machinery, raw material levels, operating characteristics, quality levels, and by-products. The relationship modeling helps predict quality upstream, formulate improved operating strategies, anticipate preventive maintenance needs, and make better use of equipment. The system aids in feature-based design and manufacturing problem solving, lowering costs, reducing environmental impact, improving efficiency and productivity, improving preventive maintenance scheduling, and reducing energy consumption. PROCESS ADVISOR can detect data patterns preceding mechanical problems and by so doing avoiding unnecessary repairs and downtime. The user may run process simulations for pilot projects or new production strategies. Process models help understand relationships and trade-offs, and to anticipate changes. *Price: $10,000*

What Financial Managers Must Know . . .

c. CAD/CHEM is a formulation modeling and multi-objective optimization system using intuitive neural networks, sensitivity analysis, data clustering, and fuzzy objective functions. It allows you to choose between design trade-offs and sees the effects of changes in formulation. CAD/CHEM aids in making better products faster, shortens the time to market, integrates the product development process, improves processing efficiency and performance, and optimizes product quality at lower costs. It improves responsiveness to customer demands, costs, resource constraints, and environmental regulations.
Price: $4,995

ACQUIRE is an expert-based knowledge acquisition system having business applications.
Price: $995

NEURO GENETIC AND TRADE is neural network software to discover and model the hidden and important relationships in such data as sales figures, financial market information, marketing research survey information, customer profiles, and demographic information. The software can detect fraud for auditor attention, evaluate processing costs and quality, forecast product/service demand, explain consumer behavior, aid in materials management, prepare forecasts, and optimize investment management.
Price: 16 inputs $295, 32 inputs $395, 64 inputs $595, etc.

BRAIN MAKER PROFESSIONAL is neural network simulation software used in solving business problems, financial forecasts of revenue and costs, conducts manufacturing analysis (e.g., safety, production yields, quality), evaluates processing costs, analyzes loan applications, performs investment analysis, predicts currency prices, predicts corporate bond ratings, predicts the S&P 500 index, appraises real estate, and performs marketing analysis. The software shows the relationship between two types of data, recognizes patterns, performs sensitivity analysis, and generates financial indicators.
Price: $795

2. Acquired Intelligence Inc.
1095 McKenzie Ave., Ste 205
Victoria, British Columbia
Canada V8P 2L5
Tel: (250) 479-8646
Fax: (205) 479-0764
WWW Site:
(http://vvv.com/ai/acquire/price.htm).

3. BioCamp Systems, Inc.
4018 148th Ave., N.E.
Redmond, Washington, 98052
Tel: (800) 716-6770
Fax: (425) 869-6850
WWW Site:
(http://www.bio-comp.com).

4. California Scientific Software
10024 Newton Road
Nevada City, California 95959
Tel: (800) 248-8112
Fax: (916) 478-9041
e-mail: sales@calsci.com
WWW Site:
(http://www.calsci.com).

Table 1 Artifical Intelligence Software (*continued*)

Vendor	Product and Descriptions
5. Elf Software Company 210 W. 101st Street New York, N.Y. 10025 Tel: (212) 316-9078	ACCESS ELF is query interface software to access Microsoft data bases. *Price: $49*
6. HNC Software Inc. 5930 Cornerstone Court West San Diego, CA 92121-3728 Tel: (619) 546-8877 Fax: (619) 452-6524	a. FALCON PAYMENT CARD FRAUD DETECTION SYSTEM is neural network software that audits and detects fraudulent transactions by customer accounts of card issuing banks and other financial institutions. The system monitors and scores card transactions for fraud. Different score thresholds may be assigned to different sets of credit cards. Fraud analysts use the system to identify potential problems (e.g., fraudulent transactions in a particular ZIP code). The neural network-based models determine the probability of fraud with each transaction by comparing it to the cardholder's known purchase patterns. If necessary, the transaction may be blocked. *Price: Varies from $250,000–$600,000 per installation plus $.02 per account per month.* b. CAPSTONE APPLICATION DECISION PROCESSING SYSTEM is software that books new payment card accounts both efficiently and profitably. It is capable of processing approximately 10,000 applications per hour with real-time credit pulls and high-speed network access for analyst workstations. The system is an intelligent neural network with user-definable rules, and the ability to incorporate traditional score cards. It has an expert rules base letting each issuer specify the decision flow that meets its needs. The system identifies and refuses poor applications. *Price: Varies from $250,000–$600,000 per installation plus $.02 per account per month.*
7. IBM Department AC 297, AS/400 P.O. Box 16848 Atlanta, Georgia 30321-0848 Tel: (800) IBM-CALL Fax: (800) 2 IBM-FAX	a. KNOWLEDGE TOOL FOR AS/400 is a troubleshooting knowledge expert base application software performing risk analysis and capacity planning. *Price: Ranging from $685 to $4,205 depending on product group purchased.* b. THE INTEGRATED REASONING SHELL FOR OS/2 RELEASE 3 is an expert system shell providing for the development of knowledge-based applications in a workstation environment. It facilitates the management of performance and growth of the business. The shell creates application solutions to business problems, improves operations, and has productivity enhancements. The shell enables large

amounts of data to be analyzed quickly, resulting in recommendations to increase the responsiveness of the company.

Price: Basic License $8,190 (one-time charge with receipt of enhancements at no additional charge). Additional License $7,875.

c. NEURAL NETWORK UTILITY PRODUCT FAMILY neural network software used to identify financial trends and patterns to guide business operations. It discovers relationships in large sets of financial data to make predictions about new data. It incorporates rules and guidelines for better decision making. The software can detect fraud, assess (score) risk, perform portfolio management, and test products.

Price: Ranging from $495 to $4,995 depending on product group purchased.

a. LEVEL 5 OBJECT PROFESSIONAL RELEASE 3.0 FOR MICROSOFT WINDOWS is a knowledge based expert system development shell tool. OBJECT is the basis to build an intelligent business support system. It shows object relationships within the company and can represent complex data structures (e.g, linked lists, queues, and trees). It aids in budgeting, scheduling of resources and activities, planning shipments, making manufacturing decisions, and managing inventory (including on-line stock reporting). OBJECT allows for targeted trouble shooting and corrective action to solve business problems. It allows for the tracking and following up of opportunities from initial identification to final contract. Different types of reports may be created using various selection criteria in extracting information from a database. It increases corporate productivity at all levels of the organization. Motorola uses this system.

Price: $2,995

b. LEVEL 5 QUEST is a fuzzy logic base query environment search engine. It scores and ranks results of a search based on their relevance and importance to the business. QUEST provides an array of match methods using artificial intelligence.

Price: $96

MULTI LOGIC EXSYS PROFESSIONAL is a knowledge based neural network development tool used in business for financial modeling and allocation of corporate resources to improve the rate of return.

Price: $2,900

8. Level 5 Research
1335 Gateway Drive, Ste. 2005
Melbourne, Florida 32901
Tel: (800) 444-4303
Tel: (407) 729-6004
Fax: (407) 727-7615
WWW site:
(http://www.L5R.com).

9. Multi Logic
Suite 312
1720 Louisiana Blvd., N.E.
Albuquerque, New Mexico 87110
Tel: (800) 676-8356
Fax (800) 256-8356
WWW Site: (http://www.exsysinfo.com/products/prices.htm).

Table 1 Artifical Intelligence Software *(continued)*

Vendor	Product and Descriptions
10. Neural Ware Inc. 202 Park West Drive Pittsburgh, Pennsylvania 15275 Tel: (800) 635-2442 Fax: (412) 787-8220 WWW Site: (http://www.neuralware.com).	NEURAL WORKS PREDICT is a neural network product used to solve prediction, modeling, and classification problems. It can be used to identify credit card and insurance fraud, loan analysis, investment analysis, financial forecasting, database marketing including market segmentation, process modeling, risk management, evaluating new customers for credit purposes, predicting future warranty claims, industrial inspection and quality control, and to rate bonds. It has features of sensitivity analysis, case-based reasoning, and explanation. *Price: $1,995*
11. Scientific Consultant Services 20 Stagecoach Road Selden, New York 11784 Tel: (516) 696-3333.	a. N-TRAIN: NEURAL NETWORK SYSTEM is neural network software aiding in solving business problems such as evaluating credit risk, trading in the financial markets, controlling manufacturing processes, and detecting and analyzing signals of difficulties arising. The system is useful in business decision making, pattern recognition of accounts, classification of financial data, and forecasting. Acceptable error measurements may be selected. *Price: $747 (Four add-on modules are available at an additional total cost of $299).* b. TRADING SYSTEMS FOR TRADE STATION are rule-based expert systems for investment portfolio selection. It includes technical analysis of stocks and commodities. It incorporates consideration of foreign currencies. *Price: $240 per system (minimum order of 5 systems for $1,200).* c. THE TRADING SIMULTOR is a simulation of trading accounts and portfolios. It can simulate systems over multiple contracts. *Price: $495*
12. Sterling Wentworth Corp. 57 West 200 South, Suite 500 Salt Lake City, Utah 84101 Tel: (800) 752-6637 Fax: (801) 355-9792.	EXPERT SERIES is expert system software used in personal financial planning for clients. It performs portfolio management, data management, risk analysis and management, estate planning, retirement planning, income tax planning, and cash flow analysis. *Price: $1,695*

CAPITAL INVESTMENT EXPERT SYSTEM is artificial intelligence software that analyzes, manages, and reports on the purchase of machinery and equipment. It includes cash flow analysis, legal aspects (e.g., conformity to environmental regulations), and installation considerations. The expert system recommends if the fixed assets should be bought or not and why. The software results in buying only financially and operationally feasible equipment.
Price: Varies with application.

MODEL WARE is an expert system involving predictive modeling. It can be used in credit analysis, forecasting stock and commodity prices, detecting faults in the manufacturing process, simulation, quality control, customer retention analysis, financial securities trading analysis, and production and inventory planning. It includes graphic capabilities. MODEL WARE can predict up to 150 variables simultaneously.
Price: $595

13. Texas Instruments Corp.
P. O. Box 660246
Mail Station 8671
Dallas, Texas 75266
Tel: (800) 336-5236
Tel: (972) 575-3542

14. Triant Technologies
20 Townsite Road, 2nd Floor
Nanainmo, British Columbia
Canada V9S 5T7
Tel: (800) 663-8611
Fax: (604) 754-2388
e-mail: mail@triant.com

preparation, analysis of costs (e.g., by category and type), financial statement analysis, preparing working papers, compliance reporting, financial statement preparation, preparing budgets and forecasts, aging customer accounts, analysis of mergers and acquisitions, converting between accounting bases (e.g., accrual to cash), and deciding whether to refinance debt.

In auditing, expert systems can reduce the cost and time in making audit decisions and in improving the audit plan and substantive testing. Expert systems can select or develop an audit program, conduct an analytical review, analyze data and evidence, select a sample and test data, determine an error rate, schedule and monitor the audit engagement, uncover illogical relationships between accounts, and evaluate assets (e.g., cash) and liabilities (e.g., accounts payable). Expert systems aid in evaluating internal control, appraising risk, determining disclosure compliance, analyzing auditor behavior, determine whether the accounting and reporting system continue to satisfy the intended objectives, and select appropriate audit software and hardware for a particular task.

In managerial accounting, expert systems may be used in making capital budgeting decisions such as selecting the right asset, the appropriate mix of products and services, keeping or selling a business segment, and buying or leasing. CASH VALUE is a commercially available expert system to assist in capital projects planning.

Expert systems may be used by multinational companies in assessing accounting, reporting and legal requirements. The expert system provides the multinational company with advice on appropriate account types, reporting formats, and conditions in the global financial market affecting the company's financial condition.

In practice management, the firm may use expert systems to make decisions about staff development and assignment. In taxation, expert systems are used in tax preparation and planning, and facilitating compliance with tax rules and procedures. Expert systems may be used in compliance matters such as in determining if the company is in compliance with government regulatory or legal requirements so as to avoid any associated penalties.

Applications to Finance

Expert systems aid in the assessment of risk (e.g., theft, fire, flood). An insurance company may use expert systems to evaluate and process claims, including highlighting suspicious claims for possible fraud. Expert systems help to optimally allocate resources based on such factors as cost, time, availability, risk and demand patterns.

In investment analysis, expert systems can recommend appropriate investments considering such factors as the state of the economy, risk preferences, tax rate, liquidity, dividend payout, capital appreciation (depreciation), desired portfolio mix, constraints and limitations, and SEC requirements. Expert systems help in timing buys and sells of securities because it integrates and considers real-time multiple external/internal data sources. A "rule generator" expert system identifies information patterns and generates trading recommendations. A "critic" expert system analyzes and reviews system recommended trades along with the explanations of doing so. An expert system can provide 24 hours trading programs so as to optimally take advantage of domestic and international market conditions such as changes in foreign exchange rates. Expert systems can recommend appropriate hedges to reduce the company's investment risk such as futures contracts, options and swaps (e.g., interest rate, currency). Expert systems will also identify and appraise arbitrage opportunities and trigger transactions.

The expert system will make a decision whether to grant a loan and if so, how much credit should be extended. It will consider profitability, risk, economic conditions, and management's policy. The expert system may approve the loan subject to certain criteria, limitations, and restrictions. The expert system may decide on the appropriate interest rate, line of credit, repayment schedule, and collateral requirements. Existing questionable loans are also identified.

Applications to Marketing

Expert systems may be used in market planning and research, making strategic marketing decisions for both products and services, new product development and enhancement, warranty service planning, product features and options, goal formulation (price, volume, profit), determining marketing mix of products and services, return policy, advertising and promotion, deriving customer profiles, setting prices, establishing discount and credit terms, sales representation, deriving the best distribution channel system, product quality appraisal, and formulation of the best style and packaging. The knowledge base of the expert system includes market structure, customer characteristics, and competition.

Applications to Management

Expert systems are used in management information systems. They generate decision models to aid in planning and control.

Fuzzy Neural Networks

New developing technology in artificial intelligence software is neural networks which allow computers to learn from a database. This is a computer model that matches the functionality of the human brain. The system obtains positive or negative responses to output from the operator and stores that data for later use in making better decisions. Although this technology is in the developmental stage, it shows promise in risk analysis, forecasting, and uncovering fraud.

Many neural network software packages that are now available are ideal for business applications. Neural network software converts the order-taking computer into a "thinking" problem solver. This development allows computers to make some of the mundane decisions previously made by accountants such as deciding on the type of lease or the type of construction accounting method. Neural network software simulates human intelligence and learns from experience. For example, each occurrence that a neural network program makes the correct decision (predetermined by the human expert) on recognizing a sequential pattern of information, the programmer reinforces the program with a stored confirmation message. On the other hand, if there is an incorrect decision a negative message is reinforced. Thus, over time experimental knowledge is built in a subject.

Business applications of neural networks are many including working capital management, analyzing customer behavior patterns, credit assessment, scanning customer purchases, internal auditing, investment portfolio management and analysis, examining spending patterns, and bankruptcy prediction. Neural network technology has also been used to predict returns on bonds, predict interest rates on Treasury Bonds, predict stock market movement, and predict currency exchange rates. Neural networks can be used by a portfolio manager to identify non-performing or undervalued securities.

Processing. Artificial intelligence systems can use either serial processing or parallel processing. While a serial processing system makes only one decision at a time, parallel processing systems are capable of making several concurrent decisions. Expert systems utilize serial processing systems whereas neural networks utilize parallel processing systems.

An expert system processes a series of *if-then* rules, matching each *if* with the respective *then* rule, till a final result is achieved. This matching process is inherently sequential. Neural networks, in contrast, use parallel processing and are able to concurrently evaluate multiple inputs.

Applications. Neural networks are proving their worth in a wide variety of business applications, and saving their users time and money. Investment groups, for example, utilize neural networks for portfolio selection and to perform at least some of their technical analysis of financial markets. Other successful applications of neural networks include forecasting applications such as bankruptcy or going-concern predictions. Many banks have successfully used neural network systems to control credit card fraud by recognizing fraudulent activity based on past charge patterns.

Neural networks can be applied in situations where traditional techniques have not yielded satisfactory results. Neural networks are also ideal where a small improvement in modeling performance can have a significant effect on operational efficiency or profits. For example, small improvements in modeling performance can lead to significant savings in direct marketing applications. The response rate in direct marketing is typically quite low and using a neural network to analyze demographic data could improve the response rate by a few percentage points and significantly reduce costs.

CONCLUSION

Managers have to get more from less, often without all the resources. Artificial intelligence is a powerful emerging technology that can be used to efficiently process information to achieve greater knowledge and improved decision making. Neural networks, in particular, offer significant advantages over traditional expert systems. Neural networks are self-adapting and can learn from information to reveal hidden patterns and relationships in the data. Artificial intelligence can be used by organizations to utilize resources more effectively, and gain a valuable competitive edge.

BUSINESS LAW

CONTRACTS

While the corporate controller is not ordinarily trained in legal matters, he or she is often relied upon to recognize situations requiring the need for legal counsel. When contracts are drawn, the controller is often consulted on accounting and other business matters. The area of contracts therefore represents an area with which the controller needs some basic familiarity.

By definition, a contract is a legally enforceable agreement, and is governed by (1) Article 2 of the Uniform Commercial Code (UCC) if the contract pertains to the sale of tangible personal property (i.e., goods), and (2) common law if the subject matter covered by the contract is real estate, services or intangibles.

Types of Contracts

Essentially, there are nine types of contracts:

1. An *executory* contract is based on conditions that have not yet been fully performed by both parties to the contract.
2. An *executed* contract is created when both parties have fully performed the conditions required by the contract.
3. An *express* contract involves an agreement expressed in words, whether spoken or written.
4. An *implied* contract is a contract that is inferred as a result of the acts or conduct of the parties involved.
5. A *bilateral* contract arises when one promise is given in exchange for another.

6. A *unilateral* contract involves an offer of a promise and an act that is committed as a result of reliance on the promise.

7. A *quasi*-contract represents an obligation created by law in order to prevent unjust enrichment.

8. A *void* contract is a contract without any legal obligations on the part of each party.

9. A *voidable* contact is a contract that may be avoided or ratified by one or more of the parties.

Elements of Contracts

The four elements required for a contract are agreement, consideration, legality, and capacity of the parties.

Agreement involves an offer and acceptance. The terms of an offer must be definite and must demonstrate an intent to incur a legal obligation. To be valid, an offer must be communicated to the offeree by the offeror (or his or her agent) and is deemed to be effective when the offeree receives it. The offeree may accept an offer until it is terminated. In general, an offer will terminate if (1) the offer has expired (i.e., it is not accepted within the time specified or within a reasonable period of time, if no time is stipulated), (2) the offer is revoked at any time prior to acceptance, (3) the offer is rejected, (4) a counter-offer is made, (5) either party dies or becomes disabled, (6) the subject matter of the offer is destroyed, or (7) the subject matter of the offer subsequently becomes illegal. In connection with point "2," it should be noted that certain offers are irrevocable. An option contract, which is irrevocable, involves an offer supported by consideration; therefore, it cannot be withdrawn prior to the expiration of the stated period of time, or a reasonable period of time if no time is specified. A firm offer, which is also irrevocable, involves a merchant who makes a written offer to buy or sell goods and specifies that the offer will remain open for a specified period. Finally, in a unilateral contract, even though the act necessary to accept the offer has not been completed, performance has begun, and the offer becomes irrevocable.

Acceptance of the offer must be unequivocal. Accordingly, the offeree cannot alter or qualify the provisions of the offer. Acceptance may be effected by any reasonable means of communication, unless a specific means of acceptance is stipulated by the offeror. Acceptance is generally effective upon dispatch (e.g., when mailed).

As noted, consideration is a necessary element of a contract. As such, both parties to the contract must give consideration. For consideration to exist, there must be legal sufficiency (i.e., something of value) and a bargained-for exchange. It should be noted, however, that some types of transactions do not require consideration for enforcement. For example, promissory estoppel, also known as the doctrine of detrimental reliance, prevents the promisor from pleading lack of consideration for his or her promise where he or she has induced the promisee to make a substantial change of position in reliance thereon. In addition, no consideration is necessary in order to modify contracts for the sale of goods.

The subject matter of a contract must be legal. An agreement will be illegal and unenforceable when formation or performance of an agreement is criminal, tortious, or otherwise opposed to public policy. In these circumstances, the contract is void.

Capacity of the parties is also necessary for a contract to be valid. While a contract made by a minor is voidable at his or her election, it may be ratified upon reaching majority. Further, a contract made by a legally insane person is generally voidable. Where one has been legally declared insane, attempted contracts are void. Lastly, with respect to an intoxicated individual, a contract is voidable if the degree of intoxication was such that the individual did not realize he or she was entering into a contract.

The Statute of Frauds

Pursuant to the statute of frauds, to be enforceable, certain executory contracts must be in writing and signed by the party to be charged with performance. The written contract may be formal or informal and may be set forth in one or more documents, but must clearly indicate the parties, specify the subject matter and essential terms, and include the signature of the party against whom enforcement is sought. The contracts covered by the statute of frauds include, but are not limited to:

1. Contracts involving the sale of goods with a price of at least $500.
2. Contracts involving the sale of investment securities.
3. Contracts conveying an interest in real property.
4. Contracts that cannot be performed within one year after the contract is made.
5. Contracts of guaranty.

Needless to say, there are exceptions to the statute of frauds. For example, with respect to sales of real property, under the doctrine of part performance, an oral contract is enforceable if the buyer makes full or partial payment, and either (1) the buyer takes possession of the property (with the seller's approval), or (2) valuable and permanent improvements have been made to the property by the buyer. With respect to the sale of goods, an oral contract will fall outside the statute of frauds if the contract covers specially manufactured goods. A written contract is also unnecessary with respect to goods that have been accepted or for which payment has been made. Finally, it should be obvious that the statute of frauds in not applicable when a party admits in court that a contract was in fact made.

The Parol Evidence Rule

Any written or oral evidence that is not contained in the written contract is known as parol evidence. The parol evidence rule stipulates that no parol evidence of any prior or contemporaneous agreement will be allowed to change or otherwise modify any of the terms or provisions of an existing written agreement. The parol evidence rule, however, is sometimes inapplicable. For example, the rule does not apply (1) to contracts that are partly written and partly verbal, (2) to an obvious clerical or typographical error, or (3) when it is necessary to explain terms that are ambiguous.

Conclusion

The controller should be able to recognize when a contract exists. Accordingly, he or she must understand the basic elements of a contract. Further, the controller needs to be cognizant of the statute of frauds and the parol evidence rule. Not being a legal expert, the controller should contact the appropriate legal counsel if he or she perceives that (1) a contract has been breached, (2) a contract is not valid, or (3) a modification to a contract is being attempted.

SALES

Generally accepted accounting principles require that a sale be afforded accounting recognition upon its execution.

In general, the concepts of contract law are applicable to sales. It should be obvious that the seller is required to deliver the full agreed-upon quantity to the buyer. Unless otherwise stipulated, if a carrier is involved, the seller's delivery obligation depends on the pertinent shipment terms (i.e., F.O.B. shipping point or F.O.B. destination point). The place of delivery is deemed to be the seller's place of business, however, if no carrier is involved. The buyer is of course entitled to full delivery and has the right to reject delivery of a partial or excess quantity. Upon acceptance, however, the buyer will be responsible for those items accepted. In general, the buyer has the right to examine goods prior to accepting them or paying for them. However, with respect to Collect on Delivery (C.O.D.) sales, payment by the buyer is necessary before inspection. Said payment does not constitute acceptance and any nonconforming goods may be rejected.

Remedies for Breach

The various remedies for breach of a sales contract are dependent upon which party caused the breach.

Seller. If the buyer causes the breach, the seller may generally withhold delivery. If a down-payment was received by the seller, and a liquidating damages clause is not included in the contract, then the seller is entitled to keep the smaller of 20% of the purchase price or $500. The excess down-payment must therefor be returned to the buyer.

A breach on the part of the buyer also entitles the seller to stop delivery of goods in transit or in possession of a third party.

Further, the seller may reclaim goods if demand is made within ten days of receipt by an insolvent buyer.

In situations where the seller has attempted to deliver nonconforming goods, the seller has the right to notify the buyer of an intent to cure and deliver conforming goods within the time limits specified in the original contract.

With respect to manufactured goods, the seller is permitted to complete manufacture of unfinished goods, identify them to the contract, and sell them, or cease their manufacture and sell the remainder for scrap. In any event the seller is entitled to recover the difference between the contract and selling prices.

Finally, in certain instances, the seller may either cancel the contract or sue for the contract price and/or damages. Legal counsel should of course be consulted if a lawsuit is contemplated.

Buyer. If the seller effectuates the breach, the buyer may reject the goods if they are nonconforming. The seller must be given notice, and if the buyer is a merchant, the buyer is required to follow the seller's reasonable instructions pertaining to the rejected goods.

When goods are not in conformity with the contract, and the nonconformity decreases the value of the goods, the buyer may generally revoke acceptance.

Alternatively, the remedy of "cover" may be available. In situations where the buyer procures the same or similar goods from another vendor, the buyer may be entitled to recover the difference between the cost of cover and the contract price, increased by any incidental damages, but reduced by any expenses saved as a result of the seller's breach.

In lieu of suing for cover, the buyer may be entitled to sue for damages. In these instances, the measure of damages is the difference between the market price at the time the buyer learned of the breach and the contract price, increased by any incidental damages, but reduced by any expenses saved as a result of the seller's breach.

INVESTMENT SECURITIES

There are two types of investment securities; those that are "certificated," and those that are "uncertificated." Only certificated securities are negotiable.

To be certificated, an investment security must be registered to a specific party or be in bearer form. A registered security states the name of the party entitled to the security or the rights it represents. Accordingly, the issuer must maintain books to record its transfer.

To be a bona fide purchase of an investment security, the purchase must be made (1) for value, (2) in good faith, and (3) without notice of any adverse claim. Investment securities should be carefully safeguarded because stolen securities, that are properly endorsed, may actually be transferred to a bona fide purchaser who takes them free of the prior party's title claim.

The transfer of a certificated security to a purchaser for value carries with it the implied warranties that the transfer is effective and rightful, the security is genuine and has not been materially altered, and the transferor is unaware of any facts that might impair the security's validity.

Endorsement of a security, by itself, does not constitute a transfer; delivery of the security on which the endorsement appears must take place for a transfer to be consummated.

The controller should also be aware that the statute of frauds is applicable to contracts involving the sale of securities; accordingly, the contract must generally be in writing.

Sometimes, no matter how tight controls are, investment securities may be lost, stolen, or accidentally destroyed. In these instances, the owner is entitled to a replacement certificate provided that (1) a request for a replacement is made before the issuer becomes aware that the security has been transferred to a bona fide purchaser, (2) a sufficient indemnity bond is filed with the issuer, and (3) all reasonable requirements of the issuer are met.

EMPLOYMENT REGULATIONS

This chapter is intended to expand on the business law concepts briefly mentioned on pages 703 and 704 of the main text. An awareness of the provisions contained in this chapter will enable the controller to interface with responsible individuals in the personnel department.

The Federal Occupational and Safety Health Act (OSHA)

The Occupational and Health Administration of the Department of Labor is authorized to administer and enforce the Act. Their objective is to promote safety in the work environment.

The Act, while not applicable to federal, state, and local governments, applies to virtually all private employers.

Under the Act, a general duty is imposed on employers to furnish a work environment that is "free from recognized hazards that are causing or are likely to cause death or serious physical harm" to employees. It should be noted, however, that an employer's liability under the Act arises only where the employer actually knew or should have known of danger. In addition to complying with the general standards of the Act, employers must also comply with certain industry-specific OSHA standards.

Workplace inspections, which are conducted without prior notification, represent the Act's simple means of enforcing compliance. To be legal, however, inspections are generally subject to employer permission. Alternatively, where the government has probable cause, a search warrant may be secured.

Employers are subject to both civil and criminal penalties for violations of the Act's provisions. Civil penalties as high as $1,000 per violation may be imposed; a $10,000 penalty may be imposed for repeated violations. An employer deemed to be a willful violator may be fined up to $10,000 and/or imprisoned for up to six months.

Finally, it is illegal to fire an employee who reveals an OSHA violation.

The Federal Fair Labor Standards Act (FLSA)

FSLA requires that employers pay a minimum hourly wage; further, employers must generally pay an overtime rate equal to time-and-a-half for work in excess of 40 hours per week. The Act, however, exempts professionals, administrative employees, executives and outside sales workers from the minimum wage and overtime provisions.

In addition, the Act regulates the employment of children in nonagricultural positions. Under the Act, children under the age of 14 may generally not be employed. However, they may be employed for newspaper delivery, acting, and working for their parents. Children between the ages of 14 and 15 may be employed to a limited extent outside of school hours in non-hazardous work. Finally, a child who is either 16 or 17 years old may be employed to perform nonhazardous tasks.

The Equal Pay Act

The Equal Pay Act makes it illegal for an employer to discriminate on the basis of gender by paying different wages for substantially equal work. The Act does, however, permit payment of different wages based on seniority, merit, quantity or quality of work, or any other factor not relating to gender. Should an employer violate the Act, it may be directed to discontinue its illegal pay structure and it may be required to provide back pay to any injured employees.

The Civil Rights Act of 1964 (CRA)

CRA makes it illegal for an employer to discriminate on the basis of race, color, religion, gender, or national origin. The Act also prohibits sexual harassment but not discrimination based on sexual preference. The Act is applicable to entities that employ 15 or more employees for 20 weeks in the current or preceding year. After enactment, the Act was modified to include The *Pregnancy Discrimination Act Amendment* which forbids employment discrimination based on pregnancy, childbirth, or related medical conditions. It should be noted that employment discrimination based on gender, religion, and national origin (but not race) is allowable if the employer can show it to be a bona fide occupational qualification. Employment practices dependent on seniority systems and work-related merit are also permitted. Violations of CRA may entitle victims to up to two years' back pay in additional to recovery of reasonable legal fees. Reinstatement, injunctive relief, and affirmative action represent possible equitable remedies.

Age Discrimination in Employment Act (ADEA)

The Act, which is applicable to nonfederal employers with 20 or more employees, forbids employment discrimination based solely on age. ADEA is applicable to all employees at least 40 years old; the Act also contains a prohibition against mandatory retirement of nonmanagerial employees based on age. Subsequent to enactment, the ADEA was amended to ban age discrimination with respect to employee benefits. The Act does, however, allow age discrimination where justified by a bona fide seniority system, a bona fide occupational qualification, or a bona fide employee benefit plan. Injured individuals may seek injunctive relief, affirmative action, and back pay.

Rehabilitation Act of 1973

The Rehabilitation Act of 1973 was enacted to prevent discrimination on the basis of handicap by any employer that is the recipient of federal assistance or contracts. While employers subject to the Act are required to make reasonable efforts to accommodate the handicapped, they are not required to hire or promote handicapped persons who are unable to perform the job after reasonable accommodations are made. Persons with physical and mental handicaps are covered by the Act while persons with alcohol or drug abuse problems are not.

Americans with Disabilities Act (ADA)

ADA, which is applicable to entities employing 15 or more individuals, prevents an employer from employment discrimination against qualified individuals with disabilities. A qualified individual with a disability is an individual who is able to perform the essential job function, with or without reasonable accommodation. A disabled person is an individual with or without a history of a physical or mental impairment that substantially limits one or more major life activities. In this connection, ADA affords protection to persons afflicted with cancer and HIV infections; recovering alcoholics and drug addicts are also protected. The Act bars employers from asking job applicants about disabilities but does allow inquiry about the applicant's ability to perform job-related tasks. Prospective employees are also protected by the Act's prohibition of pre-employment medical exams. However, if such exams are required of all other job applicants, the employer is not barred. The Act does afford protection to an employer as well. Accordingly, an employer may refuse to hire or promote a disabled person in situations where (1) accommodation would present an undue hardship, (2) the disabled person cannot fulfill job-related criteria that cannot be reasonably accommodated and (3) the disabled person would represent a direct threat to the health of other individuals.

Comprehensive Omnibus Budget Reconciliation Act of 1985 (COBRA)

COBRA mandates that employers allow voluntarily or involuntarily terminated (and certain disabled) employees to continue their group-health insurance coverage for a period not to exceed to 18 (if disabled, up to 29) months following termination. The terminated employee must, however, bear the expense of the premiums. COBRA applies to nongovernmental entities (1) employing at least 20 individuals and (2) offering an employer-sponsored health plan to employees. An employee's spouse and minor children must also be given the right to continue their group-health coverage.

Worker Adjustment and Retraining Notification Act (WARN)

WARN, which is applicable to employers of more than 100 employees, requires that employees be given 60 days notice of plant closures or mass layoffs. A plant closing is defined as the permanent or temporary closing of a single plant or parts of a plant but only if at least 50 employees will lose their jobs within a specified 30-day period. A mass layoff arises when the jobs of at least 500 employees are terminated during a 30-day period, or the jobs of at least one-third of the employees are terminated at a given site, if that one-third equals at least 50 employees.

The Family and Medical Leave Act (FMLA)

FMLA, which is applicable to entities with at least 50 employees, requires an employer to provide 12 weeks unpaid leave each year for medical or family reasons. While on leave, an employee is entitled to continued medical benefits, and upon return, an employee is entitled to the same or equivalent job.

SECURED TRANSACTIONS

A secured transaction is defined as any transaction that is aimed at creating a security interest in personal property or fixtures. When an agreement between a debtor and creditor has been reached, whereby the creditor shall have a security interest, a security agreement results. The security agreement must be in writing, signed by the debtor, and must delineate any collateral, if the agreement pertains to a nonpossessory interest.

When an interest in personal property or fixtures that secures payment or performance of an obligation exists, by definition, a security interest is created. Security interests may be either possessory or nonpossessory. Attachment must occur in order for rights of a secured party to be enforceable against the debtor. Perfection is necessary in order to make the security interest effective against most third parties.

In order for attachment to occur, (1) the secured party must have collateral pursuant to an agreement with the debtor (or the debtor must have signed a security agreement delineating collateral), (2) the creditor gives value, which may be any consideration that would support a simple contract, and (3) the debtor is afforded property rights in collateral.

Once the security interest has attached, perfection is said to have occurred. In general, the filing of a financing statement with the appropriate public official accomplishes perfection. The content of the financing statement is usually governed by state law, but generally includes, at a minimum, the names and addresses of the secured party and debtor, specification of the collateral, and (3) the signature of the debtor.

Perfection may also be accomplished by attachment alone, without filing, through the use of a purchase money security interest (PMSI) in consumer goods. This form of perfection provides protection against a debtor's other creditors and a debtor's trustee in bankruptcy.

Finally perfection is achieved when the creditor is in possession of the collateral. This means of perfection is useful for a security interest in goods, instruments, negotiable documents, and letters of credit. In the case of negotiable instruments, this is the only acceptable means of perfection.

It should be understood that there are two types of secured transactions; namely, a secured credit sale and a secured loan transaction. The former concerns a sales transaction in which the creditor is involved either as a seller or a money lender. The creditor takes a purchase money security interest (PMSI). Possession and risk of loss pass to the buyer, but the creditor retains a security interest in the goods until he or she has been paid in full. In the case of the latter, there is no sale of goods. Rather, the creditor lends money while simultaneously accepting a debtor-pledged security interest in collateral.

Essentially, there are four types of collateral; i.e., goods, negotiable instruments, intangibles and fixtures.

Goods include consumer goods, inventory and equipment. Consumer goods consist of items that are used or purchased for use primarily for personal, family, or household purposes. Inventory, on the other hand, includes goods held for sale or lease, including unfinished goods. A security interest in inventory may result in a "floating lien," whereby the lien attaches to inventory in the hands of the dealer as it is received by the dealer. Equipment, it should noted, may also be subject to a "floating lien."

Negotiable instruments include commercial paper, documents of title and investment securities.

Intangibles include both accounts receivable and contract rights.

Perfecting a Security Interest

As previously noted, to accomplish perfection, a financing statement must be filed with an appropriate public official. In instances where conflicting interests exist, the order of perfection is crucial and will decide priority, regardless of attachment. The first security interest to attach is afforded priority in cases where none of the conflicting security interests have been perfected.

If, within a ten-day period, before or after the debtor takes possession of the collateral, a purchase money security interest in noninventory collateral is filed, the creditor will be protected as of the day on which the security interest was created (i.e., the day on which the debtor takes possession of the collateral) against any nonpurchase money security interest previously filed during the ten-day period. Creditor protection also applies to previously filed floating liens. In the event that the security interest is perfected after the ten-day period, the secured party will be afforded protection as of the date of filing but will not be able to secure protection against previously perfected non-PMSI.

A PMSI in inventory takes priority over conflicting security interests (i.e., previously perfected non-PMSI) but only if both (1) the PMSI-holder perfected the interest in the inventory on or before the date the inventory was received by the debtor and (2) the PMSI-holder furnished written notice (before the debtor takes possession of the inventory) indicating the acquisition of the interest and describing the secured inventory to all holders of conflicting security interests that previously filed a financing statement pertaining to the same type of inventory.

A filing will be necessary to protect against an innocent, nonmerchant purchaser from the consumer/debtor, even though no filing is required in order to perfect a purchase money security interest in consumer goods.

The written financing statement needed to perfect a security interest must generally include the names and addresses of both the debtor and the creditor. Only the debtor must sign the statement. The financing statement must also describe the collateral covered, and is effective for a five year period commencing on the date filed. In order to extend the original five-year period for another five-years, a continuation statement, signed by the secured party, is necessary and must be filed by the secured party within the six-month period prior to the original statement's expiration date.

Rights of Parties upon Default

The secured party may, upon default by the buyer/debtor, have the right to repossess the goods without going through legal channels. Alternatively, the secured party may sell the goods and apply the proceeds to any outstanding debt.

The secured party generally will be protected against subsequent creditors and most other third parties if a security interest has been perfected. However, holders in due course will defeat the claims of any and all secured parties. Furthermore, a buyer in the ordinary course of business is not controlled by a seller-created security interest, even in instances where the security interest was perfected and the buyer was conscious of it. This is quite prevalent where inventory has been pledged as collateral.

Upon default, the secured party may exercise a privilege to notify the obligor on accounts receivable, contract rights, instruments, etc., to directly remit remuneration.

While the debtor has right to redeem collateral prior to disposition, the creditor has right to retain goods. However, unless the debtor had relinquished rights after default, the creditor must give the debtor written notice about his or her intention(s). Furthermore, except in cases involving consumer goods, the creditor must send this notice to all other interested secured parties. If the creditor receives an objection to his or her retention within a 21-day period following the sending of this notice, then the creditor is required to dispose of the property.

If the debtor has satisfied at least 60% of the obligation, and the collateral consists of consumer goods with a PMSI, then the creditor is forced to sell the collateral within 90 days of the collateral's repossession, unless the debtor has relinquished his or her rights after default. Any excess debt owed, plus repossession costs, must be returned by the secured party to the debtor.

When, for value and without knowledge of any defects in the sale, a good faith purchaser acquires collateral that was disposed of after default, the acquisition is free of any subordinate (but not superior) security interests. Finally, the debtor has no right to redeem collateral sold to a good-faith purchaser.

SURETYSHIP AND CREDITOR'S RIGHTS

Suretyship involves situations where one party agrees to be unconditionally liable for the debt or default of another party.

The parties involved in suretyship include the surety or guarantor (i.e., the party, whether compensated or not, who is responsible for the debt or obligation of another), the creditor (i.e., the party who is owed the debt or obligation), the debtor or principal debtor (i.e., the party whose obligation it is). It should be noted that co-sureties may exist. If this is the case, more than one surety is obligated for the same debt, although each co-surety may not be liable for the same amount nor may they be aware of each other's existence.

Since guaranty of collection imposes only a secondary liability upon the guarantor, the creditor must initially attempt collection from the debtor before attempting collection from the guarantor. It should be noted that, except in instances where collection is subject to some condition, guaranty and suretyship are synonymous terms.

Under the Statute of Frauds discussed earlier, a promise of guaranty must be set forth in writing and signed by the guarantor in order to be enforceable. On the other hand, a surety agreement does not have to be set forth in writing.

While the surety/guarantor need not receive consideration, consideration is needed to support the surety/guarantor's promise, and is usually represented by the creditor's granting of the loan.

Surety's Rights against Debtor or Co-Sureties

Once payment is made by the surety to the creditor, the surety is entitled to seek indemnification or reimbursement from the debtor.

In situations involving co-sureties, once the surety has made payment to the creditor, one co-surety may seek a proportionate share from any other co-sureties.

A co-surety's share of the principal debt is calculated by multiplying the amount of principal debt by a fraction, the numerator of which is the amount for which the co-surety is liable and the denominator of which is the total amount of liabilities for all co-sureties.

In the event that a co-surety is released by a creditor, any remaining co-sureties will be liable, but only to the extent of their proportionate share.

After the creditor is paid by the surety, the surety stands in the shoes of the creditor; this is known as subrogation.

If the debtor defaults, the surety may seek relief from the courts. The courts may order the debtor to pay the creditor. A surety may seek similar relief against co-sureties. This equitable right of the surety against the debtor is known as exoneration.

Defenses of a Surety

In general, a surety may raise any defense that may be raised by a party to an ordinary contract. As such, a surety may claim mutual mistake, lack of consideration, undue influence and creditor fraud.

On the other hand, a surety may not claim such defenses as death, insolvency, or bankruptcy of the debtor. The statute of limitations is similarly barred as a defense.

Another possible defense arises when the surety is not advised by the creditor about matters material to the risk when the creditor reasonably believes that the surety does not possess knowledge of such matters.

A defense also arises if the surety does not consent to material modification of the original contract. There is, however, a difference between a noncompensated surety and a compensated surety. The former is completely discharged automatically. The latter is discharged only to the extent that the material modification results in the surety sustaining a loss.

The release of the debtor by the creditor without the surety's consent may also be claimed as a defense. However, if the creditor specifically reserves his or her rights as against the surety, the reservation of rights will be effective and the surety shall remain liable pursuant to the original promise.

When the security is released or its value is impaired by the creditor, the surety is discharged but only to the extent of the security released or impaired.

Finally, the debtor's tender of payment to the creditor may be used as a defense.

Rights of the Creditor

The rights of the creditor, like the defenses of the surety, depend on the facts and circumstances of the events giving rise to the suretyship.

When improvements are made to real property and the provider is not paid for labor or materials, the creditor has the right to place a mechanic's lien on the property.

Pursuant to writ of execution, which is a postjudgment remedy, a court directs the sheriff to (1) seize and sell a debtor's nonexempt property and (2) apply the proceeds to the costs of execution and the creditor's judgment.

A writ of attachment, on the other hand, is a prejudgment remedy whereby the sheriff is directed to seize the debtor's nonexempt property. The seized property is then sold to pay the judgment, but only if a judgment against the debtor is secured. This remedy is not obtained easily and requires the creditor to post a bond sufficient to cover court costs and damages for a possible wrongful attachment action by the debtor.

Alternatively, a creditor may wish to secure a writ of garnishment. This course of action may be a prejudgment or postjudgment remedy. The writ of garnishment is aimed at a third party, such as a bank or employer, holding debtor-owned funds. The third party is directed to pay a regular portion of those funds to the creditor. The federal government's desire to prevent abusive and excessive garnishment resulted in enactment of The Consumer Credit Protection Act. Under the Act, a debtor may retain the larger of 75 percent of the weekly disposable earnings, or an amount equal to 30 hours of work at the federal minimum wage rate.

An assignment for the benefit of creditors is also a viable option. Under this option, a debtor voluntarily transfers property to a trustee who then sells the property and applies the sale proceeds on a pro-rata basis to the creditors of the debtor.

It should be noted that a homestead exemption is afforded to a debtor in bankruptcy. Accordingly, the debtor is permitted to retain a family home, or a portion of the proceeds from the sale of a family home, free from the claims of unsecured creditors and trustees. However, the protection of the homestead exemption is not available to tax liens, liens for labor or materials pertinent to real property improvements, and contract obligations for the purchase of real property.

Finally, if a debtor transfers property to a third party with the intent of defrauding the debtor's creditors, and the property becomes unavailable to the debtor's creditors, a fraudulent conveyance has taken place, and is voidable at the option of the debtor's creditors.

Federally-Enacted Statutes

The federal government passed the Truth-in-Lending Act (TLA) to require that creditors disclose finance charges and credit extension charges. TLA also sets limit on garnishment proceedings. Further, a consumer who uses his or her principal residence as security for credit purposes is given the right to cancel the transaction within three business days of the credit-transaction date, or the date the creditor provided the debtor with a required notice of the right to cancel, whichever is later. In general, TLA applies to consumer credit purchases up to $25,000. The $25,000 limit is not applicable, however, where the creditor maintains a security interest in the principal dwelling of the debtor.

TLA was later amended to include the Consumer Leasing Act (CLA) to expand its disclosure requirements to leases of consumer goods of up to $25,000. The provisions of CLA, however, are not applicable to real estate leases or leases between consumers.

Another amendment to TLA is the Fair Credit and Charge Card Disclosure Act, that requires disclosure of credit terms on credit and charge card solicitations and applications.

In an effort to ensure that there is no discrimination in the extension of credit, the Equal Credit Opportunity Act was enacted. Under the Act, it is illegal to discriminate on the basis of race, color, national origin, religion, age, gender, marital status, or receipt of income from public assistance programs.

By virtue of the Fair Credit Billing Act (FCBA), payment may be withheld by a credit card customer for supposedly defective products. FCBA regulates credit billing and establishes a mechanism enabling consumers to challenge and correct billing errors.

Finally, the Fair Debt Collection Practices Act may be useful as it affords protection to consumer-debtors from abusive, deceptive, and unfair practices by debt collectors.

DOCUMENTS OF TITLE

The controller should have a basic knowledge of documents of title because they indicate ownership of goods and emanate from shipment or storage of goods. Documents of title may be sold, transferred, or even pledged as collateral, and include bills of lading issued by a carrier to evidence the receipt of shipment, and warehouse receipts used to evidence receipt of goods by persons hired to store goods.

It should be understood that there is a difference between a negotiable document and a nonnegotiable document. In the case of the former, the document states that goods are to be delivered to "bearer" or to the "order of" a named person. Accordingly, the goods are required to be delivered to the holder of the document. A negotiable document of title is not, however, payable in money, as commercial paper is. In the case of the latter, goods are consigned to a specified person, and therefore delivery must be made to the specified person. A nonnegotiable document, also known as a straight bill of lading, represents a receipt for the goods rather than a document of title.

Transfer or Negotiation

Transfer of nonnegotiable documents is in essence an assignment, whereby the assignee is effectively subject to all defenses that are available against the assignor.

The rules applicable to negotiable documents are much more complex and depend on whether the document is order paper or bearer paper.

With respect to order paper, which is negotiable by endorsement and delivery, a transferee of an order document which was not endorsed has a right to obtain such endorsement. It should be noted that the endorsement of a document of title does not render the endorser liable for any default by the bailee or by previous endorsers.

An endorser does however warrant to the immediate purchaser (1) the genuineness of the document, (2) that the transferor has no knowledge of any fact that would impair the validity of the document and (3) that the transferor's negotiation is rightful and fully effective with respect to the document's title and the goods represented by the document.

Bearer paper, on the other hand is negotiable by delivery alone.

To be "duly negotiated," a document must be properly negotiated to a holder who, in the regular course of business or financing and not in settlement or payment of a money obligation, has purchased the document in good faith, for value, and without notice of defenses.

To secure proper negotiation of order paper, the transferor must obtain a document with proper consent of the owner, and with the owner's endorsement.

Warehouse Obligations

Goods should only be delivered to the person possessing the negotiable document, which is required to be surrendered for cancellation.

Further, a warehouse has the right to refuse delivery of the goods until payment for the goods has been made.

Finally, a completed warehouse receipt, issued with blanks and purchased in good faith, entitles the purchaser to recover from the warehouse that issued the incomplete document.

CORPORATIONS

By definition, a corporation is a separate legal entity that possesses certain powers stipulated in its charter or by governing statutes.

Classification of Corporations

There are eight classifications of corporations: public, private, domestic, foreign, publicly held, closely held, S corporation, and professional.

A *public corporation* is a corporation that is formed for governmental purposes.

A *private corporation* essentially includes all other corporations, whether publicly held or not.

A *domestic corporation* is a corporation organized under the laws of a particular state.

A *foreign corporation* is a corporation deemed to be "foreign" with respect to every state other than the state of incorporation.

A *closely held corporation* is a corporation, the stock of which is owned by a small number of persons, who are quite commonly related to each other.

A *publicly held corporation* is a corporation, the stock of which (1) is owned by a large number of persons and (2) widely traded through one of the stock exchanges.

A *professional corporation* is a corporation enabling professionals, including certified public accountants, to operate utilizing the corporate form.

An *S corporation,* as discussed in Chapter 42, is a corporation that (1) has satisfied certain IRS requirements and (2) is electing to be taxed essentially like a partnership.

Parties to a Corporation

If the decision is made to form a publicly held corporation, the services of a promoter are usually necessary. The promoter is responsible for developing ideas pertinent to the corporation, securing stock subscribers, and entering into contracts on behalf of the corporation to be established. While corporations are generally not legally bound by contracts until a preincorporation contract is assumed by the formed corporation, promoters are generally deemed to be personally liable on contracts.

An incorporator is an important party as well, since he or she is the individual charged with devising the formal application needed to create the corporation. Corporate existence only begins upon the State's issuance of the certificate of incorporation.

The stockholders are the owners of the corporation's stock. They are empowered to elect directors who will manage the entity, vote on important issues, inspect books and records, and receive financial statements. Since stockholders, as owners, share in the corporation's profits, they are entitled to receive dividends declared at the discretion of the board of directors. Stockholders may force the board to make dividend payments only when directors are found to have abused their judgment regarding dividend declaration. It should be noted that a dividend received by a stockholder during the period of a company's insolvency must be returned to the corporation.

One the greatest advantages of the corporate form, from the stockholders' point of view, is that stockholders are generally not liable beyond their investment. The courts may, however, "pierce the corporate veil," and hold the stockholders liable if, among other circumstances, the Courts determine that the corporation (1) was established in order to perpetrate a fraud or (2) is undercapitalized.

Directors, elected by the stockholders are charged with establishing the corporation's essential policies of the corporation and electing corporate officers. Since directors are employed in a fiduciary capacity, they are liable for negligence but not errors in judgment. Stockholders may commence a derivative action to cure any damage done by the directors. Directors acting in a representative capacity, however, are entitled to corporate indemnification with respect to acts performed on behalf of the corporation. While directors have the discretion to declare dividends, they will be held to be personally liable for illegal dividends; i.e., dividend payments made during the corporation's period of insolvency, or dividend payments that force the corporation into insolvency, or dividend payments made from an unauthorized account.

The corporate officers are responsible for managing the daily operations of the corporation, and their rights and powers are governed by agency law and are limited by the corporation's charter and bylaws. Corporate officers, appointed by the board of directors, while liable for negligent acts, are entitled to indemnification for acts performed within the scope of their authority, so long as they acted in good faith.

Powers and Rights of a Corporation

A corporation's sources of power include the corporation's charter and bylaws as well as relevant statutes. A corporation is normally empowered to borrow and lend money, enter into contracts, acquire and dispose property, have perpetual existence, and have exclusive use of its legal corporate name.

Dissolution or Termination of Corporations

While a corporation normally is afforded perpetual existence, there are circumstances that enable a corporation to terminate its existence. Termination may be accomplished by voluntary or involuntary dissolution.

In order to dissolve voluntarily, the board of directors must approve a corporate resolution. Approval generally requires a majority vote on the part of stockholders possessing stock with voting rights. A special shareholders' meeting is needed and all shareholders must be provided written notice of the purpose, time, date, and location of the special meeting.

Involuntary dissolution, on the other hand, may result from an administrative hearing on the part of the secretary of state, or from a judicial proceeding prompted by either a shareholder or corporate creditor.

To force an involuntary dissolution based on an administrative hearing, the secretary of state must prove that the corporation has failed to comply with state laws. Accordingly, the corporation's failure to file required annual reports or pay taxes may result in an involuntary dissolution.

A court may also force a corporation to dissolve. To do so, it must prove that the corporation fraudulently obtained its charter, the corporation was involved in ultra vires acts (i.e., those abusing or in excess of its authority), the board of directors was involved in an illegal or fraudulent act, or the assets of the corporation are being wasted or misapplied. A court forced dissolution may also result when either (1) the shareholders are deadlocked and have failed to elect directors for at least two consecutive annual meetings or (2) the directors are deadlocked, the shareholders cannot break the deadlock, and irreparable damage is threatened or being suffered by the corporation.

Consolidation or Merger

From a legal standpoint, a consolidation involves joining two or more corporations in order to form a new entity with the assets and liabilities of the old corporations. A merger, on the other hand, occurs when one corporation absorbs another. The corporation absorbed is accordingly terminated, while the other corporation (i.e., the survivor) continues its existence. The survivor logically assumes the liabilities of the corporation absorbed in the merger.

In order to effectuate a consolidation or merger, the board of directors of each corporation must ratify a formal plan, which must then be submitted to the stockholders of each corporation for their approval. Approval constitutes the consent of a majority of each corporation's voting shareholders, following due notice of a special shareholders' meeting. Furthermore, each voting shareholder must be given a copy of the merger or consolidation plan.

Any dissenting shareholders must be provided an appraisal remedy; i.e., they must be given the value of the shares immediately prior to the action to which the dissenter objects plus accrued interest, if any. In order to obtain an appraisal remedy, a dissenting shareholder must (1) file a written notice of dissent with the corporation prior to the vote of the shareholders,

(2) vote against the proposed transaction, and (3) demand in writing that an appraisal remedy be made after the shareholders' vote of approval.

Finally, articles of consolidation or merger must be filed with the absorbing corporation's state of incorporation. The merger or consolidation is effective only when this document is filed.

It should be noted that a short-form merger is often permitted when a merger of a subsidiary into a parent corporation is desired. To qualify, a parent corporation must own at least 90 percent of the outstanding shares of each class of stock in a subsidiary. It is interesting to note that only the approval of the parent corporation's board of directors is necessary. It is not necessary to secure the approval of either the shareholders of each corporation or the board of directors of the subsidiary corporation. Additionally, only the shareholders of the subsidiary corporation need be given an appraisal remedy.

BANKRUPTCY

A knowledge of bankruptcy is essential given today's economic conditions and competitive markets. This section is designed to update and expand on the material contained on pages 989 and 990 in the main text. From a legal standpoint, the primary basis for bankruptcy is insolvency in the equity sense as opposed to balance sheet insolvency. Accordingly, the entity must be unable to pay debts as they become due as opposed to merely having an excess of liabilities over assets.

Bankruptcy Reform Act of 1994

The Bankruptcy Reform Act of 1994 essentially contains two chapters applicable to corporations.

Chapter 7 permits the voluntary or involuntary liquidation of a debtor's nonexempt assets, the distribution of the proceeds to creditors, and the discharge of the remaining business and/or personal debt of the debtor. While Chapter 7 relief is available to corporations, a discharge of indebtedness is not available if the debtor is a corporation, since the limited liability of shareholders would preclude the need for a discharge. Under Chapter 7, it should be apparent that the business no longer continues to operate.

Chapter 11, on the other hand, is quite different. Chapter 11 relief, which is generally available if the entity is eligible for relief under Chapter 7, enables reorganization by the entity's business debtors, in order to keep the financially troubled business in operation. Fraud, incompetence, or gross mismanagement, however, will prevent the desired continuity.

A petition under Chapter 11 may be voluntary or involuntary, and insolvency in the balance sheet sense is not a condition precedent. The filing of a voluntary petition by an eligible debtor operates as an order for relief, effectively eliminating the need for a formal hearing.

Appointment of a committee of unsecured creditors follows an order of relief. The parties holding the seven largest unsecured claims against the debtor usually sit on the committee.

Under Chapter 11, the debtor usually remains in possession and control of the business. However, a trustee may be appointed by the Court for cause, which includes, but is not limited to, fraud on the part of the debtor or incompetence of the debtor.

The right to file a reorganization plan during the first 120 days following the order for relief rests with the debtor, unless the court has appointed a trustee. If the creditors do not accept a timely filed plan, then no other party is permitted to file a plan for reorganization during the first 180 days after the order for relief. Thereafter, however, a plan for reorganization may be filed by one or more interested parties.

In order to be effective, each class of creditors must accept the proposed plan for reorganization. Confirmation by the Bankruptcy Court is then required. Acceptance by a class of creditors requires approval by creditors holding at least two-thirds of the debt owed to that class of creditors and holding more than one-half of the allowed claims for that class.

Upon confirmation by the court, a final decree is entered, resulting in the discharge of the debtor from most pre-confirmation debts.

An expedited reorganization process is available to a qualified small business, which is defined as a business whose aggregate noncontingent liquidated secured and unsecured debts are less than $2 million. The expedited process enables elimination of creditor committees and affords the debtor the exclusive right to file a reorganization plan within 100 days.

Bankruptcy Petitions

A bankruptcy petition must be filed in order to begin bankruptcy proceedings. If the debtor files the petition, it is said to be a voluntary petition. A voluntary petition generally lists the entity's creditors, exempt property, and a description of financial condition. Upon filing a voluntary petition, an order for relief is entered.

If the creditors of the entity file the petition, it is referred to as an involuntary petition. The debtor, of course, has the right to contest the petition in court. An order for relief, however, is entered only after a court hearing.

Three petitioning creditors are required when the debtor has 12 or more creditors; only one creditor is required if the debtor has less than 12 creditors. In either situation, the petition must allege unsecured debts of at least $10,000 owed by the debtor to the petitioning creditors.

If the petition is opposed by the debtor, the court may enter an order of relief only if (1) the debtor is not paying debts as they mature, or (2) within 120 days before the petition is filed, to enforce a lien against the property, a receiver took possession of substantially all of the debtor's property.

A successful contest of an involuntary bankruptcy petition by the debtor may result in the court granting a judgment for (1) costs, (2) reasonable attorney's fees, and (3) compensatory damages. The debtor may also be awarded punitive damages should the court determine that the petition was filed in bad faith.

Priority of Claims

The priority of a claim depends on whether it is a secured claim or an unsecured claim. A creditor with a perfected secured claim against specific property of the debtor is afforded first priority to the proceeds from that property. To the extent that the proceeds of the sale of the secured asset are not sufficient to fully discharge the claim of the secured party, the creditor is considered to be an unsecured creditor.

After secured claims are satisfied, unsecured creditors are entitled to any remaining assets. Since some unsecured claims are given priority, they must be paid in full before payment is made to subordinate claims. In the event that a debtor's assets are not sufficient to fully pay unsecured creditors with the same priority, payments must be made on a pro-rata basis.

The general order of priority applicable to nonsecured claims is (1) administrative expenses, (2) debt obligations incurred after commencement of an involuntary bankruptcy case, but before the order for relief or appointment of a trustee, (3) unsecured claims for wages earned within 90 days before the filing of a bankruptcy petition or cessation of business, whichever is first, limited to $4,000 for each employee, (4) contributions to employee benefit plans based on services rendered within 180 days before the filing of the bankruptcy petition, but limited to $4,000 per employee, (5) deposits with the debtor to the extent of $1,800 per individual for the purchase, rental, or lease of property or personal services, for family or household use, (6) taxes, and (7) general creditor claims.

Discharge of Debt

While a discharge in bankruptcy generally discharges debt, certain obligations are not. Some of the more common debts that are not discharged include taxes in general, unlisted debts and debts where the creditor notice did not stipulate the debtor's name, address, and taxpayer identification number, debts for fraud, embezzlement, or larceny, liability for injury that was willful and malicious, fines and penalties, debts surviving an earlier bankruptcy proceeding, and loans used to pay federal taxes.

Discharge of debt will be denied if the debtor, within a one-year period before the petition is filed, or during the hearing of the case, (1) directly or indirectly transferred, destroyed, or concealed property, (2) concealed, destroyed, falsified, or failed to preserve any records necessary for determining financial condition, (3) committed fraud, refused to testify, or attempted bribery in connection with the bankruptcy, (4) failed to explain satisfactorily any loss or deficiency of assets, (5) refused to obey a lawful court order, (6) has been granted a discharge in a case commenced within six years before the date of the filing of the petition, or (7) executed a court-approved written waiver of discharge after the order for relief.

It should be noted that under certain conditions, a debtor and a creditor may agree to honor a discharged debt. The agreement is known as a reaffirmation agreement.

ENVIRONMENTAL LAW

Violation of environmental law may subject the corporation to stiff criminal and civil fines and penalties. As a valued member of management, the controller should possess some basic knowledge of relevant federal statutes pertinent to environmental law.

Federal statutes have been enacted to extend common law liability for nuisance (i.e., unreasonable interference with use and enjoyment of another's land) and trespass (i.e., the intentional and unlawful entry upon another's land).

The Environmental Protection Agency (EPA) is a federal administrative agency that is charged with administering federal laws designed to protect the environment.

The National Environmental Policy Act (NEPA) requires the federal government to consider the "adverse impact" of proposed legislation, rule-making, or other federal government action on the environment before the action is set in motion. Under the law, an environmental impact statement must be prepared in connection with all proposed federal legislation or major federal action that significantly impacts the quality of the human environment.

The Clean Air Act, which regulates air quality, specifically addresses (1) national ambient air quality standards, (2) stationary sources of air pollution, (3) mobile sources of air pollution, and (4) toxic air pollutants.

The Clean Water Act enables the EPA to establish water quality criteria in order to regulate the concentrations of permissible pollutants in a body of water and limit the amount of pollutants that are discharged from a particular source. Enforcement of the Act is delegated to individual states.

The Noise Control Act enables the EPA to establish noise standards for new products. Under the Act, the EPA (with the Federal Aeronautics Administration) is empowered to establish noise limits for new aircraft and to regulate, with the assistance of the Department of Transportation, noise emissions from trucks.

The Resource Conservation and Recovery Act (RCRA) authorizes the EPA to identify hazardous wastes. Further, the Act authorizes the EPA to regulate entities that generate, treat, store, and dispose of wastes deemed to be hazardous.

Finally, The Comprehensive Environmental Response, Compensation, and Liability Act (CERCLA), often referred to as the "Superfund" law, mandates that the EPA identify hazardous waste sites. The EPA must the rank the identified sites according to the severity of the environmental risk they pose.

Should the EPA have to clean up a hazardous site, it may recover the cost of the cleanup from one or more responsible parties.

FINANCIAL STATEMENT REPORTING: THE INCOME STATEMENT

FINANCIAL ACCOUNTING STANDARDS BOARD STATEMENT NUMBER 130

FASB Statement No. 130 (Reporting Comprehensive Income) requires companies to report comprehensive income and its elements in a full set of financial statements. FASB Statement Number 130 keeps the current reporting requirements for net income, but it considers net income a major element of comprehensive income. A restatement of previous years' financial statements is needed when presented for comparative purposes.

Comprehensive income applies to the change in equity (net assets) arising from either transactions or other occurrences with nonowners. Excluded are investments and withdrawals by nonowners. Comprehensive income is comprised of two components: net income and other comprehensive income. Other comprehensive income relates to all items of comprehensive income excluding net income. Thus, net income plus other comprehensive income equals total comprehensive income. Other comprehensive income includes the following:

- Foreign currency items including translation gains and losses, and gains and losses on foreign currency transactions designated as hedges of a net investment in a foreign entity.
- Unrealized losses or gains on available-for-sale securities.

- Minimum pension liability adjustments applying to the amount by which the additional pension liability exceeds the unrecognized prior service cost.
- Changes in market value of a futures contract that is a hedge of an asset reported at fair value.

FASB Statement Number 130 provides flexibility on how comprehensive income may be shown in the financial statements. There are three allowable options of reporting other comprehensive income and its components as follows:

1. Below the net income figure in the income statement, or
2. In a separate statement of comprehensive income beginning with net income, or
3. In a statement of changes in equity as long as such statement is presented as a primary financial statement. It cannot appear only in the footnotes.

Options 1 and 2 are income-statement-type formats while option 3 is a statement-of-changes-in-equity format. Options 1 and 2 are preferred.

A sample presentation under option 1 within the income statement follows:

Statement of Income and Comprehensive Income

Net Income		$600,000
Other Comprehensive Income:		
Foreign currency translation loss	($50,000)	
Unrealized gain on available-for-sale securities	70,000	
Minimum pension liability adjustment	(10,000)	
Total Other Comprehensive Income		10,000
Total Comprehensive Income		$610,000

Under the second option a separate statement of comprehensive income is presented. The reporting follows:

Income Statement

Net Income	$600,000

Statement of Comprehensive Income

Net Income		$600,000
Other Comprehensive Income:		
Foreign currency translation loss	($50,000)	
Unrealized gain on available-for-sale securities	70,000	
Minimum pension liability adjustment	(10,000)	
Total Other Comprehensive Income		10,000
Total Comprehensive Income		$610,000

Under the third option comprehensive income and its components are presented in the comprehensive income column as part of the statement of changes in equity. An illustrative format of the comprehensive income column follows:

Comprehensive Income:

Net income		xx
Other comprehensive income:		
Foreign currency items	xx	
Unrealized loss or gain on available-for-sale securities	xx	
Minimum pension liability adjustment	xx	
Total other comprehensive income		xx
Total comprehensive income		xx

In the stockholders' equity section, "accumulated other comprehensive income" is presented as one amount for all items and listed for each component separately.

The components of other comprehensive income for the period may be presented on a before-tax basis with one amount for the tax impact of all the items of other comprehensive income.

A reclassification adjustment may be required so as not to double count items reported in net income for the current period which have also been considered as part of other comprehensive income in a prior period. An example is the realized gain on an available-for-sale security sold in the current year when a holding gain was also included in other comprehensive income in a prior year. Reclassification adjustments may also apply to foreign currency translation. The reclassification adjustment applicable to a foreign exchange translation only applies to translation gains and losses realized from the sale or liquidation of an investment in a foreign entity.

Reclassification adjustments may be presented with other comprehensive income or in a footnote. The reclassification adjustment may be shown on a gross or net basis (except the minimum pension liability adjustment must be presented on a net basis).

Example 1. On January 1, 19X1, a company purchased 1,000 shares of available-for-sale securities having a market price per share of $100. On December 31, 19X1, the available-for-sale securities had a market price of $150 per share. On January 1, 19X2, the securities were sold at a market price of $130 per share. The tax rate is 30%.

The unrealized gain or loss included in other comprehensive income is determined below:

	Before Tax	Tax Effect at 30%	Net of Tax
19X1 (1,000 × $50*)	$50,000	$15,000	$35,000
19X2 (1,000 × $20**)	(20,000)	(6,000)	(14,000)
Total gain	$30,000	$9,000	$21,000

*$150 – $100 = $50
**$150 – $130 = $20

The presentation in the income statement for 19X1 and 19X2 follows:

	19X1	19X2
Net Income:		
Gross realized gain on available-for-sale securities		$30,000
Tax expense		9,000
Net realized gain		$21,000
Other Comprehensive Income:		
Unrealized gain or loss after tax	$30,000	$(9,000)
Reclassification adjustment net of tax		(21,000)
Net gain included in other comprehensive income	$30,000	$(30,000)
Total effect on comprehensive income	$30,000	$(9,000)

In interim financial statements issued to the public, FASB Statement Number 130 requires a business to present total comprehensive income. However, it is not required for interim reporting to present the individual components of other comprehensive income.

DISCLOSURES ASSOCIATED WITH OPERATIONS

Disclosure should be made of a company's major products and services including principal markets by geographic area. The information enables a proper evaluation of the entity's nature of operations. Further, AICPA Statement of Position (SOP) Number 94-6 mandates disclosure of major risks and uncertainties facing the entity. The SOP also requires disclosure in the significant accounting policies footnote that the financial information presented is based on management's estimates and assumptions. Reference should be made that actual results may differ from such estimates.

SERVICE SALES REVENUE

A transaction often involves both the sale of a product and a service. It is thus necessary to determine if the transaction should be classified primarily as a product transaction or a service transaction, or a combination of both.

For transactions having both a product and service element, the following applies:

- A transaction should be classified as primarily a service transaction if the inclusion or exclusion of the product would not change the total price of the transaction.
- If the inclusion or exclusion of the service would not alter the total transaction price, then the transaction should be classified as primarily a product transaction.
- If the inclusion or exclusion of the service or product would change the total transaction price, then the transaction should be split and the product component should be accounted for separately from the service element.

The following four methods should be used to recognize revenue from service activities:

- The specific performance method is used when performance involves a single action and the revenue is recognized when that action occurs.
- The proportional performance method is used when performance relates to a series of actions. If the transaction involves an unspecified number of actions over a stated time period, an equal amount of revenue should be recognized at fixed intervals. If the transaction relates to a specified number of similar actions, an equal amount of revenue should be recorded when each action is completed. If the transaction relates to a given number of dissimilar or unique actions, revenue

should be recognized based upon the following ratio: direct costs involved in a single action ÷ total estimated direct costs of the transaction × total revenue for the entire transaction.

- The completed performance method is used to recognize revenue when completing the final action is so critical that the entire transaction should be considered incomplete without it.

- The collection method is used to recognize revenue when there is significant uncertainty with regard to the collection of revenue. Revenue is not recognized until cash is received.

The three major cost categories that arise from service transactions are:

- Initial direct costs are incurred to negotiate and obtain a service agreement. They include commissions, credit investigation, legal fees, and processing fees.

- Direct costs arise from rendering the service such as labor charges and the cost of materials.

- Indirect costs are all the costs needed to perform the service, but cannot be classified as either initial direct costs or direct costs. Indirect costs include rent, depreciation, selling and administrative costs, allowance for bad debts, and the costs to negotiate transactions that are not consummated.

Indirect costs are expensed as incurred. Initial direct costs and direct costs are expensed only when the related revenue is recognized using either the specific performance or completed performance method. In other words, initial direct costs and direct costs should be recorded as prepaid assets and expensed once the service has been rendered. The same accounting treatment is used to expense initial direct costs under the proportional performance method; that is, initial direct costs are recorded as prepaid assets and expensed when the revenue is recognized. On the other hand, direct costs should be expensed as incurred when the proportional performance method is used. This is done because of the close relationship between the direct costs incurred and the completion of the service. If the collection method is used, both initial direct costs and direct costs are expensed as incurred.

A loss may be incurred in a service transaction. A loss should be recognized when initial direct costs and estimated total direct costs exceed the estimated revenue. The loss is first applied to reduce the prepaid asset and any remaining loss is charged against the estimated liability account.

A service transaction may involve initiation and/or installation fees. The fees are usually nonrefundable. If one can objectively determine the value of the right or privilege granted by the initiation fees, then the fees should be recognized as revenue and the associated direct costs should be expensed on the initiation date. On the contrary, if the value cannot be determined, the fees should initially be deemed unearned revenue, a liability account. Revenue should be recognized from such initiation fees using one of the service revenue recognition methods.

The accounting afforded to equipment installation fees depends upon whether the customer can buy the equipment independent of the installation. If equipment may be bought independent of installation, then the transaction is considered a product transaction and installation fees are treated as part of the product transaction. On the contrary, if both the equipment and installation are essential for service and the customer cannot buy the equipment separately, then the installation fees should be treated as unearned revenue. Unearned revenue should be recognized and the cost of installation and equipment should be amortized over the estimated service period.

CONTRACT TYPES

There are various types of construction contracts including time- and materials, unit price, fixed-price, and cost-type. Time- and materials contracts reimburse the contractor for direct labor and direct material costs. Unit price contracts provide payment to the contractor based on the amount of units completed. Fixed-price contracts are not usually subject to adjustment such as due to increasing construction costs. Cost-type contracts may either be cost without a fee or cost plus a fee. The fee is usually based on a profit margin. However, the fee may be based on some other factor such as total expected costs, uncertainty in estimating costs, project risk, economic conditions, etc. The contract costs should never be more than its net realizable value, otherwise the contract would not be financially feasible. A loss is recognized when accumulated cost exceeds net realizable value.

Contracts which are very similar may be grouped for accounting purposes. Similarity may be indicated by a similar project management, single customer, conducted sequentially or concurrently, interrelated, and negotiated as a package deal. The segmenting of a contract is segregating the larger unit into smaller ones for accounting purposes. By breaking up a unit, revenues are associated with different components or phases. In consequence, different profitability margins may apply to each different unit or phase. Segmenting of a project may be indicated when all of the following criteria are satisfied:

- The project may be segregated into its components.
- A contract bid price exists for the entire project and its major components.
- Customer approval is received.

Even if all of these conditions are not met, the project may still be segmented if all of the following exist:

- Segregation is logical and consistent.
- Risk differences are explainable.
- Each segment is negotiated.
- Cost savings arise.
- Stability exists.
- Similarity exists in services and prices.
- Contractor has a track record.

An addition or modification made to an existing contact arising from an option clause is accounted for as a separate contract if any of the following applies:

- Price of the new product or service is distinct.
- Product or service is similar to that in the original contract but differences do exist in contract pricing and cost.
- Product or service is materially different than the product or service provided for in the initial contract.

A claim is an amount above the contract price that a contractor wants customers to pay because of customer errors in specifications, customer delays, or other unanticipated causes resulting in higher costs to the contractor. The contractor may recognize additional revenue because of these claims if justification exists and the amount is determinable. The revenue is recognized only to the extent that contract costs related to the claim have been incurred. As per AICPA Statement of Position 81-1, the following benchmarks exist to establish the ability to record the additional revenue:

- Additional costs incurred were not initially expected when the contract was signed.
- The claim has a legal basis.
- The claim is verifiable and objective.
- Costs are determinable.

If the above conditions are not met, a contingent asset should be disclosed.

CONTRACT COSTS

Costs incurred to date on a contract include pre-contract costs and costs incurred after the contract date. Pre-contract costs include learning costs for a new process, design fees, and any other expenditures likely to be recouped after the contract is signed. After the contract, the pre-contract costs are considered contract costs to date.

Some pre-contract costs, such as for materials and supplies, may be deferred to an asset called Deferred Contract Costs in anticipation of a specific contract as long as recoverability is probable. If recoverability is not probable, the pre-contract costs must be immediately expensed. If excess goods are produced in anticipation of future orders, related costs may be deferred to inventory if the costs are considered recoverable.

After the status of a contract bid has been determined (accepted or rejected) a review should be conducted of the pre-contract costs. If the contract has been approved, the deferred pre-contract costs are included in contract costs. If the contract is rejected, the pre-contract costs are immediately expensed unless there are other related contracts pending that might recoup these costs.

Back charges are billable costs for work performed by one party that should have been performed by the party billed. Such an agreement is usually stipulated in the contract. Back charges are accounted for by the contractor as a receivable from the subcontractor with a corresponding reduction in contract costs. The subcontractor accounts for the back charge as contract costs and as a payable.

GOVERNMENT CONTRACTS

On cost-plus-fixed fee government contracts, fees should typically be accrued as billable. If an advance payment is received, it should not offset receivables unless the payment is for work-in-process. If any amounts are offset, disclosure is required.

If a government contract is subject to renegotiation, a renegotiation claim to which the contractor is accountable for should be charged to sales and credited to a current liability. Disclosure must be provided of the basis used to compute the anticipated refund.

If the government terminates a contract, contract costs included in inventory should be transferred to receivables. The claim against the government should be shown under current assets unless a long delay in payment is anticipated. A termination claim should be accounted for as a sale. A subcontractor's claim arising from the termination should be included in the contractor's claim against the government. Assume a contractor has a termination claim receivable of $800,000 of which $200,000 applies to the contractor's obligation to the subcontractor. In this situation, a liability should be accrued for $200,000. The termination claim is reduced by any inventory applying to the contract that the contractor is retaining. Disclosure should be provided of the terms of terminated contracts.

Direct costs are included in contract costs such as material, labor, and subcontracting costs. Indirect costs are allocated to contracts on an appropriate basis. Allocable costs include quality control, insurance, contract supervision, repairs and maintenance, tools, and inspection. Learning and startup costs should be charged to existing contracts. The entry for an expected loss on a contract is to make a loss provision.

REVENUE RECOGNITION WHEN A RIGHT OF RETURN EXISTS

A reasonable estimate of returned merchandise may be impaired if the products are not similar, lack of previous experience in estimating returns because the product is new or circumstances have changed, a long time period exists for returns, and the product has a high degree of obsolescence.

Example 2. On March 1, 19X5, product sales of $1,000,000 were made. The cost of the goods is $600,000. A 60-day return privilege exists. The anticipated return rate of goods is 10%. On April 15, 19X5, a customer returns goods having a selling price of $80,000. The criteria to recognize revenue when the right of return exits have been satisfied. The journal entries follow:

March 1, 19X5

Accounts Receivable	1,000,000	
Sales		1,000,000
Cost of Sales	600,000	
Inventory		600,000
Sales Returns	100,000	
Allowance for Sales Returns		100,000

$1,000,000 × 10% = $100,000

Inventory	40,000	
Cost of Sales		40,000

$100,000 × 40% (gross profit rate) = $40,000

April 15, 19X5

Allowance for Sales Returns	80,000	
Accounts Receivable		80,000

Cost of Sales	8,000	
Inventory		8,000*
*Inventory assumed returned ($100,000 × 40%)		$40,000
Less: Amount returned ($80,000 × 40%)		32,000
Adjustment to inventory		$ 4,000

SOFTWARE REVENUE RECOGNITION

As per AICPA Statement of Position 97-2, revenue should be recorded when the software contract does not involve major production, change, or customization as long as the following conditions exist:

1. The contract is enforceable.
2. The software has been delivered.
3. Receipt of payment is probable.
4. The selling price is fixed or known.

Separate accounting is required for the service aspect of a software transaction if the following conditions exist:

1. The services are required for the software transaction.
2. A separate provision exists in the contract covering services so a price for such services is provided for.

A software contract may include more than one component such as upgrade, customer support subsequent to sale, add-ons, and return or exchange provision. The total selling price of the software transaction should be allocated to the contractual components based on their fair values. If fair value is not ascertainable, revenue should be deferred until it is determinable or when all components of the transaction have been delivered. NOTE: The four revenue criteria stipulated above must be met before any allocation of the fee to the contractual elements may be made. Additionally, the fee for a contractual component is ascertainable if the element is sold separately.

WARRANTY AND MAINTENANCE REVENUE

Extended warranty and product maintenance contracts are often provided by retailers as separately priced services in addition to the sale of their products. Any warranty or maintenance agreements that are not separately priced should be accounted for as contingencies. Services under contracts may be provided at fixed intervals, a certain number of times, or as required to keep the product operational.

Revenues and incremental direct cost from separately priced extended warranty and product maintenance contracts should be initially deferred. Revenue should be recorded on a straight line basis over the contract period. The associated incremental direct costs should be expensed proportionately to the revenue recognized. Incremental direct costs arise from obtaining the contract. Other costs, such as the cost of services rendered, general and administrative costs, and the costs of contracts not consummated, should be expensed as incurred.

Losses from these contracts should be recognized when the anticipated costs of rendering the service plus the unamortized portion of acquisition cost exceeds the corresponding deferred revenue. To ascertain loss, contracts should be grouped in a consistent manner. Losses are not recognized on individual contracts but instead apply to a grouping of similar contracts. Loss is recognized by initially reducing unamortized acquisition costs. If this is insufficient, a liability is recorded.

CONTRIBUTIONS

FASB Statement Number 116 applies to the accounting and reporting for contributions received and contributions made. Cash, other monetary and nonmonetary assets, services, or unconditional promises to give assets or services qualify as contributions. Contributions may involve either donor imposed restrictions or donor imposed conditions. If the donor restricts the way a contribution is to be used (such as to build a research laboratory), it is considered a restriction and the revenue from such a contribution and any associated costs are recognized immediately. However, if the donor imposes a condition, such as, the donee must obtain matching funds, that condition must be met before revenue may be recognized.

A donor may make an unconditional or conditional promise. An unconditional promise exists if the donor has no right to take back the donated asset and the contribution would be available after some stated time period or on demand. Unconditional promises to give contributions are recognized immediately. A conditional promise is contingent upon the happening of a future occurrence. If that event does not take place, the donor is not obligated by the promise. A vague promise is considered conditional. Conditional promises are recorded only when its terms are met. A conditional promise may be treated as an unconditional promise if the possibility that the condition will not be satisfied is remote.

There must be supporting evidence to substantiate that a promise has been made. Such evidence includes information about the donor (e.g., donor's name and address), the amount the donor commits to give such as in a public announcement, when the amount promised will be given, and to whom the promise to give was made. The donor may have taken certain actions relying on the promise. The donor may have made partial payments. A recorded promise should be at the fair market value of the consideration. If the amount will be collected beyond one year, a discounted cash flow calculation may be made. If discounting is done, the interest is accounted for as contribution income, not interest income.

Contributed services should be recognized if specialized skills are rendered by the donor and those skills would have been purchased by the donee if they were not donated. Contributions received should be recorded at fair value by debiting the asset and crediting revenue. Quoted market prices or market prices for similar assets, appraisal by independent experts, or valuation techniques such as discounted cash flows, should be used to compute fair value. The value of contributed services should be based on quoted market prices for those services.

Disclosures are required in the financial statements of recipients of contributions. For unconditional promises to give, the amount of receivables due within one year, in one to five years, and more than five years should be disclosed along with the amount expected to be uncollected. For conditional promises to give, disclosure is required of promised amounts along with a description of the promise. Promises with similar characteristics may be grouped. Disclosure should be made of the nature and degree of contributed services, limitations or conditions set by the donor, and the programs or activities benefiting from contributed services. Companies are encouraged to disclose the fair value of services received but not recorded as revenue.

The donor should record an expense and a corresponding decrease in assets, or an increase in liabilities, at fair value, in the year in which the contribution is made. If fair value differs from carrying value, a loss or gain on disposition is recorded.

ADVERTISING COSTS

American Institute of CPAs' Statement of Position 93-7 (Reporting on Advertising Costs) requires the expensing of advertising as incurred when the advertising program first occurs. However, the cost of direct-response advertising may be deferred if the major purpose of the promotion is to elicit sales to customers who respond specifically to the advertising and for which future benefit exists. For example, the former condition is satisfied if the response card is specially coded. The latter condition is met if the resulting future revenues exceed the future costs to be incurred. The deferred advertising is amortized over the expected benefit period using the revenue method (current year revenue to total revenue). The cost of a billboard should also be capitalized and amortized. Advertising expenditures incurred after revenue is recognized should be accrued. These advertising costs should be expensed when the related revenues are recognized.

RESTRUCTURING CHARGES

Securities and Exchange Commission Staff Accounting Bulletin Number 67 requires restructuring charges to be expensed and presented as a component in computing income from operations.

In general, an expense and liability should be accrued for employee termination benefits in a restructuring. Disclosure should be made of the group and number of workers laid off.

An exit plan requires the recognition of a liability for the restructuring changes incurred if there is no future benefit to continuing operations. The expense for the estimated costs should be made on the commitment date of the exit plan. Expected gains from assets to be sold in connection with the exit plan should be recorded in the year realized. These gains are not allowed to offset the accrued liability for exit costs. Exit costs incurred are presented as a separate item as part of income from continuing operations. Disclosures associated with an exit plan include the terms of the exit plan, description and amount of exit costs incurred, activities to be exited from, method of disposition, expected completion date, and liability adjustments.

ORGANIZATION COSTS

Organization costs (e.g., legal and accounting fees to start a business) must be expensed as incurred.

Startup Costs

Under SOP 98-5, startup (preoperating, preopening) costs must be expensed as incurred. Startup costs include the one-time costs of opening a new business, introducing a new product or service, conducting business in a new territory, or having business with a new class of customer.

Costs to Develop or Obtain Computer Software for Internal Use

AICPA Statement of Position 98-1 (Accounting for the Costs of Computer Software Developed or Obtained for Internal Use) deals with software development or purchase for internal (not external) use. The company has no plan to sell the software.

The three stages of computer development are:

1. *Preliminary project stage.* This stage may involve such activities as structuring an assembly team, appraising vendor proposals, and think-

ing about reengineering efforts. A software development strategy or vendor has not yet been decided upon. During this stage, all costs should be expensed as incurred without separate presentation in the income statement.

2. *Application development stage.* A determination has been made as to how the software development work will be carried out. Costs incurred during this stage are capitalized provided it is probable the project will be completed successfully. Typical costs that should be capitalized include direct material and/or services contributing to the project, payroll costs, and any interest costs incurred during the development process, testing and installation. General and administrative costs, overhead, and training costs are not deferred.

3. *Post-implementation/operation stage.* The stage begins when the internal use software is put in service. Capitalized costs should be amortized on a straight-line basis over the estimated useful life of the internally-used software. Because the estimated life is typically short it should be reappraised periodically. Capitalized costs of any existing software that is to be replaced by newly developed software should be expensed when the new software is ready for use.

Costs for upgrades or enhancements should only be capitalized if they result in additional functionality beyond the original software.

Manual data conversion costs should be expensed. However, costs to develop bridging software should be capitalized.

If internally developed computer software is used in R&D activities, it should be accounted for under FASB Statement Number 2 (Accounting for Research and Development Costs). The software development costs included as R&D expenditures are (1) software acquired to be used in R&D activities where the software has no alternative future use and (2) software applicable to a specific pilot R&D projects.

In the event it is later decided to sell computer software initially developed for internal use, the sales proceeds (in excess of direct incremental costs) should be netted against the book value of the deferred software costs. When book value is reduced to zero, profit is recognized on the excess amount. Under EITF Issue 97-13 (Accounting for Costs Incurred in Connection with a Consulting Contract or an Internal Project That Combines Business Process Reengineering and Information Technology Transformation) business process reengineering costs are expensed irrespective of whether such reengineering efforts are performed as a separate project or as an element of a larger project encompaassing software development.

EARNINGS PER SHARE

FASB Statement Number 128 (Earnings Per Share) covers the computation, reporting and disclosures associated with earnings per share. The pronouncement makes some major changes in the computation of earnings per share as previously existed under APB Opinion Number 15. Presentation of both basic and diluted earnings per share is mandated.

Basic earnings per share takes into consideration only the actual number of outstanding common shares during the period (and those contingently issuable in certain cases).

Diluted earnings per share includes the effect of common shares actually outstanding and the effect of convertible securities, stock options, stock warrants, and their equivalents. Diluted earnings per share should not assume the conversion, exercise, or contingent issuance of securities having an antidilutive effect (increasing earnings per share or decreasing loss per share) because it violates conservatism.

BASIC EARNINGS PER SHARE

Basic earnings per share equals net income available to common stockholders divided by the weighted average number of common shares outstanding. Common stock equivalents are no longer presented in this computation. When a prior period adjustment occurs that causes a restatement of previous years' earnings, basic EPS should be restated.

Example 3. The following data are presented for a company:

Preferred stock, $10 par, 6% cumulative, 30,000 shares issued and outstanding	$300,000
Common stock, $5 par, 100,000 shares issued and outstanding	$500,000
Net income	$400,000

The cash dividend on the preferred stock is $18,000 (6% × $300,000).

Basic EPS equals $3.82 as computed below.

Earnings available to common stockholders:

Net income	$400,000
Less: Preferred dividends	(18,000)
Earnings available to common stockholders	$382,000

Basic EPS = $382,000/100,000 shares = $3.82

Example 4. On January 1, 19X3, David Company had the following shares outstanding:

6% Cumulative preferred stock, $100 par value 150,000 shares
Common stock, $5 par value   500,000 shares

During the year, the following took place:

- On April 1, 19X3, the company issued 100,000 shares of common stock.
- On September 1, 19X3, the company declared and issued a 10% stock dividend.
- For the year ended December 31, 19X3, the net income was $2,200,000.

Basic earnings per share for 19X3 equals $2.06 ($1,300,000/632,500 shares) computed below.

Earnings available to common stockholders:

Net income	$2,200,000
Less: Preferred dividend (150,000 shares x $6)	(900,000)
Earnings available to common stockholders	$1,300,000

Weighted-average number of outstanding common shares is determined as follows:

1/1/19X3 - 3/31/19X3 (500,000 x 3/12 x 110%)	137,500
4/1/19X3 - 8/31/19X3 (600,000 x 5/12 x 110%)	275,000
9/1/19X3 - 12/31/19X3 (660,000 x 4/12)	220,000
Weighted average outstanding common shares	632,500

DILUTED EARNINGS PER SHARE

If potentially dilutive securities exist that are outstanding, such as convertible debt, convertible preferred stock, stock options, or stock warrants, then both basic and diluted earnings per share must be shown.

FASB Statement Number 128 retains the "if converted method" to account for convertible securities in earnings per share determination. The pronouncement also retains the "treasury stock method" to account for stock options and warrants.

If options are granted as part of a stock-based compensation agreement, the assumed proceeds from the exercise of the options under the treasury stock method includes deferred compensation and the ensuing tax benefit that would be credited to paid-in capital arising from the exercise of the options.

The denominator of diluted earnings per share equals the weighted average outstanding common shares for the period plus the assumed issue of common shares arising from convertible securities plus the assumed shares issued because of the exercise of stock options or stock warrants, or their equivalent.

Table 1 shows in summary form the earnings per share fractions.

Table 1. Earnings Per Share Fractions

BASIC EARNINGS PER SHARE = Net Income Available to Common Stockholders/Weighted Average Number of Common Shares Outstanding

DILUTED EARNINGS PER SHARE = Net Income Available to Common Stockholders + Net of Tax Interest and/or Dividend Savings on Convertible Securities/Weighted Average Number of Common Shares Outstanding + Effect of Convertible Securities + Net Effect of Stock Options

---

Example 5. Assume the same information as in the prior example dealing with basic earnings per share for David Company. Assume further that potentially diluted securities outstanding include 5% convertible bonds (each $1,000 bond is convertible into 25 shares of common stock) having a face value of $5,000,000. There are options to buy 50,000 shares of common stock at $10 per share. The average market price for common shares is $25 per share for 19X3. The tax rate is 30%. Diluted earnings per share for 19X3 is $1.87 ($1,475,000/787,500 shares) as computed below.

Income for diluted earnings per share:

Earnings available to common stockholders		$1,300,000
Interest expense on convertible bonds ($5,000,000 × .05)	$250,000	
Less: Tax savings ($250,000 × .30)	(75,000)	
Interest expense (net of tax)		175,000
Income for diluted earnings per share		$1,475,000
Shares outstanding for diluted earnings per share:		
Weighted average outstanding common shares		632,500
Assumed issued common shares for convertible bonds (5,000 bonds × 25 shares)		125,000
Assumed issued common shares from exercise of option	50,000	
Less: Assumed repurchase of treasury shares (50,000 × $10 = $500,000/$25)	(20,000)	30,000
Shares outstanding for diluted earnings per share		787,500

Basic earnings per share and diluted earnings per share (if required) must be disclosed on the face of the income statement. A reconciliation is required of the numerators and denominators for basic and diluted earnings per share.

FINANCIAL STATEMENT REPORTING: THE BALANCE SHEET

LOANS RECEIVABLE

FASB Statement Number 91 (Accounting for Nonrefundable Fees and Costs Associated With Originating or Acquiring Loans and Initial Direct Costs of Leases) applies to both the incremental direct costs of originating a loan, and internally incurred costs directly related to loan activity. Loan origination fees are netted with the related loan origination costs and are accounted for in the following manner:

- For loans held for resale, the net cost is capitalized and recognized at the time the loan is sold.
- For loans held for investment, the net cost is capitalized and amortized over the loan period using the interest method.

Loan commitment fees are initially deferred and recognized in earnings as follows:

- If the commitment is exercised, the fee is recognized over the loan period by the interest method.
- If the commitment expires, the fee is recognized at the expiration date.
- If, based upon previous experience, exercise of the commitment is remote, amortize the fee over the commitment period using the straight-line method.

IMPAIRMENT OF LOANS

FASB Statement Number 114 (Accounting by Creditors for Impairment of a Loan) provides that a loan is a contractual obligation to receive money either on demand or at a fixed or determinable date. Loans include accounts receivable and notes if their maturity date exceeds one year. If it is probable that some or all of the principal or interest is uncollectible, the loan is deemed impaired. A loss on an impaired loan is recorded immediately by debiting bad debt expense and crediting a valuation allowance.

Determining the Value of an Impaired Loan

The loss on an impaired loan is the difference between the investment in loan and the discounted value of future cash flows using the effective interest rate on the original loan. In general, the investment in loan is the principal plus accrued interest. In practical terms, the value of a loan may be based on its market price, if available. The loan value may also be based on the fair value of the collateral, less estimated selling costs, if the loan is collateralized and the security is expected to be the only basis of repayment.

Example 1. On December 31, 2000, Debtor Inc. issues a five-year, $100,000 note at an annual interest rate of 10% payable to Creditor Inc. The market interest rate for the loan is 12%. The discounted value of the principal is $56,742 (based on a principal of $100,000 discounted at 12% for 5 years). The discounted value of the interest payments is $36,048 (based on annual interest of $10,000 for 5 years discounted at 12%). Thus, the discounted value of the loan is $92,790 ($56,742 plus $36,048). Discount on Notes Receivable is $7,210 ($100,000 less $92,790). The discount will be amortized using the effective interest method. Creditor Inc. records the note as follows:

Notes Receivable	100,000	
Discount on Notes Receivable		7,210
Cash		92,790

On December 31, 2002, Creditor Inc. determines that it is probable that Debtor Inc. will only be able to repay interest of $8,000 per year (rather than $10,000 per year) and $70,000 (rather than $100,000) of face value at maturity. This loan impairment requires the immediate recognition of a loss. The discounted value of future cash flows discounted for 3 years at 12% for $70,000 is $49,824, and for $8,000 is $19,215. Therefore, the total present value of future cash flows is $69,039 ($49,824 plus $19,215). On 12/31/02, the carrying value of the investment in loan is $95,196. As a result, the impairment loss is $26,157 ($95,196 less $69,039). The journal entry to record the loss is:

| Bad Debts | 26,157 | |
| Allowance for Bad Debts | | 26,157 |

Interest income from an impaired loan may be recognized using several methods including cash-basis, cost-recovery, or a combination.

If the creditor's charging off of some part of the loan results in recording an investment in an impaired loan below its present value of future cash flows, no additional impairment is to be recorded.

In determining the collectibility of a loan, consideration should be given to the following:

- Financial problems of borrower
- Borrower is in an unstable or unhealthy industry
- Regulatory reports
- Compliance exception reports
- Amount of loan
- Prior loss experience
- Lack of marketability of collateral

A loan is not considered impaired when the delay in collecting is insignificant.

Disclosures

The following should be disclosed either in the body of the financial statements or in the footnotes:

- The creditor's policy of recognizing interest income on impaired loans, including the recording of cash receipts.
- The average recorded investment in impaired loans, the related interest revenue recognized while the loans were impaired, and the amount of interest revenue recognized using the cash basis while the loans were impaired.
- The total investment in impaired loans including (1) the amount of investments for which a related valuation allowance exists and (2) the amount of investments for which a valuation allowance does not exist.

PATENTS

The legal life of patents is 20 years.

DONATION OF FIXED ASSETS

FASB Statement Number 116 (Accounting for Contributions Received and Contributions Made) requires a donated fixed asset to be recorded at its fair market value by debiting the fixed asset and crediting contribution revenue.

According to FASB Statement 116, the company donating a nonmonetary asset recognizes an expense for the fair value of the donated asset. The difference between the carrying value and the fair value of the donated asset is a gain or loss.

Example 2. Hartman Company donates land costing $100,000 with a fair value of $130,000. The journal entry is:

Contribution Expense	130,000	
Land		100,000
Gain on Disposal of Land		30,000

If a company pledges unconditionally to give an asset in the future, accrue contribution expense and a payable. However, if the pledge is conditional, an entry is not made until the asset is transferred.

IMPAIRMENT OF FIXED ASSETS

FASB Statement Number 121 (Accounting for the Impairment of Long-Lived Assets and for Long-Lived Assets to be Disposed Of) states that a noncurrent asset is considered impaired if the total (undiscounted) expected future cash flows from using it is below its carrying value. (In ascertaining whether asset impairment has occurred, its carrying value should include any associated goodwill.) If this recoverability test for asset impairment is satisfied, an impairment loss must be computed as the excess of the asset's book value over its fair value. Fair value is the amount at which the asset could be purchased or sold between willing participants; fair value is not based on a forced or liquidation sale. Possible methods to determine fair market value include the market price in an active market, price of similar assets, or value based on a valuation technique (e.g., present value of future cash flows, options pricing model).

If the fair market value is not determinable and the discounted value of future cash flows is used, the asset should be grouped at the lowest level at which the cash flows are separately identifiable.

An impairment loss is charged against earnings with a similar reduction in the recorded value of the impaired fixed asset. After impairment, the reduced carrying value becomes the new cost basis for the fixed asset. Thus, the fixed asset cannot be written up for a subsequent recovery in market value. Therefore, the impaired loss cannot be restored. Depreciation is based on the new cost basis.

In the event that the impaired asset is to be disposed of instead of being kept in service, the impaired asset should be recorded at the lower of cost or net realizable value.

An impairment may arise from a major change in how the asset is used, a decline in market value, continued expected losses from the asset, excess construction costs over expected amounts, adverse business conditions, or legal problems.

Example 3. A company has a fixed asset with a cost of $1,000,000 and accumulated depreciation of $200,000. In applying the recoverability test to ascertain if an impairment has taken place, it is determined that the total (undiscounted) expected future net cash flows is $840,000. No impairment exists because the undiscounted future expected net cash flows ($840,000) is more than the carrying value of the asset ($800,000).

Example 4. Assume the same data as in the prior example except that the total (undiscounted) future net cash flows is $700,000. The recoverability test now shows an impairment loss because the total (undiscounted) cash flows ($700,000) is less than the book value ($800,000) of the fixed asset. Assuming the fixed asset has a fair market value of $680,000, the impairment loss equals $120,000 (book value of $800,000 less fair market value of $680,000). The journal entry to record the impairment is:

Loss on Impairment of Fixed Asset	120,000	
Accumulated Depreciation		120,000

The following must be footnoted in connection with impaired fixed assets:
- Identifying the asset impaired
- Amount of loss
- Method used to determine fair market value
- Cause of impairment
- Business segment experiencing the impairment in asset value

If an impaired asset is to be disposed of instead of used, the impaired asset is presented at the lower of cost or net realizable value (fair value less cost to sell). The selling costs include brokerage commissions and transfer fees. However, insurance, security services, utility expenses and costs to protect or maintain the asset are usually not deemed selling costs in determining net realizable value. The present value of costs to sell may be used when the fair value of the asset is based on the discounted cash flows and the sale is expected to take place after one year.

If the asset is to be disposed of shortly, the net realizable value is a better measure of the cash flows that one can expect to receive from the impaired asset. Assets held for disposal are not depreciated. Conceptually, these assets are more like inventory because they are expected to be sold in the near term.

STOCK-BASED COMPENSATION

FASB Statement Number 123 (Accounting for Stock-Based Compensation) applies to stock option plans, nonvested stock, employee stock purchase plans, and stock compensation awards that are to be settled by cash payment.

Stock Option Plans

Employers may account for stock option plans using either the "intrinsic value" method or the "fair value" method.

The "intrinsic value" method is the one in place before FASB Statement Number 123. It is already discussed in the main volume. The "fair value" method under FASB Statement Number 123 is discussed in this supplement.

Under the fair value method, fair value is computed by using an option-pricing model that takes into account several factors. A popular option pricing model is Black and Scholes. It is used to compute the equilibrium value of an option. The model provides insight into the valuation of debt relative to equity. This model may be programmed into computer spreadsheets and some pocket calculators. The Black-Scholes model makes it possible to determine the present value of hypothetical financial instruments. Some assumptions of this model are that 1) the stock options are freely traded and 2) the total return rate (considering the change in price plus dividends) may be determined based on a continuous compounding over the life of the option. Under FASB Statement Number 123 the option life is the expected time period until the option is exercised rather than the contractual term. By reducing the option's life its value is reduced. It is a random variable derived from a normal bell curve distribution. The Black-Scholes model was developed based on European-style options exercisable only at expiration. However, most employee stock options are American-style and are exercisable at any time during the option life once vesting has taken place. The Black-Scholes model uses the volatility expected for the option's life. NOTE: Difficulties arise in determining option values when there is an early option exercise and variability in stock price and dividends. The Black-Scholes model may also be used in valuing put options by modifying computations. See chapter on Financial Derivatives Products and Financial Engineering for more information on Black-Scholes.

Other models may be used for option pricing such as the more complicated binomial model.

Before the current value of an option may be computed, consideration must be given to its expiration value.

Compensation expense is based on the fair value of the award at the grant date, and is recognized over the period between the grant date and the vesting date, in a way similar to the intrinsic value method.

Under the fair value method, the stock option is accounted for in a similar way as the journal entries under the intrinsic value method, except the fair value of the option would be recognized as deferred compensation and amortized over the period from the grant date to the date the option is initially exercisable.

Note: Non-compensatory stock option plans may also exist. Such plans are characterized by having stock offered to employees on some basis (e.g., equally, percent of salary), participation by full-time employees, a reasonable time period for the exercise of the options, and the discount to employees to buy the stock is not better than that afforded to company stockholders. If any of these criteria are not satisfied, than the plan is compensatory in nature. The objective of a non-compensatory plan is to obtain funds and to have greater widespread ownership in the company among employees. It is not primarily designed to provide compensation for services performed. Therefore, no compensation expense is recognized.

Nonvested Stock

Nonvested stock is stock that cannot be sold currently because the employee who was granted the shares has not yet satisfied the vesting requirements to earn the right to the shares. The fair value of a share of nonvested stock awarded to an employee is measured at the market price per share of nonrestricted stock on the grant date unless a restriction will be imposed after the employee has a vested right to it, in which case the fair value is approximated considering the restriction.

Employee Stock Purchase Plans

An employee stock purchase plan allows employees to buy stock at a discount. It is noncompensatory if the discount is minor (5% or less), most full-time employees may participate, and the plan has no option features.

Stock Compensation Awards Required to Be Settled by Paying Cash

Some stock-based compensation plans require an employer to pay an employee, either on demand or at a particular date, a cash amount based on the appreciation in the market price of the employer's stock. A ceiling stock price may be established depending on the plan. The compensation cost applicable to the award is the amount of change in stock price.

Disclosures

The following should be disclosed regarding the fair value method to account for stock options as well as for stock-based compensation plans in general:

- Weighted-average grant date fair value of options and/or other equity instruments granted during the year.
- A description of the method and assumptions used to estimate fair value of options.
- Major changes in the terms of stock-based compensation plans.
- Amendments to outstanding awards.

Tax Aspects

Compensation expense is deductible for tax reporting when paid but deducted for financial reporting when accrued. This results in interperiod income tax allocation involving a deferred income tax credit. If for some reason reversal of the temporary difference does not occur, a permanent difference exists which does not impact profit. The difference should adjust paid-in-capital in the year the accrual occurs.

ACCOUNTING AND DISCLOSURES

SEGMENTAL DISCLOSURES

FASB Statement Number 131 (Disclosures About Segments of an Enterprise and Related Information) requires that the amount reported for each segment item should be based on what is used by the "chief operating decision-maker" in formulating a determination as to how much resources to assign to a segment and how to appraise the performance of that segment. The term "chief operating decision maker" may apply to the chief executive officer or chief operating officer or to a group of executives. *Note:* The reference of "chief operating decision-maker" may apply to a function and not necessarily to a specific person(s).

Revenue, gains, expenses, losses, and assets should only be allocated to a segment if the chief operating decision maker considers it in measuring a segment's earnings for purposes of making a financial or operating decision. The same is true with regard to allocating to segments eliminations and adjustments applying to the company's general purpose financial statements. Any allocation of financial items to a segment should be rationally based.

In measuring a segment's earnings or assets, the following should be disclosed for explanatory purposes:

- Measurement or valuation basis used.
- Differences in measurements used for the general-purpose financial statements relative to the financial information of the segment.

- A change in measurement method relative to prior years.
- A symmetrical allocation meaning an allocation of depreciation or amortization to a segment without a related allocation to the associated asset.

Segmental information is required in annual financial statements. Some segmental disclosures are required in interim financial statements.

Segmental Attributes

An operating segment is a distinct revenue-producing component of the business for which internal financial data are produced. Expenses are recognized as incurred in that segment. *Note:* A start-up operation would qualify as an operating segment even though revenue is not being earned. An operating segment is periodically reviewed by the chief operating decision-maker to evaluate performance and to determine what and how much resources to allocate to the segment.

A reportable segment requiring disclosure is one which is both an operating segment and meets certain percentage tests discussed in the next section.

An aggregation may be made of operating segments if they are similar in terms of products or services, customer class, manufacturing processes, distribution channels, legal entity, and regulatory control.

Percentage Tests

A reportable segment satisfies one of the following criteria:

- Revenue including unaffiliated and intersegment sales or transfers is 10% or more of total (combined) revenue of all operating segments.
- Operating profit or loss is 10% or more of total operating profit of all operating segments.
- Assets are 10% or more of total assets of all operating segments.

After the 10% tests have been made, additional segments may be reported on if they do not satisfy the 10% tests until at least 75% (constituting a substantial portion) of total revenue of all operating segments have been included. As a practical matter, no more than 10 segments (upper limit) should be reported because to do otherwise would result in too cumbersome or detailed reporting. In this case, combined reporting should be of those operating segments most closely related.

If a segment does not meet the 10% test for reportability in the current year but met the 10% test in prior years and is expected to be reportable in future years, it should still be reported in the current year.

If a segment passes the 10% test in the current year because of some unusual and rare occurrence, it should be excluded from reporting in the current year.

Reconciliation

A company does not have to use the same accounting principles for segmental purposes as that used to prepare the consolidated financial statements. There must be a reconciliation between segmental financial data and general purpose financial statements. The reconciliation is for revenue, operating profit or loss, and assets. Any differences in measurement approaches between the company as a whole and its segments should be explained. If measurement practices have changed over the years regarding the operating segments, that fact should be disclosed and explained. The business must describe its reasoning and methods in deriving the composition of its operating segments.

Restatement

If the business structure changes, this may require a restatement of segmental information presented in prior years to aid in comparability. If restatement occurs, appropriate footnote disclosure should be made.

Disclosures

Disclosure should be provided of major sources of foreign revenue constituting 10% or more of total revenue. Further, disclosure is necessary if a foreign area constitutes 10% or more of total operating profit or loss, or of total assets. The foreign area and the percentage derived therein should be disclosed.

Disclosure should exist of the dollar sales to major customers comprising of 10% or more of total revenue. A single customer may refer to more than one customer if under common control (e.g., subsidiaries of a parent). A single customer may also be defined as government agencies.

Information about foreign geographic areas and customers are required even if this information is not used by the business in formulating operating decisions.

Disclosure should be made of major contracts to other entities and governments.

Disclosure should be made of how reporting segments were determined (e.g., customer class, products or services, geographic areas). Disclosure should be given identifying those operating segments that have been aggregated. The following should be disclosed for each reportable segment:

- Types of products and services.
- Revenue to outside customers as well as intersegment revenue.
- Operating profit or loss.
- Total assets.
- Capital expenditures.
- Depreciation, depletion and amortization.
- Major noncash revenues and expenses excluding that immediately above.
- Interest revenue and interest expense.
- Extraordinary and unusual items.
- Equity in earnings of investee.
- Tax effects.

Example 1. A company reports the following information for its reportable segments:

Segment	Total Revenue	Operating Profit	Identifiable Assets
1	$500	$50	$200
2	250	10	150
3	3,500	200	1,950
4	1,500	100	900
Total	$5,750	$360	$3,200

The revenue test is 10% × $5,750 = $575. Segments 3 and 4 satisfy this test.

The operating profit (loss) test is 10% × $360 = $36. Segments 1, 3 and 4 satisfy this test.

The identifiable assets test is 10% × $3,200 = $320. Segments 3 and 4 satisfy this test. Therefore, the reportable segments are 1,3 and 4.

DISCLOSURE OF CAPITAL STRUCTURE INFORMATION

FASB Statement Number 129 (Disclosure of Information About Capital Structure) requires footnote disclosure regarding the rights and privileges of common and preferred stockholders such as dividend preferences, participation privileges, conversion terms, unusual voting rights, sinking fund requirements, and terms for additional issuances. In a liquidation situation, footnote information must be made of liquidation preferences such as dividend arrearages and liquidation values for preferred stock. In the case of redeemable stock, disclosure must be made of redemption requirements for each of the next five years.

RELATED PARTY DISCLOSURES

FASB Statement Number 57 deals with disclosures for related party transactions. Such transactions occur when a transacting party can significantly influence or exercise control of another transaction party because of a financial, common ownership, or familial relationship. It may also arise when a nontransacting party can significantly impact the policies of two other transacting parties. Related party transactions include those involving:

- Joint ventures.
- Activities between a subsidiary and parent.
- Activities between affiliates of the same parent company.
- Relationships between the company and its principal owners, management, or their immediate families.

Related party transactions often occur in the ordinary course of business and may include such activities as granting loans or incurring debt, sales, purchases, services performed or received, guarantees, allocating common costs as the basis for billings, compensating balance requirements, property transfers, rentals, and filing of consolidated tax returns.

Related party transactions are presumed not to be at arm's length. They are usually not derived from competitive, free-market dealings. Some possible examples follow:

- A "shell" company (with no economic substance) purchases merchandise at inflated prices.
- A lease at "bargain" or excessive prices.
- Unusual guarantees or pledges.
- A loan at an unusually low or high interest rate
- Payments for services at inflated prices.

Related party disclosures include the following:

- Nature and substance of the relationship.
- Amount of transaction.

- Terms of transaction.
- Year-end balances due or owed.
- Any control relationships that exist.

DISCLOSURES FOR DERIVATIVES

The Securities and Exchange Commission requires certain disclosures for the accounting and reporting for derivatives including financial instruments and commodities. Derivative commodity instruments include futures, forwards, options and swaps. These disclosures include:

- The types and nature of derivative instruments to be accounted for.
- The accounting method used for derivatives such as the fair value method, accrual method, and deferral method. Disclosure should be made where gains and losses associated with derivatives are reported.
- The risks associated with the derivatives.
- Distinguishment of derivatives used for trading or nontrading purposes.
- Derivatives used for hedging purposes including explanation.

INFLATION INFORMATION

FASB Statement Number 89 (Financial Reporting and Changing Prices) permits an entity to voluntarily disclose inflation information so management and financial statement readers can better evaluate the impact of inflation on the business. Selected summarized financial information should be presented based on current costs and adjusted for inflation (in constant purchasing power) for a five-year period. The Consumer Price Index for All Urban Consumers may be used. Inflation disclosures include those for sales and operating revenue stated in constant purchasing power, income from continuing operations (including per share amounts) on a current cost basis, cash dividends per share in constant purchasing power, market price per share restated in constant purchasing power, purchasing power gain or loss on net monetary items, inflation adjusted inventory, restated fixed assets, foreign currency translation based on current cost, net assets based on current cost, and the Consumer Price Index used.

ENVIRONMENTAL REPORTING AND DISCLOSURES

Companies are faced with federal and local compliance requirements regarding environmental issues. Environmental laws provide rigorous specifications with which companies must comply. The costs of compliance could significantly increase a company's expected cost of projects and processes. Failure to abide by environmental dictates could result in substantial costs and risks including civil and criminal prosecution and fines. The company must police itself to avoid legal defense fees and penalties. An effective compliance program, such as having preventive and detective controls, is crucial in minimizing environmental risks. The corporate manager must be assured that appropriate accounting, reporting, and disclosures for environmental issues are being practiced by the firm.

Legislation

The Environmental Protection Agency (EPA) enforces Federal laws regulating pollution, sold waste disposal, water supply, pesticide and radiation control and ocean dumping. EPA regulations require adherence to specific pollution detection procedures, such as leak testing, and installation of corrosion protection and leak detection systems applicable to underground storage tanks.

The Clean Air Act of 1963 concentrates on issues such as acid rain, urban smog, air-borne toxins, ozone-depleting chemicals and other air pollution problems. The Clean Water Act established controls of water pollution and wetlands preservation.

The Environmental Response Compensation and Liability Act (Superfund) relates to uncontrolled or abandoned hazardous waste disposal sites. Companies must disclose emergency planning, spills or accidents of hazardous materials, and when chemicals are released into surrounding areas. The chemicals must be disclosed to prospective buyers, employees, and tenants.

To go from a reactive position (the company just complies with regulations) to a proactive policy (the company envelops environmental concerns into its daily business practices), the entity must formulate financial information to complement technical and scientific data. Further, environmental expenditures have to be segregated so as to improve decision making and accountability for environmental responsibilities. There should be an appraisal model for setting priorities as the basis for resource allocations.

Accounting and Reporting

Securities and Exchange Commission Staff Accounting Bulletin Number 92 deals with how environmental liabilities are determined, future contingencies, "key" environmental factors, and disclosures of environmental problems. Depending on the circumstances a liability and/or footnote disclosure would be required. Examples are:

- Information on site remediation projects such as current and future costs, and remediation trends. Site remediation includes hazard waste sites.
- Contamination due to environmental health and safety problems.
- Legal and regulatory compliance issues such as with regard to cleanup responsibility.
- Water or air pollution.

Environmental problems should be addressed immediately to avoid significant future costs including additional cleanup costs, penalties, and legal fees.

Environmental costs should be compared to budgeted amounts, and variances may be computed and tracked. Forecasted information should be changed as new information is available. Internal controls must be established over the firm's environmental responsibility, including internal checks, safeguarding of assets, and segregation of duties.

A financial analysis of environmental costs should be conducted by analyzing cost trends over the years within the company, comparisons to competing companies, and comparisons to industry averages. Additionally, comparisons should be made between projects within the company.

Environmental costs should be allocated across departments, products, and services. Environmental cost information is useful in product and service mix decisions, pricing policies, selecting production inputs, appraising pollution prevention programs, and evaluating waste management policies.

KEY FINANCIAL ACCOUNTING AREAS

LEASES

Transfer of Lease Receivable

The lessor may transfer a lease receivable. The gain on sale equals the cash received less both the portion of the gross investment sold and unearned income related to the minimum lease payments.

Example 1. A lessor has on its books a lease receivable with an unguaranteed residual value. Unlike guaranteed residual value, unguaranteed residual value does not qualify as a financial asset. The lessor sells an 80% interest in the minimum lease payments for $100,000. The lessor keeps a 20% interest in the minimum lease payments and a 100% interest in the unguaranteed residual value. Other information follows:

Minimum lease payments		$110,000
Unearned income in minimum lease payments		75,000
Gross investment in minimum lease payments		185,000
Add: Unguaranteed residual value	7,000	
Unguaranteed income in residual value	13,000	
Gross investment in residual value		20,000
Gross investment in lease receivable		$205,000

The journal entry for the sale of the lease receivable is:

Cash	100,000	
Unearned income ($75,000 × 80%)	60,000	
Lease receivable ($185,000 × 80%)		148,000
Gain		12,000

Related Parties

In a related party lease where substantial influence exists, the lease should be accounted for based on its economic substance rather than its legal form. If substantial influence is absent, the related party lease should be classified and accounted for as if the participants were unrelated.

FASB Statement Number 13 requires that a parent must consolidate a subsidiary whose principal business operations is leasing property from a parent or other affiliates.

A related party lease agreement involving significant influence may require consolidation accounting for the lessor and lessee if all of the following conditions are present:

- Most of the lessor's activities apply to leasing assets to one specific lessee.
- The lessee incurs the risks and rewards applicable with rented property along with any related debt. This may occur if the lease agreement gives the lessee control and management over the leased property, the lessee guarantees the lessor's debt or residual value of the leased item, and the lessee has the right to purchase the property at a lower than fair value price.
- The lessor's owners do not have a significant residual equity capital investment at risk.

If the consolidation conditions are not met, combined financial statements instead of consolidated financial statements may be appropriate.

FASB Statement Number 57 requires disclosure of the nature and degree of leasing transactions among related parties.

Money-Over-Money Lease

A money-over-money lease occurs when an entity manufactures or purchases an asset, leases it to the lessee, and receives nonrecourse financing exceeding the cost of the asset. The collateral for the borrowing is the leased asset and any future rental derived therefrom. The lessor is prohibited from offsetting the asset (in an operating lease) or the lease receivable (in other than an operating lease) and the nonrecourse obligation unless a legal right of setoff exists. The leasing and borrowing are considered separate transactions.

Business Combinations

A business combination by itself has no bearing on lease classification. In a purchase transaction, the acquirer may assign a new value to a capitalized lease because of the allocation of acquisition price to the net assets of the acquired entity. However, provided the lease terms are not modified, the lease should be accounted for using the original terms and classification. A similar treatment is afforded under the pooling-of-interest method in that the new lease would retain its classification.

With respect to a leveraged lease when the purchase method is used the following guidelines are followed:

- The classification continues as a leveraged lease.
- The net investment in the leveraged lease should be recorded at fair market value including tax effects.
- The usual accounting for a leveraged lease should be practiced.

Disposal of a Business Segment

The expected costs directly associated with a disposal of a business segment decision includes future rental payments less amounts to be received from subleases. The difference between the unamortized cost of the leased property and the discounted value of the minimum lease payments to be received from the sublease is recognized as a gain or loss.

PENSION PLANS

Employers Having More Than One Defined Benefit Plan

If an employer has more than one pension plan, it has to prepare separate calculations of pension expense, fair value of plan assets, and liabilities for each plan.

The employer is prohibited from offsetting assets or liabilities of different pension plans unless a legal right exists to use the assets of one plan to pay the debt or benefits of another plan.

Disclosures may be combined for all pension plans kept by the employer with the following exceptions:

- U.S. pension plans may not be aggregated with foreign pension plans unless there exist similar assumptions.
- A minimum pension asset of one plan may not be used to offset a minimum pension liability of another, and vice versa.

Multiemployer Plans

A multiemployer plan typically includes participation of two or more unrelated employers. It often arises from a collective-bargaining contract with the union. The plan is typically administered by a Board of Trustees. In this instance, plan assets contributed by one employer may be used to pay employee benefits of another participating employer. Hence, the assets are combined for all employers and are available and unrestricted to pay benefits to all employees irrespective of whom they are employed by. In other words, there is no segregation of assets in a particular employer's account or any restrictions placed on that employer's assets. An example is a plan contributed to by all employers employing the members of a particular union regardless of whom the employees work for. Retirees of different employers receive payment from the same combined fund. An example is the teamster's union.

In a multiemployer plan, the employer's pension expense equals its contribution to the plan for the year. If a contribution is accrued, the employer must record a liability.

If an employer withdraws from the multiemployer plan, it may incur a liability for its share of the unfunded benefit obligation of the plan. If an employer would probably incur a liability if it withdraws from the plan and the amount is reasonably ascertainable, a loss must be accrued with a concurrent liability. However, if the loss is reasonably possible, only footnote disclosure is needed.

Footnote disclosure for employers involved with a multiemployer plan include:

- A description of the plan including employees covered.
- The benefits to be provided.
- Nature of matters affecting the comparability of information for the years presented.
- Pension expense for the period.

Multiple-Employer Plans

These plans have similarities to multiemployer plans. They also consist of two or more unrelated employers. However, multiple-employer plans are in effect aggregated single-employer plans that are combined so that assets of all may be totaled so as to lower administrative costs. The assets are merged so as to improve the overall rate of return from investing them. In many instances, participating employers may use different benefit formulas for their respective pension contributions. Each employer in the plan accounts for its particular interest separately. An example of such an arrangement is when businesses in an industry have their trade group handle the plans of all the companies. Each company retains its responsibilities only for its own workers. Multiple-employer plans are typically not associated with collective- bargaining agreements.

Annuity Contracts

An employer may sign a valid and irrevocable insurance contract to pay benefit obligations arising from a defined benefit plan. Annuity contracts are used to transfer the risk of providing employee benefits from the employer to the insurance company.

If the annuity contracts are the basis to fund the pension plan and to pay plan obligations, the employer's insurance premium is the pension expense for the period covering all currently earned benefits. In this instance, the company and plan do not report plan assets, accumulated benefit obligation, or a projected benefit obligation. On the contrary, if the annuity contracts only cover part of the benefit obligation, the employer is liable for the uncovered obligation.

In a participating annuity contract, the insurer pays the employer part of the income earned from investing the insurance premiums. In most instances, income earned (e.g., interest, dividends) reduces pension expense. A disadvantage to the employer of a participating contract is that it costs more than one which is nonparticipating due to the participation privilege. This additional cost applicable to the participation right should be recognized as a pension plan asset. Therefore, except for the cost of participation rights, pension plan assets exclude the cost of annuity contracts. In later years, fair value should be used in valuing the participation right included in plan assets. In the event that fair value may not be reasonably determined, the asset should be recorded at cost with amortization based on the dividend period stipulated in the contract. However, unamortized cost cannot exceed the net realizable value of the participation right. If the terms of the participating annuity contract is such that the employer retains all or most of the risk applicable to the benefit obligation, the purchase of this contract does not constitute a settlement of the employer's obligations under the pension plan.

Insurance contracts other than annuity contracts are considered investments. They are reported as pension plan assets and reported at fair value. Fair value may be in terms of conversion value, contract value, cash surrender value, etc., depending on the circumstances.

The definition of an annuity contract is *not* met if one or more of the following exist:

- There exists uncertainty as to whether the insurance company will be able to pay its debts due to financial difficulties.
- There is a captive insurance company, meaning that the insurance entity has as its major client the employer or any of its associated parties.

An employer has to record a loss when it assumes the obligation to pay retirees because the insurance company is financially unable to do so. The loss is recorded at the lower of any gain associated with the original insurance contract or the amount of benefit assumed. An unrecognized additional loss should be treated as an amendment to the pension plan.

Employee Retirement Income Security Act (ERISA)

The Act generally provides for full vesting of pension benefits if an employee has worked for 15 years. Past service costs must be funded over a period not more than 40 years.

Employer's Accounting for Postemployment Benefits

FASB Statement Number 112 provides authoritative guidance in accounting and reporting for postemployment benefits. The pronouncement relates to benefits to former or inactive employees, their beneficiaries, and dependents after employment, but before retirement. Former or inactive employees include individuals on disability and those that have been laid off. However, individuals on vacation or holiday or who are ill are not considered inactive.

Postemployment benefits are different from postretirement benefits. Postemployment benefits may be in cash or in kind and include salary continuation benefits, supplemental unemployment benefits, severance benefits, disability related benefits, job training and counseling benefits, life insurance benefits, and healthcare benefits.

An accrual is made for postemployment benefits if the following conditions are met:

- The amount of benefits is reasonably determinable.
- Benefits apply for services already rendered.
- Payment of benefits is probable.
- Benefit obligations vest or accumulate.

PROFIT SHARING PLANS

A profit sharing plan may be discretionary (contributions are at the discretion of the Board of Directors) or nondiscretionary (contributions are based on a predetermined formula and depend on attaining a specified earnings level). In a discretionary plan, an accrual of expense is made when set by the Board. The entry is to debit profit sharing expense and credit accrued profit sharing liability. In a nondiscretionary arrangement, an accrual is made when required under the plan terms.

INCOME TAX ACCOUNTING

Multiple Tax Jurisdictions

The determination for federal reporting purposes may differ from that of local reporting requirements. As a result, temporary differences, permanent differences, and loss carrybacks or carryforwards may differ between federal and state and/or city reporting. If temporary differences are significant, separate deferred tax computations and recording will be required.

Tax Status Changes

The impact of any change in tax status affecting a business requires an immediate adjustment to deferred tax liabilities (or assets) and to income tax expense. An example of a tax status change requiring an adjustment on the accounts is a company opting for C corporation status. There should be a footnote describing the nature of the status change and its impact on the accounts.

Business Combinations

In a business combination accounted for under the purchase method the costs assigned to the acquired entity's net assets may differ from the valuation of those net assets on the tax return. This may cause a temporary difference arising in either a deferred tax liability or deferred tax asset reported on the acquirer's consolidated financial statements.

The amortization of goodwill for tax purposes is over a mandatory 15-year period while for books goodwill may be amortized over a 40-year period. This gives rise to a temporary difference. Negative goodwill may also result in a temporary difference arising from the difference of depreciation expense for book and tax purposes.

A company may have unrecognized tax benefits applicable to operating losses or tax credits arising from a purchase business combination. This may give rise to other similar tax advantages after the combination date. The tax benefits realized should be apportioned for book reporting between pre- and post-acquisition tax benefits.

Under the pooling-of-interest method, if the combined entity will be able to use an operating loss or tax credit carryforward, the deferred tax benefits should be recognized when previous year's financial statements are restated.

In some cases, a pooling-of-interests is taxable requiring a step up of the net assets of a combining company for tax reporting. The difference between the stepped-up basis and the book value of net assets on the books constitutes a temporary difference.

Separate Financial Statements of a Subsidiary

If separate financial statements are prepared, the consolidated income tax expense should be allocated to each of the subsidiaries.

Employee Stock Ownership Plans

Retained earnings is increased for the tax benefit arising from deductible dividends paid on unallocated shares held by an ESOP. However, dividends paid on allocated shares are includable in income tax expense.

Quasi Reorganization

The tax benefits applicable with deductible temporary differences and carryforwards on the date of a quasi-reorganization should usually be recorded as an increase in paid-in-capital if the tax benefits will occur in later years.

DERIVATIVE PRODUCTS

FASB Statement Number 133 (Accounting for Derivative Investments and Hedging Activities) deals with the accounting and reporting requirements for derivative instruments and for hedging activities. Derivatives are rights and obligations and must be presented in the financial statements. Financial instruments must be reported at fair value.

FASB Statement Number 133 defines a derivative as a financial instrument or contract having the following three components:

1. Underlying Price or Rate on an Asset or Liability. It is not the asset or liability itself. Examples of an underlying might be stock or commodity

price, index of prices, interest rate, and foreign exchange rate. Further there is either a notational amount (number of shares, pounds, or currency units stipulated in the contract) or payment provisions (fixed or determinable amount required to settle the underlying instrument such as interest rate).

2. A required or allowable net settlement exists.
3. There exists no net investment or a smaller initial net investment than would be anticipated for a contract with similar terms linked to changing market conditions.

There are many examples of derivatives including futures contracts, forward contracts, interest rate swaps, and stock option contracts.

A company must report derivatives at fair value as either assets or liabilities. Depending on the circumstances, a derivative must be a hedge of exposure of either:

1. Changes in the fair value of a recognized asset or liability or an unrecognized firm commitment.
2. Variable cash flows applicable to a forecasted transaction.
3. Foreign currency risk of a net investment in a foreign operation, foreign-currency denominated forecasted transaction, available-for-sale security, or an unrecognized firm commitment.

How the change in fair value of a derivative (gain or loss) is accounted for varies with the planned use of the derivative as follows:

- A derivative designed to hedge vulnerability to changes in the fair value of a recognized asset or liability or firm commitment will have the gain or loss included in net income in the year of change coupled with the offsetting loss or gain on the hedged item associated with the hedged risk. The net impact of this accounting is to include in net income the degree to which the hedge is not effective in offsetting changes in fair value.
- A derivative hedging exposure to variable cash flows of a forecasted transaction (cash flow hedge) will have the effective part of the derivatives gain or loss initially presented as an element of other comprehensive income (outside of earnings) and later reclassified into earnings when the forecasted transaction impacts earnings. The ineffective part of the gain or loss is immediately presented in earnings. If a cash flow hedge is discontinued because it is probable that the initial forecasted transaction will not take place, the net gain or loss in accumulated other comprehensive income shall be immediately reclassified into earnings.

- A derivative whose purpose is to hedge foreign currency exposure of a net investment in a foreign activity will have the gain or loss presented under other comprehensive income as an element of the cumulative translation adjustment. The hedge of the foreign currency exposure may apply to an unrecognized firm commitment or an available-for-sale security.

NOTE: If a derivative is not to hedge an instrument, the gain or loss is included in net income in the period of change.

A company opting to use hedge accounting must disclose the method it will use to evaluate the success of the hedging derivative and the measurement means to ascertain the ineffective part of the hedge. The methods chosen must conform to the company's risk management policy.

Accounting for the change in fair value (gain or loss) of a derivative depends on whether or not it qualifies as part of a hedging arrangement and, if such is the case, the purpose of holding the derivative. Either all or a proportion of a derivative may be considered a hedging instrument. The proportion must be stated as a percentage of the whole derivative so that the risk in the hedging part of the derivative is the same as the entire derivative.

Two or more derivatives, or parts thereof, may be considered in combination and jointly designated as a hedging instrument.

If an impairment loss is recorded on an asset or liability associated with a hedged forecasted transaction, any offsetting net gain associated with that transaction in accumulated other comprehensive income should be reclassified immediately into net income of the period. In a similar manner, a recovery of the asset or liability resulting in a reduction of the net loss should be shown in earnings.

Required disclosures include identifying derivatives, time period for intended hedging, risk management policies of the company, where net gain or loss associated with derivatives are presented in the financial statements, and description of transactions or other events that will result in reclassification into earnings of gain and loss reported in accumulated other comprehensive income.

ACCOUNTING FOR MULTINATIONAL OPERATIONS

INTRODUCTION: ACCOUNTING DIMENSIONS OF INTERNATIONAL BUSINESS

Today, the world economy is truly internationalized and globalized. Advances in information technology, communications, and transportation have enabled businesses to service a world market. Many U.S. companies, both large and small, are now heavily engaged in international trade. The foreign operations of many large U.S. multinational corporations now account for a significant percentage (10% to 50%) of their sales and/or net income.

The basic business functions (i.e., finance/accounting, production, management, marketing) take on a new perspective when conducted in a foreign environment. There are different laws, economic policies, political frameworks, and social/cultural factors which all have an effect on how business is to be conducted in that foreign country. From an accounting standpoint, global business activities are faced with three realities:

1. Accounting standards and practices differ from country to country. Accounting is a product of its own economic, legal, political, and sociocultural environment. Since this environment changes from country to country, the accounting system of each country is unique and different from all others.

2. Each country has a strong "accounting nationalism": it requires business companies operating within its borders to follow its own accounting standards and practices. Consequently, a foreign company

operating within its borders must maintain its books and records and prepare its financial statements in the local language, using the local currency as a unit of measure, and in accordance with local accounting standards and procedures. In addition, the foreign company must comply with the local tax laws and government regulations.

3. Cross-border business transactions often involve receivables and payables denominated in foreign currencies. During the year, these foreign currencies must be translated (converted) into the local currencies for recording in the books and records. At year-end, the foreign currency financial statements must be translated (restated) into the parent's reporting currency for purposes of consolidation. Both the recording of foreign currency transactions and the translation of financial statements require the knowledge of the exchange rates to be used and the accounting treatment of the resulting translation gains and losses.

The biggest mistake a company can make in international accounting is to not be aware of, or even worse, to ignore these realities. It should know that differences in accounting standards, tax laws, and government regulations do exist; and that these differences need to be an integral part of formulating their international business plan.

FOREIGN CURRENCY EXCHANGE RATES

Exchanges rates are used to convert one currency into another currency. An exchange rate is the price of one currency in terms of another currency, i.e. the amount of one currency that must be given to buy one unit of another currency. Because U.S. firms have to prepare their financial statements in U.S. dollars, we shall focus on foreign currency exchange rates in terms of U.S. dollars.

Foreign currency exchange rates are quoted daily in the financial press. Two different rates are quoted for each day:

- A direct quote, which is the amount in U.S. dollar of one unit of foreign currency:

  1 British pound = US$ 1.5505

- An indirect quote, which is the amount of foreign currency equivalent to 1 U.S. dollar:

  US$ 1 = .6450 British pound

The above quotes are called spot rates, which are rates quoted for transactions to be settled within two business days. For some major currencies, forward rates are also quoted for future delivery (30-day, 60-day, 180-day forward) of the foreign currency.

Currencies are bought and sold like other goods. Under the current system of floating exchange rates, foreign exchange rates (like stock prices) are constantly fluctuating, depending on the forces of supply and demand. Because current exchange rates are both volatile and unpredictable, international business transactions are subject to the additional risk of exchange rate fluctuations.

ACCOUNTING FOR FOREIGN CURRENCY TRANSACTIONS

International business transactions are cross-border transactions, therefore two national currencies are usually involved: the currency of the buyer and the currency of the seller. For example, when a United States corporation sells to a corporation in Germany, the transaction can be settled in U.S. dollars (the seller's currency) or in German marks (the buyer's currency).

TRANSACTIONS DENOMINATED IN U.S. CURRENCY

When the foreign transaction is settled in U.S. dollars, no measurement problems occur for the U.S. corporation. As long as the U.S. corporation receives U.S. dollars, the transaction can be recorded in the same way as a domestic transaction.

Example 1. A U.S. firm sells on account equipment worth $100,000 to a German company. If the German company will pay the U.S. firm in U.S. dollars, no foreign currency is involved and the transaction is recorded as usual:

Accounts Receivable	100,000	
Sales		100,000

To record sales to German company

TRANSACTIONS DENOMINATED IN FOREIGN CURRENCY

However, if the transaction above is settled in German marks, the U.S. corporation will receive foreign currency (German marks) which must be translated into U.S. dollars for purposes of recording on the U.S. company's books. Thus, a foreign currency transaction exists when the transaction is settled in a currency other than the company's home currency.

A foreign currency transaction must be recorded in the books of accounts when it is begun (date of transaction), then perhaps at interim reporting dates (reporting date), and finally when it is settled (settlement date). On each of these three dates, the foreign currency transaction must be recorded in U.S. dollars, using the spot rate on that date for translation.

Accounting at Transaction Date

Before any foreign currency transaction can be recorded, it must be first translated into the domestic currency, using the spot rate on that day. For the U.S. company, this means that any receivable and payable denominated in a foreign currency must be recorded in U.S. dollars.

Example 2. Assume a U.S. firm purchases merchandise on account from a French company on December 1, 20X1. The cost is 50,000 French Francs, to be paid in 60 days. The exchange rate for French francs on December 1 is $.20. Using the exchange rate on December 1, the U.S. firm translates the FFr 50,000 into $10,000 and records the following entry:

Dec. 1   Purchases   10,000

                Accounts Payable   10,000

                To record purchase of merchandise on account
                (FFr 50,000 x $.20 = $10,000).

Accounting at Interim Reporting Date

Foreign currency receivables and payables that are not settled at the balance sheet date are adjusted to reflect the exchange rate at that date. Such adjustments will give rise to foreign exchange gains and losses which are to be recognized in the period when exchange rates change.

Example 3. Assume that on December 31, 20X1, the exchange rate for the French franc is $0.22. The U.S. firm will make the following adjusting entry:

Dec. 31   Foreign Exchange Loss   1,000

                Accounts Payable   1,000

                To adjust accounts payable to current exchange rate
                (FrF 50,000 x $0.22 = $11,000; $11,000 – $10,000
                = $1,000)

Accounting at Settlement Date

When the transaction is settled, if the exchange rate changes again, the domestic value of the foreign currency paid on the settlement date will be different from that recorded on the books. This difference gives rise to translation gains and losses which must be recognized in the financial statements.

Example 4.   To continue our example, assume that on February 1, 20X2, the exchange rate for the French franc is $0.21. The settlement will be recorded as follows:

Feb. 1	Accounts Payable	11,000	
	Cash		10,500
	Foreign Exchange Gain		500

To record payment of accounts payable
(FrF 50,000 x $0.21 = $10,500) and foreign exchange gain.

To summarize: In recording foreign currency transactions, SFAS 52 adopted the two-transaction approach. Under this approach, the foreign currency transaction has two components: the purchase/sale of the asset, and the financing of this purchase/sale. Each component will be treated separately and not netted with the other. The purchase/sale is recorded at the exchange rate on the day of the transaction and is not adjusted for subsequent changes in that rate. Subsequent fluctuations in exchange rates will give rise to foreign exchange gains and losses. They are considered as financing income or expense and are recognized separately in the income statement in the period the foreign exchange fluctuations happen. Thus, exchange gains and losses arising from foreign currency transactions have a direct effect on net income.

TRANSLATION OF FOREIGN CURRENCY FINANCIAL STATEMENTS

When the U.S. firm owns a controlling interest (more than 50%) in another firm in a foreign country, special consolidation problems arise. The subsidiary's financial statements are usually prepared in the language and currency of the country in which it is located, and in accordance with the local accounting principles. Before these foreign currency financial statements can be consolidated with the U.S. parent's financial statements, they must first be adjusted to conform with U.S. GAAP, and then translated into U.S. dollars.

Two different procedures may be used to translate foreign financial statements into U.S. dollars: (1) translation procedures and (2) remeasurement procedures. Which one of these two procedures is to be used depends on the determination of the functional currency for the subsidiary.

THE FUNCTIONAL CURRENCY

SFAS 52 defines the functional currency of the subsidiary as the currency of the primary economic environment in which the subsidiary operates. It is the currency in which the subsidiary realizes its cash flows and conducts its operations. To help management determine the functional currency of its subsidiary, SFAS 52 provides a list of six salient economic indicators regarding cash flows, sales price, sales market, expenses, financing, and intercompany transactions. Depending on the circumstances:

- The functional currency can be the local currency. For example, a Japanese subsidiary manufactures and sells its own products in the local market. Its cash flows, revenues, and expenses are primarily in Japanese yen. Thus its functional currency is the local currency (Japanese yen).
- The functional currency is the U.S. dollar. For foreign subsidiaries which are operated as an extension of the parent and integrated with it, the functional currency is that of the parent. For example, if the Japanese subsidiary is set up as a sales outlet for its U.S. parent, i.e. it takes orders, bills and collects the invoice price, and remits its cash flows primarily to the parent, then its functional currency would be the U.S. dollar.

The functional currency is also the U.S. dollar for foreign subsidiaries operating in highly inflationary economies (defined as having a cumulative inflation rate of more than 100% over a three-year period). The U.S. dollar is deemed the functional currency for translation purposes because it is more stable than the local currency.

Once the functional currency is determined, the specific conversion procedures are selected as follows:

- Foreign currency is the functional currency—use translation procedures.
- U.S. dollar is the functional currency—use remeasurement procedures.

Translation Procedures

If the local currency is the functional currency, the subsidiary's financial statements are translated using the current rate method. Under this method:

- All assets and liabilities accounts are translated at the current rate (the rate in effect at the financial statement date)

- Capital stock accounts are translated using the historical rate (the rate in effect at the time the stock was issued).
- The income statement is translated using the average rate for the year.
- All translation gains and losses are reported on the balance sheet, in an account called "Cumulative Translation Adjustments" in the stockholders' equity section.

The purpose of these translation procedures is to retain, in the translated financial statements, the financial results and relationships among assets and liabilities that were created by the subsidiary's operations in its foreign environment.

Example 5. To illustrate, suppose that the following trial balance, expressed in the local currency (LC) is received from a foreign subsidiary, XYZ Company. The year-end exchange rate is 1 LC = $1.50, and the average exchange rate for the year is 1 LC = $1.25. Under the current rate method, XYZ Company's trial balance would be translated as follows:

Figure 1 shows the translation procedures applied to XYZ Company's trial balance. Note that the translation adjustment is reflected as an adjustment of stockholders' equity in U.S. dollars.

Remeasurement Procedures

If the U.S. dollar is considered to be the functional currency, the subsidiary's financial statements are then remeasured into the U.S. dollar by using the temporal method. Under this method:

- Monetary accounts such as cash, receivable, and liabilities are remeasured at the current rate on the date of the balance sheet.
- Non-monetary accounts such as inventory, fixed assets, and capital stock are remeasured using the historical rates.
- Revenues and expenses are remeasured using the average rate, except for cost of sales and depreciation expenses which are remeasured using the historical exchange rates for the related assets.
- All remeasurement gains and losses are recognized immediately in the income statement.

The objective of these remeasurement procedures is to produce the same U.S. dollar financial statements as if the foreign entity's accounting records had been initially maintained in the U.S. dollar. Figure 2 shows these remeasurement procedures applied to XYZ Company's trial balance. Note that the translation gain/loss is included in the income statement.

Figure 1 Translation Procedures XYZ Company Trial Balance 12/31/01

	Local Currency		Exchange Rate	U.S. Dollars	
	Debit	Credit		Debit	Credit
Cash	LC 5,000		(1 LC = $1.50)	$7,500	
Inventory	15,000		"	22,500	
Fixed Assets	30,000		"	45,000	
Payables		LC 40,000	"		$60,000
Capital Stock		4,000	Historical rate		5,000
Retained Earnings		6,000	to balance		10,000
Sales		300,000	(1 LC = $1.25)		375,000
Cost of Goods Sold	210,000		"	262,500	
Depreciation Expense	5,000		"	6,250	
Other Expenses	85,000		"	106,250	
	LC 350,000	LC 350,000		$450,000	$450,000

Figure 2 Remeasurement Procedures XYZ Company Trial Balance 12/31/01

	Local Currency		Exchange Rate	U.S. Dollars	
	Debit	Credit		Debit	Credit
Cash	LC 5,000		(1 LC = $1.50)	$7,500	
Inventory	15,000		(1 LC = $1.30)	19,500	
Fixed Assets	30,000		(1 LC = $0.95)	28,500	
Payables		LC 40,000	(1 LC = $1.50)		$60,000
Capital Stock		4,000	—		5,000
Retained Earnings		6,000			7,000
Sales		300,000	(1 LC = $1.25)		375,000
Cost of Goods Sold	210,000		(1 LC = $1.30)	273,000	
Depreciation Expense	5,000		(1 LC = $0.95)	4,750	
Other Expenses	85,000		(1 LC = $1.25)	106,250	
				439,500	
Translation Gain/Loss				7,500	
	LC 350,000	LC 350,000		447,000	447,000

INTERPRETATION OF FOREIGN FINANCIAL STATEMENTS

To evaluate a foreign corporation, we usually analyze the financial statements of the foreign corporation. However, the analysis of foreign financial statements needs special considerations:

1. We often have the tendency of looking at the foreign financial data from a home country perspective. For example, a U.S. businessman has the tendency of using U.S. Generally Accepted Accounting Principles (GAAP) to evaluate the foreign financial statements. However, U.S. GAAP are not universally recognized and many differences exist between U.S. GAAP and the accounting principles of other countries (industrialized or nonindustrialized).

2. Because of the diversity of accounting principles worldwide, we have to overcome the tendency of using our home country GAAP to evaluate foreign financial statements. Instead, we should try to become familiar with the foreign GAAP used in the preparation of these financial statements and apply them in our financial analysis.

3. Business practices are culturally based. Often they are different from country to country and have a significant impact on accounting measurement and disclosure practices. Therefore, local economic conditions and business practices should be taken into consideration to correctly analyze foreign financial statements.

HARMONIZATION OF ACCOUNTING STANDARDS

The diversity of accounting systems is an obstacle in the development of international trade and business and the efficiency of the global capital markets. Many concerted efforts have been made to reduce this diversity through the harmonization of accounting standards. Also, as international business expands, there is a great need for international accounting standards which can help investors make decisions on an international scale. The agencies working toward the harmonization of accounting standards are:

A. The International Accounting Standards Committee (IASC)

The IASC was founded in 1973. At that time, its members consisted of the accountancy bodies of Australia, Canada, France, Japan, Mexico, the Netherlands, the United Kingdom, Ireland, the United States, and West Germany. Since its founding, membership has grown to around 116 accountancy bodies from approximately 85 countries.

IASC's fundamental goal is the development of international accounting standards. It is also working towards the improvement and harmonization of accounting standards and procedures relating to the presentation and comparability of financial statements (or at least through enhanced disclosure, if differences are present). To date, it has developed a conceptual framework and issued a total of 32 International Accounting Standards (IAS) covering a wide range of accounting issues. It is currently working on a project concerned with the core standards in consultation with other international groups, especially the International Organization of Securities Commissions (IOSCO), to develop worldwide standards for all corporations to facilitate multi-listing of foreign corporations on various stock exchanges.

B. The International Federation of Accountants (IFAC)

IFAC was founded in 1977 by 63 accountancy bodies representing 49 countries. By 1990, IFAC membership had grown to 105 accountancy bodies from 78 different countries. Its purpose is to develop "a coordinated worldwide accountancy profession with harmonized standards." It concentrated on establishing auditing guidelines to help promote uniform auditing practices throughout the world. It also promoted general standards for ethics, education and accounting management.

In addition to the IASC and IFAC, there are a growing number of regional organizations involved in accounting harmonization at the regional level. These organizations included, among others, the Inter-American Accounting Association (established in 1949), the ASEAN Federation of Accountants (AFA) (established in 1977), and the Federation des Experts Comptables Europeens (FEE), created by the merger in 1986 of the former Union Europeenne des Experts Comptables Economiques et Financiers (UEC) and the Groupe d'Etude (GE).

C. The European Economic Community (EEC)

The EEC, although not an accounting body, has made great strides in harmonizing the accounting standards of its member countries. During the 1970s, it began the slow process of issuing EEC directives to harmonize the national accounting legislation of its member countries. The directives must go through a three-step process before they are finalized. First, they are proposed by the EEC Commission and presented to the national representatives of the EEC members. Second, if the proposal is satisfactory to the nations, it is adopted by the Commission. Finally, it must be issued by the Council of Ministers of the EEC, before it can be enforced on the members.

The most important directives in the harmonization of accounting standards among EEC members are:

- *The Fourth Directive* (1978) regarding the layout and content of annual accounts, valuation methods, annual report, publicity and audit of public and private company accounts
- *The Seventh Directive* (1983) regarding the consolidation of accounts for certain groups of enterprises and
- *The Eighth Directive* (1984) regarding the training, qualification and independence of statutory auditors

COST-VOLUME-PROFIT ANALYSIS AND LEVERAGE

BREAK-EVEN AND COST-VOLUME-REVENUE ANALYSIS FOR NONPROFIT ORGANIZATIONS

By definition, the goal of a nonprofit entity is *not* to earn a profit. The nonprofit organization's objective is to render as much suitable service as possible with as little human and physical services, as needed. Ideally, the performance in a nonprofit organization is to break even. This means that, by and large and on a short-term basis, revenues should equal costs. If you generate a surplus, a possibility is that you may not receive the same amount from the funding agency as last year. On the other hand, if you produce a deficit, you may run into insolvency, a danger for survival. Further, chances are that you may not be able to borrow money from the bank, as not-for-profit entities often can, because of your weak financial stance. One thing is clear; over the long run, nonprofit entities cannot survive without reserves and cannot sustain persistent deficits.

Cost-volume-revenue (CVR) analysis, together with cost behavior information, helps nonprofit managers perform many useful analyses. CVR analysis deals with how revenue and costs change with a change in the service level. More specifically, it looks at the effects on revenues of changes in such factors as variable costs, fixed costs, prices, service level, and mix of services offered. By studying the relationships of costs, service volume, and revenue, nonprofit management is better able to cope with many planning decisions.

Break-even analysis, a branch of CVR analysis, determines the break-even service level. The break-even point—the financial crossover point where revenues exactly match costs—does not show up in financial reports, but nonprofit financial managers find it an extremely useful measurement in a variety of ways. It reveals which programs are self-supporting and which are subsidized.

Questions Answered by CVR Analysis

CVR analysis tries to answer the following questions:

(a) What service level is (or what units of service are) required to break even?

(b) How would changes in price, variable costs, fixed costs, and service volume affect a surplus?

(c) How do changes in program levels and mix affect aggregate surplus/deficit?

(d) What alternative break-even strategies are available?

Analysis of Revenues. Revenues for nonprofit entities are typically classified into the following categories:

- Grants from governments.
- Grants from private sources.
- Cost reimbursements and sales.
- Membership fees.
- Public contributions received directly or indirectly.
- Legacies and memorials.
- Other revenues such as investment income (e.g., interest, dividends).

For managerial purposes, however, each type of revenue is grouped into its fixed and variable parts. Fixed revenues are those that remain unchanged regardless of the level of service, such as gifts, grants, and contracts. In colleges, for example, donations, gifts, and grants have no relationship to enrollment. Variable revenues are the ones that vary in proportion to the volume of activity. Examples are cost reimbursements and membership fees. In colleges, tuition and fees are variable in relation to the number of students. Different nonprofit entities may have different sources of revenue: variable revenue only, fixed revenue only, or a combination of both. In this chapter, we will cover all three cases in treating break-even and CVR questions.

Analysis of Cost Behavior. For external reporting purposes, costs are classified by managerial function (such as payroll, occupancy, and office), and also by programs and supporting services. A model functional classification is *IRS Form 990 Part II—Statement of Functional Expenses,* an excerpt from which is shown below.

IRS Form 990

Line No.	Functional expense category
26	Salaries and wages
27	Pension plan contributions
28	Other employee benefits
29	Payroll taxes
30	Professional fundraising fees
31	Accounting fees
32	Legal fees
33	Supplies
34	Telephone
35	Postage and shipping
36	Occupancy
37	Equipment rental and maintenance
38	Printing and publications
39	Travel
40	Conferences, conventions, meetings
41	Interest
42	Depreciation, depletion, etc.
43	Other expenses (itemize)

For managerial purposes (such as planning, control, and decision making), further classification of costs is desirable. One such classification is by behavior. Depending on how a cost will react or respond to changes in the level of activity, costs may be viewed as variable or fixed. This classification is made within a specified range of activity, called the relevant range. The relevant range is the volume zone within which the behavior of variable costs, fixed costs, and prices can be predicted with reasonable accuracy.

Typical activity measures are summarized as follows.

Measures of the Service Level

Nonprofit Types	Units of Service
Hospital or health care	Bed-days, patient contact hours, patient-days, service hours
Educational	Number of enrollments, class size, full-time equivalents (FTE) hours
Social clubs	Number of members served

Variable Costs. Variable costs vary in total with changes in volume or level of activity. Examples of variable costs include supplies, printing and publications, telephone, and postage and shipping.

Fixed Costs. Fixed costs do not change in total regardless of the volume or level of activity. Examples include salaries, accounting and consulting fees, and depreciation.

The following table shows the fixed-variable breakdown of IRS Form 990 functional expenses.

IRS Form 990 Line No.	Expense Category
	FIXED COSTS
26	Salaries and wages
27	Pension plan
28	Other benefits
29	Payroll taxes
30	Fund-raising fees
31	Accounting fees
32	Legal fees
36	Occupancy
37	Equipment rental/maintenance
41	Interest
42	Depreciation
43	Other
	VARIABLE COSTS
33	Supplies
34	Telephone
35	Postage and shipping

38	Printing and publications
39	Travel
40	Conferences, meetings
43	Other

Types of Fixed Costs—Program-Specific or Common. Fixed costs of nonprofit entities are subdivided into two groups. Direct or program-specific fixed costs are those that can be directly identified with individual programs. These costs are avoidable or escapable if the program is dropped. Examples include the salaries of the staff whose services can be used only in a given program, and depreciation of equipment used exclusively for the program. Common fixed costs would continue even if an individual program were discontinued.

CVR Analysis with Variable Revenue Only

For accurate CVR analysis, a distinction must be made between costs as either variable or fixed. In order to compute the break-even point and perform various CVR analyses, note the following important concepts.

Contribution Margin (CM). The contribution margin is the excess of revenue(R) over the variable costs (VC) of the service. It is the amount of money available to cover fixed costs (FC) and to generate surplus. Symbolically, CM = R − VC.

Unit CM. The unit CM is the excess of the unit price (P) over the unit variable cost (V). Symbolically, unit CM = P − V.

CM Ratio. The CM ratio is the contribution margin as a percentage of revenue, i.e.,

$$\text{CM ratio} = \frac{CM}{R} = \frac{R - VC}{R} = 1 - \frac{VC}{R}$$

The CM ratio can also be computed using per-unit data as follows:

$$\text{CM ratio} = \frac{\text{Unit CM}}{P} = \frac{P - V}{P} = 1 - \frac{V}{P}$$

Note that the CM ratio is 1 minus the variable cost ratio. For example, if variable costs are 40 percent of revenue, then the variable cost ratio is 40 percent and the CM ratio is 60 percent.

Example 1. To illustrate the various concepts of CM, assume that Los Altos Community Hospital has an average revenue of $250 per patient day. Variable costs are $50 per patient day. Total fixed costs per year are $650,000. Expected number of patient days is 4,000. The projected statement of revenue and expenditures follows:

	Total	Per Unit	Percentage
Revenue (4,000 days)	$1,000,000	$250	100%
Less: Variable costs	200,000	50	20
Contribution margin	$ 800,000	$200	80%
Less: Fixed costs	650,000		
Net income	$ 150,000		

From the data listed above, CM, unit CM, and the CM ratio are computed as:

CM = R - VC = $1,000,000 - $200,000 = $800,000
Unit CM = P - V = $250 - $50 = $200

$$\text{CM ratio} = \frac{CM}{R} = \frac{\$\ 800,000}{\$1,000,000} = 1 - \frac{\$\ 200,000}{\$1,000,000}$$
$$= 0.8 = 80\%$$

$$\text{or} = \frac{\text{Unit CM}}{P} = \frac{\$200}{\$250} = 0.8 = 80\%$$

Break-Even Analysis

The break-even point represents the level of revenue that equals the total of the variable and the fixed costs for a given volume of output service at a particular capacity use rate. Generally, the lower the break-even point, the higher the surplus and the less the operating risk, other things being equal. The break-even point also provides nonprofit managers with insights into surplus/deficit planning. To develop the formula for the break-even units of service, use the following variables:

R = Total revenue
P = Price or average revenue per unit
U = Units of service
VC = Total variable costs
V = Unit variable cost
FC = Total fixed costs

To break even means: Total revenue − total costs = 0

$$R - VC - FC = 0 \text{ or } PU - VU - FC = 0$$

To solve, factor U out to get $(P - V)U - FC = 0$
Rearrange as $(P - V)U = FC$ and divide by $(P - V)$ to isolate U.

$$U = \frac{FC}{(P - V)}$$

In words,

$$\text{Break-even point in units} = \frac{\text{Fixed costs}}{\text{Unit CM}}$$

If you want break-even point in dollars, use

$$\text{Break-even point in dollars} = \frac{\text{Fixed Costs}}{\text{CM ratio}}$$

Example 2. Using the same data as given in Example 1, where unit CM = $250 − $50 = $200 and CM ratio = 80%, we get:

Break-even point in units = $650,000/$200 = 3,250 patient days
Break-even point in dollars = $650,000/0.8 = $812,500

Or, alternatively,

3,250 patient days × $250 = $812,500. The hospital needs 3,250 patient days to break even.

Graphical Approach in a Spreadsheet Format. The graphical approach to obtaining the break-even point is based on the so-called *break-even (B-E) chart* as shown in Figure 1. Sales revenue, variable costs, and fixed costs are plotted on the vertical axis while volume, x, is plotted on the horizontal axis. The break-even point is the point where the total revenue line intersects the total cost line. The chart can effectively report surplus potentials over a wide range of activity and therefore can be used as a tool for discussion and presentation.

The *surplus-volume (S-V) chart* as shown in Figure 2, focuses on how surplus varies with changes in volume. Surplus is plotted on the vertical axis, while units of output are shown on the horizontal axis. The S-V chart provides a quick condensed comparison of how alternatives on pricing, variable costs, or fixed costs may affect surplus (or deficit) as volume changes. The

S-V chart can be easily constructed from the B-E chart. Note that the slope of the chart is the unit CM.

Determination of Target Surplus Volume. Besides determining the break-even point, CVR analysis determines the volume to attain a particular level of surplus. The formula is:

$$\text{Target surplus level} = \frac{\text{Fixed costs plus target surplus}}{\text{Unit CM}}$$

Example 3. Using the same data as given in Example 1, assume the hospital wishes to accumulate a surplus of $250,000 per year. Then, the target surplus service level would be:

$$\frac{\$650,000 + \$250,000}{\$250 - \$50} = \frac{\$900,000}{\$200} = 4,500 \text{ patient days}$$

Figure 1.   Break-Even Chart

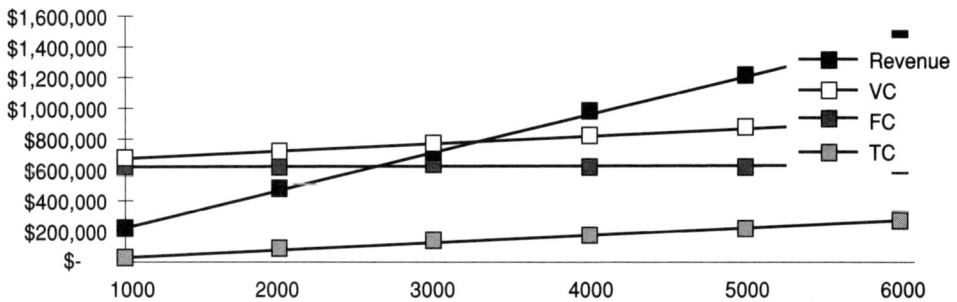

Figure 2.   Surplus-Volume (S-V) Chart

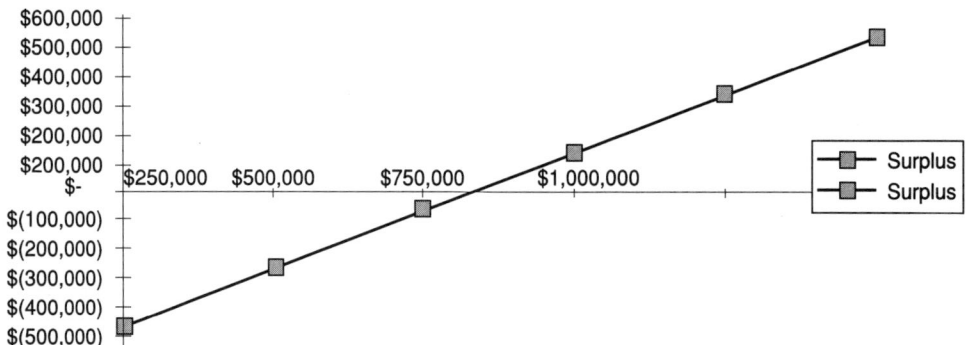

Margin of Safety. The margin of safety is a measure of difference between the actual level of service and the break-even service level. It is the amount by which revenue may drop before deficits begin, and is expressed as a percentage of expected service level:

$$\text{Margin of safety} = \frac{\text{Expected level} - \text{Break-even level}}{\text{Expected level}}$$

The margin of safety is used as a measure of operating risk. The larger the ratio, the safer the situation since there is less risk of reaching the break-even point.

Example 4. Assume that Los Altos Hospital projects 4,000 patient days with a break-even level of 3,250. The projected margin of safety is

$$\frac{4,000 - 3,250}{4,000} = 18.75\%$$

Example 5. A nonprofit college offers a program in management for executives. The program has been experiencing financial difficulties. Operating data for the most recent year are shown below.

Tuition revenue (40 participants @$7,000)	$280,000
Less variable expenses (@$4,000)	160,000
Contribution margin	$120,000
Less fixed expenses	150,000
Operating deficit	$(30,000)

The break-even point is $150,000/($7,000 – $4,000) = 50 participants.

Example 6. In Example 5, the dean of the school is convinced that the class size can be increased to more economical levels without lowering the quality. He is prepared to spend $15,000 per year in additional promotional and other support expenses. If that is the case, the new break-even point is 55 participants ($165,000/($7,000 – $4,000).

To generate a surplus of $30,000, the school must get 60 participants [$150,000 + $30,000)/$3,000].

Some Applications of CVR Analysis and What-If Analysis. The concepts of contribution margin and the contribution income statement have many applications in surplus/deficit planning and short-term decision making. Many "what-if" scenarios can be evaluated using them as planning tools, especially utilizing a spreadsheet program such as *Microsoft Excel* or *Lotus 1-2-3*. Some applications are illustrated below using the same data as in Example 1.

Example 7. Recall from Example 1 that Los Altos Hospital has unit CM = $250 – $50 = $200, CM ratio = 80%, and fixed costs of $650,000. Assume that the hospital expects revenues to go up by $250,000 for the next period. How much will surplus increase?

Using the CM concepts, we can quickly compute the impact of a change in the service level on surplus or deficit. The formula for computing the impact is:

$$\text{Change in surplus} = \text{Dollar change in revenue} \times \text{CM ratio}$$

Thus:

$$\text{Increase in surplus} = \$250,000 \times 80\% = \$200,000$$

Therefore, the income will go up by $200,000, assuming there is no change in fixed costs. If we are given a change in service units (e.g., patient days) instead of dollars, then the formula becomes:

$$\text{Change in surplus} = \text{Change in units} \times \text{Unit CM}$$

Example 8. Assume that the hospital expects patient days to go up by 500 units. How much will surplus increase? From Example 1, the hospital's unit CM is $200. Again, assuming there is no change in fixed costs, the surplus will increase by $100,000, as computed below.

$$500 \text{ additional patient days} \times \$200 \text{ CM per day} = \$100,000$$

Example 9. Referring back to Example 5, another alternative under consideration is to hold the present program without any change in the regular campus facilities instead of in rented outside facilities that are better located. If adopted, this proposal will reduce fixed costs by $60,000. The variable costs will decrease by $100 per participant. Is the move to campus facilities advisable if it leads to a decline in the number of participants by 5?

	Present		Proposed
S(40 × $7,000)	$280,000	(35 × $7,000)	$245,000
VC(40 × $4,000)	160,000	(35 × $3,900)	136,500
CM	$120,000		$108,500
FC	150,000		90,000
Surplus	$(30,000)		$ 18,500

The answer is yes, since the move will turn into a surplus.

CVR Analysis with Variable and Fixed Revenues. Many nonprofit organizations derive two types of revenue: fixed and variable. In this situation, the formulas developed previously need to be modified. The following example illustrates this.

Example 10. ACM, Inc., a mental rehabilitation provider, has a $1,200,000 lump-sum annual budget appropriation to help rehabilitate mentally ill clients. The agency charges each client $600 a month for board and care. All the appropriation must be spent. The variable costs for rehabilitation activity average $700 per patient per month. The agency's annual fixed costs are $800,000. The agency manager wishes to know how many patients can be served.

Let U = units of service = number of clients to be served.

We set up: Total revenue – Total expenses = 0

Lump sum appropriation + R – VC – FC = 0
Lump sum appropriation + PU – VU – FC = 0
$1,200,000 + $7,200 U – $8,400 U – $800,000 = 0
($7,200 – $8,400)U = $800,000 – $1,200,000
$$-\$1,200\ U = -\$400,000$$
$$U = \$400,000/\$1,200$$
$$U = 333 \text{ clients}$$

Alternatively, you may use the following formula:

$$\text{Break-even point in units} = \frac{\text{Fixed costs} - \text{Fixed revenue}}{\text{Unit CM}}$$

Thus,

$$\text{Break-even number of patients} = \frac{\$800,000 - \$1,200,000}{-\$1,200}$$
$$= \$400,000/\$1,200 = 333 \text{ clients}$$

We will investigate the following two "what-if" scenarios:

Example 11. In Example 10, suppose the manager of the agency is concerned that the total budget for the coming year will be cut by 10 percent to $1,080,000. All other things remain unchanged. The manager wants to know how this budget cut affects the next year's service level. Using the formula yields:

$$\text{Break-even number of clients} = \frac{\$800,000 - \$1,080,000}{-\$1,200}$$

$$U = -\$280,000/-\$1,200$$

$$U = 233 \text{ clients}$$

Example 12. In Example 10, the manager does not reduce the number of patients served despite a budget cut of 10 percent. All other things remain unchanged. How much more does he or she have to charge clients for board and care? We let V = board and care charge per year and set up

$$\$1,200,000 + \$7,200\,U - \$8,400\,U - \$800,000 = 0$$

$$(\$7,200 - \$8,400)U = \$800,000 - \$1,200,000$$

$$-\$1,200\,U = -\$400,000$$

$$U = \$400,000/\$1,200$$

$$U = 333 \text{ clients}$$

$$\$1,080,000 + 333V - \$8,400\,(333) - \$800,000 = 0$$

$$333V = \$2,797,200 + \$800,000 - \$1,080,000$$

$$333V = \$2,517,200$$

$$V = \$2,517,200/333 \text{ clients}$$

$$V = \$7,559$$

Thus, the monthly board and care charge must be increased to $630 (7,559/12 months).

Use of Spreadsheet Software. "What-If" scenarios can be easily analyzed using popular spreadsheet software such as *Microsoft Excel, Lotus 1-2-3*, or *QuattroPro*. Examples 11 and 12 can be solved using the GoalSeek command. For example, in Excel, you find this command under Tools Bar.

CVR Analysis with Fixed Revenue Only. Some nonprofit entities may have only one source of revenue, typically a government budget appropriation. In this case, the break-even formula becomes:

$$\text{Break-even points in units} = \frac{\text{Fixed revenue} - \text{Fixed costs}}{\text{Unit variable cost}}$$

Example 13. A social service agency has a government budget appropriation of $750,000. The agency's main mission is to assist disabled people who are unable to seek or hold jobs. On the average, the agency supplements each individual's income by $6,000 annually. The agency's fixed costs are

$150,000. The agency CEO wishes to know how many people could be served in a given year. The break-even point can be computed as follows:

$$\frac{\$750,000 - \$150,000}{\$6,000} = 100$$

Example 14. In Example 13, assume that the CEO is concerned that the total budget for the year will be reduced by 10 percent to a new amount of 90%($750,000) = $675,000. The new break-even point is:

$$\frac{\$675,000 - \$150,000}{\$6,000} = 88 \text{ (rounded)}$$

The CEO has the options of cutting the budget in one or more of three ways: (1) cut the service level, as computed above, (2) reduce the variable cost, the supplement per person, and (3) seek to cut down on the total fixed costs.

Program Mix Analysis

Previously, our main concern was to determine program-specific break-even volume. But as we are aware, most nonprofit companies are involved in multiservice, multiprogram activities. One major concern is how to plan aggregate break-even volume, surplus, and deficits. Break-even analysis and cost-volume-revenue analysis require additional computations and assumptions when an organization offers more than one program. In multiprogram organizations, program mix is an important factor in calculating an overall break-even point. Different rates and different variable costs result in different unit CMs. As a result, break-even points and Cost-Volume-Revenue relationships vary with the relative proportions of the programs offered, called the *program mix.*

When the product is defined as a package, the multiprogram problem is converted into a single-program problem. The first step is to determine the number of packages that need to be served to break even. The following example illustrates a multiprogram, multiservice situation.

Example 15. The Cypress Counseling Services is a nonprofit agency offering two programs: psychological counseling (PC) and alcohol addiction control (AAC). The agency charges individual clients an average of $10 per hour of counseling provided under the PC program. The local Chamber of Commerce reimburses the company at the rate of $20 per hour of direct service provided under the AAC. The nonprofit agency believes that this billing variable rate is low enough to be affordable for most clients and also high enough to derive clients' commitment to the program objectives. Costs of administering the two programs are given below.

	PC	AAC
Variable costs	$4.6	$11.5
Direct fixed costs	$120,000	$180,000

There are other fixed costs that are common to the two programs, including general and administrative and fund raising, of $255,100 per year. The projected surplus for the coming year, segmented by programs, follows:

	PC	AAC	Total
Revenue	$500,000	$800,000	$1,300,000
Program mix in hours	(50,000)	(40,000)	
Less: VC	(230,000)	(460,000)	(690,000)
Contribution margin	$270,000	$340,000	$610,000
Less: Direct FC	(120,000)	(180,000)	(300,000)
Program margin	$150,000	$160,000	$310,000
Less: Common FC			(255,100)
Surplus			$54,900

First, based on program-specific data on the rates, the variable costs, and the program mix, we can compute the package (aggregate) value as follows:

Program	P	V	Unit CM	Mix*	Package CM
PC	$10	$4.6	$5.4	5	$27
AAC	20	11.5	8.5	4	34
Package total					$61

*The mix ratio is 5:4 (50,000 hours for PC and 40,000 hours for AAC).

We know that the total fixed costs for the agency are $555,100. Thus, the package (aggregate) break-even point is

$$\frac{\$555,100}{\$61} = 9,100 \text{ packages}$$

The agency must provide 45,500 hours of PC (5 × 9,100) and 36,400 hours of AAC (4 × 9,100) to avoid a deficit. To prove,

	PC	AAC	Total
Revenue	$455,000 (a)	$728,000 (b)	$1,183,000
Program mix in hours	(45,500)	(36,400)	
Less: VC	(209,300) (c)	(418,600)(d)	(627,900)
Contribution margin	$245,700	$309,400	$ 555,100
Less: Direct FC	(120,000)	(180,000)	(300,000)
Program margin	$125,700	$129,400	$ 255,100
Less: Common FC			(255,100)
Surplus			$ 0

(a) 45,500 × $10   (c) 45,500 × $4.60
(b) 36,400 × $20   (d) 36,400 × $11.50

Example 16. Assume in Example 15 that 56,000 hours of PC services are budgeted for the next period. The agency wants to know how many hours of AAC services are necessary during that period to avoid an overall deficit. The answer is 29,729 hours, as shown below.

Direction: Set surplus = 0 and PC units of service = $56,000 and let Goal Seeking determine ACC units of service.

Input Data	PC	AAC
Rates	$ 10	$ 20
Units of service (Hours)	56,000	29,729
Variable cost per unit	$ 4.6	$ 11.5

Contribution Statement of Surplus or Deficit

	PC	AAC	Total
Revenue	$560,000	$594,588	$1,154,588
Less: Variable Costs	257,600	341,888	599,488
Contribution margin	$302,400	$252,700	$ 555,100
Less: Direct fixed costs	120,000	180,000	300,000
Program margin	$182,400	$ 72,700	$ 255,100
Less: Common fixed costs			255,100
Surplus		$	(0)

Management Options

Cost-volume-revenue analysis is useful as a frame of reference, as a vehicle for expressing overall managerial performance, and as a planning device via break-even techniques and "what-if" scenarios. In many practical situations, management will have to resort to a combination of approaches to reverse a deficit, including:

1. Selected changes in volume of activity.
2. Planned savings in fixed costs at all levels.
3. Some savings in variable costs.
4. Additional fund drives or grant seeking.
5. Upward adjustments in pricing.
6. Cost reimbursement contracts.

All these approaches will have to be mixed to form a feasible planning package. Many nonprofit managements fail to develop such analytical approaches to the economics of their operations. Further, the accounting system is not designed to provide information to investigate cost-volume-revenue relations.

THE USE OF CAPITAL BUDGETING IN DECISION MAKING

COMPARING PROJECTS WITH UNEQUAL LIVES

A replacement decision typically involves two mutually exclusive projects. When these two mutually exclusive projects have significantly different lives, an adjustment would be necessary. We discuss two approaches: (1) the replacement chain (common life) approach and (2) the equivalent annual annuity approach.

The Replacement Chain (Common Life) Approach

This procedure extends one or both projects until an equal life is achieved. For example, Project A has a 6-year life, while Project B has a 3-year life. Under this approach, the projects would be extended to a common life of 6 years. Project B would have an adjusted NPV equal to the NPV_B plus the NPV_B discounted for 3 years at the project's cost of capital. Then the project with the higher NPV would be chosen.

Example 1. Sims Industries, Inc. is considering two machines to replace an old machine. Machine A has a life of 10 years, will cost $24,500, and will produce net cash savings of $4,800 per year. Machine B has an expected life of 5 years, will cost $20,000, and will produce net cash savings in operating costs of $6,000 per year. The company's cost of capital is 14 percent. Project A's NPV is

$NPV_A = PV - I = \$4{,}800\ PVIFA_{10,14} - \$24{,}500$

$\qquad = \$4{,}800(5.2161) - \$24{,}500 = \$25{,}037.28 - \$24{,}500$

$\qquad = \$537.28$

Project B's extended time line can be set up as follows:

0	1	2	3	4	5	6	7	8	9	10
−200	60	60	60	60	60	60	60	60	60	60
						−200				(in hundredths)

$Adjusted\ NPV_B = PV - I = \$6{,}000\ PVIFA_{10,14} - \$20{,}000\ PVIF_{5,14} - \$20{,}000$

$\qquad = \$6{,}000(5.2161) - \$20{,}000(0.5194) - \$20{,}000$

$\qquad = \$31{,}296.60 - \$10{,}388.00 - \$20{,}000$

$\qquad = \$908.60$

Or, alternatively,

$NPV_B = PV - I = \$6{,}000\ PVIFA_{5,14} - \$20{,}000$

$\qquad = \$6{,}000(3.4331) - \$20{,}000$

$\qquad = \$20{,}598.60 - \$20{,}000$

$\qquad = \$598.60$

$Adjusted\ NPV_B = NPV_B + NPV_B\ discounted\ for\ 5\ years$

$\qquad = \$598.60 + \$598.60\ PVIF_{5,14}$

$\qquad = \$598.60 + \$598.60(0.5194)$

$\qquad = \$598.60 + \$310.91$

$\qquad = \$909.51\ (due\ to\ rounding\ errors)$

The Equivalent Annual Annuity (EAA) Approach. It is often cumbersome to compare projects with different lives. For example, one project might have a 4-year life versus a 10-year life for the other. This would require a replacement chain analysis over 20 years, the lowest common denominator of the two lives. In such a case, it is often simpler to use an alternative approach, the *equivalent annual annuity method.*

This procedure involves three steps:

1. Determine each project's NPV over its original life.
2. Find the constant annuity cash flow or EAA, using

$$\frac{\text{NPV of each project}}{\text{PVIFA}_{n,i}}$$

3. Assuming infinite replacement, find the infinite horizon (or perpetuity) NPV of each project, using

$$\frac{\text{EAA of each}}{\text{cost of capital}}$$

Example 2. From Example 1, $\text{NPV}_A = \$537.28$ and $\text{NPV}_B = \$598.60$. To obtain the constant annuity cash flow or EAA, we do the following:

$$\text{EAA}_A = \$537.28/\text{PVIFA}_{10,14} = \$537.28/5.2161 = \$103.00$$
$$\text{EAA}_B = \$598.60/\text{PVIFA}_{5,14} = \$598.60/3.4331 = \$174.36$$

Thus, the infinite horizon NPVs are as follows:

Infinite horizon $\text{NPV}_A = \$103.00/0.14 = \$735.71$
Infinite horizon $\text{NPV}_B = \$174.36/0.14 = \$1,245.43$

The Concept of Abandonment Value

The notion of abandonment value recognizes that abandonment of a project before the end of its physical life can have a significant impact on the project's return and risk. This distinguishes between the project's economic life and physical life. Two types of abandonment can occur:

1. Abandonment of an unprofitable asset.
2. Sale of the asset to some other party who can extract more value than the original owner.

Example 3. ABC Company is considering a project with an initial cost of $5,000 and net cash flows of $2,000 for next three years. The expected abandonment cash flows for years 0,1,2, and 3 are $5,000, $3,000, $2,500, and $0. The firm's cost of capital is 10 percent. We will compute NPVs in three cases.

Case 1. NPV of the project if kept for 3 years.
$$\text{NPV} = \text{PV} - \text{I} = \$2,000 \ \text{PVIFA}_{10,3} = \$2,000(2.4869) - \$5,000$$
$$= -\$26.20$$

Case 2. NPV of the project if abandoned after Year 1

$$\text{NPV} = \text{PV} - \text{I} = \$2{,}000\ \text{PVIF}_{10,1} + \$3{,}000\ \text{PVIF}_{10,2} - \$5{,}000$$
$$= \$2{,}000(0.9091) + \$3{,}000(0.9091) - \$5{,}000$$
$$= \$1{,}818.20 + \$2{,}727.30 - \$5{,}000 = -\$454.50$$

Case 3. NPV of the project if abandoned after Year 2

$$\text{NPV} = \text{PV} - \text{I} = \$2{,}000\ \text{PVIF}_{10,1} + \$2{,}000\ \text{PVIF}_{10,2} + \$2{,}500\ \text{PVIF}_{10,2} - \$5{,}000$$
$$= \$2{,}000(0.9091) + \$2{,}000(0.8264) + \$2{,}500(0.8264) - \$5{,}000$$
$$= \$1{,}818.20 + \$1{,}652.80 + \$2{,}066.00 - \$5{,}000 = \$537$$

The company should abandon the project after Year 2.

HOW INCOME TAXES AFFECT INVESTMENT DECISIONS

Income taxes make a difference in many capital budgeting decisions. The project which is attractive on a before-tax basis may have to be rejected on an after-tax basis and vice versa. Income taxes typically affect both the amount and the timing of cash flows. Since net income, not cash inflows, is subject to tax, after-tax cash inflows are not usually the same as after-tax net income.

How to Calculate After-Tax Cash Flows

Let us define:

S = Sales

E = Cash operating expenses

d = Depreciation

t = Tax rate

Then, before-tax cash inflows (or cash savings) = $S - E$ and net income = $S - E - d$

By definition,

> After-tax cash inflows = Before-tax cash inflows − Taxes = $(S - E)$ − $(S - E - d)\ (t)$

Rearranging gives the short-cut formula:

> After-tax cash inflows $= (S - E)\ (1 - t) + (d)(t)$ or
> $= (S - E - d)\ (1 - t) + d$

As can be seen, the deductibility of depreciation from sales in arriving at taxable net income reduces income tax payments and thus serves as a *tax shield.*

> Tax shield = Tax savings on depreciation = $(d)(t)$

Example 4. Assume:

$$S = \$12,000$$
$$E = \$10,000$$
$$d = \$500 \text{ per year using the straight line method}$$
$$t = 30\%$$

Then,

$$
\begin{aligned}
\text{After-tax cash inflow} \ &= (\$12,000 - \$10,000)\,(1 - .3) + (\$500)(.3) \\
&= (\$2,000)(.7) + (\$500)(.3) \\
&= \$1,400 + \$150 = \$1,550
\end{aligned}
$$

$$
\begin{aligned}
\text{Note that a tax shield} \ &= \text{tax savings on depreciation} = (d)(t) \\
&= (\$500)(.3) = \$150
\end{aligned}
$$

Since the tax shield is dt, the higher the depreciation deduction, the higher the tax savings on depreciation. Therefore, an accelerated depreciation method (such as double-declining balance) produces higher tax savings than the straight-line method. Accelerated methods produce higher present values for the tax savings which may make a given investment more attractive.

Example 5. The Navistar Company estimates that it can save $2,500 a year in cash operating costs for the next ten years if it buys a special-purpose machine at a cost of $10,000. No residual value is expected. Depreciation is by straight-line. Assume that the income tax rate is 30%, and the after-tax cost of capital (minimum required rate of return) is 10%. After-tax cash savings can be calculated as follows:

Note that depreciation by straight-line is $10,000/10 = $1,000 per year. Thus,

$$
\begin{aligned}
\text{After-tax cash savings} \ &= (S - E)\,(1 - t) + (d)(t) \\
&= \$2,500(1 - .3) + \$1,000(.3) \\
&= \$1,750 + \$300 = \$2,050
\end{aligned}
$$

To see if this machine should be purchased, the net present value can be calculated.

$$PV = \$2,050 \ T4(10\%, 10 \text{ years}) = \$2,050 \ (6.145) = \$12,597.25$$

Thus, NPV = PV – I = $12,597.25 – $10,000 = $2,597.25

Since NPV is positive, the machine should be bought.

Capital Budgeting Decisions and the Modified Accelerated Cost Recovery System (MACRS)

Although the traditional depreciation methods still can be used for computing depreciation for book purposes, 1981 saw a new way of computing depreciation deductions for tax purposes. The current rule is called the *Modified Accelerated Cost Recovery System* (MACRS) rule, as enacted by Congress in 1981 and then modified somewhat in 1986 under the Tax Reform Act of 1986. This rule is characterized as follows:

1. It abandons the concept of useful life and accelerates depreciation deductions by placing all depreciable assets into one of eight age property classes. It calculates deductions, based on an allowable percentage of the asset's original cost (see Tables 1 and 2).

With a shorter asset tax life than useful life, the company would be able to deduct depreciation more quickly and save more in income taxes in the earlier years, thereby making an investment more attractive. The rationale behind the system is that this way the government encourages the company to invest in facilities and increase its productive capacity and efficiency. (Remember that the higher d, the larger the tax shield (d)(t)).

2. Since the allowable percentages in Table 1 add up to 100%, there is no need to consider the salvage value of an asset in computing depreciation.

3. The company may elect the straight line method. The straight-line convention must follow what is called the *half-year convention*. This means that the company can deduct only half of the regular straight-line depreciation amount in the first year. The reason for electing to use the MACRS optional straight-line method is that some firms may prefer to stretch out depreciation deductions using the straight-line method rather than to accelerate them. Those firms are the ones that just start out or have little or no income and wish to show more income on their income statements.

Example 6. Assume that a machine falls under a 3-year property class and costs $3,000 initially. The straight line option under MACRS differs from the traditional straight line method in that under this method the company would deduct only $500 depreciation in the first year and the fourth year ($3,000/3 years =$1,000; $1,000/2=$500). The table below compares the straight line with half-year convention with the MACRS.

Year	Straight line (half-year) Depreciation	Cost		MACRS %	MACRS deduction
1	$ 500	$3,000	×	33.3%	$ 999
2	1,000	3,000	×	44.5	1,335
3	1,000	3,000	×	14.8	444
4	500	3,000	×	7.4	222
	$3,000				$3,000

The Use of Capital Budgeting in Decision Making

Example 7. A machine costs $10,000. Annual cash inflows are expected to be $5,000. The machine will be depreciated using the MACRS rule and will fall under the 3-year property class. The cost of capital after taxes is 10%. The estimated life of the machine is 4 years. The salvage value of the machine at the end of the fourth year is expected to be $1,200. The tax rate is 30%.

The formula for computation of after-tax cash inflows $(S - E)(1 - t) + (d)(t)$ needs to be computed separately. The NPV analysis can be performed as follows:

	Present value factor @ 10%	Present value
Initial investment: $10,000	1.000	$(10,000.00)
$(S - E)(1 - t)$:		
$5,000 (1 - .3) = $3,500 for 4 years	3.170(a)	$11,095.00
(d)(t):		

Year	Cost		MACRS %	d	(d)(t)		
1	$10,000	×	33.3%	$3,330	$ 999	.909(b)	908.09
2	$10,000	×	44.5	4,450	1,335	.826(b)	1,102.71
3	$10,000	×	14.8	1,480	444	.751(b)	333.44
4	$10,000	×	7.4	740	222	.683(b)	151.63

Salvage value:

$1,200 in year 4: $1,200 (1 - .3) =

840(c)	.683(b)	573.72
Net present value (NPV)		$4,164.59

(a) Present value of an annuity of $1 = 3.170 (from Table A-4 in the Appendix).
(b) Present values of $1 obtained (from Table A-3 in the Appendix).
(c) Any salvage value received under the MACRS rules is a *taxable gain* (the excess of the selling price over book value, $1,200 in this example), since the book value will be zero at the end of the life of the machine.

Since NPV = PV − I = $4,164.59 is positive, the machine should be bought.

Example 8. A firm is considering the purchase of an automatic machine for $6,200. The machine has an installation cost of $800 and zero salvage value at the end of its expected life of five years. Depreciation is by the straight-line method with the *half-year convention*. The machine is considered a five-year property. Expected cash savings before tax is $1,800 per year over the five years. The firm is in the 40 percent tax bracket. The firm has determined the cost of capital (or minimum required rate of return) of 10 percent after taxes.

Year(s)	Having Cash Flows	Amount of Cash Flows	10% PV Factor	PV
Initial investment	Now	$(7,000)	1.000	$(7,000)
Annual cash inflows:				
$1,800				
× 60%				
$1,080	1-5	1,080	3.791	4,094

Depreciation deductions:

Year	Depreciation	Tax Shield at 40%					
1	$700	$280	1	280	0.909	255
2	1,400	560	2	560	0.826	463
3	1,400	560	3	560	0.751	421
4	1,400	560	4	560	0.683	382
5	1,400	560	5	560	0.621	348
6	700	280	6	280	0.564	158
Net Present Value						$(879)

The firm should not buy the automatic machine since its NPV is negative.

Example 9. The Wessels Corporation is considering installing a new conveyor for materials handling in a warehouse. The conveyor will have an initial cost of $75,000 and an installation cost of $5,000. Expected benefits of the conveyor are: (a) Annual labor cost will be reduced by $16,500, and (b) breakage and other damages from handling will be reduced by $400 per month. Some of the firm's costs are expected to increase as follows: (a) Electricity cost will rise by $100 per month, and (b) annual repair and maintenance of the conveyor will amount to $900.

Assume the firm uses the MACRS rules for depreciation in the five-year property class. No salvage value will be recognized for tax purposes. The conveyor has an expected useful life of eight years and a projected salvage value of $5,000. The tax rate is 40 percent. We will determine the project's NPV at 10 percent. Should the firm buy the conveyor?

Annual cash inflows are computed as follows:

$16,500	Reduction in labor cost
4,800	Reduction in breakage
−1,200	Increase in electricity costs
−900	Increase in repair and maintenance cost
$19,200	

Initial amount of investment is:

$75,000 + $5,000 = $80,000

Year(s)

		Having Cash Flows	Amount of Cash Flows	10% PV Factor	PV
Initial investment		Now	$(80,000)	1.000	$(80,000)
Annual cash inflow:					
	$19,200				
	× 60%				
After-tax cash inflow:	$11,520	1-8	11,520	5.335	61,459.20
Depreciation deduction:					

Year	Cost	MACRS	Depreciation	Tax Shield				
1	$80,000	20%	$16,000	$ 6,400	1	6,400	0.909	5,817.60
2	80,000	32	25,600	10,240	2	10,240	0.826	8,458.24
3	80,000	19.2	15,360	6,144	3	6,144	0.751	4,614.14
4	80,000	11.5	9,200	3,680	4	3,680	0.683	2,513.44
5	80,000	11.5	9,200	3,680	5	3,680	0.621	2,285.28
6	80,000	5.8	4,640	1,856	6	1,856	0.564	1,046.78
								$24,735.48

Salvage value, fully taxable since book value will be

zero:

$5,000					
× 60%					
$3,000		8	3,000	0.467	1,401.00
Net present value					$ 7,595.68

The Wessels Corporation should buy and install the conveyor since it brings a positive NPV.

Table 1 Modified Accelerated Cost Recovery System Classification of Assets

Property class

Year	3-year	5-year	7-year	10-year	15-year	20-year
1	33.3%	20.0%	14.3%	10.0%	5.0%	3.8%
2	44.5	32.0	24.5	18.0	9.5	7.2
3	14.8a	19.2	17.5	14.4	8.6	6.7
4	7.4	11.5a	12.5	11.5	7.7	6.2
5		11.5	8.9a	9.2	6.9	5.7
6		5.8	8.9	7.4	6.2	5.3
7			8.9	6.6a	5.9a	4.9
8			4.5	6.6	5.9	4.5a
9				6.5	5.9	4.5
10				6.5	5.9	4.5
11				3.3	5.9	4.5
12					5.9	4.5
13					5.9	4.5
14					5.9	4.5
15					5.9	4.5
16					3.0	4.4
17						4.4
18						4.4
19						4.4
20						4.4
21						2.2
Total	100%	100%	100%	100%	100%	100%

a Denotes the year of changeover to straight-line depreciation.

Table 2 MACRS Tables by Property Class

MACRS Property Class & Depreciation Method	Useful Life (ADR Midpoint Life) "a"	Examples of Assets
3-year property 200% declining balance	4 years or less	Most small tools are included; the law specifically excludes autos and light trucks from this property class.
5-year property 200% declining balance	More than 4 years to less than 10 years	Autos and light trucks, computers, typewriters, copiers, duplicating equipment, heavy general-purpose trucks, and research and experimentation equipment are included.
7-year property 200% declining balance	10 years or more to less than 16 years	Office furniture and fixtures and most items of machinery and equipment used in production are included.
10-year property 200% declining balance	16 years or more to less than 20 years	Various machinery and equipment, such as that used in petroleum distilling and refining and in the milling of grain, are included.
15-year property 150% declining balance	20 years or more to less than 25 years	Sewage treatment plants, telephone and electrical distribution facilities, and land improvements are included.
20-year property 150% declining balance	25 years or more	Service stations and other real property with an ADR midpoint life of less than 27.5 years are included.
27.5-year property Straight-line	Not applicable	All residential rental property is included.
31.5-year property Straight-line	Not applicable	All nonresidential real property is included.

"a" The term ADR midpoint life means the "useful life" of an asset in a business sense; the appropriate ADR midpoint lives for assets are designated in the Tax Regulations.

TOTAL QUALITY MANAGEMENT (TQM) AND QUALITY COSTS*

TOTAL QUALITY MANAGEMENT

In order to be globally competitive in today's world-class manufacturing environment, firms place an increased emphasis on quality and productivity. *Total quality management (TQM)* is an effort in this direction. Simply put, it is a system for creating competitive advantage by focusing the organization on what is important to the customer. Total quality management can be broken down into: "Total": that is the whole organization is involved and understands that customer satisfaction is everyone's job. "Quality": the extent to which products and services satisfy the requirements of internal and external customers. "Management": the leadership, infrastructure and resources that support employees as they meet the needs of those customers.

TQM is essentially an endless quest for perfect quality. It is a *zero-defects* approach. It views the optimal level of quality costs as the level where zero defects are produced. This approach to quality is opposed to the traditional belief, called *acceptable quality level (AQL),* which allows a predetermined level of defective units to be produced and sold. AQL is the level where the number of defects allowed minimizes total quality costs. The rationale behind the traditional view is that there is a tradeoff between prevention and appraisal costs and failure costs. Quality experts maintain that the optimal quality level should be about 2.5% of sales.

---

* This chapter was coauthored by Anique Qureshi, Ph.D., CPA, CIA, associate professor of accounting at Queens College, and an accounting professional.

Principles of TQM

Making a product right the first time is one of the principal objectives of TQM. Implementing a successful TQM program will in fact reduce costs rather than increase them. There is no question that better quality will result in better productivity. This is based on the principle that when less time is spent on rework or repair, more time is available for manufacturing, which will increase productivity.

When an organization maintains accurate records of its cost of quality, TQM will demonstrate that effective quality assurance geared towards prevention versus correction will pay for itself. A good example of this is the situation where it is possible to eliminate 100% inspection with a good statistical process control (SPC) program. Elimination of high reject rates results in fewer products being repaired, reworked or scrapped with the obvious reductions in cost.

Tying the cost of quality to TQM is necessary in order to motivate management who is cost motivated in both industry and government. In a TQM environment, management will start utilizing the cost data to measure the success of the program. The corporate financial planner can determine that overall product costs are being reduced by the TQM program. Given this success in the prevention of defects, the following failure costs will be reduced or eliminated:

1. Rework or repair
2. Inspection of rework
3. Testing of rework
4. Warranty costs
5. Returned material
6. Discounts, adjustments and allowances

It is quite obvious that the cost of prevention in TQM is minor when taken against the above listed failure costs.

A checklist of TQM features are as follows:

- A systematic way to improve products and services
- A structured approach in identifying and solving problems
- Long term
- Conveyed by management's actions
- Supported by statistical quality control
- Practiced by everyone

Elements of TQM

The principle elements of TQM are straightforward and embrace a commonsense approach to management. However, each of the individual elements must be integrated into a structured whole to succeed. The elements are as follows:

1. *A Focus on the Customer*

   Every functional unit has a customer, whether it be an external consumer or an internal unit. TQM advocates that managers and employees become so customer-focused that they continually find new ways to meet or exceed customers' expectations. We must accept the concept that quality is defined by the customer and meeting the customer's needs and expectations is the strategic goal of TQM.

2. *A Long-Term Commitment*

   Experience in the U.S. and abroad shows that substantial gains come only after management makes a long-term commitment, usually five years or more, in improving quality. Customer-focus must be constantly renewed to keep that goal foremost.

3. *Top Management Support and Direction*

   Top management must be the driving force behind TQM. Senior managers must exhibit personal support by using quality improvement concepts in their management style, incorporating quality in their strategic planning process, and providing financial and staff support.

4. *Employee Involvement*

   Full employee participation is also an integral part of the process. Each employee must be a partner in achieving quality goals. Teamwork involves managers, supervisors, and employees in improving service delivery, solving systemic problems, and correcting errors in all parts of work processes.

5. *Effective and Renewed Communications.*

   The power of internal communication, both vertical and horizontal, is central to employee involvement. Regular and meaningful communication from all levels must occur. This will allow an agency to adjust its ways of operating and reinforce the commitment of TQM at the same time.

6. *Reliance on Standards and Measures*

   Measurement is the springboard to involvement, allowing the organization to initiate corrective action, set priorities and evaluate progress. Standards and measures should reflect customer requirements and changes that need to be introduced in the internal business of providing those requirements. The emphasis is on "doing the right thing right the first time."

7. *Commitment to Training*

   Training is absolutely vital to the success of TQM. The process usually begins with awareness training for teams of top-level managers. This is followed by courses for teams of mid-level managers, and finally by courses for non-managers. Awareness training is followed by an identification of areas of concentration, or of functional areas where TQM will first be introduced. Implementing TQM requires additional skills training, which is also conducted in teams.

8. *Importance of Rewards and Recognition*

   Most companies practicing TQM have given wide latitude to managers in issuing rewards and recognition. Here, a common theme is that individual financial rewards are not as appropriate as awards to groups or team members, since most successes are group achievements.

QUALITY COSTS

Costs of quality are costs that occur because poor quality may exist or actually does exist. More specifically, quality costs are the total of the costs incurred by (1) investing in the prevention of nonconformances to requirements; (2) appraising a product or service for conformance to requirements; and (3) failure to meet requirements.

Quality costs are classified into three broad categories: prevention, appraisal, and failure costs. *Prevention costs* are those incurred to prevent defects. Amounts spent on quality training programs, researching customer needs, quality circles, and improved production equipment are considered in prevention costs. Expenditures made for prevention will minimize the costs that will be incurred for appraisal and failure. *Appraisal costs* are costs incurred for monitoring or inspection; these costs compensate for mistakes not eliminated through prevention. *Failure costs* may be internal (such as scrap and rework costs and reinspection) or external (such as product returns due to quality problems, warranty costs, lost sales due to poor product performance, and complaint department costs. Market shares of many U.S. firms have eroded because foreign firms have been able to sell higher-quality products at lower prices.

Studies indicate that costs of quality for American companies are typically 20 to 30% of sales. Quality experts maintain that the optimal quality level should be about 2.5% of sales.

Two Different Views Concerning Optimal Quality Costs

There are two views concerning optimal quality costs:

1. the traditional view that uses an acceptable quality level
2. the world-class view that uses total quality control

Optimal Distribution of Quality Costs: Traditional View. The traditional approach uses an *acceptable quality level (AQL)* that permits a predetermined level of defective units to be produced and sold. AQL is the level where the number of defects allowed minimizes total quality costs. The reasoning of the traditional approach is that there is a tradeoff between failure costs and prevention and appraisal costs. As prevention and appraisal costs increase, internal and external failure costs are expected to decrease. As long as the decrease in failure costs is greater than the corresponding increase in prevention and failure costs, a company should continue increasing its efforts to prevent or detect defective units.

Optimal Distribution of Quality Costs: World-Class View. The world-class view uses total quality control and views the optimal level of quality costs as the level where zero defects are produced. The zero-defects approach uses a quality performance standard that requires:

1. all products to be produced according to specifications and
2. all services to be provided according to requirements

Zero defects reflect a total quality control philosophy used in Just-in-Time (JIT) manufacturing. Figure 1 illustrates the relationship between these two cost components under two different views.

QUALITY COST AND PERFORMANCE REPORTS

The principal objective of reporting quality costs is to improve and facilitate managerial planning, control, and decision making. Potential uses of quality cost information include:

(a) quality program implementation decisions
(b) evaluation of the effectiveness of quality programs
(c) strategic pricing decisions (For example, a reduction in quality costs might enable a firm to reduce its selling price, improve its competitive position, and increase market share.)

Figure 1

Traditional View

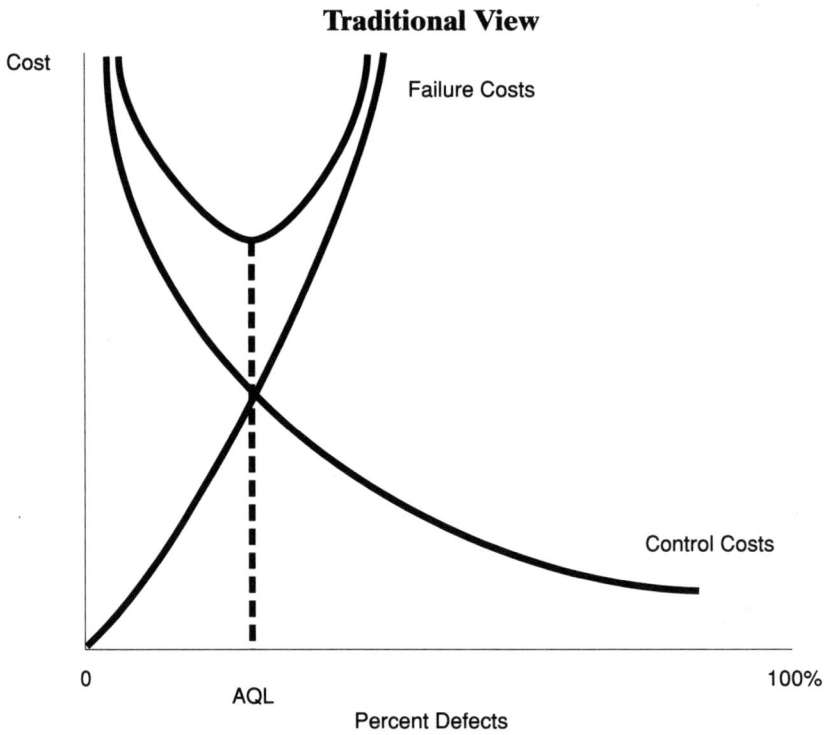

Cost

Failure Costs

Control Costs

0

AQL

100%

Percent Defects

World-Class View

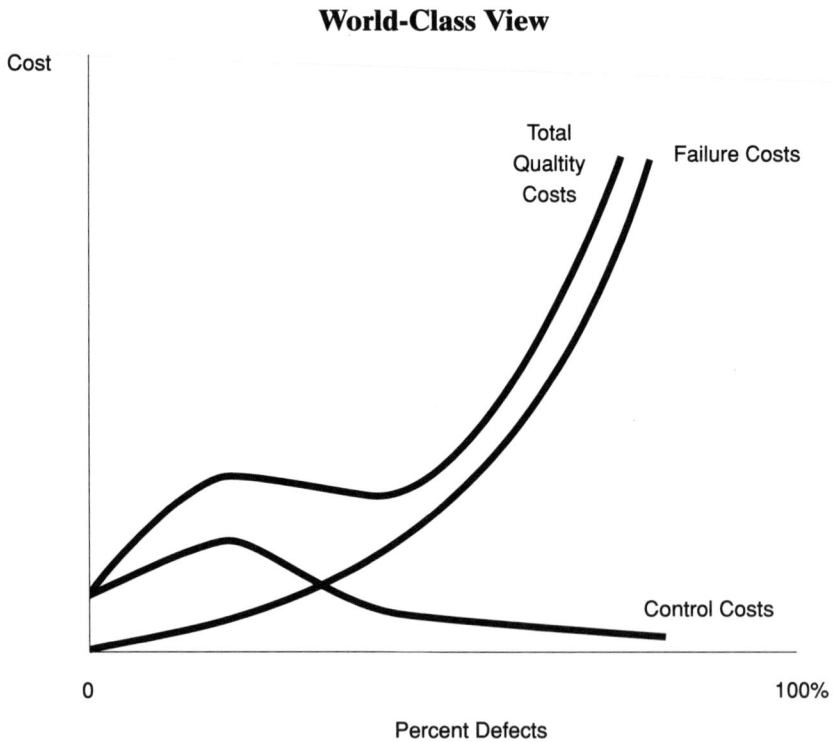

Cost

Total
Qualtity
Costs

Failure Costs

Control Costs

0

100%

Percent Defects

The control process involves comparing actual performance with quality standards. This comparison provides feedback that can be used to take corrective action if necessary. The first step in a quality cost reporting system is to prepare a detailed listing of actual quality costs by category. Furthermore, each category of quality costs is expressed as a percentage of sales. This serves two purposes: (a) it permits managers to assess the financial impact of quality costs, and (b) it reveals the relative emphasis currently placed on each category.

Figure 2   Quality Costs—General Description

Prevention Costs

The costs of all activities specifically designed to prevent poor quality in products or services. Examples are the costs of new product review, quality planning, supplier capability surveys, process capability evaluations, quality improvement team meetings, quality improvement projects, quality education and training.

Appraisal Costs

The costs associated with measuring, evaluating or auditing products or services to assure conformance to quality standards and performance requirements. These include the costs of incoming and source inspection/test of purchased material, in process and final inspection/test, product, process, or service audits, calibration of measuring and test equipment, and the costs of associated supplies and materials.

Failure Costs

The costs resulting from products or services not conforming to requirements or customer/user needs. Failure costs are divided into internal and external failure cost categories.

Internal Failure Costs

Failure costs occurring prior to delivery or shipment of the product, or the furnishing of a service, to the customer. Examples are the costs of scrap, rework, reinspection, retesting, material review, and downgrading.

External Failure Costs

Failure costs occurring after delivery or shipment of the product, and during or after furnishing of a service, to the customer. Examples are the costs of processing customer complaints, customer returns, warranty claims, and product recalls.

Total Quality Costs

The sum of the above costs. It represents the difference between the actual cost of a product or service, and what the reduced cost would be if there was no possibility of substandard service, failure of products, or defects in their manufacture.

Quality cost reports (Figure 3) can be used to point out the strengths and weaknesses of a quality system. Improvement teams can use them to describe the monetary benefits and ramifications of proposed changes. Return-on-investment (ROI) models and other financial analyses can be constructed directly from quality cost data to justify proposals to management. In practice, quality costs can define activities of quality program and quality improvement efforts in a language that management can understand and act on—dollars.

The negative effect on profits, resulting from product or service of less than acceptable quality or from ineffective quality management, is almost always dynamic. Once started, it continues to mushroom until ultimately the company finds itself in serious financial difficulties due to the two-pronged impact of an unheeded increase in quality costs coupled with a declining performance image. Management that clearly understands this understands the economics of quality.

In the quality cost report, quality costs are grouped into one of four categories:

1. prevention costs
2. appraisal costs
3. internal failure costs
4. external failure costs

In addition, each category of quality costs is expressed as a percentage of sales. There are four types of performance reports to measure a company's quality improvement. They are:

1. *Interim quality performance report.* It measures the progress achieved within the period relative to the planned level of progress for the period (see Figure 4).

2. *One-year quality trend report.* It compares the current year's quality cost ratio with the previous year's ratio. More specifically, it compares (1) the current year's variable quality cost ratio with the previous year's variable quality cost ratio, and the current year's actual fixed quality costs with the previous year's actual fixed quality costs (see Figure 5).

3. *Long-range quality performance report.* It compares the current year's actual quality costs with the firm's intended long-range quality goal (see Figure 6).

Activity-Based Management and Optimal Quality Costs

Activity-based management supports the zero-defect view of quality costs.

Activity-based management classifies activities as: (1) value-added activities and (2) nonvalue-added activities.

Quality-related activities (internal and external failure activities, prevention activities, and appraisal activities) can be classified as value-added and nonvalue-added.

Internal and external failure activities and their associated costs are nonvalue-added and should be eliminated.

Prevention activities that are performed efficiently are value-added. (Costs caused by inefficiency in prevention activities are nonvalue-added costs.)

Appraisal activities may be value-added or nonvalue-added depending upon the activity. For example, quality audits may serve a value-added objective.

Once the quality-related activities are identified for each category, resource drivers can be used to improve cost assignments to individual activities. Root or process drivers can also be identified and used to help managers understand what is causing the cost of the activities.

Using Quality Cost Information

The principal objective of reporting quality costs is to improve and facilitate managerial planning, control, and decision making.

Potential uses of quality cost information include:

1. quality program implementation decisions
2. evaluation of the effectiveness of quality programs
3. strategic pricing decisions (For example, improved reporting of quality costs might be used by managers to target specific quality costs for reductions. A reduction in quality costs might enable a firm to reduce its selling price, improve its competitive position, and increase market share.)
4. inclusion of quality costs in cost-volume-profit analysis (For example, overlooking quality cost savings results in a higher breakeven and possible rejection of a profitable project.)

The control process involves comparing actual performance with quality standards. This comparison provides feedback that can be used to take corrective action if necessary.

Figure 3

Allison Products
Quality Cost Report
For the Year Ended March 31, 19x2

	Quality Costs		Percentage of Sale(a)
Prevention costs:			
Quality training	$30,000		
Reliability engineering	79,000	$109,000	3.73%
Appraisal costs:			
Materials inspection	$19,000		
Product acceptance	10,000		
Process acceptance	35,000	$64,000	2.19%
Internal failure costs:			
Scrap	$40,000		
Rework	34,000	$74,000	2.53%
External failure costs:			
Customer complaints	$24,000		
Warranty	24,000		
Repair	15,000	$63,000	2.16%
Total quality costs		$310,000	10.62% (b)

(a) Actual sales of $2,920,000
(b) $310,000/$2,920,000 = 10.62 percent. Difference is rounding error.

Figure 4

Allison Products
Interim Standard Performance Report
For the Year Ended March 31, 19x2

	Actual Costs	Budgeted Costs(a)	Variance
Prevention costs:			
Quality training	$30,000	$30,000	$0
Reliability engineering	79,000	80,000	1,000 F
Total prevention	$109,000	$110,000	$1,000 F
Appraisal costs:			
Materials inspection	$19,000	$28,000	$9,000 F
Product acceptance	10,000	15,000	5,000 F
Process acceptance	35,000	35,000	0
Total appraisal	$64,000	$78,000	$14,000 F

Total Quality Management (TQM) and Quality Costs

Internal failure costs:

Scrap	$40,000	$44,000	$4,000 F
Rework	34,000	36,500	2,500 F
Total internal failure	$74,000	$80,500	$6,500 F

External failure costs:

Fixed:

Customer complaints	$24,000	$25,000	$1,000 F

Variable:

Warranty	24,000	20,000	(4,000) U
Repair	15,000	17,500	2,500 F
Total external failure	$63,000	$62,500	($500) U
Total quality costs	$310,000	$331,000	$21,000 F
Percentage of actual sales	10.62%	11.34%	0.72% F

(a) Based on actual sales
(b) Actual sales of $2,920,000

Figure 5

Allison Products
Quality Cost, One-Year Trend
For the Year Ended March 31, 19x2

	Actual Costs 19x2(a)	Budgeted Costs 19x1	Variance
Prevention costs:			
Quality training	$30,000	$36,000	$6,000 F
Reliability engineering	79,000	120,000	41,000 F
Total prevention	$109,000	$156,000	$47,000 F
Appraisal costs:			
Materials inspection	$19,000	$33,600	$14,600 F
Product acceptance	10,000	16,800	6,800 F
Process acceptance	35,000	39,200	4,200 F
Total appraisal	$64,000	$89,600	$25,600 F
Internal failure costs:			
Scrap	$40,000	$48,000	$8,000 F
Rework	34,000	40,000	6,000 F
Total internal failure	$74,000	$88,000	$14,000 F
External failure costs:			
Fixed:			
Customer complaints	$24,000	$33,000	$9,000 F

Variable:			
Warranty	24,000	23,000	(1,000) U
Repair	15,000	16,400	1,400 F
Total external failure	$63,000	$72,400	$9,400 F
Total quality costs	$310,000	$406,000	$96,000 F
Percentage of actual sales	10.62%	13.90%	3.29% F

(a) Based on actual sales = $2,920,000

Figure 6

Allison Products
Long-Range Performance Report
For the Year Ended March 31, 19x2

	Actual Costs	Target Costs(a)	Variance
Prevention costs:			
Quality training	$30,000	$14,000	($16,000) U
Reliability engineering	79,000	39,000	(40,000) U
Total prevention	$109,000	$53,000	($56,000) U
Appraisal costs:			
Materials inspection	$19,000	$7,900	($11,100) U
Product acceptance	10,000	0	(10,000) U
Process acceptance	35,000	12,000	(23,000) U
Total appraisal	$64,000	$19,900	($44,100) U
Internal failure costs:			
Scrap	$40,000	$0	($40,000) U
Rework	34,000	0	(34,000) U
Total internal failure	$74,000	$0	($74,000) U
External failure costs:			
Fixed:			
Customer complaints	$24,000	$0	($24,000) U
Variable:			
Warranty	24,000	0	(24,000) U
Repair	15,000	0	(15,000) U
Total external failure	$63,000	$0	($63,000) U
Total quality costs	$310,000	$72,900	($237,100) U
Percentage of actual sales	10.62%	2.50%	–8.12% U

(a) Based on actual sales of $2,920,000. These costs are value-added costs.

RISK MANAGEMENT AND ANALYSIS

Risk management involves identifying risk exposure, analyzing risk, measuring potential loss, determining the best insurance strategy (or whether to self-insure), cost projections and control, volatility of operations, timing of adverse events, claims adjustment, proper cost allocation, and the use of risk management software.

Risks facing a business may negatively affect its reputation, "bottom-line," cost and availability of financing, credit rating, market price of stock, regulatory or legislative changes, and elimination of barriers to entry.

An evaluation must be made of the tradeoff between risk and return. A higher risk mandates a higher rate of return to justify taking the extra risk.

A risk program must be in place. The program must have built-in flexibility to adjust, as conditions require. The program must conform to the goals, objectives, and policies of the business.

The company must have a workable contingency plan such as a recovery plan. Employees must be instructed what to do in such eventualities. Test runs should be practiced. Contingency plans must be updated periodically to incorporate new technologies, changing staff, and new areas of business activity.

Areas of risk must be identified and corrective action taken to reduce those risks. Unusually high risk will not only have negative effects on earnings but might also place in question the continuity of the operation.

Models and quantitative approaches including actuarial techniques may be used to appraise potential catastrophic losses, product/service liability, intellectual property losses, and business interruption. Probability distributions should be arrived at of expected losses based on the model or quantitative technique used.

APPRAISAL OF RISK

The "red flags" of undue risk must be identified and controlled. "Red flags" include poor employee training and performance, inadequate planning, fragmentation, poor communication, lateness, improper focus, failure to observe government regulations or laws (e.g., the federal Comprehensive Environmental Response, Compensation and Liability Act covering the release and disposal of hazardous substances and wastes), overconfidence, and "hostile" attitudes.

When appraising a particular situation, evaluate the risk profile, financial status, and acceptable risk exposure. What is the entity's risk tolerance level? To what extent does the risk of a situation exceed predetermined maximum risk levels? Has management received proper approval to undertake the high-risk level? Has proper planning been performed to take into account the adverse effects on the business if things do not work out? For example, if losses are incurred that significantly exceed the entity's traditional insurance program, the company might be permanently crippled. Examples include a business interruption resulting from a terrorist bombing, loss of a major vendor, misinterpretation of law, or a product recall.

In appraising risk, consideration must be given to the company's liquidity and solvency position to withstand loss. A determination must be made of the costs associated with various risks.

Risk should be evaluated and minimized. Risk may be reduced through the following means:

- Vertically integrate to reduce the price and supply risk of raw materials.
- Take out sufficient insurance coverage for possible asset and operating losses (including foreign risk protection). A lower trend in insurance expense to the asset insured may indicate inadequate coverage.
- Diversify activities, product/service line, market segments, customer bases, geographic areas, and investments.
- Sell to diversified industries to protect against cyclical turns in the economy.
- Sign a forward contract to take delivery of raw materials at fixed prices at a specified future date so the entity insulates itself from price increases.
- Enter into foreign currency futures contracts to lock in a fixed rate.
- Participate in joint ventures and partnerships with other companies. In so doing, obligations of the parties must be taken into account. For example, questions to be asked are: *Which company is to absorb most of the losses? What is our company's duties and exposure under the agreement?*

- Sell low-priced products as well as more expensive ones to protect against inflationary and recessionary periods.
- Change suppliers who prove unreliable.
- Take steps so the company is less susceptible to business cycles (e.g., inelastic demand products, negatively correlated products/services).
- Add products/services having different seasonal attractiveness and demand.
- Emphasize a piggyback product base (similar merchandise associated with the basic business).
- Balance the company's financing mix.

In analyzing the company's product/service line, determine:

- Extent of correlation between products. Positive correlation means high risk because the demand for all the products go in the same direction. Negative correlation minimizes the risk. No correlation means indifference between products.
- Product demand elasticity equal to the percentage change in quantity relative to the percentage change in price. Elastic demand means that a minor change in price has a significant impact on quantity demanded. This indicates higher risk. Inelastic product demand minimizes risk because a change in price will have little effect on quantity demanded.

In analyzing the risk associated with multinational companies, compute:

- Total assets in high-risk foreign countries to total assets.
- High-risk foreign revenue to total revenue. High-risk revenue is based on risk ratings of companies in published sources (e.g., International Country Risk Guide).
- High-risk foreign revenue to net income.
- Percentage of earnings associated with foreign government contracts.
- Fluctuation in foreign exchange rates.

TYPES OF RISK

The corporate financial manager needs to take into account the various types of risk the entity faces. For example, corporate risk may be in the form of overrelying on a few key executives or the underinsurance of assets. Industry risk may be the high technological environment, or an industry scrutinized under the "public eye," or a capital-intensive business. Moving toward a variable cost-oriented business may minimize industry risk. Economic risk includes susceptibility to the business cycle. This risk may be reduced by having a low-priced substitute for a high priced-one.

Social risk occurs when a company experiences customer boycott or discrimination cases. A way to reduce this risk is to be engaged in community involvement and sensitivity training.

A company must properly instruct its personnel not to intrude with electronic mail, slander others, or commit libel. The company must carefully train and monitor staff to guard against possible infractions causing employee lawsuits or federal/local government investigation.

Political risk applies to relations with U.S. and local government agencies and foreign governments when operations are carried out overseas. This risk may be reduced through lobbying efforts and avoiding activities and placing assets in high-risk foreign areas.

Environmental risk includes product lines and services susceptible to changes in the weather. Having counter-seasonal goods and services, or moving to another geographic location may reduce this risk. Multinational entities are susceptible to environmental risk, particularly in the former "Iron Curtain" countries. There are often problems with the land and resource use, including pollution and hazardous waste. The acquiring company must be cautious of not only the cleanup costs, but also associated penalties and fines. Prior to acquisition, the acquirer must be assured that there is a contract under which the seller will be responsible for all or part of the environmental obligations. A high-risk premium applies to corporate investments in countries with environmental problems. Insurance companies, for example, should reject potential clients that are not environmentally certified or fail to meet particular environmental norms. Banks need to be concerned with the collectibility of loans to companies with major environmental exposure. If a company is "dirty," it may have difficulty obtaining adequate insurance or loans. Further, the effect of impending government environmental laws on the business must be considered. Environmental problems and disasters may significantly hurt earnings.

Terrorism is also of concern to certain types of businesses. Security measures must be in place to guard against bombing.

A determination must be made as to how the risks facing a business interact. A model must consider alternative scenarios.

RISK ANALYSIS AND MANAGEMENT SOFTWARE

Software is available to assess, evaluate, and control the risks facing a company. A risk management information system (RMIS) includes hardware and software components. However, we consider here software availability, implications, benefits, and applications. The software selected should be that which offers a proper "fit" to the environment and circumstances of the company.

In deciding on the "right" software the financial manager should consider the company's requirements and expectations, corporate culture, report preparation needs, regulatory reporting mandates, product/service line, nature of operations, claims processing and administration, government compliance laws, business policies and procedures, insurance coverage, technological resources, employee background and experience, levels of communication, legal liability aspects, organizational structure, and work flow. The risk management and analysis software should include the ability to manipulate data into risk patterns.

Are the "right" managers being provided with the appropriate information on a timely basis? A determination must also be made of the communication and distribution features of the software. The software should be flexible so that reports may be customized depending on the data needed and for whom. For example, a factory foreman or manager wants to know how many employee injuries occurred and of what nature. On the other hand, the accounting department manager wants to know the negative financial effects the accidents have on the company's financial position and operating performance.

Software may be used to evaluate safety statistical data by division, department, responsibility unit, geographic location, and manager. Potential difficulties may be highlighted. An example of a risk management software application is providing a report on how many employee injuries took place by department, operation, and activity. Is the client's incidence rate above or below expected ranges? How does the client injury rate compare to competitors and industry averages? There should be a software feature, such as an expert system, on how to correct the problem of a high rate of employee accidents and offer other relevant recommendations.

If a company is exchanging risk information with others (e.g., insurance company, investment banker, and government agencies), then software compatibility is needed. Further, there should exist appropriate operating systems and network support. A company may use its Intranet to expand risk management throughout the company. It is important that there be proper user interfaces.

RISK CONTROL

Risk control includes environmental compliance, periodic inspections, and alarm systems. Loss prevention and control must consider physical and human aspects. For example, "safer" machines may be used to prevent worker injury. Appropriate sprinklers may be installed to prevent fires. Consultants may be retained in specialized areas such as industrial hygiene.

Product labeling should be appraised as to appropriateness and representation. Any consumer complaints should be immediately investigated to avoid possible government action or litigation.

The financial manager must determine the best kind, term, and amount of insurance to carry to guard against losses. Insurance coverage may be taken out for losses to plant, property and equipment, product/service deficiencies, and employee conduct. The financial manager should consider insuring areas not typically insured against, such as industrial espionage, loss of intellectual property, or employee theft. An example of the latter is employment practice liability insurance (EPLI). This policy is available from many insurance companies such as Chubb and Lexington. Unfortunately even this type of policy often excludes coverage for bodily injury, workers' compensation, and infractions under ERISA. It is not unusual for an employee to sue because of an employer's promotion and hiring policies. The insurance premium may be lowered by increasing the deductible or changing to less expensive insurance carriers.

The financial manager must carefully monitor the entity's fiduciary responsibilities, working conditions, contractual commitments, and employment practices. Systems must be checked on an ongoing basis for defects in functioning such as fire alarm devices. The company must be certain that its employee policies are fair and in conformity with federal and local laws.

Risk control includes provisions against terrorist acts related to loss of life, product losses, and property damage. Security procedures including access controls must be strong in high-risk areas such as in a foreign country with extremist groups. Employees must be instructed to use safety precautions.

RISK SOFTWARE PACKAGES AND PRODUCTS

There are many risk management software packages available to financial managers. Some useful packages are described below.

Decision Support Systems' The Expert Business Impact Analysis System provides risk appraisal factors and protection strategy recommendations. It has a database of global threats, vulnerability assessments, comparative analysis, and reporting capabilities (including by location). It contains threat probabilities with documented statistical sources, outage durations, and regional segmentation. It has interactive "what-if" analysis features for scenario planning to evaluate the benefits of alternative solutions and to perform comparisons with the current and historical background. (For information telephone: (800) 788-6447, e-mail: BIAsys@aol.com or write to Decision Support Systems, 380 S. State Road 434, Suite 1004-117, Altamonte Springs, Florida 32714.)

Strohl Systems offers contingency planning software products to plan for unexpected disruptions on the company's operations. It is better to anticipate interruptions before they turn into major problems. BIA Professional is a business impact analysis tool allowing the company to quickly and easily define the effects of disaster and helps target critical functions for contingency planning. Living Disaster Recovery Planning Systems (LDRPS) is continuity (recovery) planning software including a question and answer feature, sample documents and diagrams, graphics, report writer, recover strategies and contingency planning, and presentation of recovery activities in the form of Program Evaluation and Review Technique (PERT) and Gantt charts. Plans and procedures cover emergency response, crisis management, notification, facilities relocation, security, asset management and retrieval, vital records, contamination, safety, and health. (For information write: Strohl Systems, 500 North Gulph Road, King of Prussia, PA 19406, telephone: (610) 768-4120, fax: (610) 768-4138, or Web: http://www.strohl-systems.com.)

CSCI's Recovery PAC is business recovery planning software including comprehensive business impact analysis and risk assessment. It identifies critical business functions and applications and sets priorities for recovery. It also identifies risk exposures that can potentially turn into a disaster. (For information telephone: (800) 925-CSCI.)

Business Foundations' Internal Operations Risk Analysis software evaluates a company's areas of risk and internal control structure. It is an expert system developed around 180 interview questions. Based on the answers to the questions, the software prepares a management report highlighting the strengths and weaknesses in the operations of the business. A risk rating (high, medium, and low) is assigned to categories of risk. Relevant management and analytical reports are generated. Operational areas evaluated by the software include working environment, objects, planning, and personnel. It has database capabilities. It recommends for problem areas corrective steps. There is an upgrade for industry-specific components.

Price Waterhouse's Controls assists in risk analysis by documenting, evaluating, and testing the company's internal controls. Areas of risk exposure are identified. Control weaknesses are highlighted with resultant recommendations for improvement. Control effectiveness may be evaluated at different levels within the company (e.g., by activity, by business unit). A comparison and analysis may be made of the relative control performance of different operating units. (For information fax: (201) 292-3800 or Web: http://www.pw.com.)

Pleier and Associates' ADM Plus performs risk management, planning, and analysis.

Corporate Systems' CS EDGE Series offers a risk management information system providing claim processing and evaluation, accident analysis, management of fixed assets, and risk reporting and appraisal. (For information telephone: (800) 9-CS-EDGE or Web: http://www.csedge.com.)

American International Group (AIG)'s IntelliRisk is a risk management information system providing claims information, asset management, risk reduction strategies, account information, payment history, report preparation, searches and sorting, and communication online features with underwriters, brokers, and adjusters. (For information telephone: Alan Louison, Director of Risk Management Information Services at (800) 767-2524 or write: American International Group, Department A, 70 Pine Street, New York, N.Y. 10270.)

Dorn Technology Group's RISK MASTER/WIN integration package has many features including incident reporting, claim adjustments and reporting, policy management, workers' compensation, actuarial reporting, and reserve analysis. (For information telephone (800) 587-1440 or (313) 462-5800; fax (3l3) 462-5809; or Web: http://dorn.com.)

Health Management Technologies' RETURN is software for workers' compensation, disability, and group health plans. It manages cases, channels information to network providers, monitors both work status and return to work, and documents activity and case outcome. It offers an electronic Rolodex of providers, treatment centers, resources, and contacts. The package evaluates provider performance and results in cost savings. The features include a standard letter generator, report writer, accounts receivable for case management, bill repricing, and job analysis. (For information telephone: (800) 647-7007 or write: Health Management Technologies, 1150 Moraga Way, Suite 150, Moraga, California 94556.)

California Interactive Computer's Claims and Risk Management Systems has modules for workers' compensation, group medical, property and casualty, disability management, and general risk management. The software can be customized for your particular needs by the vendor. (For information telephone: (805) 294-1300, fax: (805) 294-1310, write: California Interactive Computing, 25572 Avenue Stanford, Valencia, California 91355, Web: http://calinteractive.com.)

Conway Computer Group's Pabblo and Paccasso are a windows-based client/server solution for workers compensation and property/casualty insurance administration. (For information telephone: (601) 957-7400 or write: Conway Computer Group, P.O. Box 12801, Jackson, Mississippi 39211, Web: http://www.ccg.com.)

PC Solutions' Certifitra keeps track of insurance certificates, aids in insurance auditing, and prepares reports of insurance status (e.g., coverage, expiration dates). (For information telephone: (704) 525-9330, fax: (704) 525-9539, or e-mail: pcsoln@vnet.net.)

CCH Incorporated's Safety Compliance Assistant is interactive software to comply with the U.S. Occupational Safety and Health Administration (OSHA) General Industry Standards. It provides inspection and training checklists, detects OSHA compliance violations, maintains required documents, and corrects violations. (For information telephone: (800) 228-8353.)

CIC Incorporated's Back Track software verifies employees' background for hiring purposes. (For information telephone: (800) 321-HIRE extension 126, or fax: (813) 559-0232.)

QA Systems QASYS is innovative flexible risk management software for insurance companies. (For information telephone: (800) 946-1717 or (212) 599-1717, or write: QA Systems, 220 E. 42nd St., New York, N.Y. 10017.)

RISK MODELING SOFTWARE APPLICATIONS

Risk modeling is a decision-making aid to the financial manager. Models may be used in analyzing risks while financial models can evaluate the financial consequences arising from accidents or other adverse developments. Risk models may be developed for measuring the financial impact due to catastrophes (fire, flood, earthquake, nuclear). The probable loss arising from the accident, disaster, or other event may be estimated. The model may also determine the probable effects on business activities as well as possible competitive reactions. A contingency model may help in planning an appropriate strategy and response. A "what-if" scenario analysis may be formulated to see the end-result effects of changing input variables and factors. An example of a scenario modeling analysis is to simulate the possible operating and financial consequences on the company from various possibilities arising from a hurricane. The company's risk vulnerability from such an event may be "mapped" and appraised. The "best-case," "worst-case," and "likely" scenarios may be depicted and reviewed. The model simulation has the benefit of aiding the company in determining beforehand how to best minimize the damage operationally and financially and how to provide proper protective measures.

The software enables the company to determine the areas, types, and degrees of risk facing the business. A minimum-maximum range of loss figure may be derived.

Risk modeling may be used to identify and define the type and amount of risks related to various exposures. A priority ranking based on risk and uncertainty may also be prepared and studied. Risk problem areas may be analyzed along with a set of appropriate alternative responses.

RISK MANAGEMENT INFORMATION SYSTEMS (RMIS) TESTING LABORATORY

Deloitte and Touche, CPAs has started the first independent risk management systems testing laboratory that tests software, develops systems solutions, evaluates software usefulness, provides benchmarking information, and customizes applications. Deloitte and Touche, CPAs will compare software products, compare reporting and application features, and appraise effectiveness in meeting your needs. (For information contact David Duden, RMIS/Lab Director at telephone: (860) 543-7341, e-mail: dduden@ dttus.com, or Web: http://www.rmislab.com.)

ONLINE RISK MANAGEMENT DATA BASE SERVICES

There are many online services available providing important risk management information. For example, the National Council on Compensation Insurance (NCCI) Inc. provides an online InsNet Workers Compensation Characteristic Series containing claims data useful in having a cost-effective workers compensation system. The service aids in evaluating risks, determining and appraising workers compensation costs including frequency data, specifying injury claim characteristics, providing demographic and body claim characteristics, and specifying benefit type information. (For information about NCCI's InsNet online service telephone: (800) 622-4123, access the Web site: http://www.ncci.com, or write to National Council on Compensation Insurance, 750 Park of Commerce Drive, Boca Raton, Florida 33487.)

REENGINEERING AND OUTSOURCING THE BUSINESS

Reengineering includes downsizing and restructuring. It should be properly balanced. Outsourcing is contracting out production or service functions performed by the company to save on costs or to establish efficiencies. The financial manager must identify problems within the organization and recommend solutions. The financial manager must therefore understand what reengineering and outsourcing are about, how they affect the business, and how they may be implemented correctly. The financial manager needs to analyze, evaluate, offer suggestions, and comment on the company's existing or possible efforts to reengineer, downsize, restructure, and outsource the business.

REENGINEERING

A strategy is the implementation of a company's plans and tactics. A company may downsize or right size to its "core" to create value. Reengineering is defined as a multidisciplinary approach to making fundamental changes in how operations, activities, functions, and procedures are conducted within a business. The objective of such change is to improve performance, productivity, and profitability. Reengineering should be undertaken if the benefit exceeds the cost of doing so considering money and time. There should be a "road map" of the steps in the reengineering process. Reengineering may be for the company as a whole, one or more business units, and particular geographic locations. There is a risk in reengineering of not enough or too much change. For reengineering to succeed the following should be present: employee understanding and cooperation, good project planning and management, timely assessment, benchmarks, and realistic expectations. Reengineering may take different forms of approach including business process redesign (redesigning processes to achieve efficiencies and enhance service quality) and process innovation (making fundamental changes to improve the importance of processes). Reengineering attempts continual improvement in business procedures.

In reengineering, the focus should be on the current and potential customer and then corporate structure and processes designed accordingly. In other words, reengineering from the outside in. Managers must monitor and track the current and emerging satisfaction needs of customers and formulate the products and services they demand. New product innovation and creativity may be required. Reengineering must create "real value" to the customer. In so doing, consider if the current product/service line helps in keeping present customers and expanding the customer base.

Objectives for cost reduction should be established such as time for each job (task, operation, activity), expected maintenance, and compatibility.

Employees must understand the why to reengineering so their support, contribution, and continued morale to the process may be obtained. Cultural differences have to be taken into account. Disproportionate downsizing is a mistake. The company must be restructured logically and practically. Proper planning is required to avoid any surprises.

Reengineering may aid in developing new products and/or services, improving product distribution, and achieving growth. A successful strategy includes joint ventures and franchishing. The purposes of reengineering include:

- Cost control and reduction (e.g., employee costs)
- Revenue, profit, and rate of return maximization
- Growth and capacity therefor
- Reduction in risk
- Appreciation in stock and bond price
- Improvement in bond rating
- Lowering in the cost of financing
- Inventory reduction
- Improved market share
- Remaining competitive
- Reduction in headcount
- Change in corporate culture
- Additional flexibility
- Spinoff of a segment or operation

- Improved quality
- Improved integration
- Streamlining production and distribution
- Keeping up-to-date with the latest technology
- Improved productivity
- Improved interaction and communication
- Improved product delivery and service
- Change the product/service mix

In reengineering, consideration should be given to the cost and time of doing so, new ideas, developing products and services, managing operations and projects, portfolio management, retraining, acquisitions and mergers, joint ventures, automation, amount of restructuring needed, change to equipment, employee training, inspection requirements, infrastructure, risk profile, whether fundamental or incremental change is needed, reassignment (if any) of displaced employees, and legal and contractual provisions and limitations.

The right resources must be at the right places at the right time. Processes may be redesigned to improve service quality and promote efficiencies. Continuous improvement in processes and procedures, job descriptions, and work flow mandate commitment and follow-through. However, be careful not to make inappropriate or incorrect changes to the system or process. The effect of current changes on the future must be taken into account. A manager does not want to make a change now having just an immediate benefit but having a long-term negative effect. An example is laying off experienced supervisors who will be needed in the future to train employees when business picks up. Questions to be answered in reengineering follow:

- Should the reengineering effort be centralized or decentralized? If decentralized, how will integration be accomplished?
- Where does reengineering begin and end?
- What expectations are there to be achieved?
- What is the role of technology in the reengineering effort?
- What are the logistics throughout the project's life?
- What effect does reengineering efforts have on the environmental program of the business?
- How much value does the reengineering plan achieve?
- What uncertainties and risks does reengineering have and what steps have been undertaken to reduce such risks? The risks associated

with reengineering include financial, technological, operational, and political.

- What legal issues and contract commitments are raised because of the reengineering program?

- If, and to what extent, will outside consultants be involved?

- When, and how will periodic reviews (reports) take place?

- Is reengineering proceeding as scheduled? If not, what is the problem and how may it be rectified?

- Who will be assigned to the reengineering effort, and why? What are their qualifications and time commitment?

Before full-scale reengineering takes place at the entire company, a pilot program and prototyping should be conducted to identify problems, learn from mistakes, and formulate sound strategies and approaches based on experience. By developing solutions to expected problems before full scale implementation, the company may save in cost and time as well as reduce risks. It is best to complete one reengineering project before proceeding to the next because the manager becomes more focused and learns from experience.

Scenario analysis should be undertaken looking at high, low, and average situations. Probabilities, weights, and rankings may be assigned to alternative scenario situations as part of the evaluative process. There is a link between scenario planning and business reengineering. Scenario analysis considers uncertainties, range of possibilities (outcomes), what is critical and what is not, controllable and uncontrollable factors, the effect of implementing a strategy in one area on other areas, contingent possibilities (a course of action is valuable only in particular scenario settings). Scenario analysis considers advisable steps to take now or in the future, or if a particular change in circumstance occurs. It is similar to a simulation to determine what will happen in the "real world." "Red flags" should be recognized and corrective action taken. What are the positive and negative outcomes from implementing a particular procedure or strategy? Scenario analysis assists in reducing risk and focusing on reengineering efforts. The scenario program provides "visions" as to the future. Its results include what activities should be emphasized or deemphasized, and what actions should be eliminated. Scenario analysis looks at the alternative possibilities available and aids in timely implementation. A priority ranking of alternatives may be established.

Reengineering in the plant may take the form of automating operations, updating manufacturing approaches, and accomplishing greater flexibility. It may involve reorganizing the human resource function to achieve economies and eliminate duplication. Internal organizational processes and product/service deliveries may be redesigned.

One must be careful that reengineering does not result in "dumbsizing" when the entity's long-term financial position and operating results are adversely impacted. Does the reengineering program layoff experienced personnel, cut vital services, increase risk, result in legal liability, cause conflicts with vendors or customers, result in worker mistrust, cause injuries or malfunctioning of equipment, or cause other negative aspects that outweigh any benefits achieved? The authors are aware of instances when in fact a reengineering program that was improperly administered was counterproductive.

The reengineering team should consist of those who are representative of those to be affected within the department by the ultimate outcome of the proposed reengineering. The group should be a cross-section of individuals within the company. In other words, there should be organizational diversity. Determine who is responsible for what and how, and how often performance will be measured. If individuals are trying to sabotage the reengineering effort, take necessary steps to remove the roadblock such as dismissing uncooperative employees.

OUTSOURCING AND INSOURCING

A corporate policy must be established regarding outsourcing. Outsourcing is contracting to others work that was formerly done within the company. It includes buying goods and services from vendors. As a general rule, outsourcing is more appropriate for "core" activities than "noncore" operations. Companies more suitable for outsourcing are those that are decentralized, engaged in restructuring (e.g., downsizing), and are out-of-date.

There are many outsourcing service providers in areas such as finance, administration, engineering, manufacturing, buying, human resources, customer service, real estate management, computer systems, marketing and sales, investment management, maintenance, product procurement, distribution (e.g., shipping) and logistics, technology, and transportation. For example, information technology services are provided by Integrated Systems Solutions of White Plains, New York. Xerox Corporation offers many business services related to office work and duplication functions.

Before outsourcing, consideration should be given to whether it makes sense in light of expectations, company objectives and needs, business plans, major sources of revenue, cost (including conversion costs), risk (including business uncertainties), contract period, legal liability, availability, security, confidentiality, time constraints (including time to implement and schedule), capacity limitations, employee expertise and proficiency, employee morale, time concerns, nature of item (e.g., critical importance), compatibility, corporate culture, degree of control sought, innovation and creativity, logistics, and cost of redeployment and relocation. A company may be able to outsource an aspect of its operations for less than it costs to train and manage employees to conduct the same function within the business. If a function is "mission critical," it probably should not be outsourced because management would want to retain control over it. An activity that gives the company a significant competitive advantage (differentiation) should most likely stay within the company.

Outsourcing allows a business to be more efficient and effective, engage in subcontracting legacy systems, reduce costs (e.g., staff), reduce risk, streamline and simplify operations, improve quality, focus on core activities and competencies, free up capital and human resources, improve existing processes, improve delivery of activities, generate efficiencies and effectiveness, enhance flexibility, obtain a competitive advantage, redeploy staff and assets, achieve economies, enhance productivity, convert fixed costs to variable costs, and obtain improved up-to-date technology.

In selecting an outsourcing vendor, consider reputation, contacts, references, reliability, experience, specialty and focus, fees, flexibility, stability, expertise (specialized skills), cost, quality of service, creativity and innovation, upgrade potential, communications, commitment, contract provisions and restrictions (e.g., penalty and cancellation clauses), and "fit."

Ask the outsource vendor for a "trial period" to see how things are going before entering into a regular contract. However, avoid long-term contracts especially those that are rigid in its terms. You want flexibility and do not want to be locked in for the long-term. We recommend renewable short-term contracts. The contract should be updated as the environment and circumstances change.

Insist that outsourcing contracts contain provisions regarding performance expectations (e.g., service level goals) and measurement guidelines. Undertake periodic performance appraisals. Customer satisfaction with the outsourcer's services is crucial so surveys should be periodically conducted.

Insourcing is the self-manufacture of goods or services. Instead of buying the items from outside, the company produces the product or renders the service in an attempt to lower costs, improve quality, hasten availability, and be less reliant on outsiders. The cost-benefit of insourcing must be carefully evaluated.

FORECASTING AND FINANCIAL PLANNING

Financial management in private organizations typically operates under conditions of uncertainty or risk. Probably the most important function of business is forecasting. A forecast is a starting point for planning. The objective of forecasting is to reduce risk in decision making. In business, forecasts are the basis for capacity planning, production and inventory planning, personnel planning, planning for sales and market share, financial planning and budgeting, planning for research and development and top management's strategic planning. Sales forecasts are especially crucial aspects of many financial management activities, including budgets, profit planning, capital expenditure analysis, and acquisition and merger analysis.

Figure 1 illustrates how sales forecasts relate to various managerial functions of business.

WHO USES FORECASTS?

Forecasts are needed for marketing, production, purchasing, personnel, and financial planning. Further, top management needs forecasts for planning and implementing long-term strategic objectives and planning for capital expenditures. More specifically, marketing managers use sales forecasts to determine 1) optimal sales force allocations, 2) set sales goals, and 3) plan promotions and advertising. Other things such as market share, prices, and trends in new product development are required.

Production planners need forecasts in order to:

- Schedule production activities
- Order materials

Figure 1 Sales Forecasts and Managerial Functions

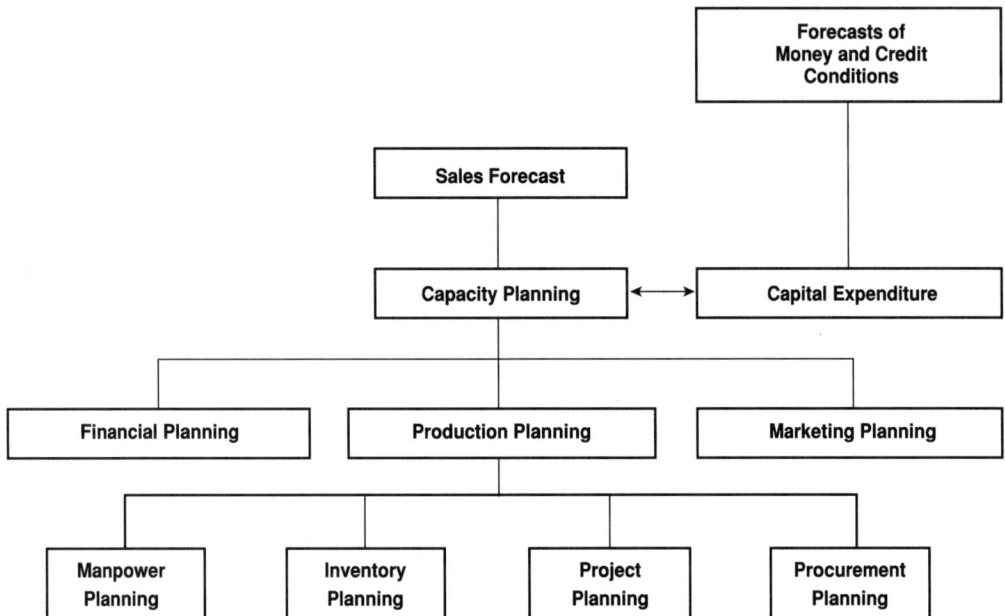

- Establish inventory levels
- Plan shipments

Some other areas which need forecasts include material requirements (purchasing and procurement), labor scheduling, equipment purchases, maintenance requirements, and plant capacity planning.

As shown in Figure 1, as soon as the company makes sure that it has enough capacity, the production plan is developed. If the company does not have enough capacity, it will require planning and budgeting decisions for capital spending for capacity expansion.

On this basis, the financial manager must estimate the future cash inflow and outflow. She must plan cash and borrowing needs for the company's future operations. Forecasts of cash flows and the rates of expenses and revenues are needed to maintain corporate liquidity and operating efficiency. In planning for capital investments, predictions about future economic activity are required so that returns or cash inflows accruing from the investment may be estimated.

Forecasts must also be made of money and credit conditions and interest rates so that the cash needs of the firm may be met at the lowest possible cost. The finance and accounting functions must also forecast interest rates to support the acquisition of new capital, the collection of accounts receivable to help in planning working capital needs, and capital equipment expenditure rates to help balance the flow of funds in the organization. Sound predictions of foreign exchange rates are increasingly important to financial managers of multinational companies (MNCs).

Long-term forecasts are needed for the planning of changes in the company's capital structure. Decisions as to whether to issue stock or debt in order to maintain the desired financial structure of the firm require forecasts of money and credit conditions.

The personnel department requires a number of forecasts in planning for human resources in the business. Workers must be hired and trained, and there must be benefits provided that are competitive with those available in the firm's labor market. Also, trends that affect such variables as labor turnover, retirement age, absenteeism, and tardiness need to be forecast as input for planning and decision making in this function.

The service sector which today accounts for 2/3 of the U.S. gross domestic product (GDP), including banks, insurance companies, restaurants, and cruiseships, need various projections for their operational and long-term strategic planning. Take a bank, for example. The bank has to forecast demands of various loans and deposits, as well as money and credit conditions so that it can determine the cost of money it lends.

TYPES OF FORECASTS

The types of forecasts used by businesses and other organizations may be classified in several categories, depending on the objective and the situation for which a forecast is to be used. Four types are discussed below.

Sales Forecasts

As discussed in the previous section, the sales forecast gives the expected level of sales for the company's goods or services throughout some future period and is instrumental in the company's planning and budgeting functions. It is the key to other forecasts and plans.

Financial Forecasts

Although the sales forecast is the primary input to many financial decisions, some financial forecasts need to be made independently of sales forecasts. This include forecasts of financial variables such as the amount of external financing needed, earnings, and cash flows and prediction of corporate bankruptcy.

Economic Forecasts

Economic forecasts, or statements of expected future business conditions, are published by governmental agencies and private economic forecasting firms. Business can use these forecasts and develop its own forecasts about external business outlook that will affect its product demand. Economic forecasts cover a variety of topics including GDP, levels of employment, interest rates, and foreign exchange rates.

Technological Forecasts

A technological forecast is an estimate of rates of technological progress. Certainly, software makers are interested in the rates of technological advancement in computer hardware and its peripheral equipment. Technological changes will provide many businesses with new products and materials to offer for sale, while other companies will encounter competition from other businesses. Technological forecasting is probably best performed by experts in the particular technology.

FORECASTING METHODS

There is a wide range of forecasting techniques which the company may choose from. There are basically two approaches to forecasting: qualitative and quantitative. They are as follows:

1. Qualitative approach—forecasts based on judgement and opinion.
   - Executive opinions
   - Delphi technique
   - Sales force polling
   - Consumer surveys
   - Techniques for eliciting experts' opinions—PERT-derived
2. Quantitative approach
   a) Forecasts based on historical data
      - Naive methods
      - Moving averages
      - Exponential smoothing
      - Trend analysis
      - Decomposition of time series
      - Box-Jenkins

b) Associative (Causal) forecasts
- Simple regression
- Multiple regression
- Econometric modeling

c) Forecasts based on consumer behavior—Markov approach

d) Indirect methods
- Market surveys
- Input-output analysis
- Economic indicators

Figure 2 summarizes the forecasting methods.

Quantitative models work superbly as long as little or no systematic change in the environment takes place. When patterns or relationships do change, by themselves, the objective models are of little use. It is here where the qualitative approach based on human judgment is indispensable. Because judgmental forecasting also bases forecasts on observation of

Figure 2 Forecasting Methods

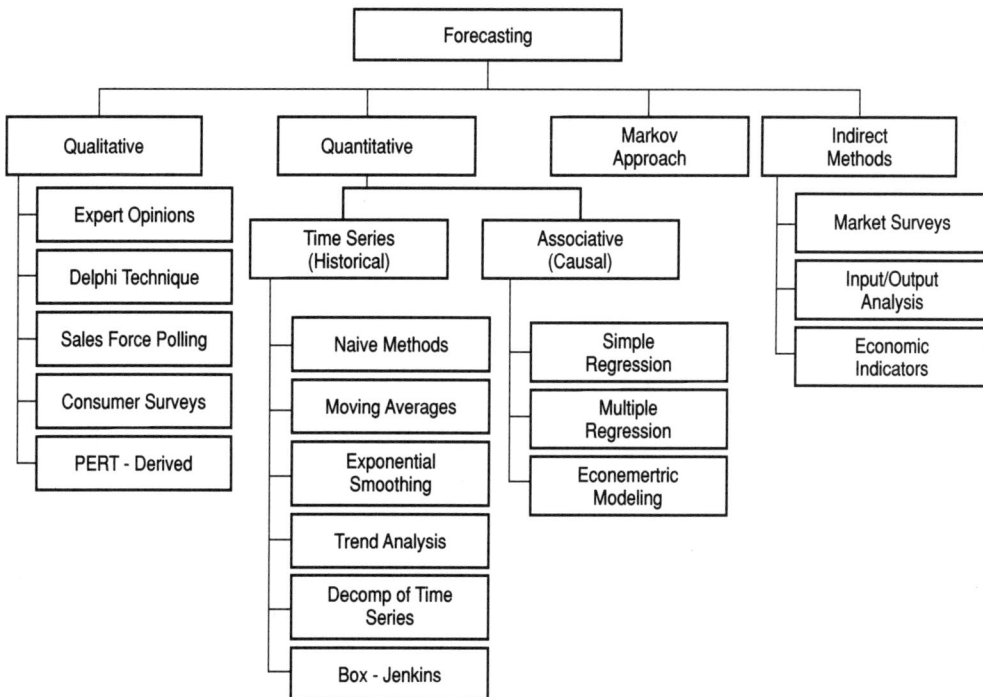

existing trends, they too are subject to a number of shortcomings. The advantage, however, is that they can identify systematic change more quickly and interpret better the effect of such change on the future.

We will discuss the qualitative method here in this chapter, while various quantitative methods along with their illustrations will be taken up in subsequent chapters.

SELECTION OF FORECASTING METHOD

The choice of a forecasting technique is significantly influenced by the stage of the product life cycle, and sometimes by the firm or industry for which a decision is being made.

In the beginning of the product life cycle, relatively small expenditures are made for research and market investigation. During the first phase of product introduction, these expenditures start to increase. In the rapid growth stage, considerable amounts of money are involved in the decisions; therefore a high level of accuracy is desirable. After the product has entered the maturity stage, the decisions are more routine, involving marketing and manufacturing. These are important considerations when determining the appropriate sales forecast technique.

After evaluating the particular stages of the product, and firm and industry life cycles, a further probe is necessary. Instead of selecting a forecasting technique by using whatever seems applicable, decision makers should determine what is appropriate. Some of the techniques are quite simple and rather inexpensive to develop and use, whereas others are extremely complex, require significant amounts of time to develop, and may be quite expensive. Some are best suited for short-term projections, whereas others are better prepared for intermediate- or long-term forecasts.

What technique or techniques to select depends on the following criteria:

1. What is the cost associated with developing the forecasting model compared with potential gains resulting from its use? The choice is one of benefit-cost trade-off.
2. How complicated are the relationships that are being forecasted?
3. Is it for short-run or long-run purposes?
4. How much accuracy is desired?
5. Is there a minimum tolerance level of errors?
6. How much data are available? Techniques vary in the amount of data they require.

THE QUALITATIVE APPROACH

The qualitative (or judgmental) approach can be useful in formulating short-term forecasts and also can supplement the projections based on the use of any of the qualitative methods. Four of the better known qualitative forecasting methods are Executive Opinions, the Delphi Method, Sales Force Polling, and Consumer Surveys.

Executive Opinions

The subjective views of executives or experts from sales, production, finance, purchasing and administration are averaged to generate a forecast about future sales. Usually this method is used in conjunction with some quantitative method such as trend extrapolation. The management team modifies the resulting forecast based on their expectations.

The advantage of this approach is that the forecasting is done quickly and easily, without need of elaborate statistics. Also, the jury of executive opinions may be the only feasible means of forecasting in the absence of adequate data. The disadvantage, however, is that of "group think." This is a set of problems inherent to those who meet as a group. Foremost among these problems are high cohesiveness, strong leadership, and insulation of the group. With high cohesiveness, the group becomes increasingly conforming through group pressure which helps stifle dissension and critical thought. Strong leadership fosters group pressure for unanimous opinion. Insulation of the group tends to separate the group from outside opinions, if given.

The Delphi Method

It is a group technique in which a panel of experts are individually questioned about their perceptions of future events. The experts do not meet as a group in order to reduce the possibility that consensus is reached because of dominant personality factors. Instead, the forecasts and accompanying arguments are summarized by an outside party and returned to the experts along with further questions. This continues until a consensus is reached by the group, especially after only a few rounds. This type of method is useful and quite effective for long-range forecasting.

The technique is done by "questionnaire" format and thus it eliminates the disadvantages of group think. There is no committee or debate. The experts are not influenced by peer pressure to forecast a certain way, as the answer is not intended to be reached by consensus or unanimity. Low reliability is cited as the main disadvantage of the Delphi Method, as well as lack of consensus from the returns.

Figure 3 An Example of the Use of the Delphi Method

1 Population (in Millions)	2 Midpoint	3 Number of Panelists	4 Probability Distribution of Panelists	5 Weighted Average (2×4)
30 and above	00	0	.00	0
20-30	25	1	.05	1.25
15-19	17	2	.10	1.70
10-14	12	2	.10	1.20
5-9	7	7	.35	2.45
2-4	3	8	.40	1.20
Less than 2	1	0	.00	0
Total		20	1.00	7.80

Case example: "In 1982, a panel of 20 representatives, with college educations, from different parts of the U.S.A., were asked to estimate the population of Bombay, India. None of the panelists had been to India since World War I.

"The population was estimated to be 7.8 million, which is very close to the actual population."

Source: Singhvi, Surendra. "Financial Forecast: Why and How?" *Managerial Planning.* March/April, 1984.

Sales-Force Polling

Some companies use as a forecast source sales people who have continual contacts with customers. They believe that the sales force who are closest to the ultimate customers may have significant insights regarding the state of the future market. Forecasts based on sales-force polling may be averaged to develop a future forecast. Or they may be used to modify other quantitative and/or qualitative forecasts that have been generated internally in the company. The advantages to this way of forecast are that (1) it is simple to use and understand, (2) it uses the specialized knowledge of those closest to the action, (3) it can place responsibility for attaining the forecast in the hands of those who most affect the actual results, and (4) the information can be easily broken down by territory, product, customer or salesperson.

The disadvantages include salespeople being overly optimistic or pessimistic regarding their predictions, and inaccuracies due to broader economic events that are largely beyond their control.

Consumer Surveys

Some companies conduct their own market surveys regarding specific consumer purchases. Surveys may consist of telephone contacts, personal interviews, or questionnaires as a means of obtaining data. Extensive statistical analysis is usually applied to survey results in order to test hypotheses regarding consumer behavior.

PERT-Derived Forecasts

A technique known as PERT (Program Evaluation and Review Technique) has been useful in producing estimates based on subjective opinions such as executive opinions or sales force polling. The PERT methodology requires that the expert provide three estimates: (1) pessimistic (a), (2) the most likely (m), and (3) optimistic (b). The theory suggests that these estimates combine to form an expected value, or forecast, as follows:

$$EV = (a + 4m + b)/6$$

with a standard deviation of

$$\sigma = (b - a)/6$$

where

EV = expected value (mean) of the forecast

σ = standard deviation of the forecast

For example, suppose that management of a company believes that if the economy is in recession, the next year's sales will be $300,000 and if the economy is in prosperity $330,000. Their most likely estimate is $310,000. The PERT method generates an expected value of sales as follows:

$$EV = (\$300,000 + 4(\$310,000) + \$330,000)/6 = \$311,667$$

with a standard deviation of

$$\sigma = (\$330,000 - \$300,000)/6 = \$5,000$$

Advantages:

1. It is often easier and more realistic to ask the expert to give optimistic, pessimistic and most likely estimates than a specific forecast value.

2. The PERT method includes a measure of dispersion (the standard deviation), which makes it possible to develop probabilistic statements regarding the forecast. For example, in the above example the forecaster is 95 percent confident that the true value of the forecasted sales lies between plus or minus two standard deviations from the mean ($311,667). That is the true value can be expected between $211,667 and $411,667.

A Word of Caution

It is also important to realize that forecasting is not an exact science like mathematics, it is an art. The quality of forecasts tends to improve over time as the forecaster gains more experience. Evidence, however, shows that forecasts using qualitative techniques are not as accurate as those using quantitative techniques:

> Humans possess unique knowledge and inside information not available to quantitative methods. Surprisingly, however, empirical studies and laboratory experiments have shown that their forecasts are not more accurate than those of quantitative methods. Humans tend to be optimistic and underestimate the future uncertainty. In addition, the cost of forecasting with judgmental methods is often considerably higher than when quantitative methods are used.[1]

Note: Therefore, a forecaster must use both qualitative as well as quantitative techniques to create a reasonable forecast.

COMMON FEATURES AND ASSUMPTIONS INHERENT IN FORECASTING

As pointed out, forecasting techniques are quite different from each other. But there are certain features and assumptions that underlie the business of forecasting. They are:

1. Forecasting techniques generally assume that the same underlying causal relationship that existed in the past will continue to prevail in the future. In other words, most of our techniques are based on historical data.

---

[1] "Science of Forecasting," *International Journal of Forecasting,* Vol. 2, 1986, p. 17.

2. Forecasts are very rarely perfect. Therefore, for planning purposes, allowances should be made for inaccuracies. For example, the company should always maintain a safety stock in anticipation of stockouts.

3. Forecast accuracy decreases as the time period covered by the forecast (that is, the time horizon) increases. Generally speaking, a long-term forecast tends to be more inaccurate than a short-term forecast because of the greater uncertainty.

4. Forecasts for groups of items tend to be more accurate than forecasts for individual items, since forecasting errors among items in a group tend to cancel each other out. For example, industry forecasting is more accurate than individual firm forecasting.

STEPS IN THE FORECASTING PROCESS

There are five basic steps in the forecasting process. They are:

1. Determine the what and why of the forecast and what will be needed. This will indicate the level of detail required in the forecast (for example, forecast by region, forecast by product, etc.), the amount of resources (for example, computer hardware and software, manpower, etc.) that can be justified, and the level of accuracy desired.

2. Establish a time horizon, short-term or long-term. More specifically, project for the next year or next five years, etc.

3. Select a forecasting technique. Refer to the criteria discussed before.

4. Gather the data and develop a forecast.

5. Identify any assumptions that had to be made in preparing the forecast and using it.

6. Monitor the forecast to see if it is performing in a manner desired. Develop an evaluation system for this purpose. If not, go to step 1.

Figure 4 The Forecasting Process

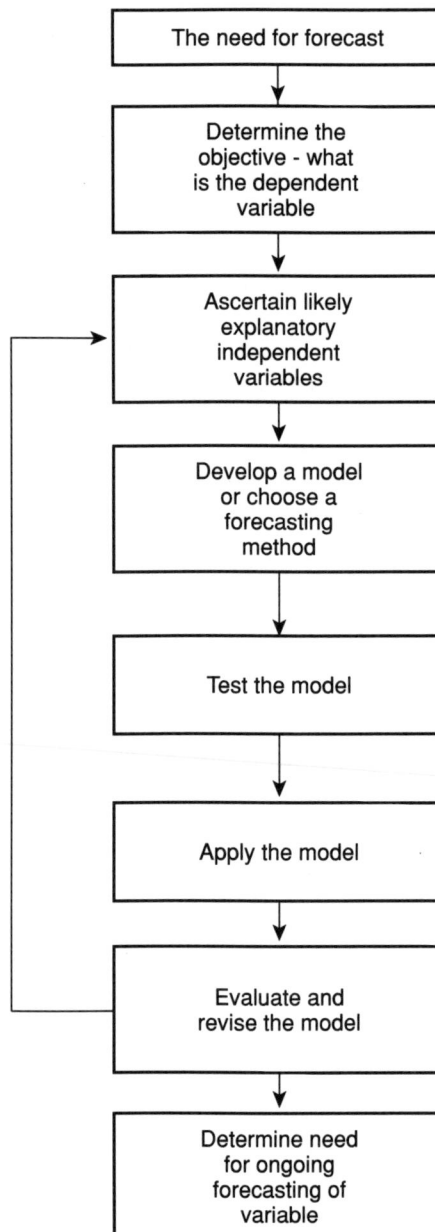

```
              ┌──────────────────────┐
              │  The need for forecast │
              └───────────┬──────────┘
                          ↓
              ┌──────────────────────┐
              │     Determine the     │
              │    objective - what   │
              │    is the dependent   │
              │       variable        │
              └───────────┬──────────┘
                          ↓
          ┌─→ ┌──────────────────────┐
          │   │    Ascertain likely   │
          │   │      explanatory      │
          │   │      independent      │
          │   │       variables       │
          │   └───────────┬──────────┘
          │               ↓
          │   ┌──────────────────────┐
          │   │    Develop a model    │
          │   │     or choose a       │
          │   │      forecasting      │
          │   │        method         │
          │   └───────────┬──────────┘
          │               ↓
          │   ┌──────────────────────┐
          │   │     Test the model    │
          │   └───────────┬──────────┘
          │               ↓
          │   ┌──────────────────────┐
          │   │    Apply the model    │
          │   └───────────┬──────────┘
          │               ↓
          │   ┌──────────────────────┐
          └───│     Evaluate and      │
              │    revise the model   │
              └───────────┬──────────┘
                          ↓
              ┌──────────────────────┐
              │    Determine need     │
              │     for ongoing       │
              │    forecasting of     │
              │       variable        │
              └──────────────────────┘
```

FINANCIAL AND EARNINGS FORECASTING

Financial forecasting, an essential element of planning, is the basis for *budgeting* activities. It is also needed when estimating future financing requirements. The company may look either internally or externally for financing. Internal financing refers to cash flow generated by the company's normal operating activities. External financing refers to capital provided by parties external to the company. You need to analyze how to estimate *external* financing requirements. Basically, forecasts of future sales and related expenses provide the firm with the information to project future external financing needs. The chapter discusses (1) the *percent-of-sales method* to determine the amount of external financing needed, (2) the CPA's involvement in prospective financial statements, and (3) earnings forecast.

THE PERCENT-OF-SALES METHOD

Percentage of sales is the most widely used method for projecting the company's financing needs. This method involves estimating the various expenses, assets, and liabilities for a future period as a percent of the sales forecast and then using these percentages, together with the projected sales, to construct pro forma balance sheets.

Basically, forecasts of future sales and their related expenses provide the firm with the information needed to project its future needs for financing. The basic steps in projecting financing needs are:

1. Project the firm's sales. The sales forecast is the initial most important step. Most other forecasts (budgets) follow the sales forecast.
2. Project additional variables such as expenses.

3. Estimate the level of investment in current and fixed assets required to support the projected sales.
4. Calculate the firm's financing needs.

The following example illustrates how to develop a pro forma balance sheet and determine the amount of external financing needed.

Example 1. Assume that sales for 19x1 = $20, projected sales for 19x2 = $24, net income = 5% of sales, and the dividend payout ratio = 40%. Figure 1 illustrates the method, step by step. All dollar amounts are in millions.

Figure 1   Pro Forma Balance Sheet (in millions of dollars)

	Present *(19X1)*	*% of Sales* *(19X1 Sales = $20)*	*Projected* *(19X2 Sales = $24)*	
ASSETS				
Current assets	2	10	2.4	
Fixed assets	4	20	4.8	
Total assets	6		7.2	
LIABILITIES AND STOCKHOLDERS' EQUITY				
Current liabilities	2	10	2.4	
Long-term debt	2.5	n.a.	2.5	
Total liabilities	4.5		4.9	
Common stock	0.1	n.a.	0.1	
Paid-in-capital	0.2	n.a.	0.1	
Retained earnings	1.2		1.92 (a)	
Total equity	1.5		2.22	
Total liabilities and stockholders' equity	6		7.12	Total financing provided
			0.08 (b)	External financing needed
			7.2	Total

(a) 19X2 retained earnings = 19X1 retained earnings + projected net income − cash dividends paid
  = $1.2 + 5% ($24) − 40% [5% ($24)]
  = $1.2 + $1.2 − $0.48
  = $2.4 − $0.48
  = $1.92
(b) External financing need = project total assets − (projected total liabilities + projected equity)
  = $7.2 − ($4.9 + $2.22)
  = $7.2 − $7.12
  = $0.08

The steps for the computations are outlined as follows:

Step 1. Express those balance sheet items that vary directly with sales as a percentage of sales. Any item such as long-term debt that does not vary directly with sales is designated "n.a.," or "not applicable."

Step 2. Multiply these percentages by the 19x2 projected sales = $24 to obtain the projected amounts as shown in the last column.

Step 3. Simply insert figures for long-term debt, common stock and paid-in-capital from the 19x1 balance sheet.

Step 4. Compute 19x2 retained earnings as shown in (b).

Step 5. Sum the asset accounts, obtaining a total projected assets of $7.2, and also add the projected liabilities and equity to obtain $7.12, the total financing provided. Since liabilities and equity must total $7.2, but only $7.12 is projected, we have a shortfall of $0.08 "external financing needed."

Although the forecast of additional funds required can be made by setting up pro forma balance sheets as described above, it is often easier to use the following formula:

External funds needed (EFN)	=	Required increase in assets	−	Spontaneous increase in liabilities	−	Increase in retained earnings
EFN	=	(A/S) ΔS	−	(L/S) ΔS	−	(PM)(PS)(1 − d)

where

A/S = Assets that increase spontaneously with sales as a percentage of sales.
L/S = Liabilities that increase spontaneously with sales as a percentage of sales.
ΔS = Change in sales.
PM = Profit margin on sales.
PS = Projected sales
d = Dividend payout ratio.

Example 2. In Example 1,

A/S = $6/$20 = 30%
L/S = $2/$20 = 10%
ΔS = ($24 − $20) = $4

PM = 5% on sales

PS = $24

d = 40%

Plugging these figures into the formula yields:

EFN = 0.3($4) – 0.1($4) – (0.05)($24)(1 – 0.4)

= $1.2 – $0.4 – $0.72 = $0.08

Thus, the amount of external financing needed is $800,000, which can be raised by issuing notes payable, bonds, stocks, or any combination of these financing sources.

The major advantage of the percent-of-sales method of financial forecasting is that it is simple and inexpensive to use. One important assumption behind the use of the method is that the firm is operating at full capacity. This means that the company has no sufficient productive capacity to absorb a projected increase in sales and thus requires additional investment in assets. Therefore, the method must be used with extreme caution if excess capacity exists in certain asset accounts.

To obtain a more precise projection of the firm's future financing needs, however, the preparation of a cash budget may be required.

THE CPA'S INVOLVEMENT AND RESPONSIBILITY WITH PROSPECTIVE FINANCIAL STATEMENTS

The American Institute of Certified Public Accountants (AICPA) in *Statement of Position 45-4* provides guidelines for business enterprises which publish financial forecasts. Improved financial forecasting should be of concern to the AICPA and the Securities and Exchange Commission as a basis for financial decision making, security analysis, and in affecting the future market value of securities through investor expectations. Figure 2 presents an excerpt from the 1983 Annual Report of Masco Corporation which contains (1) a five-year cash flow forecast, (2) forecasts of a five-year growth rate for sales, and (3) key assumptions used in the forecasts.

There are three types of functions that CPAs can perform with respect to prospective financial statements that will be relied upon by third parties: examination, compilation, and application of agreed-upon procedures. CPAs must prepare prospective financial statements according to AICPA standards. There must be disclosure of the underlying assumptions.

Prospective financial statements may be for general use or limited use. General use is for those not directly dealing with the client. The general user

Figure 2 Management Forecast Disclosure by Masco Corporation

FIVE-YEAR FORECAST

We have included in the annual report a sales forecast for each of our major product lines and operating groups for 1988.

While we recognize that long-term forecasts are subject to many variables and uncertainties, our experience has been that our success is determined more by our own activities than by the performance of any industry or the economy in general. In addition, the balance and diversity of our products and markets have been such that a shortfall in expected performance in one area has been largely offset by higher than expected growth in another.

Although variations may occur in the forecast for any individual product line, we have a relatively high level of confidence that our overall five-year growth forecast is achievable.

ASSUMPTIONS USED IN FORECAST

1. Average 2-3 percent annual real growth in GNP.
2. Average inflation 5-7 percent.
3. Present tax structure to continue.
4. No change in currency exchange rates.
5. No acquisitions.
6. No additional financing.
7. Dividend payout ratio 20 percent.
8. Four percent after-tax return on investment of excess cash.
9. No exercise of stock options.

FIVE-YEAR CASH-FLOW FORECAST

(In thousands)	1984-1988
Net Income	$ 850,ooo
Depreciation	280,000
	1,130,000
	(230,000)
	(280,000)
	(260,000)
	(170,000)
Net Cash Change	190,000
Beginning Cash, 1-84	210,000
Cash, 12-31-88	$ 400,000

SALES GROWTH BY PRODUCTS

	Sales Forecast		Actual Sales		(In thousands)
	5-Year Growth Rate 1984-1988	1988	5-Year Growth Rate 1979-1983	1983	1978
Products for the Home and Family	14%	$1,225,000	16%	$ 638,000	$308,000
Products for Industry	16%	875,000	9%	421,000	278,000
Total Sales	15%	$2,100,000	13%	$1,059,000	$585,000

SALES GROWTH BY SPECIFIC MARKETS AND PRODUCTS (1) (2)

	Forecast		Actual		(In thousands)
	5-Year Growth Rate 1984-1988	1988	5-Year Growth Rate 1979-1983	1983	1978
Masco Faucet Sales (3)	15%	$490,000	9%	$243,000	$155,000
Faucet Industry Sales-Units	7%	35,000	(5)%	25,000	32,000
Masco Market Share-Units	2%	38%	5%	34%	27%
Housing Completions	4%	1,700	(4)%	1,400	1,700
Independent Cold Extrusion Industry Sales	13%	$580,000	1%	$310,000	$290,000
Masco Cold Extrusion Sales (3)	14%	$170,000	5%	$ 88,000	$ 70,000
Truck Production	7%	3,400	(8)%	2,400	3,700
Auto Production	4%	8,200	(6)%	6,800	92,00
Masco Auto Parts Sales	13%	$210,000	8%	$113,000	$ 76,000

(1) Excludes foreign sales.   (2) Industry data Masco estimates.   (3) Includes foreign sales.

Source: 1983 Annual Report of Masco Corporation, p. 42.

may take the deal or leave it. Limited use is for those having a direct relationship with the client.

Prospective financial statements may be presented as a complete set of financial statements (balance sheet, income statement, and statement of cash flows). However, in most cases, it is more practical to present them in summarized or condensed form. At a minimum, the financial statement items to be presented are:

- Sales
- Gross margin
- Nonrecurring items
- Taxes
- Income from continuing operations
- Income from discontinued operations
- Net income
- Primary and fully diluted earnings per share
- Material changes in financial position

Not considered prospective financial statements are pro-forma financial statements and partial presentations.

The American Institute of CPA's Code of Professional Ethics includes the following guidelines regarding prospective financial statements:

- Cannot vouch for the achieveability of prospective results
- Must disclose assumptions
- Accountant's report must state the nature of the work performed and the degree of responsibility assumed

CPAs are not permitted to furnish services on prospective financial statements if the statements are solely appropriate for limited use but are distributed to parties not involved directly with the issuing company. They are not allowed to use plain-paper services on prospective financial statements for third-party use.

A prospective financial statement may be classified as either a forecast or a projection.

Financial Forecast

A financial forecast presents management's expectations, and there is an expectation that all assumptions will take place. *Note:* A financial forecast encompasses a presentation that management expects to occur but that is not necessarily most probable. A financial forecast may be most useful to general users, since it presents the client's expectations. A financial forecast and not a financial projection may be issued to passive users, or those not negotiating directly with the client.

A financial forecast may be given a single monetary amount based on the best estimate, or as a reasonable range. *Caution:* This range must not be chosen in a misleading manner.

Irrespective of the accountant's involvement, management is the only one who has responsibility for the presentation because only management knows how it plans to run the business and accomplish its plans.

Financial Projection

A financial projection presents a "what-if" scenario that management does not necessarily expect to occur. However, a given assumption may actually occur if management moves in that direction. A financial projection may be most beneficial for limited users, since they may seek answers to hypothetical questions based on varying assumptions. These users may wish to alter their scenarios based on anticipated changing situations. A financial projection, like a forecast, may contain a range.

A financial projection may be presented to general users only when it supplements a financial forecast. Financial projections are not permitted in tax shelter offerings and other general-use documents.

Types of Engagements

The following five types of engagements may be performed by the CPA in connection with prospective financial statements:

Plain Paper. The CPA's name is not associated with the prospective statements. This service can only be conducted if all of the following conditions are satisfied:

- The CPA is not reporting on the presentation.
- The prospective statements are on paper not identifying the accountant.
- The prospective financial statements are not shown with historical financial statements that have been audited, reviewed, or compiled by the CPA.

Internal Use. The prospective financial statements are only assembled, meaning mathematical and clerical functions are performed. Assembling financial data is permitted if the following two criteria exist:

- Third parties will not use the statements.
- The CPA's name is associated with the statement.

Note that assembling prospective financial statements is limited only to internal use. Appropriate language on the statements might be "For Internal Use Only."

Compilation. This is the lowest level of service performed for prospective financial statements directed for third parties. The compilation engagement involves:

- Assembling prospective data.
- The conduct of procedures to ascertain whether the presentation and assumptions are appropriate.
- Preparation of a compilation report.

With a compilation, no assurance is given regarding the presentation or assumptions, but rather it serves to identify obvious matters to be investigated further. Working papers have to be prepared to show there was proper planning and supervision of the work, as well as compliance with required compilation procedures. The CPA must also obtain a management letter from the client regarding representations given to him.

Warning: A compilation should not be made when the forecasted financial statements exclude disclosure of the significant assumptions or when the financial projections exclude the hypothetical assumptions.

Agreed-upon Procedures. This relates to applying procedures agreed to or requested by specific users, and issuing a report. The report identifies the procedures undertaken, gives the accountant's findings, and restricts distribution of the report to the particular parties. The specified users have to participate in establishing the nature and procedures. Also, the procedures undertaken must be more than just reading the prospective data.

Examination. The CPA appraises the preparation underlying the supporting assumptions and the presentation of prospective financial information in accordance with AICPA standards. A report is then issued on whether AICPA guidelines have been adhered to and whether the assumptions are reasonable. It is the highest level of assurance. An adverse opinion must be given if there is a failure to disclose a material assumption or if disclosed assumptions are unreasonable. For example, there may be not reasonable expectation that the actual figure will fall within the range of assumptions presented in a forecast having a range. A disclaimer opinion is necessary in the event of a scope limitation, such as when a required examination procedure cannot be performed because of client restrictions or inappropriate circumstances.

EARNINGS FORECAST

For many years, financial analysts have predicted earnings per share and stock price performance. Considerable emphasis has been placed on such forecasts in order to provide guidance to investors. Recently, management forecast disclosures in financial statements have placed greater emphasis on the development of forecasting methodology in this area. The accuracy of these earnings forecasts has been given much attention recently primarily due to the SEC's position on financial forecasts and issuance of a Statement of Position by the AICPA.

Security Analysts vs. Time-Series Models

Forecasts of earnings per share for business firms are published by both management and security analysts. Unfortunately, however, the accuracy of EPS forecasts by security analysts have been shown to be little if any better than that produced by some "naive" models such as extrapolating the past trend of earnings. Indeed, it increasingly appears that the change in EPS may be a random variable.

Projections of EPS are frequently made by independent security analysts. Examples of forecast sources include (1) Value Line Investment Survey, (2) Lynch, Jones and Ryan's Institutional Brokers Estimate System (IBES), (3) Standard & Poor's The Earnings Forecaster, and (4) Zacks Investment Research's Icarus Service. Figure 3 presents an excerpt from the monthly report from Lynch, Jones, and Ryan's IBES Service which contains various earnings forecasts by individual security analysts.

Figure 3   Extract from Monthly Summary Report of the IBES Service

A. Description of Data

Price–Price as of the day prior to date of report: shown in eighths.

Actual–Fiscal Year and EPS
Earnings per share for the most recently reported fiscal year end. Industry and Sector aggregates are computed by share-weighting the EPS of each constituent company.

Estimates–Fiscal Year One and Fiscal Year Two
Mean–Average of all available estimates. Aggregates are share weighted.

Percent Change–Actual– Percent change of mean estimates from last year's actual EPS.

Relative– Percent change of mean estimate from last year's actual EPS relative to the average change for all I/B/E/S Summary Data companies (unweighted).

6 mo.– Percent change of mean estimates from its level 6 months ago.

Revisions –% up– Percent of estimates revised up since last month.

% down – Percent of estimates revised down since last month.

*Coefficient of Variation–Coefficient of variation–*Industry and sector aggregates are net income weighted, i.e., individual coefficients of variation are weighted by their shares times mean estimate.

*Estimated 5 Yr. Growth Rate–*The medium or mid-point in the series of reported estimates. Aggregates are net income weighted.

S.D.– Standard devaluation of estimates for long term growth; indicates the range in percentage points within which 2/3rds of the estimated growth rates fall. Aggregates are net income weighted.

B. Data for International Oils (Industry and Firm Level), March 1985

Sector/Industry/Company	Price	Actual Fiscal Year	Actual EPS	FY1 Mean	FY1 %Chg Actual	FY1 %Chg Relative	FY1 %Chg 6 mo.	FY1 Rev %Up	FY1 Rev %Down	FY1 Coeff. of Var.	FY2 Mean	FY2 %Chg Actual	FY2 %Chg Relative	FY2 %Chg 6 mo.	FY2 Rev %Plus	FY2 Rev %Down	FY2 Coeff. of Var.	5 Yr Growth Median	5 Yr Growth S.D.
INTERNATIONAL OILS			5.77	6.23	8.1	0.88	-4.8	5	20	5.4	6.87	19.1	0.79	-1.8	NA	5	6.8	7	3
CHEVRON CORP.	34.1	12/84	4.48	4.69	4.6	0.83	-15.5	3	24	8.1	5.82	30.0	0.86	NA			16.1	7	4
EXXON	49.2	12/84	6.77	6.84	1.1	0.80	-0.1	14	20	3.9	7.47	10.3	0.73	NA			2.7	7	3
MOBIL CORP.	29.5	12/84	3.12	3.54	13.4	0.90	-18.4		36	9.8	4.20	34.6	0.89	NA			12.4	7	3
ROYAL DUTCH PETE	54.0	12/83	9.59	11.12	18.0	0.92	3.4	12	4	5.5	11.61	21.0	0.80	-1.1	8	8	4.6	7	3
SHELL TRANS&TRAD	33.7	12/83	5.79	7.00	20.9	0.98	1.2			1.5	7.41	28.0	0.85	-2.9			7.1	10	1
TEXACO	35.2	12/84	4.45	4.81	3.7	0.82	-17.5		42	10.1	4.93	10.9	0.74	NA			6.1	7	3

Source: Lynch, Jones, and Ryan, IBES Monthly Summary Data (New York, N.Y.)

Figure 4 summarizes the pros and cons of both approaches.

Figure 4 Pros and Cons of Security Analyst and Univariate Time-Series Model Approaches to Forecasting

Security Analysts Approach to Forecasting

Pros

1. Ability to incorporate information from many sources.
2. Ability to adjust to structural change immediately.
3. Ability to update continually as new information becomes available.

Cons

1. High initial setup cost and high ongoing cost to monitor numerous variables, make company visits, and so on.
2. Heavy dependence on the skills of a single individual.
3. Analyst may have an incentive not to provide an unbiased forecast (e.g., due to pressure to conform to consensus forecasts).
4. Analyst may be manipulated by company officials (at least in the short run).

Univariate Time-Series Model Approach to Forecasting

Pros

1. Ability to detect and exploit systematic patterns in the past series.
2. Relatively low degree of subjectivity in the forecasting (especially given the availability of computer algorithms to identify and estimate models).
3. Low cost and ease of updating.
4. Ability to compute confidence intervals around the forecasts.

Cons

1. Limited number of observations available for newly formed firms, firms with structural change, and so on.
2. Financial statement data may not satisfy distributional assumptions of time-series model used.
3. Inability to update forecasts between successive interim or annual earnings releases.
4. Difficulty of communicating approach to clients (especially the statistical methodology used in identifying and estimating univariate models).

Source: Foster, George, *Financial Statement Analysis,* 2nd ed., Prentice Hall, Englewood Cliffs, N.J., 1986, p. 278.

Table 1 shows sources of earnings forecasting data preferred by financial analysts.

Table 1 What Are Your Present Sources of Earnings Forecasting Data?

Rank	1	2	3	4	5
Company contacts	56	28	24	8	9
Own research	55	15	5	1	
Industry statistics	19	14	14	7	
Other analysis	12	17	2	8	11
Historical financial data	8	12	8	5	4
Economic forecasts	7	7	10	3	
Competition	1	7	2	6	1
Computer simulation					2
Field trips		1			
Government agencies			2		
Industry & trade sources	1	7	17	3	5
Public relations of a promotional nature					1
Retired directors					1
Rumor					2
Wall Street sources	1	4	9	3	4

Rank   1 = most preferred

5 = least preferred

Source: Carper, Brent W., Barton Jr., Frank M., Wunder Haroldene F. "The Future of Forecasting." *Management Accounting.* August, 1997. pp. 27-31.

This section compares various forecasting methods using a sample drawn from the Standard and Poor's 400. It also examines the ability of financial analysts to forecast earnings per share performance based on the relationship of past forecasts of future earnings by financial analysts and through the use of recent univariate time-series models.

Our sample of Earnings Per Share (EPS) was drawn from the 1984 through 1988 time period using the quarterly *Compustat Industrial* data tapes available from S & P. Included in our sample are 30 firms randomly selected from the Standard & Poor 400 index for manufacturing firms over the period January 1984 to July 1988, using monthly data as reported to the public security markets. To collect data on financial analyst forecasts, we have selected the *Value Line Forecasting Survey* which is one of several reporting agencies that employ financial analysts and report their forecasts on a weekly basis.

In order to compare the forecasting ability of financial analysts with extrapolative models, seven time-series models were used to forecast earnings per share. The popular computer forecasting software *RATS* was used to estimate the models.

Data for the resulting sample of firms were used over the five-year time period studied (i.e., January, 1984-June, 1987) to estimate the models. This period was a relatively short time period to avoid the possibility of structural changes in the economy affecting the results of the study.

Next, forecasts were derived from July, 1987 to June, 1988 using monthly data. The accuracy of the forecasts from each of the models for the period were evaluated using the two measures: (1) MAPE (mean absolute percentage error) and (2) MSE (mean square error).

Forecasting Methodology

In this section, we present each forecasting model. These models relate to various models proposed by earnings forecasters in the accounting, finance, and forecasting literature. They are the following:

1. Exponential Smoothing Model with Additive Seasonal Effect.
2. Single Exponential Smoothing Model.
3. Exponential Smoothing Model with Linear Trend and Seasonal Additive Effects.
4. Exponential Smoothing Model with Exponential Trend and Seasonal Additive Effects.
5. Box-Jenkins Analysis SARIMA(1,0,0) (0,1,0) s = 12

   A seasonal autoregressive integrated moving average (SARIMA) model is identified with first order autoregressive parameters and a 12-month seasonal adjustment.
6. Box-Jenkins Analysis SARIMA(1,0,0) (0,1,1) s = 12

   A seasonal autoregressive integrated moving average (SARIMA) model is identified with first order autoregressive parameters and a 12-month seasonal adjustment. It also contains a seasonal moving average.
7. Linear Trend Analysis
8. Value Line Forecast

Forecasting Accuracy

In Table 2, the Sample Average Forecast Error was estimated for each of 12 months based on earlier data. From July 1987 through June 1988, the monthly forecast errors are presented using the MAPE measure. From this analysis there is some variation in forecasting accuracy. The exponential forecasting methods performed well for methods 1, 2, and 3. The Box-Jenkins approaches for methods 5 and 6, and the linear trend analysis for method 7 were reasonably successful. Overall, however, the monthly Value Line forecast resulted in the largest forecast errors.

Table 2 Sample Average Forecast Errors from 30 Companies Mean Absolute Percentage Error (MAPE)

Method	1	2	3	4	5	6	7	8
1987:7	0.28	0.30	0.39	1.54	0.42	0.64	0.57	1.77
1987:8	0.24	0.23	0.29	1.51	0.72	0.95	0.58	1.39
1987:9	0.19	0.22	0.16	1.51	1.00	1.23	0.56	0.70
1987:10	0.19	0.22	0.16	1.55	1.28	1.54	0.56	0.70
1987:11	0.24	0.43	0.46	1.48	1.72	1.98	0.56	1.73
1987:12	0.27	0.71	0.71	1.48	2.09	2.35	0.69	4.28
1988:1	0.42	0.83	1.11	1.46	2.47	2.60	0.55	4.97
1988:2	0.42	0.83	1.11	1.46	2.47	2.60	0.55	4.97
1988:3	0.67	2.15	2.10	2.00	3.31	3.45	0.73	6.01
1988:4	0.78	3.17	1.48	1.72	3.53	3.65	0.73	9.00
1988:5	0.81	1.44	1.44	1.80	0.86	0.99	0.68	8.62
1988:6	0.81	1.44	1.44	1.80	0.86	0.99	0.68	8.62

Table 2 presents the MSE results. Generally, the mean square error reflected similar conclusions (see Table 3).

Table 3 Sample Average Forecast Errors from 30 Companies Mean Square Error (MSE)

Method	1	2	3	4	5	6	7	8
1987:7	0.42	0.34	0.39	6.27	0.12	0.12	1.21	1.59
1987:8	0.31	0.23	0.40	6.17	0.13	0.13	1.26	1.63
1987:9	0.31	0.23	0.33	5.93	0.14	0.14	1.31	1.69
1987:10	0.31	0.21	0.33	5.93	0.14	0.14	1.31	1.69
1987:11	0.32	0.64	0.76	6.22	0.48	0.47	1.47	2.19
1987:12	0.34	0.78	0.87	5.93	0.55	0.53	1.62	2.39
1988:1	0.71	1.32	1.38	5.91	0.97	0.95	1.45	0.99
1988:2	0.71	1.32	1.38	5.91	0.97	0.95	1.45	0.99
1988:3	1.40	5.48	1.81	5.68	3.89	3.86	2.28	0.85
1988:4	1.20	6.10	1.40	5.33	3.45	3.43	1.95	0.82
1988:5	1.21	7.29	1.41	5.21	3.35	3.34	2.03	0.74
1988:6	1.21	7.29	1.41	5.21	3.35	3.34	2.03	0.74

CONCLUSION

Financial forecasting, an essential element of planning, is a vital function of financial managers. It is needed where the future financing needs are being estimated. Basically, forecasts of future sales and their related expenses provide the firm with the information needed to project its financing requirements. Furthermore, financial forecasting involves earnings forecasts which provide useful information concerning the expectations of a firm's future total market return. This is of interest to security analysts and investors. Different forecasting methods of earnings were compared in terms of their accuracy. Also presented was a CPA's involvement with prospective financial statements.

CASH FLOW FORECASTING

A forecast of cash collections and potential writeoffs of accounts receivable is essential in *cash budgeting* and in judging the appropriateness of current credit and discount policies. The critical step in making such a forecast is estimating the cash collection and bad debt percentages to be applied to sales or accounts receivable balances. This chapter discusses several methods of estimating *cash collection rates* (or *payment proportions*) and illustrates how these rates are used for cash budgeting purposes.

The first approach, which is based on the *Markov model,* involves the use of a probability matrix based on the estimates of what is referred to as transition probabilities. This method is described on a step-by-step basis using an illustrative example. The second approach involves a simple average. The third approach offers a more pragmatic method of estimating collection and bad debt percentages by relating credit sales and collection data. This method employs regression analysis. By using these approaches, a financial planner should be able to:

- Estimate future cash collections from accounts receivable
- Establish an allowance for doubtful accounts
- Provide a valuable insight into better methods of managing accounts receivable

MARKOV APPROACH

The Markov (probability matrix) approach has been around for a long time. This approach has been successfully applied by Cyert and others to accounts receivable analysis, specifically to the estimation of that portion of the accounts receivable that will eventually become uncollectible. The method requires classification of outstanding accounts receivable according to age categories that reflect the stage of account delinquency, e.g., current accounts, accounts one month past due, accounts two months past due, and so forth. Consider the following example. XYZ department store divides its accounts receivable into two classifications: 0 to 60 days old and 61 to 120 days old. Accounts that are more than 120 days old are declared uncollectible by XYZ. XYZ currently has $10,000 in accounts receivable: $7,000 from the 0-60-day-old category and $3,000 from the 61-120-day-old category. Based on an analysis of its past records, it provides us with what is known as the matrix of transition probabilities. The matrix is given as shown in Table 1.

Table 1   Probability Matrix

From To	Collected	Uncollectible	0-60 Days Old	61-120 Days Old
Collected	1	0	0	0
Uncollectible	0	1	0	0
0-60 days old	.3	0	.5	.2
61-120 days old	.5	.1	.3	.1

Transition probabilities are nothing more than the probability that an account receivable moves from one age stage category to another. We note three basic features of this matrix. First, notice the squared element, 0 in the matrix. This indicates that $1 in the 0-6-day-old category cannot become a bad debt in one month's time. Now look at the two circled elements. Each of these is 1, indicating that, in time, all the accounts receivable dollars will either be paid or become uncollectible. Eventually, all the dollars do wind up either as collected or uncollectible, but XYZ would be interested in knowing the probability that a dollar of a 0-60-day-old or a 61-120-day-old receivable would eventually find its way into either paid bills or bad debts. It is convenient to partition the matrix of transition probabilities into four submatrices, as follows.

$$\begin{array}{cc} I & O \\ R & Q \end{array}$$

so that

$$I = \begin{bmatrix} 1 & 0 \\ 0 & 1 \end{bmatrix} \qquad O = \begin{bmatrix} 0 & 0 \\ 0 & 0 \end{bmatrix}$$

$$R = \begin{bmatrix} .3 & 0 \\ .5 & .1 \end{bmatrix} \qquad Q = \begin{bmatrix} .5 & .2 \\ .3 & .1 \end{bmatrix}$$

Now we are in a position to illustrate the procedure used to determine:

- Estimated collection and bad debt percentages by age category
- Estimated allowance for doubtful accounts

Step-by-step, the procedure is as follows:

Step 1. Set up the matrix $[I - Q]$.

$$[I - Q] = \begin{bmatrix} 1 & 0 \\ 0 & 1 \end{bmatrix} - \begin{bmatrix} .5 & .2 \\ .3 & .1 \end{bmatrix} = \begin{bmatrix} .5 & -.2 \\ -.3 & .9 \end{bmatrix}$$

Step 2. Find the inverse of this matrix, denoted by N.

$$N = [I - Q]^{-1} = \begin{bmatrix} 2.31 & .51 \\ .77 & 1.28 \end{bmatrix}$$

Note: The inverse of a matrix can be readily performed by spreadsheet programs such as *Microsoft's Excel, Lotus 1-2-3,* or *Quattro Pro.*

Step 3. Multiply this inverse by matrix R.

$$NR = \begin{bmatrix} 2.31 & .51 \\ .77 & 1.28 \end{bmatrix} \begin{bmatrix} .3 & 0 \\ .5 & .1 \end{bmatrix} = \begin{bmatrix} .95 & .05 \\ .87 & .13 \end{bmatrix}$$

NR gives us the probability that an account will eventually be collected or become a bad debt. Specifically, the top row in the answer is the probability that $1 of XYZ's accounts receivable in the 0-60-day-old category will end up in the collected and bad debt category will be paid, and a .05 probability that it will eventually become a bad debt. Turning to the second row, the two entries represent the probability that $1 now in the 61-120-day-old category will end up in the collected and bad debt categories. We can see from this row that there is a .87 probability that $1 currently in the 61-120-day-category will be collected and a .13 probability that it will eventually become uncollectible.

If XYZ wants to estimate the future of its $10,000 accounts receivable ($7,000 in the 0-60 day category and $3,000 in the 61-120 day category), it must set up the following matrix multiplication:

$$[7,000 \quad 3,000] \begin{bmatrix} .95 & .05 \\ .87 & .13 \end{bmatrix} = [9,260 \quad 740]$$

Hence, of its $10,000 in accounts receivable, XYZ expects to collect $9,260 and to lose $740 to bad debts. Therefore, the estimated allowances for the collectible accounts is $740.

The variance of each component is equal to

$$A = be\,(cNR - (cNR)_{sq})$$

where $c_i = b_i/\sum\limits_{i=1}^{2} b_i$ and e is the unit vector.

In our example, $b = (7{,}000 \quad 3{,}000)$, $c = (.7 \quad .3)$. Therefore,

$$A = [7{,}000 \quad 3{,}000]\begin{bmatrix}1\\1\end{bmatrix}\left\{[.7 \quad .3]\begin{bmatrix}.95 & .05\\.87 & .13\end{bmatrix} - [.7 \quad .3]\begin{bmatrix}.95 & .05\\.87 & .13\end{bmatrix}_{sq}\right\}$$

$$= 10{,}000\,[\,[.926 \quad .074] - [.857476 \quad .005476]\,]$$

$$= [685.24 \quad 685.24]$$

which makes the standard deviation equal to $26.18 (\sqrt{\$685.24}$). If we want to be 95 percent confident about our estimate of collections, we would set the interval estimate at $9,260 + 2(26.18)$, or $9,207.64 -$9,312.36, assuming $t = 2$ as a rule of thumb. We would also be able to set the allowance to cover the bad debts at $740 + 2(26.18)$, or $792.36.

SIMPLE AVERAGE

The most straightforward way to estimate collection percentages is to compute the average value realized from past data, i.e.,

$$P'_i = AVE\,(C_{t+i}/S_t)$$

$$= \frac{1}{N}\sum_{t=1}^{N}\frac{C_{t+i}}{S_t}, \quad i = 0,1,2 \ldots$$

where

        P'_t = an empirical estimate of collection percentages,

        C_{t+i} = cash collection in month t+i from credit sales in month t,

        S_t = credit sales in month t, and

        N = the number of months of past data to compute the average.

LAGGED REGRESSION APPROACH

A more scientific approach to estimating cash collection percentages (or payment proportions) is to utilize *multiple regression*. We know that there is typically a time lag between the point of a credit sale and realization of cash. More specifically, the lagged effect of credit sales and cash inflows is distributed over a number of periods, as follows:

$$C_t = b_1 S_{t-1} + b_2 S_{t-2} + \ldots b_i S_{t-i}$$

where

C_t = cash collection in month t

S_t = credit sales made in period t

$b_1, b_2, \ldots b_i$ = collection percentages (the same as P'_i) and

i = number of periods lagged

By using the regression method discussed previously, we will be able to estimate these collection rates. We can utilize "Regression" of Excel or special packages such as *SPSS, MicroTSP, SAS,* or *Systat.*

It should be noted that the cash collection percentages, $(b_1, b_2, \ldots, b_i)$ may not add up to 100 percent because of the possibility of bad debts. Once we estimate these percentages by using the regression method, we should be able to compute the bad debt percentage with no difficulty.

Table 2 shows the regression results using actual monthly data on credit sales and cash inflows for a real company. Equation I can be written as follows:

$$C_t = 60.6\% (S_{t-1}) + 24.3\% (S_{t-2}) + 8.8\% (S_{t-3})$$

This result indicates that the receivables generated by the credit sales are collected at the following rates: first month after sale, 60.6 percent; second month after sale, 24.3 percent; and third month after sale, 8.8 percent. The bad debt percentage is computed as 6.3 percent (100–93.7%).

It is important to note, however, that these collection and bad debt percentages are probabilistic variables; that is, variables whose values cannot be known with precision. However, the standard error of the regression coefficient and the 5-value permit us to assess the probability that the true percentage is between specified limits. The confidence interval takes the following form:

$$b \pm t\, S_b$$

where S_b = standard error of the coefficient.

Table 2   Regression Results for Cash Collection (C_t)

Independent Variables	Equation I	Equation II
S_{t-1}	0.606[a]	0.596[a]
	(0.062)[b]	(0.097)
S_{t-2}	0.243[a]	0.142
	(0.085)	(0.120)
S_{t-3}	0.088	0.043
	(0.157)	(0.191)
S_{t-4}		0.136
		(0.800)
R^2	0.754	0.753
Durbin-Watson	2.52[c]	2.48[c]
Standard Error of the estimate(S_e)	11.63	16.05
Number of monthly observations	21	20
Bad debt percentages	0.063	0.083

[a]Statistically significant at the 5% significance level.
[b]This figure in the parentheses is the standard error of the e estimate for the coefficient (S_b).
[c]No autocorrelation present at the 5% significance level.

Example 1. To illustrate, assuming $t = 2$ as rule of thumb at the 95 percent confidence level, the true collection percentage from the prior month's sales will be

$$60.6\% \pm 2(6.2\%) = 60.6\% \pm 12.4\%$$

Turning to the estimation of cash collections and allowance for doubtful accounts, the following values are used for illustrative purposes:

$S_{t-1} = \$77.6$, $S_{t-2} = \$58.5$, $S_{t-3} = \$76.4$, and forecast average monthly net credit sales = $\$75.2$

Then, (a) the forecast cash collection for period t would be

$$C_t = 60.6\%(77.6) + 19.3\%(58.5) + 8.8\%(76.4) = \$65.04$$

If the financial manager wants to be 95 percent confident about this forecast value, then the interval would be set as follows:

$$C_t \pm t\, S_e$$

where S_e = standard error of the estimate.

To illustrate, using t = 2 as a rule of thumb at the 95 percent confidence level, the true value for cash collections in period t will be

$65.04 ± 2(11.63) = $65.04 ± 23.26

(b) the estimated allowance for uncollectible accounts for period t will be

6.3% ($75.2) = $4.74

By using the limits discussed so far, financial planners can develop flexible (or probabilistic) cash budgets, where the lower and upper limits can be interpreted as pessimistic and optimistic outcomes, respectively. They can also simulate a cash budget in an attempt to determine both the expected change in cash collections for each period and the variation in this value.

In preparing a conventional cash inflow budget, the financial manager considers the various sources of cash, including cash on account, sale of assets, incurrence of debt, and so on. Cash collections from customers are emphasized, since that is the greatest problem in this type of budget.

Example 2. The following data are given for Erich Stores:

	September Actual	October Actual	November Estimated	December Estimated
Cash sales	$ 7,000	$ 6,000	$ 8,000	$ 6,000
Credit sales	50,000	48,000	62,000	80,000
Total sales	$57,000	$54,000	$70,000	$86,000

Past experience indicates net collections normally occur in the following pattern:

- No collections are made in the month of sale
- 80% of the sales of any month are collected in the following month
- 19% of sales are collected in the second following month
- 1% of sales are uncollectible

We can project total cash receipts for November and December as follows:

	November	December
Cash receipts		
Cash sales	$ 8,000	$ 6,000
Cash collections		
September sales		

50,000 (19%)	9,500	
October sales		
48,000 (80%)	38,400	
48,000 (19%)		9,120
November sales		
62,000 (80%)		49,600
Total cash receipts	$55,900	$64,720

CONCLUSION

Two methods of estimating the expected collectible and uncollectible patterns were presented. One advantage of the Markov model is that the expected value and standard deviation of these percentages can be determined, thereby making it possible to specify probabilistic statements about these figures. We have to be careful about these results, however, since the model makes some strong assumptions. A serious assumption is that the matrix of transition probabilities is constant over time. We do not expect this to be perfectly true. Updating of the matrix may have to be done, perhaps through the use of such techniques as exponential smoothing and time series analysis.

The regression approach is relatively inexpensive to use in the sense that it does not require a lot of data. All it requires is data on cash collections, and credit sales. Furthermore, credit sales values are all predetermined; we use previous months' credit sales to forecast cash collections, that is, there is no need to forecast credit sales. The model also allows you to make all kinds of statistical inferences about the cash collection percentages and forecast values.

Extensions of these models can be made toward setting credit and discount policies. Corresponding to a given set of policies, there is an associated transition matrix in the Markov model, and associated collection percentages in the regression model. By computing long-term collections and bad debts for each policy, an optimal policy can be chosen that maximizes expected long-run profits per period.

INTEREST RATE FORECASTING

While there have been a number of efforts devoted to evaluating the accuracy of forecasts of sales and earnings per share, there has been little attention given to the reliability of interest forecasts. Noting that interest rates and earnings are closely linked more than ever before, interest rates need to be forecast accurately.

Furthermore, many corporate financial decisions, such as the timing of a bond refunding, are dependent on anticipated changes in interest rates. Especially for financial institutions, changes in the level of interest rates can be one of the most important variables determining the success of the enterprise since both lending and investing decisions are influenced heavily by anticipated movements in interest rates. Clearly, the accuracy of interest rate forecasts is important from the perspective of the producer and the consumer of such forecasts.

Whether refinancing a mortgage, changing the mix of investment portfolios, or completing a multimillion-dollar acquisition, the future direction of interest rates is a key factor. It is important to develop a tracking and forecasting system that considers not only economic factors but also psychological and political forces.

INTEREST RATE FUNDAMENTALS

Today's supply of and demand for credit determines today's short-term interest rate. Expectations about the future supply of and demand for credit determine the long-term interest rate. Therefore, it is safe to say that short- and long-term interest rates are impacted by similar factors.

Then what are the specific factors that determine interest rates? The business cycle is one factor. The cycle tends to dictate credit demands by the government and businesses. Economic growth is "credit and liquidity driven" in our economy. As the demand for funds strengthens during an expansion, there is an upward pressure on interest rates. The reverse would occur during a business contraction.

Although the demand side is stressed in this explanation of the cyclical effect on interest rates, the supply side of credit and liquidity should not be ignored. For example, foreign credit supplies are certainly an important factor these days. The larger the trade deficit, the larger will be the trade deficit of foreign capital into the U.S.—which, all things being equal, helps lower interest rates.

Any gap between the demand and supply will be accentuated by monetary policy. The Federal Reserve is supposed to "lean against the wind." Thus, the Fed's net addition to liquidity (growth of the monetary aggregates) will tend to raise interest rates near cyclical peaks and diminish them at cyclical troughs.

In addition, inflation impacts short- and long-term interest rates. One key factor is compensation for anticipated inflation, which would otherwise erode the purchasing power of principal and interest and hence ruin the supply of savings.

The stage is set for interest rate forecasting. Interest rates are the dependent variable within a multiple regression framework in which the state of the business cycle, monetary policy, and inflation anticipations are the right-hand explanatory variables.

The difficulties, however, are that the correct measurement of the explanatory factors are hard to find. For example, how do you represent the business cycle? It can be characterized by a multitude of business conditions and their statistical representations. The Fed's monetary policy is another example. Finding the right "proxies" would be a burdensome task.

Furthermore, the interest rate as the dependent variable is also hard to define since there are short-term rates, intermediate-term rates, and long-term rates. Table 1 presents a guide to selecting the dependent variable and conceivable independent variables. This table is by no means an exhaustive list and is only a suggest guide, based on a review of past efforts at forecasting interest rates.

Table 2 provides a list of variables that emerged from some selected prior empirical testing by interest rate experts.

STATISTICAL METHODOLOGY AND A SAMPLE MODEL

Despite many difficulties, statistical forecasts of interest rates are commonly attempted by business economists and frequently structured along the lines of the sample equation shown in Table 3. Multiple regression analysis appears to be the dominant approach to building the model for interest rate forecasting.

Table 1   Commonly Used Variables in Interest Rate Forecasting

---

Dependent Variables

1. *Short-Term Rates*

    U.S. Treasury bill rates (notably three-month)

    Federal funds rate

    Prime rate

2. *Long-Term Rates*

    New AA utility bond yields

    20-year U.S. Treasury bond yields

    30-year U.S. Treasury bond yields

    10-year U.S. Treasury bond yields

    Commercial mortgage rates

    Residential mortgage rates

Independent Variables

1. *Real Economic Activity*

    Real GDP

    Change in real GDP

    Change in non-agricultural payroll employment

    Confidence index

    Leading economic indicators

2. *Capacity Utilization*

    Rate of growth in productivity

    Vendor performance

    New capacity utilization estimates

    Manufacturers capacity utilization

    Operating rates to preferred rates

    Utilization rate . . . Manufacturing

    Capacity utilization . . . Primary materials

    Capacity utilization . . . Advanced processing

    Buying policy

    Business equipment/consumer goods

    Help wanted/unemployment

    Number of initial jobless claims

    Change in unfilled orders

    Output/capacity

3. *Credit Demands by Government and Businesses*
   Income velocity (GDP/M-1)
   Federal budget deficit/GDP
   Change in mortgage debt
   Change in bank loans to business
   Change in installment debt
4. *Inflation Rate*
   Change in CPI (Consumer Price Index)
   Change in PPI (Producer Price Index)
5. *Monetary Aggregates*
   Change in money supply (M-1)
   Change in money supply (M-2)
   Real money base—Money supply in constant dollars (M-1)
6. *Liquidity*
   Money supply (M-1)/GDP
   Money supply (M-2)/GDP
7. *Banking*
   Member bank borrowing
   Loans/deposits . . . Commercial banks
   Loans/investments . . . Commercial banks
8. *Households*
   Change in household net worth (flow of funds)
9. *Corporations*
   Internal cash flow/business capital spending
10. *Foreign Credit Supplies and Foreign Influences*
    Size of current account (i.e., foreign trade) deficit/GDP
    Foreign interest rates
11. *Expectational-type Variables*
    Moving average of prior years of actual inflation
    Moving average of the change in the 3-month T-bill yield
    Polynomial distributed lag of the percentage change in the CPI

In Table 3, we show the 20-year U.S. Treasury bond yield as a function of the unemployment rate, the growth in money supply, a weighted average of past inflation, and volatility in the three-month Treasury bill.

Table 2 Key Variables in Interest Rate Forecasting Found in the Literature

Dependent Variable	Independent (Explanatory) Variables
1. *Roger Williams*[1]	
Federal fund rate	Vendor performance
	Change in money supply M-1 or M-2
	Rate of change in the CPI
New AA utility bond yields	Vendor performance
	Rate of change in the CPI lagged one period
	Ratio of bank loans to investments lagged one period
2. *The Prudential*[2]	
10-year Treasury bond yields	Government deficits/GDP
	Foreign trade/GDP
	Rate of growth in productivity
	Moving average of the five prior years of actual inflation
	Lagged change in GDP
	Foreign interest rates
	Variance and momentum indexes
3. *Schott*[3]	
20-year Treasury bond yields	Log (unemployment rate)
	Percentage change in M-1
	Polynomial distributed lag of the percentage change in the CPI
	Volatility = moving average of the change in the three-month T-bill.
4. *Horan*[4]	
New AA utility bond yield	Income volatility (GDP/M-1)
	Moving average of CPI change
	Commercial paper rate
	RHO (autoregressive error term)

[1]Roger Williams, "Forecasting Interest Rates and Inflation," *Business Economics,* January 1979, pp. 57-60.
[2]The Prudential, "Understanding Long-Term Interest Rates," *Economic Review,* July 1991, pp. 1-8.
[3]Francis H. Scott, "Forecasting Interest Rates: Methods and Application," *Journal of Business Forecasting,* Fall 1986, pp. 11-19.
[4]Lawrence J. Horan, "Forecasting Long-Term Interest Rates—A New Method," *Business Economics,* September 1978, pp. 5-8.

Table 3 Model and Values of Parameters

Model

20-Year T-Bond Yield =

$b_0 + b_1 \times \log$ (Unemployment Rate) $+ b_2 \times$ % Change in M-1
$+ b_3 \times$ Change in CPI, Annualized $+ b_4 \times$ Volatility

Value of Parameters

Independent Variable	Coefficient	t-Value*
1. Constant	11.137	4.36
2. Log (unemployment rate)	–3.297	–3.65
3. Percentage change in M-1	–0.026	–2.16
4. Polynomial distributed lag of the percentage change in the CPI annualized; lag of 4 quarters, 2nd degree polynomial	–0.24	2.73
5. Volatility; 4-year moving average of the absolute value of the change in the 3-month T-bill	1.726	2.05

n = 47
S_e = 0.4709
R^2 = 0.975
Durbin-Watson = 1.64**

---

*Statistically significant at the 5 percent significance level.
**No autocorrelation (serial correlation) at the 1 percent level.
Source: Schott, Francis H., "Forecasting Interest Rates, Methods and Application," *Journal of Business Forecasting,* Fall 1986, p. 18.

CHECKLIST FOR SCREENING OUT EXPLANATORY FACTORS

In order to pick the best regression equation for interest forecasting, you should pretty much follow the same criteria as in Multiple Regression Analysis:

1. Many independent variables listed in Table 2 tend to be highly correlated with each other (*muticollinearity*). This will help lead to the elimination of a number of overlapping series.
2. Variables cannot be retained unless the positive or negative signs of regression coefficients are consistent with theoretical expectations.
3. Traditional yardsticks such as R^2, t-test, F-test, and Durbin-Watson test must be used to select preliminary equations.

4. The predictive performance of the preliminary models needs to be tested based on *ex ante* and *ex post* forecasts.

   a. It is usually measured by such metrics as MPE, RSME, MSE, MAD, and/or Henry Theil U Coefficient.

   b. Compare the forecasts with some "naive" (but much less costly) approach, such as assuming that rates in the future will be the same as today.

   c. Compare quantitative approaches such as econometric forecasting with judgmental forecasts. Judgment can be the overriding factor in interest rate forecasting.

   d. In addition to these evaluations, a separate evaluation of *turning point errors* needs to be made. A turning point error takes place when either you project an increase in interest levels when rates declined or when you anticipated its decline when rates increased. It often is argued that the ability of forecasters to anticipate reversals of interest rate trends is more important than the precise accuracy of the forecast. Substantial gains or losses may arise from a move from generally upward moving rates to downward rate trends (or vice versa), but gains or losses from incorrectly predicting the extent of a continued increase or decrease in rates may be much more limited.

A WORD OF CAUTION

No reasonable business planners should rely solely on statistical methods such as multiple regression. Other quantitative methods need to be attempted. It is important to realize that differences among forecasting methods and assumptions and in a choice of proxies regarding the explanatory variables can yield vastly different results from analyst to analyst. Judgments and expert opinions can help determine the future direction of interest rates. The right marriage between a quantitative evaluation and expert judgments is a must. Consensus forecasts such as those of the National Association of Business Economists (NABE), which receives wide coverage in the financial press, and econometric forecasts made by consulting firms such as The Wharton Econometric Associates, Chase Econometrics, and DRI/McGraw-Hill should be consulted as well.

The cost of errors in interest rate forecasting can be as severe as that of exchange rate forecasting mistakes. Schott at Equitable Life suggests that businesses use specific strategies and policies to reduce their exposure to interest rate forecasting mistakes (e.g., asset/liability maturity matching and hedging with futures).

CONCLUSION

Interest rate forecasting is as treacherous as other economic forecasting, such as the prediction of corporate earnings and foreign exchange rates. The chapter briefly touched upon fundamentals: business cycles, the outlook for the demand and supply of credits, monetary policy, and the inflation rate. It also presented a sample model that reflects on the fundamental theory. The forecasting ability of the model also should be judged in terms of its ability to anticipate major changes in the direction (or turning point) of rates.

FORECASTING FOREIGN EXCHANGE RATES*

This chapter addresses the problem of forecasting foreign exchange rates. It explores the need for managers to forecast the exchange rates. It then establishes a framework of the international exchange markets and explores the relationship between exchange rates, interest rate, and inflation rate. The chapter focuses on the different types of forecasting techniques used to predict the foreign exchange rates and concludes by setting up a framework within which forecasts can be evaluated.

WHY FORECAST EXCHANGE RATES?

Frequently companies are faced with a decision regarding forecasting foreign exchange rates. Some companies choose to ignore forecasting, while others often rely on their banks for the answer. Very few companies dedicate resources to forecast foreign exchange rate.

Many companies argue that the forecasts of international exchange rates are often inaccurate and hence invalid. Therefore, there is no need to forecast. These companies, however, fail to understand that forecasting is not an exact science but rather an art form where quality of forecasts generally tend to improve as companies and managers gain more experience in forecasting.

In today's global environment, companies trading across the national boundaries are often exposed to transaction risk, the risk that comes from fluctuation in the exchange rate between the time a contract is signed and when the payment is received. Historically, exchange rates have been fixed and there have been very few fluctuations within a short time period. However, most exchange rates today are floating and can easily vary as much as 5% within a week. Moreover, the recent crisis in the European

---

* This chapter was coauthored by Anique Qureshi, Ph.D., CPA, CIA, associate professor of accounting at Queens College, and an accounting consultant.

monetary market illustrates the need for accurate exchange rate information. There are four primary reasons why it is imperative to forecast the foreign exchange rates.

Hedging Decision

Multinational companies (MNCs) are constantly faced with the decision of whether or not to hedge payables and receivables in foreign currency. An exchange rate forecast can help MNC's determine if it should hedge its transactions. As an example, if forecasts determine that the Swiss franc is going to appreciate in value relative to the dollar, a company expecting payment from a Swiss partner in the future may not decide to hedge the transaction. However, if the forecasts showed that the Swiss franc is going to depreciate relative to the dollar, the U.S. partner should hedge the transaction.

Short-Term Financing Decision for MNC

A large corporation has several sources of capital market and several currencies in which it can borrow. Ideally, the currency it would borrow would exhibit low interest rate and depreciate in value over the financial period. For example, A U.S. firm could borrow in German marks; during the loan period, the marks would depreciate in value; at the end of the period, the company would have to use fewer dollars to buy the same amount of marks and would benefit from the deal.

International Capital Budgeting Decision

Accurate cash flows are imperative in order to make a good capital budgeting decision. In case of international projects, it is not only necessary to establish accurate cash flows but it is also necessary to convert them into an MNC's home country currency. This necessitates the use of a foreign exchange forecast to convert the cash flows and there after, evaluate the decision.

Subsidiary Earning Assessment for MNC

When an MNC reports its earnings, international subsidiary earnings are often translated and consolidated in the MNC's home country currency. For example, when IBM makes a projection for its earnings, it needs to project its earnings in Germany, then it needs to translate these earnings from Deutsche marks to dollars. A depreciation in marks would decrease a subsidiary's earnings and vice versa. Thus, it is necessary to generate an accurate forecast of marks to create a legitimate earnings assessment.

SOME BASIC TERMS AND RELATIONSHIPS

At this point, it is necessary to address some of the basic terminology used in foreign exchange as well as address the fundamental laws of international monetary economics. It is also necessary to establish a basic international monetary framework before forecasting.

Spot Rate

Spot rate can be defined as the rate that exists in today's market. Table 1 illustrates a typical listing of foreign exchange rates found in the *Wall Street Journal*. The British pound is quoted at 1.6708. This rate is the spot rate. It means you can go to the bank today and exchange $1.6708 for £1.00. How this works is, say, for example, your need £10,000 for a paying off an import transaction on a given day, you would ask your bank to purchase £10,000. The bank would not hand you the money, but instead it would instruct its English subsidiary to pay £10,000 to your English supplier and it would debit you account by (10,000 × 1.6708) $16,708.

Forward Rate

Besides the spot rate, Table 1 also quotes the forward rate. The 90-day forward rate for the pound is quoted as 1.6637. In forward market, you buy and sell currency for a future delivery date, usually, one, three, or six months in advance. If you know you need to buy or sell currency in the future, you can hedge against a loss by selling in the forward market. For example, let's say you are required to pay £10,000 in 3 months to your English supplier. You can purchase £10,000 today by paying $16,637 (10,000 × 1.6637). These pounds will be delivered in 90 days. In the meantime you have protected yourself. No matter what the exchange rate of pound or U.S. dollar is in 90 days, you are assured delivery at the quoted price.

As can be seen in the example, the cost of purchasing pounds in the forward market ($16,637) is less than the price in the spot market ($16,708). This implies that the pound is selling at a forward discount relative to the dollar, so you can buy more pounds in the forward market. It could also mean that the U.S. dollar is selling at a forward premium.

Interest Rate Parity Theory

The interest rate parity theory says that interest rate differential must equal the difference between the spot and the forward rate. The validity of this theory can be easily tested by a simple example. Lets assume that the interest rate in the U.S. is 10%. An identical investment in Switzerland yields 5%.

Table 1 Sample Listing of Foreign Exchange Rates

Thursday, April 30, 1998

The New York foreign exchange selling rates below apply to trading among banks in amounts of $1 million and more, as quoted at 4 p.m. Eastern time by Dow Jones and other sources. Retail transactions provide fewer units of foreign currency per dollar.

Country	U.S. $ equiv.		Currency per U.S. $	
	Thu	Wed	Thu	Wed
Argentina (Peso)	1.0001	1.0001	.9999	.9999
Australia (Dollar)	.6500	.6494	1.5385	1.5399
Austria (Schilling)	.07911	.07913	12.640	12.638
Bahrain (Dinar)	2.6525	2.6525	.3770	.3770
Belgium (Franc)	.02698	.02698	37.065	37.060
Brazil (Real)	.8744	.8736	1.1436	1.1447
Britain (Pound)	1.6708	1.6697	.5985	.5989
1-month forward	1.6682	1.6672	.5994	.5998
3-months forward	1.6637	1.6625	.6011	.6015
6-months forward	1.6575	1.6566	.6033	.6036
Canada (Dollar)	.6988	.6959	1.4310	1.4369
1-month forward	.6993	.6964	1.4301	1.4369
3-months forward	.7001	.6971	1.4284	1.4345
6-months forward	.7012	.6981	1.4261	1.4324
Chile (Peso)	.002208	.002209	452.85	452.65
China (Renminbi)	.1208	.1208	8.2781	8.2782
Colombia (Peso)	.0007322	.0007292	1365.72	1371.35
Czech. Rep. (Koruna)	....	....	....	....
Commercial rate	.03031	.03017	32.995	33.149
Denmark (Krone)	.1460	.1460	6.8475	6.8490
Ecuador (Sucre)	....	....	....	....
Floating rate	.0001996	.0001996	5010.00	5010.00
Finland (Markka)	.1836	.1835	5.4480	5.4490
France (Franc)	.1661	.1661	6.0195	6.0200
1-month forward	1.664	1.664	6.0088	6.0092
3-months forward	1.670	1.670	5.9886	5.9888
6-months forward	1.678	1.678	5.9605	5.9594

Furthermore, the exchange rate is .7097 dollar per franc. Now an investor can invest $100,000 in the U.S. and earn interest of $5,000 (100,000 × .10/2) in six months. The same investor can today purchase 140,905 francs (100,000/.7097) and invest in a Swiss bank to earn 144,428 francs. Now when the investor decides to transfer his currency to the U.S., what will be the exchange rate? If the investor has sold francs in the 180-day forward market, the exchange rate should be 0.7270 and investor earnings would transfer to $ 105,000. If the exchange rate were lower, i.e., 0.7100, the amount would be $102,543 and no one would be interested to invest in Switzerland. All Swiss investors would want to invest in U.S., so they would buy dollars and drive down the exchange rate until the exchange rate was 0.7270 and excess profits disappeared.

Fisher Price Effect

Fisher Price effect states that difference in interest rates must equal expected difference in inflation rates. Interest rate is made up several different components:

Interest Rate = $K_r + K_i + K_{drp}$

where

K_i = the inflation premium
K_{drp} = the default risk premium
K_r = the real interest rate

Fisher argued that the real interest rate remains the same for all countries. Thus the differences in exchange rate are a direct result of differences in inflation rate. (It is assumed that the investments are identical and therefore default risk would be the same.) If the real interest rates were different, it provides an excellent opportunity for currency arbitrage and eventually, the market would make the exchange rates such that the real interest rate was identical.

Purchasing Power Parity

The law of purchasing power parity states that the expected difference in inflation rate equals the difference between the forward and the spot rate. This can be easily proven. According to the interest rate parity theory, the difference in interest rate equals the difference between the forward and spot rate. According to the Fisher price effect, the difference between interest rates also equals the difference between inflation rates. Therefore, the difference between the inflation rates should equal the difference between the forward and spot rate.

The three previously described theories form the cornerstone of international finance. These theories are very important in that they are used in developing some fundamental forecasting models. These three models have been kept relatively simple although real life is not this simple. Frequently these models are modified to account for real world and market imperfections.

FORECASTING TECHNIQUES

The international financial markets are very complex. Therefore, a variety of forecasting techniques are used to forecast the foreign exchange rate. A certain method of forecasting may be more suited to one particular exchange rate or scenario. There are four major ways of forecasting foreign exchange rates: Fundamental forecasting, market-based forecasting, technical forecasting, and a mixture of the three.

Fundamental Forecasting

Fundamental forecasting is based on fundamental relationships between economic variables and exchange rates. Given current values of these variables along with their historical impact on a currency's value, corporations can develop exchange rate projections. In previous sections, we established a basic relationship between exchange rates, inflation rates, and interest rates. This relationship can be used to develop a simple linear forecasting model for the Deutsche mark.

$$DM = a + b (INF) + c (INT)$$

where

DM = the quarterly percentage change in the German mark

INF = quarterly percentage change in inflation differential (US inflation rate – German inflation rate)

INT = quarterly percentage change in interest rate differential (US interest rate – German interest rate)

Note: This model is relatively simple with only two explanatory variables. In many cases, several other variables are added but the essential methodology remains the same.

Example 1. The following example illustrates how exchange rate forecasting can be accomplished using the fundamental approach. Table 2 shows the basic input data for the ten quarters. Table 3 shows a summary of the regression output, based on the use of *Microsoft Excel.*

Table 2

Period	US CPI	US INF	G CPI	G INF	US INT	G INT	DM/$	INF Diff	INT Diff
Apr 95	123.7	1.56%	104.0	0.87%	9.64%	6.97%	1.8783	0.69%	2.67%
Jul 95	124.7	0.81%	104.5	0.48%	9.51%	6.87%	1.8675	0.33%	2.64%
Oct 95	125.9	0.96%	105.2	0.67%	9.92%	7.40%	1.8375	0.29%	2.52%
Jan 96	128.1	1.75%	105.9	0.67%	10.82%	8.50%	1.6800	1.08%	2.32%
Apr 96	129.4	1.01%	106.4	0.47%	11.42%	8.87%	1.6820	0.54%	2.55%
Jul 96	131.6	1.70%	107.3	0.85%	11.25%	8.93%	1.5920	0.85%	2.32%
Oct 96	133.8	1.67%	108.4	1.03%	10.83%	9.00%	1.5180	0.65%	1.83%
Jan 97	134.9	0.82%	108.7	0.28%	10.06%	9.70%	1.4835	0.55%	0.36%
Apr 97	135.7	0.59%	108.7	0.00%	10.16%	8.40%	1.7350	0.59%	1.76%
Jul 97	136.6	0.66%	109.7	0.92%	9.84%	8.60%	1.7445	−0.26%	1.24%
Oct 97	137.8	0.88%	111.8	1.91%	9.62%	8.40%	1.6750	−1.04%	1.36%
Jan 98	138.8	0.73%	1112.7	0.81%	9.36%	8.00%		−0.08%	1.36%

Period	Quarterly % Change INF Diff.	INT Diff.	DM/$
Jul 95	−0.5231	−0.01124	−0.00575
Oct 95	−0.1074	−0.04545	−0.01606
Jan 96	2.6998	−0.07937	−0.08571
Apr 96	−0.4984	0.099138	0.00119
Jul 96	0.5742	−0.0902	−0.05351
Oct 96	−0.2431	−0.21121	−0.04648
Jan 97	−0.1565	−0.80328	−0.02273
Apr 97	0.0874	3.888889	0.169532
Jul 97	−1.4329	−0.29545	0.005476
Oct 97	3.0346	−0.01613	−0.03984
Jan 98	−0.9234	0.114754	

Source: The raw data was derived from *International Economic Conditions,* August 1998.

Table 3 Microsoft *Excel* Repression Output

Analysis of Variance	df	Sum of Squares	Mean Square	F	Significance F
Regression	2	0.039325	0.01966	41.317	0.00013
Residual	7	0.003331	0.00048		
Total	9	0.042656			

	Coefficients	Standard Error	t-Statistic	P-value	Lower 95%	Upper 95%
Intercept	−0.0149	0.0072502	−2.057589	0.06975	−0.0321	0.00223
INF Diff.	−0.0171	0.0050964	−3.352584	0.00849	−0.0291	−0.005
INT Diff.	0.04679	0.0055715	8.39862	15E−05	0.0336	0.05997

Regression Statistics

Multiple R	0.9602
R Square	0.9219
Adjusted R Square	0.8996
Standard Error	0.0218
Observations	10

Our forecasting model that can be used to predict the DM/$ exchange rate for the next quarter is:

$$DM = -0.0149 - 0.0171 \, (INF) + 0.0468 \, (INT)$$
$$R^2 = 92.19\%$$

Ex post predictions are summarized in Table 4 and plotted against actual values in Figure 1.

Assuming that INT = −0.9234 and INF = 0.1148 for the next quarter,

$$DM = -0.0149 - 0.0171 \, (-0.9234) + 0.0468 \, (0.1148) = 0.00623$$
$$DM/\$ = (1 + 0.00623) \times (1.6750) = 1.6854$$

According to the forecast, the exchange rate in first quarter of 98 should be 1.6854. The actual rate was 1.6392. The error in the forecast was .0462 (1.6854 − 1.6392) and the mean percentage error (MPE) of forecast was 2.78%.

This example presents a simple fundamental forecasting model for foreign exchange rates. This model is especially useful if the exchange rates are

Table 4

Observation	Predicted Y	Residuals	Standardized Residuals	Percentile	DM/$
1	−0.00651	0.000756	0.034667	5	−0.0857
2	−0.01521	−0.00085	−0.039159	15	−0.0535
3	−0.06476	−0.02095	−0.960496	25	−0.0465
4	−0.00176	0.002953	0.135359	35	−0.0398
5	−0.02895	−0.02456	−1.125773	45	−0.0227
6	−0.02065	−0.02584	−1.184324	55	−0.0161
7	−0.04983	0.027104	1.242462	65	−0.0057
8	0.165562	0.00397	0.181967	75	0.0012
9	−0.00426	0.009735	0.446276	85	0.0055
10	−0.06752	0.027684	1.269022	95	0.1695

Figure 1 Plot of Predicted and Actual Y Values

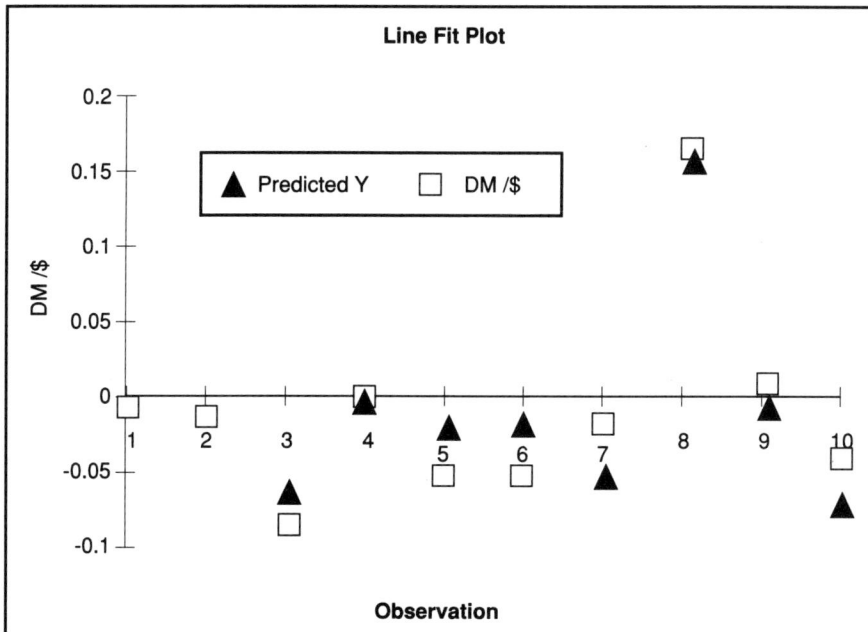

freely floating and there is minimum government or central bank intervention in the currency market. Note that this model relies on relationships between macro-economic variables.

However, there are certain problems with this forecasting technique. First, this technique will not be very effective with fixed exchange rates. This technique also relies on forecast to forecast. That is, one needs to project the future interest rate and the future inflation rate in order to compute the differentials that are the used to compute the exchange rate. Note: These estimates are frequently published in trade publications and bank reports. Second, this technique often ignores other variables that influence the foreign exchange rate.

Market-Based Forecasting

The process of developing forecasts from market indicators is known as *market-based forecasting*. This is perhaps the easiest forecasting model. While it is very simple, it is also very effective. The model relies on the spot rate and the forward rate to forecast the price. The model assumes that the spot rate reflects the foreign exchange rate in the near future. Let us suppose that the Italian lira is expected to depreciate vs. the U.S. dollar. This would encourage speculators to sell Lira and later purchase them back at the lower (future) price. This process if continued would drive down the prices of lira until the excess (arbitrage) profits were eliminated.

The model also suggests that the forward exchange rate equals the future spot price. Again, let us suppose that the 90-day forward rate is .987. The market forecasters believe that the exchange rate in 90 days is going to be .965. This provides an arbitrage opportunity. Markets will keep on selling the currency in the forward market until the opportunity for excess profit is eliminated.

This model, however, relies heavily on market efficiency. It assumes that capital markets and currency markets are highly efficient and that there is perfect information in the market place. Under these circumstances, this model can provide accurate forecasts. Indeed, many of the world currency markets such as the market for U.S. dollar, German mark, and Japanese Yen are highly efficient and this model is well suited for such markets. However, market imperfections or lack of perfect information reduces the effectiveness of this model. In some cases, this model cannot be used.

Technical Forecasting

Technical forecasting involves the use of historical exchange rates to predict future values. It is sometimes conducted in a judgmental manner, without statistical analysis. Often, however, statistical analysis is applied in technical forecasting to detect historical trends. There are also time series models that examine moving averages. Most technical models rely on the past to predict the future. They try to identify a historical pattern that seems to repeat and then try to forecast it. The models range from a simple moving average to a complex auto regressive integrated moving average (ARIMA). Most models try to break down the historical series. They try to identify and remove the random element. Then they try to forecast the overall trend with cyclical and seasonal variations.

A moving average is useful to remove minor random fluctuations. A trend analysis is useful to forecast a long-term linear or exponential trend. Winter's seasonal smoothing and Census XII decomposition are useful to forecast long-term cycles with additive seasonal variations. ARIMA (auto regressive integrated moving average) is useful to predict cycles with multiplicative seasonality. Many forecasting and statistical packages such as *Forecast Pro, Sibyl/Runner, Minitab,* and *SAS* can handle these computations. An example of technical forecasting follows.

Example 2. This example uses the past six years of monthly data of the German mark (DM/$) exchange rate to forecast the DM/$ for the first 9 months in 1998. The data is given Table 5 and plotted in Figure 2.

Table 5   Germany Currency 7-Year Monthly Closings

Month	1992	1993	1994	1995	1996	1997	1998
January	2.3892	1.8298	1.6785	1.8646	1.6805	1.4835	1.6190
February	2.2185	1.8268	1.6884	1.8296	1.6930	1.5195	1.6395
March	2.3175	1.8028	1.8219	1.8927	1.6947	1.7000	1.6445
April	2.1865	1.7985	1.6773	1.8783	1.6822	1.7350	1.6590
May	2.1327	1.8215	1.7015	1.9858	1.6913	1.7255	1.6080
June	2.1986	1.8249	1.8211	1.9535	1.6645	1.8120	1.5255
July	2.0940	1.8590	1.8810	1.8675	1.5920	1.7445	1.4778
August	2.0520	1.8145	1.8748	1.9608	1.5680	1.7425	1.4055
September	2.0207	1.8460	1.8798	1.8730	1.5650	1.6612	1.4105
October	2.0630	1.7255	1.7684	1.8353	1.5180	1.6750	
November	1.9880	1.6375	1.7354	1.7895	1.5030	1.6327	
December	1.9188	1.5713	1.7803	1.6915	1.4955	1.5175	

Source: The raw data was derived from *Business International,* December 1998.

Figure 2 Plot of 6-Year DM/$ Rate

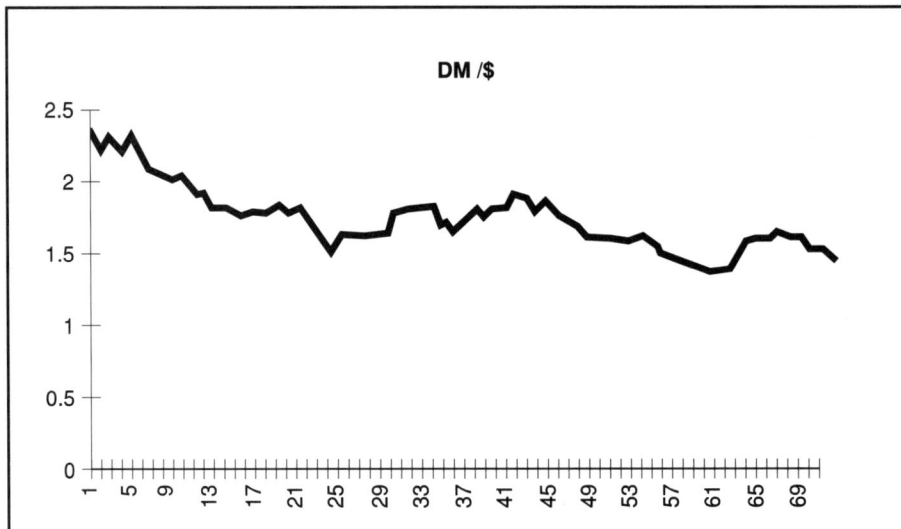

The data pattern seems to show a mild cycle with additive seasonality. Winter's seasonal smoothing is the ideal method under these situations. The data was run in *Forecast Pro for Windows*, a PC software package. The summary of the forecast is presented in Table 6 and plotted against actual values in Figure 3. Table 6 also summarizes the predictive performance of the model. The mean percentage error (MPE) was somewhat low (1.19%), which is generally indicative of a good forecast.

Table 6 Summary of Forecast

Forecast	Actual	Error	% Error
1.6080	1.6190	−0.0110	−0.68%
1.6507	1.6395	0.0112	0.68%
1.7248	1.6445	0.0803	4.77%
1.6593	1.6590	0.0003	0.02%
1.6079	1.6080	−0.0001	−0.01%
1.5879	1.5255	0.0624	4.01%
1.4863	1.4778	0.0085	0.57%
1.4526	1.4055	0.0471	3.30%
1.3834	1.4105	−0.0271	−1.94%
	Average:	0.0191	1.19%

Figure 3   Plot of Actual Versus Smoothed Values

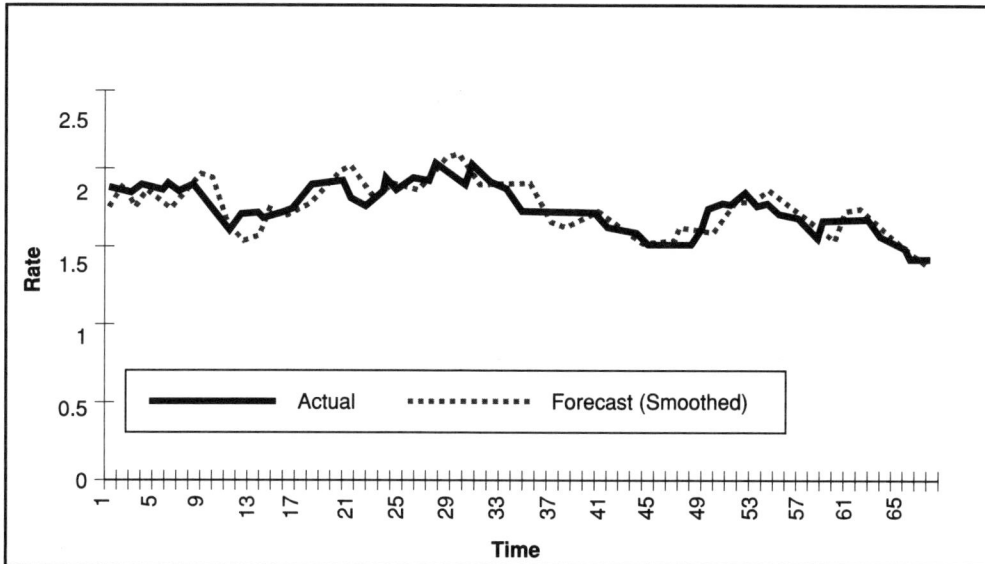

Mixed Forecasting

Mixed forecasting in not a unique technique but rather a combination of the three previously discussed methods. In some cases, a mixed forecast is nothing but a weighted average of a variety of the forecasting techniques. The techniques can be weighted arbitrarily or by assigning a higher weight to the more reliable technique. Mixed forecasting may often lead to a better result than relying on one single forecast.

A FRAMEWORK FOR EVALUATING FORECASTS

Forecasting foreign exchange is an ongoing process. Due to the dynamic nature of international markets, forecasts may not be accurate. However, the quality of a forecast does improve with a forecaster's experience. Therefore, it is necessary to set up some kind of framework within which a forecast can be evaluated.

The simplest framework would be to measure the errors in forecasting, which are discussed in detail in the next chapter (*Evaluation of Forecasts*). Several measures such as MAD, MSE, and MPE can be calculated and tracked. If more than one forecasting technique is used, i.e., a mixed forecast is used, a company may be able to decide which technique is superior. It may then adjust the weighting scale in a mixed forecast.

A good framework makes it easy for a company to predict errors in forecasting. For example, if a forecaster is consistently forecasting the foreign exchange rate for the German mark above its actual rate this would suggest that a forecaster needs to adjust the forecast for this bias. Furthermore, a tracking signal and the turning point error needs to be systematically monitored.

CONCLUSION

In reality, currency forecasting is neglected in many multinational firms. They often argue that forecasting is useless since it does not provide an accurate estimate. They do not even have a hedging strategy. Failure to accurately forecast currency can have a disastrous impact on earnings. Moreover, it is important to realize that forecasting is often undertaken so the corporation has a general idea about the overall trend of the future and that the companies are not caught off guard. While currency forecasts are not 100% accurate, they do provide some advance warning of future trends.

It is also important to realize that forecasting is not an exact science. The quality of forecasts tends to improve over time as the forecaster gains more experience. One cannot ignore the value of judgement and intuition in forecasting, although evidence shows that forecasts using qualitative techniques are not as accurate as those using quantitative techniques.

Note: An experienced forecaster uses both qualitative as well as quantitative techniques to create a reasonable forecast.

EVALUATION OF FORECASTS

The cost of a prediction error can be substantial. Forecasters must always find ways to improve their forecasts. That means that they might want to examine some objective evaluations of alternative forecasting techniques. This section presents the guidelines they need. Two evaluation techniques are presented here. The first is in the form of a checklist. A forecaster could use it to evaluate either a new model he or she is in the process of developing or an existing model. The second is a statistical technique for evaluating a model.

COST OF PREDICTION ERRORS

There is always a cost involved with a failure to predict a certain variable accurately. It is important to determine the cost of the prediction error in order to minimize the potential detrimental effect on future profitability of the company. The cost of the prediction error can be substantial, depending upon the circumstances. For example, failure to make an accurate projection on sales could result in poor production planning, too much or too little purchase of labor, and so on, thereby causing potentially huge financial losses.

The cost of the prediction error is basically the contribution or profit lost on an inaccurate prediction. It can be measured in terms of lost sales, disgruntled customers, and idle machines.

Example 1. Assume that a company has been selling a toy doll having a cost of $.60 for $1.00 each. The fixed cost is $300. The company has no privilege of returning any unsold dolls. It has predicted sales of 2,000 units. However, unforeseen competition has reduced sales to 1,500 units. Then the cost of its prediction error (that is, its failure of predict demand accurately) would be calculated as follows:

1. Initial predicted sales = 2,000 units.

   Optimal decision: purchase 2,000 units.

   Expected net income = $500 [(2,000 units × $.40 contribution) – $300 fixed costs]

2. Alternative parameter value = 1,500 units.

   Optimal decision: purchase 1,500 units.

   Expected net income = $300 [(1,500 units × $.40 contribution) – $300 fixed costs]

3. Results of original decision under alternative parameter value.

   Expected net income:

   Revenue (1,500 units × $1.00) – Cost of dolls (2,000 units × $.60) – $300 fixed costs

   = $1,500 – $1,200 – $300 = $0.

4. Cost of prediction error, (2) – (3) = $300.

CHECKLIST

Two main items to be checked are the data and the model with its accompanying assumptions. The questions to be raised are the following:

1. Is the source reliable and accurate?
2. In the case of use of more than one source that is reliable and accurate, is the source used the best?
3. Are the data the most recent available?
4. If the answer to question 3 is yes, are the data subject to subsequent revision?
5. Is there any known systematic bias in the data which may be dealt with?

The model and its accompanying assumptions should be similarly examined. Among other things, the model has to make sense from a theoretical standpoint. The assumptions should be clearly stated and tested as well.

MEASURING ACCURACY OF FORECASTS

The performance of a forecast should be checked against its own record or against that of other forecasts. There are various statistical measures that can be used to measure performance of the model. Of course, the performance

Evaluation of Forecasts

is measured in terms of forecasting error, where error is defined as the difference between a predicted value and the actual result.

$$\text{Error (e)} = \text{Actual (A)} - \text{Forecast (F)}$$

MAD, MSE, RMSE, and MAPE

The commonly used measures for summarizing historical errors include the *mean absolute deviation* (MAD), the *mean squared error* (MSE), the *root mean squared error* (RMSE), and the *mean absolute percentage error* (MAPE). The formulas used to calculate MAD, MSE, and RMSE are

$$\text{MAD} = \Sigma \, |e| \, / \, n$$
$$\text{MSE} = \Sigma \, e^2 \, / \, (n-1)$$
$$\text{RMSE} = \sqrt{(\Sigma \, e^2/n)}$$

Sometimes it is more useful to compute the forecasting errors in percentages rather than in amounts. The MAPE is calculated by finding the absolute error in each period, dividing this by the actual value of that period, and then averaging these absolute percentage errors, as shown below.

$$\text{MAPE} = \Sigma \, |e|/A \, / \, n$$

The following example illustrates the computation of MAD, MSE, and RMSE, and MAPE.

Example 2. Sales data of a microwave oven manufacturer are given below:

Period	Actual (A)	Forecast (F)	e (A–F)	|e|	e^2	Absolute Percent Error |e|/A
1	217	215	2	2	4	.0092
2	213	216	–3	3	9	.0014
3	216	215	1	1	1	.0046
4	210	214	–4	4	16	.0190
5	213	211	2	2	4	.0094
6	219	214	5	5	25	.0023
7	216	217	–1	1	1	.0046
8	212	216	–4	4	16	.0019
			–2	22	76	.0524

Using the figures,

$$\text{MAD} \quad = \Sigma \, |e| \, /n = 22/8 = 2.75$$

$$\text{MSE} \quad = \Sigma \, e^2 \, / \, (n-1) = 76/7 = 10.86$$

$$\text{RMSE} \quad = \sqrt{\Sigma \, e^2} \, / \, n = \sqrt{76/8} = \sqrt{9.5} = 3.08$$

$$\text{MAPE} \quad = \Sigma \, |e| \, /A \, / \, n = .0524/8 = .0066$$

One way these measures are used is to evaluate forecasting ability of alternative forecasting methods. For example, using either MAD or MSE, a forecaster could compare the results of exponential smoothing with alphas and elect the one that performed best in terms of the lowest MAD or MSE for a given set of data. Also, it can help select the best initial forecast value for exponential smoothing.

THE U STATISTIC AND TURNING POINT ERRORS

There is still a number of statistical measures for measuring accuracy of the forecast. Two standards may be identified. First, one could compare the forecast being evaluated with a naive forecast to see if there are vast differences. The naive forecast can be anything; for instance, the same as last year, moving average, or the output of an exponential smoothing technique. In the second case, the forecast may be compared against the outcome when there is enough to do so. The comparison may be against the actual level of the variable forecasted, or the change observed may be compared with the change forecast.

The Theil U Statistic is based upon a comparison of the predicted change with the observed change. It is calculated as:

$$U = 1/n \, \Sigma \, (F - A)^2 \, / \, (1/n)\Sigma \, F^2 + (1/n)\Sigma \, A^2$$

As can be seen, $U = 0$ is a perfect forecast, since the forecast would equal actual and $F - A = 0$ for all observations. At the other extreme, $U = 1$ would be a case of all incorrect forecasts. The smaller the value of U, the more accurate are the forecasts. If U is greater than or equal to 1, the predictive ability of the model is lower than a naive no-change extrapolation. *Note:* Many computer software packages routinely compute the U Statistic.

Still other evaluation techniques consider the number of *turning point errors* which is based on the total number of reversals of trends. The turning point error is also known as "error in the direction of prediction." In a certain case, such as interest rate forecasts, the turning point error is more serious than the accuracy of the forecast. For example, the ability of forecasters to anticipated reversals of interest rate trends is more important—perhaps substantially more important—than the precise accuracy of the forecast. Substantial gains or losses may arise from a move from generally upward moving rates to downward rate trends (or vice versa) but gains or losses from incorrectly forecasting the extent of a continued increase or decrease in rates may be much more limited.

CONTROL OF FORECASTS

It is important to monitor forecast errors to insure that the forecast is performing well. If the model is performing poorly based on some criteria, the forecaster might reconsider the use of the existing model or switch to another forecasting model or technique. The forecasting control can be accomplished by comparing forecasting errors to predetermined values, or limits. Errors that fall within the limits would be judged acceptable while errors outside of the limits would signal that corrective action is desirable (See Figure 1).

Figure 1   Monitoring Forecast Errors

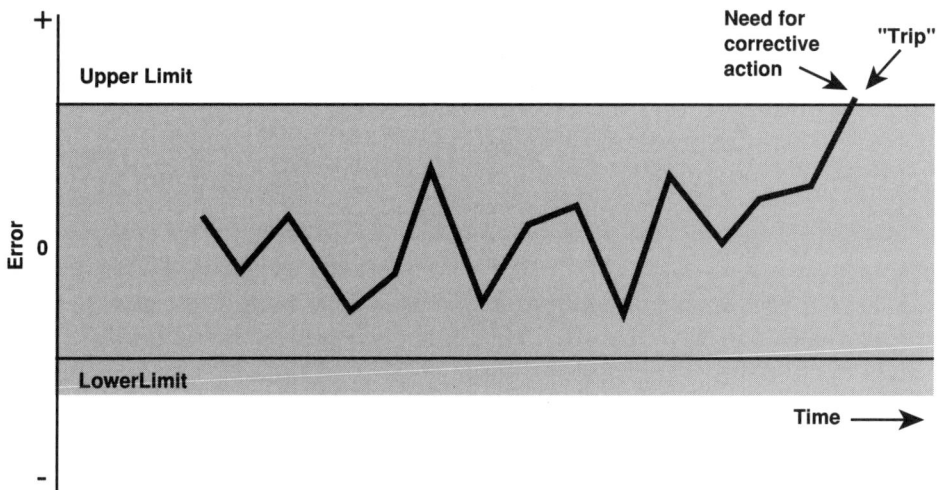

Forecasts can be monitored using either tracking signals or control charts.

Tracking Signals

A tracking signal is based on the ratio of cumulative forecast error to the corresponding value of MAD.

$$\text{Tracking signal} = \Sigma(A - F) / MAD$$

The resulting tracking signal values are compared to predetermined limits. These are based on experience and judgement and often range from plus or minus three to plus or minus eight. Values within the limits suggest that the forecast is performing adequately. By the same token, when the signal goes beyond this range, corrective action is appropriate.

Example 3. Going back to Example 2, the deviation and cumulative deviation have already been computed:

$$MAD = \Sigma \ |A - F| \ / \ n = 22 \ / \ 8 = 2.75$$
$$\text{Tracking signal} = \Sigma \ (A - F) \ / \ MAD = -2 \ / \ 2.75 = -0.73$$

A tracking signal is as low as –0.73, which is substantially below the limit (–3 to –8). It would not suggest any action at this time.

Note: After an initial value of MAD has been computed, the estimate of the MAD can be continually updated using exponential smoothing.

$$MAD_t = \alpha(A - F) + (1 - \alpha) \ MAD_{t-1}$$

Control Charts

The control chart approach involves setting upper and lower limits for individual forecasting errors instead of cumulative errors. The limits are multiples of the estimated standard deviation of forecast, S_f, which is the square root of MSE. Frequently, control limits are set at 2 or 3 standard deviations.

$$\pm \ 2 \ (\text{or } 3) \ S_f$$

Note: Plot the errors and see if all errors are within the limits, so that the forecaster can visualize the process and determine if the method being used is in control.

Example 4. For the sales data below, using the naive forecast, we will determine if the forecast is in control. For illustrative purposes, we will use 2 sigma control limits.

Year	Sales	Forecasts	Error	Error^2
1	320			
2	326	320	6	36
3	310	326	−16	256
4	317	310	7	49
5	315	317	−2	4
6	318	315	3	9
7	310	318	−8	64
8	316	310	6	36
9	314	316	−2	4
10	317	314	3	9
			−3	467

Evaluation of Forecasts

First, compute the standard deviation of forecast errors

$$S_f = \sqrt{e^2 / (n - 1)} = \sqrt{467/(9 - 1)} = 7.64$$

Two sigma limits are then plus or minus $2(7.64) = -15.28$ to $+15.28$.

Note that the forecast error for year 3 is below the lower bound, so the forecast is not in control (See Figure 2). The use of other methods such as moving average, exponential smoothing, or regression would possibly achieve a better forecast.

Figure 2 Control Chart for Forecasting Errors

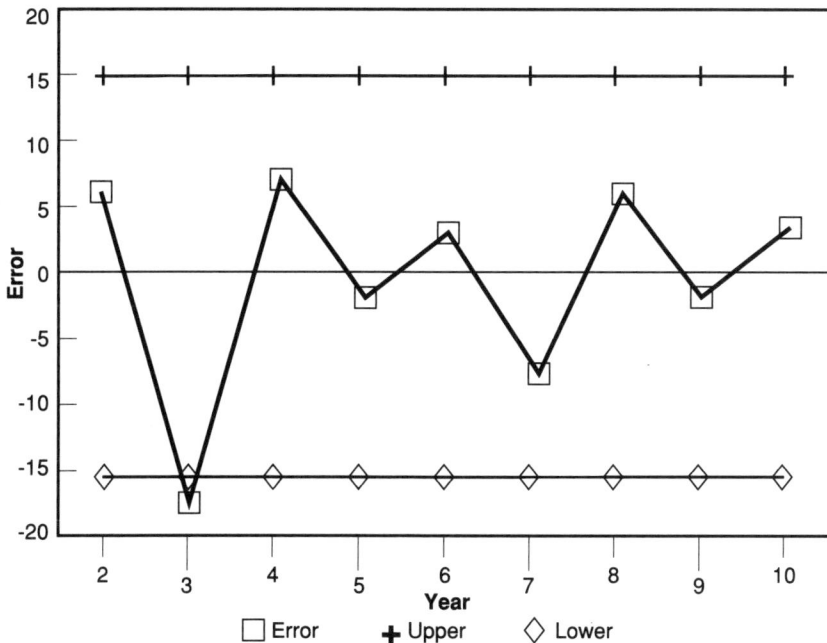

Note: A system of monitoring forecasts needs to be developed. The computer may be programmed to print a report showing the past history when the tracking signal "trips" a limit. For example, when a type of exponential smoothing is used, the system may try a different value of α (so the forecast will be more responsive) and to continue forecasting.

CONCLUSION

There is always a cost associated with a failure to predict a certain variable accurately. Because all forecasts tend to be off the mark, it is important to provide a measure of accuracy for each forecast. Several measures of forecast accuracy and a measure of turning point error can be calculated.

These quite often are used to help managers evaluate the performance of a given method as well as to choose among alternative forecasting techniques. Control of forecasts involves deciding whether a forecast is performing adequately, using either a control chart or a tracking signal. Selection of a forecasting method involves choosing a technique that will serve its intended purpose at an acceptable level of cost and accuracy.

FORECASTING TOOLS AND SOFTWARE

The life cycle of a typical new product is divided into four major stages: introduction, growth, maturity, and saturation (decline). Depending upon the nature of the market, a right choice of forecasting methodology is called for. Table 1 shows life cycle effects upon forecasting methodology. Table 2 summarizes the forecasting methods that have been discussed in this book. It is organized in the following format:

1. Description
2. Accuracy
3. Identification of turning point
4. Typical application
5. Data required
6. Cost
7. Time required to develop an application and make forecasts

Furthermore, in an effort to aid forecasters in choosing the right methodology, Table 3 provides rankings of forecasting methodology by:

1. Accuracy: Why do you need the forecast?
2. Cost: How much money is involved?
3. Timing: When will the forecast be used?
4. Form: Who will use the forecast?
5. Data: How much data are available?

Table 1 Life Cycle Effects on Forecasting Methodology

Introduction

Data:	No data available; Rely on qualitative methods.
Time:	Need long horizon.
Methods:	Qualitative (judgement) such as market surveys and Delphi.

Growth

Data:	Some data available for analysis.
Time:	Still need long horizon; trends and cause-effect relationships important.
Methods:	Market surveys still useful. Regression, time series and growth models justified.

Maturity

Data:	Considerable data available.
Time:	More uses of short-term forecasts; still need long-term projections, but trends change only gradually.
Methods:	Quantitative methods more useful. Time series helpful for trend, seasonal. Regression and exponential smoothing very useful.

Decline

Data:	Abundant data.
Time:	Shorter horizon.
Methods:	Continue use of maturity methods as applicable. Judgement and market surveys may signal changes.

Table 2 Summary of Commonly Used Forecasting Methods

Summary of Commonly Used Qualitative (Judgmental) Forecasting Techniques

Technique	PERT-Derived	Sales Force Polling	Consumer Surveys
Description	Based on three estimates provided by experts: pessimistic, most likely, and optimistic.	Based on sales force opinions; tend to be too optimistic.	Based on market surveys regarding specific consumer purchases.
Accuracy:			
Short-term (0-3 mon)	Fair	Fair to good	Fair to good
Medium-term (3 mon-2 yr)	Poor	Poor	Poor
Long-term (2 yr and over)	Poor	Poor	Poor
Identification of turning point	Poor to fair	Poor to good	Poor
Typical application	Same as expert opinions.	Forecasts of short-term sales forecasts.	Forecasts of short-term sales forecasts.
Data required	Same as expert opinions.	Data by regional and product line breakdowns.	Telephone contacts, personal interviews or questionnaires.
Cost of forecasting with a computer	Minimal	Minimal	Minimal
Time required to develop an application and make forecasts	Two weeks	Two weeks	More than a month

Continued on next page

Table 2   Summary of Commonly Used Forecasting Methods *(continued)*

Summary of Commonly Used Quantitative Forecasting Methods

Technique	PERT-Derived	Sales Force Polling	Consumer Surveys
Description	Functionally relates sales to other economic, competitive, or internal variables and estimates an equation using the least-squares technique.	A system of interdependent regression equations that describes some sector of economic sales or profit activity. The parameters of the regression equations are usually estimated simultaneously.	Models based on learned behavior: Consumers tend to repeat their part brand loyalty.
Accuracy:			
Short-term (0-3 mon)	Good to very good	Good to very good	Excellent
Medium-term (3 mon-2 yr)	Good to very good	Very good to excellent	Poor
Long-term (2 yr and over)	Poor	Good	Poor
Identification of turning point	Good	Excellent	Good
Typical application	Forecast of sales by product classes, forecasts of earnings, and other financial data.	Forecasts of sales by product classes, forecasts of earnings.	Forecasts of sales and cash collections.
Data required	At least 30 observations are recommended for acceptable results.	The same as for regression.	Data required for transaction probabilities.
Cost of forecasting with a computer	Varies with application	Expensive	Expensive
Time required to develop an application and make forecasts	Depends on ability to identify relationships	More than a month	More than a month

Continued on next page

Table 2 Summary of Commonly Used Forecasting Methods *(continued)*

Summary of Commonly Used Time Series Methods

Technique	Classical Decomposition	Box-Jenkins
Description	Decomposes a time series into seasonals, trend cycles, and irregular elements. Primarily used for detailed time-series analysis (including estimating seasonals)	Iterative procedure that produces an autoregressive, integrated moving average model, adjusts for seasonal and trend factors, estimates appropriate weighting parameters, tests the model, and repeats the cycle as appropriate.
Accuracy:		
Short-term (0-3 mon)	Very good to excellent	Very good to excellent
Medium-term (3 mon-2 yr)	Good	Poor to good
Long-term (2 yr and over)	Very poor	Very poor
Identification of turning point	Very good	Fair
Typical application	Tracking and warning, forecasts of sales and financial data.	Production and inventory control for large volume items, forecasts of cash balances and earnings.
Data required	A minimum of three years' history to start. Thereafter, the complete history.	Production and inventory control for large volume items, forecasts of cash balances and earnings.
Cost of forecasting with a computer	Minimal	Expensive
Time required to develop an application and make forecasts	One day	Two days

Source: Heavily adapted from Chambers, John, S. Mullick and D. Smith, "How to Choose the Right Forecasting Technique," *Harvard Business Review,* Vol. 49, no. 4, July-August 1971.

Table 3   The Forecasting Decision Matrix

Techniques	Timing: When Will the Forecast Be Used?		Rankings
Qualitative or Judgmental	Short Lead Time ↑↓ Long Lead Time		Expert Opinion Consensus Opinion Sales Force Polling Market Surveys Delphi
Time Series	Short Lead Time ↑↓ Long Lead Time		Trend Analysis Moving Average Exponential Smoothing Classical Decomposition Box-Jenkins
Causal, Markov, and Direct	Short Lead Time ↑↓ Long Lead Time		Markov Regression Leading Indicator Life Cycle Analysis Surveys Econometric Input-Outpur Analysis

Techniques	Form: Who Will Use the Forecast?		Rankings
Qualitative or Judgmental	Precise Forecast ↑↓ Imprecise Forecast		Market Surveys Expert Opinion Sales Force Polling Delphi
Time Series	Precise Forecast ↕ Imprecise Forecast		All Similar, Giving Precise Forecasts
Causal, Markov, and Indirect	Precise Forecast ↕ Imprecise Forecast		All Similar, Giving Precise Forecasts

Techniques	Data: How Much Are Available?		Rankings
Qualitative or Judgmental	Considerable Data Required ↑↓ Little Data Required		Generally All Similar, Little Historical Data Needed
Time Series	Considerable Data Required ↑↓ Little Data Required		All Similar, At Least Two Years' Data Usually Required
Causal, Markov, and Indirect	Considerable Data Required ↑↓ Little Data Required		Input-Out Analysis Econometric Life Cycle Analysis Markov Leading Indicator Regression Surveys

FORECASTING AND STATISTICAL SOFTWARE

There are numerous computer software that are used for forecasting purposes. They are broadly divided into two major categories: forecasting software and general purpose statistical software. Some programs are standalone, while others are spreadsheet add-ins. Still others are templates. A brief summary of some popular programs follows.

1. Sales & Market Forecasting Toolkit

Sales & Market Forecast Toolkit is a *Lotus 1-2-3 template* that produces sales and market forecasts, even for new products with limited historical data. It provides eight powerful methods for more accurate forecasts, and includes spreadsheet models, complete with graph, ready-to-use with your numbers. The Sales & Market Forecasting Toolkit offers a variety of forecasting methods to help you generate accurate business forecasts, even in new or changing markets with limited historical data.

The forecasting methods include:

- Customer Poll
- Whole Market Penetration
- Chain Method
- Strategic Modeling
- Moving Averages, exponential smoothing, and linear regressions

The Customer Poll method helps build a forecast from the ground up, by summing the individual components such as products, stores, or customers. Whole Market Penetration, Market Share, and the Chain Method are top-down forecasting methods used to predict sales for new products and markets lacking sales data. The Strategic Modeling method develops a forecast by projecting the impact of changes to pricing and advertising expenditures. Statistical forecasting methods include exponential smoothing, moving averages, and linear regression.

You can use the built-in macros to enter data into your forecast automatically. For example, enter values for the first and last months of a 12-month forecast. The compounded-growth-rate macro will automatically compute and enter values for the other ten months.

It is available from:

Lotus Selects
P.O. Box 9172
Cambridge, MA 02139-9946
(800) 635-6887   (617) 693-3981

2. Forecast! GFX

Forecast! GFX is a *stand-alone* forecasting system that can perform five types of time-series analysis: seasonal adjustment, linear and nonlinear trend analysis, moving-average analysis, exponential smoothing, and decomposition. Trend analysis supports linear, exponential, hyperbolic, S-curve, and polynomial trends. Hyperbolic trend models are used to analyze data that indicate a decline toward a limit, such as the output of an oil well or the price of a particular model of personal computer. *Forecast! GFX* can perform multiple-regression analysis with up to 10 independent variables.

> Intex Solutions
> 35 Highland Cir.
> Needham, MA 01294
> (617)449-6222   (617)444-2318 (fax)

3. ForeCalc

ForeCalc, Lotus and *Symphony Add-in,* feature the following:

- Uses nine forecasting techniques and includes both automatic and manual modes
- Eliminates the need to export or reenter data

You can use it in either automatic or manual mode. In automatic mode, just highlight the historical data in your spreadsheet, such as sales, expenses, or net income; then *ForeCalc* tests several exponential-smoothing models and picks the one that best fits your data.

Forecast results can be transferred to your spreadsheet with upper and lower confidence limits. *ForeCalc* generates a line graph showing the original data, the forecasted values, and confidence limits.

ForeCalc can automatically choose the most accurate forecasting technique:

- Simple one-parameter smoothing
- Holt's two-parameter smoothing
- Winters' three-parameter smoothing
- Trendless seasonal models
- Dampened versions of Holt and Winters's smoothing

ForeCalc's manual mode lets you select the type of trend and seasonality-yielding nine possible model combinations. You can vary the type of trend (constant, linear, or dampened), as well as the seasonality (nonseasonal, additive, or multiplicative).

Business Forecast Systems, Inc.
68 Leonard St.
Belmont, MA 02178
(617)484-5050

4. StatPlan IV

StatPlan IV is a *stand-alone* program for those who understand how to apply statistics to business analysis. You can use it for market analysis, trend forecasting, and statistical modeling.

StatPlan IV lets you analyze data by range, mean, median, standard deviation, skewdness, kurtosis, correlation analysis, one- or two-way analysis of variance (ANOVA), cross tabulations, and t-test.

The forecasting methods include multiple regression, stepwise multiple regression, polynomial regression, bivariate curve fitting, autocorrelation analysis, trend and cycle analysis, and exponential smoothing.

The data can be displayed in X-Y plots, histograms, time-series graphs, autocorrelation plots, actual vs. forecast plots, or frequency and percentile tables.

It is available from:

Lotus Selects
P.O. Box 9172
Cambridge, MA 02139-9946
(800) 635-6887   (617) 693-3981

5. Geneva Statistical Forecasting

Geneva Statistical Forecasting, a *stand-alone* software, can batch-process forecasts for thousands of data series, provided the series are all measured in the same time units (days, weeks, months, and so on). The software automatically explores as many as nine different forecasting methods, including six linear and nonlinear regressions and three exponential-smoothing techniques, before picking the one that best fits your historical data.

The program incorporates provisions that simplify and accelerate the process of reforecasting data items. Once you complete the initial forecast, you can save a data file that records the forecasting method assigned to each line item. When it is time to update the data, simply retrieve the file and reforecast, using the same methods as before.

Geneva Statistical Forecasting tries as many as nine forecasting methods for each line item.

Pizzano & Co.
800 W. Cummings Park
Woburn, MA 01801
(617)935-7122

6. SmartForecasts

SmartForecasts, a *stand-alone* forecasting software, does the following:

- Automatically chooses the right statistical method
- Lets you manually adjust forecasts to reflect your business judgement
- Produces forecast results

SmartForecasts combines the benefits of statistical and judgmental forecasting. It can determine which statistical method will give you the most accurate forecast, and handle all the math.

Forecasts can be modified using the program's EYEBALL utility. You may need to adjust a sales forecast to reflect an anticipated increase in advertising or a decrease in price. *SmartForecasts* summarizes data with descriptive statistics, plots the distribution of data values with histograms, plots variables in a scattergram, and identifies leading indicators.

You can forecast using single- and double-exponential smoothing, and simple- and linear-moving averages. It even builds seasonality into your forecasts using Winters's exponential smoothing, or you can eliminate seasonality by using times series decomposition and seasonal adjustment.

In addition, *SmartForecasts* features simultaneous multiseries forecasting of up to 60 variables and 150 data points per variable, offers multivariate regression to let you relate business variables, and has an Undo command for mistakes.

Smart Software, Inc.
4 Hill Rd.
Belmont, MA 02178
(800)762-7899   (617)489-2748 (fax)

7. Tomorrow

Tomorrow, a *stand-alone* forecasting software, uses an optimized combination of linear regression, single exponential smoothing, adaptive rate response single exponential smoothing, Brown's one-parameter double exponential smoothing, Holt's two-parameter exponential smoothing, Brown's one-parameter triple exponential smoothing, and Gardner's three-parameter damped trend. Some of the main features include:

- There's no need to reformat your existing spreadsheets. *Tomorrow* recognizes and forecasts formula cells (containing totals and subtotals, for example). It handles both horizontally and vertically oriented spreadsheets. It accepts historical data in up to 30 separate ranges.
- Allows you to specify seasonality manually, or calculates seasonality automatically.
- Allows you to do several forecasts of different time series (for example, sales data from different regions) at once.
- Recognizes and forecasts time series headings (names of months, etc.).
- Forecast optionally becomes normal part of your spreadsheet.
- Undo command restores original spreadsheet.
- Browse feature allows you to look at any part of the spreadsheet (including the forecast) without leaving *Tomorrow*.
- Checks for and prevents accidental overlaying of nonempty or protected cells.
- Optional annotation mode labels forecast cells, calculates MAPE, and, when seasonality is automatically determined, describes the seasonality.
- Comprehensive context-sensitive on-line help.

Isogon Corp.
330 Seventh Ave.
New York, NY 10001
(212)967-2424

8. Forecast Pro

Forecast Pro, a *stand-alone* forecasting software, uses artificial intelligence. A built-in expert system examines your data. Then it guides you to exponential smoothing, Box-Jenkins, or regression, whichever method suits the data best.

Business Forecast Systems, Inc.
68 Leonard St.
Belmont, MA 02178
(617)484-5050   (617)484-9219

9. MicroTSP

MicroTSP is a *stand-alone* software that provides the tools most frequently used in practical econometric and forecasting work. It covers the following:

1. Descriptive statistics
2. A wide range of single equation estimation techniques including ordinary least squares (multiple regression), two-stage least squares, non-linear least squares, and probit and logit.

Forecasting tools includes:

1. Exponential smoothing including single exponential, double exponential, and Winters smoothing.
2. Box-Jenkins methodology.

Quantitative Micro Software
4521 Campus Drive, Suite 336
Irvine, CA 92715
(714) 856-3368

10. Sibyl/Runner

Sibyl/Runner is an interactive, *stand-alone* forecasting system. In addition to allowing the usage of all major forecasting methods, the package permits analysis of the data, suggests available forecasting methods, compares results, and provides several accuracy measures in such a way that it is easier for the user to select an appropriate method and forecast needed data under different economic and environmental conditions. For details, see Makridakis, S., Hodgsdon, and S. Wheelwright, "An Interactive Forecasting System," *American Statistician,* November 1974.

Applied Decision Systems
Lexington, MA 02173
(614) 424-9820

11. Forecast Plus

Forecast Plus, a *stand-alone* forecasting software, uses artificial intelligence. A built-in expert system examines your data. Then it guides you to thirteen forecasting methods including exponential smoothing, Box-Jenkins, or regression, whichever method suits the data best.

The software features the following:

- A simple to use menu system
- High resolution graphic capability
- An ability to choose an appropriate forecasting technique
- An ability to handle all phases of forecasting analysis

- An ability to save forecasted data
- Optimization of smoothing constants

StatPac, Inc.
3814 Lyndale Avenue South
Minneapolis, MN 55409
(612) 822-8252

12. Other Forecasting Software

There are many other forecasting software such as *Autocast II* and *4 Cast* (Delphus, Inc. 103 Washington St. #348 Morristown, NJ 07960, (201) 267-9269) and *Trendsetter Expert Version* (Concentric Data Systems 110 Turnpike Rd., Westborough, MA 01581, (800) 325-9035).

13. General Purpose Statistical Software

There are numerous statistical software widely in use that can be utilized in order to build a forecasting model. Some of the more popular ones include Systat, SAS Application System, Statgraphics, SPSS, PC-90, Minitab, RATS, and BMD.

CHOOSING THE RIGHT PACKAGE

Since different software packages apply different techniques for many of the same tasks, it is a good idea to select a package that explains which method it is using and why, so you can eventually learn the most appropriate technique for your specific forecasting task. Figure 1 spells out your options in choosing the right package.

CONCLUSION

Today's financial managers have some powerful tools at hand to simplify the forecasting process and increase its accuracy. Several forecasting models are available, and the automated versions of these should be considered by any manager who is regularly called upon to provide forecasts. A personal computer with a spreadsheet is a good beginning, but the stand-alone packages currently available provide the most accurate forecasts and are the easiest to use. In addition, they make several forecasting models available and can automatically select the best one for a particular data set.

Figure 1 Which Forecasting Software Is Right for You? Know Your Options

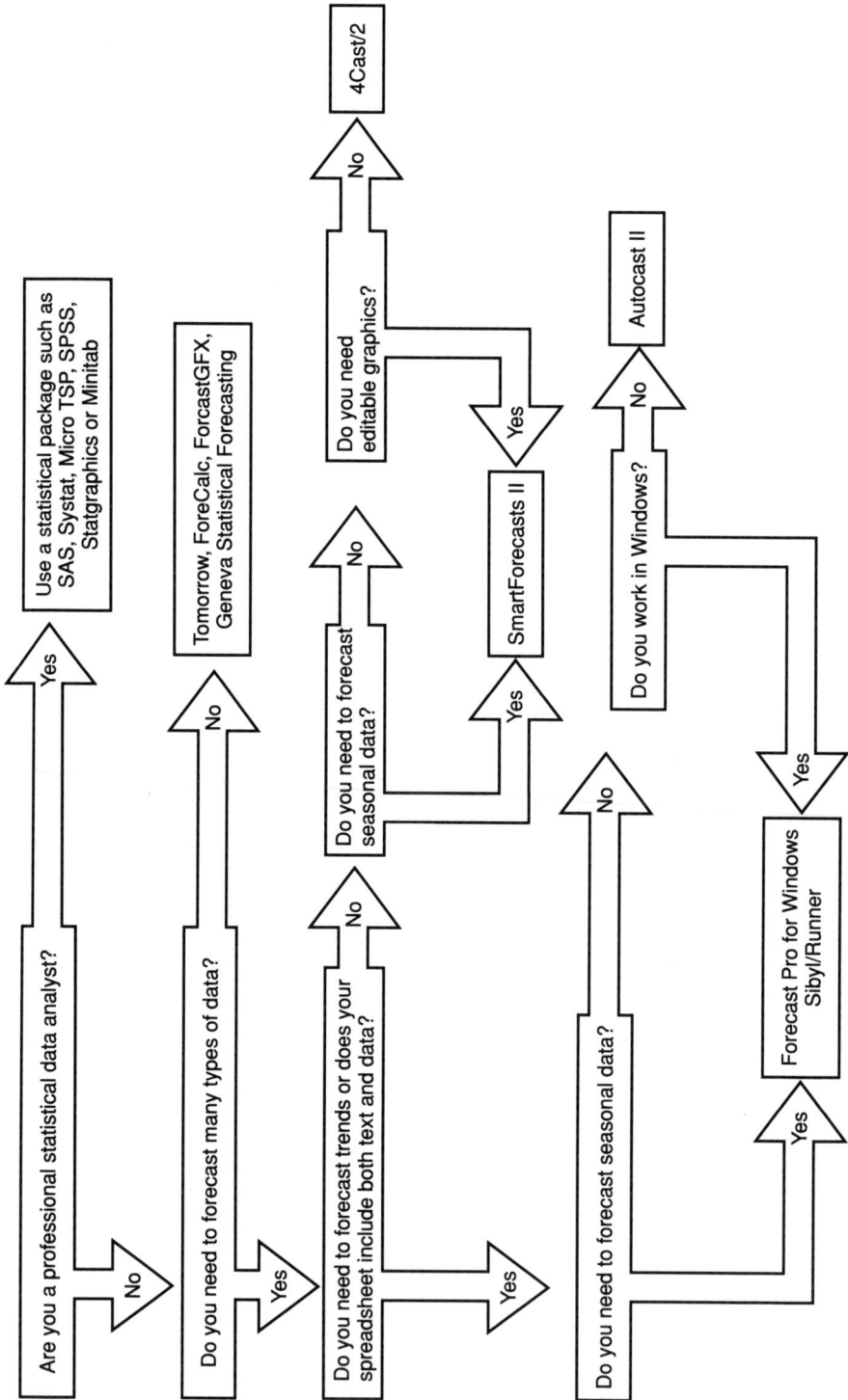

THE USE OF COMPUTER SOFTWARE IN MANAGERIAL ACCOUNTING*

Computer software is available for most areas of managerial accounting, including cost systems, activity-based costing (ABC), forecasting, budgeting and planning, inventory evaluation, material requirement appraisal, project management, capital budgeting, risk analysis, linear programming, and flow-charting. There are stand-alone packages, templates, and spreadsheet add-ins. The purpose of this chapter is to alert you to software useful in managerial accounting, including their features, applications, and suitability to meet a particular company's needs.

PLANNING AND BUDGETING

In the areas of planning and budgeting, many useful software exist.

Planet Corporation's *Business Maestro* generates operational and strategic business plans, while its *Budget Maestro* accounts for projects and evaluates trends in human resources and related costs.

Orange Systems' *ALCIE* provides capacity planning, purchasing job shop control, inventory management, and distribution.

Comshare's *Commander Budget* does budgeting with the use of spreadsheets and prepares management reports. It performs multidimensional analysis, analyzes budgeted figures and how they impact on the business, performs variance analysis, looks at "what-if" scenarios, performs

*This chapter was coauthored by Anique A. Qureshi, Ph.D., CPA, CIA, associate professor of accounting and information systems at Queens College.

exception analysis, and prepares management reports. It has application interfaces to financial databases.

Adaytum Software's *Planning* integrates budgeting links between cost centers, expense/sales, production plans, and cash flow analysis. Variance analysis is performed.

KCI Computing's *Control* is multidimensional and dynamic in handling budgets, planning models, consolidations, foreign currency translation, and cost allocations.

SAS Institute's *CFO Vision* software does costing by project, job, customer, and business segment. It performs financial consolidations, reporting, and analysis. It examines the reasons behind the figures and improves the timeliness and availability of business reporting.

Design Data Systems' *DDS Financial* integrates financial distribution, project management, and sales force modules.

TM1 software does multidimensional budgeting, forecasting, and reporting. It looks at various pricing scenarios, and evaluates the consequences of budget options.

Walker Interactive's *Business Framework Series* is used for budgeting, planning, forecasting, and analysis of cost and profitability.

Software 2000 Incorporated's *Infinium Financial Manager* performs purchase management, order processing, inventory control, quality control, and master production scheduling. It also does financial analysis, cost allocation, budgeting, specialized reporting, project management and currency management.

M-USA Business Systems' *Pacioli 2000* has modules for inventory control, job costing, budgeting, project control, cash management, assembly control and sales history.

Alcar is a strategic planning and appraisal software for Fortune 1000 companies. Users can assess if a plan or acquisition can be sufficiently funded by internal cash flow or outside financing.

Arbor Software's *Essbase* is a multidimensional database for business planning, evaluation, and management reporting.

Big Software's *Big Business* is a business management system integrating sales, marketing, inventory, and finance. It monitors inventory and tracks customers.

Synex Systems' *F9 Universal* software integrates budget reports.

Chief financial officers may use *CFO Spreadsheet Applications,* a spreadsheet template, for selecting optimal alternative capital investments and to manage cash flows.

Budget Express is a spreadsheet add-in facilitating "what-if" analysis comparing current to future values based on inputted changes. It makes the preparation of budgets and forecasts easy. For instance, by automatically totaling columns and rows, and calculating summary information by month, quarter, and year.

Pro Plan is a template used for financial planning and reporting. It prepares such financial statements as the income statement, balance sheet, and statement of cash flows. Ratio reports are also generated.

Profit Planner is a template used to project sales, cost of sales, operating expenses, assets, liabilities, and stockholders' equity. The financial figures for a company are compared to industry averages.

What-if Solver is an optimization add-in used to solve optimization problems subject to various constraints.

SRC Software's *Advisor Series* includes decision support, planning and forecasting, currency translations, and international consolidations. It handles complex budgeting and financial reporting situations.

Microcompass Systems' *QL Financials* is a software containing budget management, sales and purchase ordering, and inventory management. It has multicurrency features.

Social Systems' *Simplan* is used for integrated, multipurpose planning and budgeting. It can be used for revenue forecasting, econometric modeling, and time series analysis. In projecting sales, variables to be considered include selling price, units, availability of materials, interest rates, and market share.

Comshare's *Interactive Financial Planning System* (IFPS) is a multipurpose, interactive financial modeling system aiding in constructing, solving, and asking "what-if" questions of financial models. Interrelationships of data are considered. The output is in the form of spreadsheet. Data inputted into the model include revenue, selling price, volume, growth rate, variable cost, fixed cost, gross margin, contribution margin, net present value, internal rate of return, departmental figures, assets, working capital and market position. Alternative options to result in a desired outcome may also be presented. Information may be summarized in final form in terms of department, geographic region, product line, service line, customer, and supplier. IFPS has statistical functions that may be performed such as moving average, regression, and autocorrelation. Leading and lagging variables may be considered such as estimating future cash collections based on prior credit sales. There is a sampling routine based on examining the population considering the probability distribution. Sensitivity analysis (considering the effect of changing a variable on an outcome) is another feature of IFPS. There is also a goal seeking mode. Variables are analyzed as to their overall contributions. The software has graphic capabilities.

EXPRESS is used for financial planning and analysis including pro forma financial statements and risk analysis. There are statistical and analytical features such as percent difference, sorting, maximum-minimum, and leads and lags. Statistical functions include regression, cluster analysis, factor analysis, exponential smoothing, deseasonalization, and time series. There are graphic displays.

Ferox Microsystems' *ENCORE! PLUS* performs analytical functions and risk evaluation.

Micro Data Base's *GURU* is an expert system shell used to prepare reports, statistical analysis, and data management. The software provides managerial and financial advice for routine decisions.

Financial modeling for profit planning and budgeting can be done using a powerful spreadsheet program such as *Lotus 1-2-3, VP Planner, Javelin, Excel, SuperCalc, Quattro Pro, Educom Financial Planning Model* (EFPM), *XSIM, Empire, Foresight, Orion,* and *Venture.*

Ernst and Young's *Prosper* performs corporate financial planning and analysis of financial data. It prepares budgets and cash flow reports along with various visual presentations. It also performs investment analysis.

Smart Shop's *Cash Wise* prepares and evaluates cash flow projected statements to meet a company's strategic planning needs. It responds to "what-if" scenarios.

FuziWare Inc's *FuziCalc* is a unique spreadsheet that allows the decision maker to benefit from the structure of quantitative decision analysis, without forcing the user to provide very precise numerical inputs. The spreadsheet is based on the fuzzy set theory and fuzzy logic; it takes the computational complexity out of fuzzy arithmetic. Its primary strength is in modeling under uncertainty. As a spreadsheet, *FuziCalc* offers only the very basic features. Many features that one is accustomed to in conventional spreadsheets are lacking in *FuziCalc*. Most users will probably want *FuziCalc* to supplement, rather than replace, their conventional spreadsheet. *FuziCalc* is easy to use and offers powerful features to model decision making under uncertainty.

FORECASTING AND STATISTICS

There are numerous software for forecasting financial and nonfinancial information. Further, a spreadsheet template can produce sales and market forecasts for new products and services based on historical data.

Spreadware's *Pro Forma* prepares and analyzes pro forma financial statements. It tracks cash inflows and outflows, and conducts "what-if" evaluation among alternatives. Variance analysis is performed.

Business Matters Incorporated's *Cashe* is a comprehensive business forecasting and modeling software product. Financial planning is made easier through built-in formulas and linked relationships which may be adjusted with changing information. In-depth analysis is performed including that for changes in assumptions or scenarios. External factors are taken into account when forecasting such as changing interest rates. Analysis of variances, break-even, and risk evaluations are performed. It allows for the modification of business assumptions so financial forecasts may be reviewed, updated, and compared easily.

Geneva's *Statistical Forecasting* is a stand-alone package of forecasting data series over a specified time period (e.g., monthly). It includes linear and nonlinear regressions and exponential smoothing techniques.

Tomorrow is a forecasting software based on a mix of exponential smoothing and regression. Data used may be in up to 30 separate ranges. Seasonality adjustments are made. Forecasts may be made in different time series such as revenue by different geographic areas.

Forecast! GFX is a software for doing time series analyses (adjusted for seasonality), exponential smoothing, moving average, and decomposition. Trend applications are used to appraise data moving toward a lower limit. There is a multiple regression feature for a maximum of 10 explanatory variables used to explain a dependent variable.

Forecast Pro uses artificial intelligence in forecasting data while *Forecast Plus* uses artificial intelligence to evaluate data, and then selects an appropriate forecasting method among 13 available ones. There is optimization of smoothing constants and excellent graphics features.

ForeCalc is an add-in forecasting program. It can take historical data in a spreadsheet and, using exponential smoothing, determine the optimal projection based on the best fit of the data. The software also provides confidence limits. Information may be graphically displayed. Seasonal factors are considered in the model.

Sibyl/Runner is an interactive, stand-alone forecasting package allowing for data appraisal. It recommends the appropriate forecasting method for the given facts, compares results, and provides various accuracy measures.

Stat Plan IV is stand-alone software using statistics to solve business problems. It is very useful in management decision making. Data may be evaluated by range, standard deviation, mean, correlation, analysis of variance, and statistical significance. The forecasting methods include regression, autocorrelation, and exponential smoothing. Data may be graphically plotted including comparing actual to budget figures. Applications include trend depictions, financial modeling, and market appraisal.

Smart Forecasts automatically selects the best statistical technique to use based on the facts in a particular case. The approach allows for flexibility based on desired changes of the user via the program's *EYEBALL* utility. For example, the revenue projection is changed as changes are made in selling price, promotion plan, and consumers' disposal income. Forecasting may be in the form of moving averages and exponential smoothing. Seasonality can be adjusted, such as by using time series decomposition. It considers up to 60 variables.

Micro TSP involves econometric forecasting including descriptive statistics, multiple regression, and exponential smoothing.

Infordata Systems' *INQUIRE* is a special-purpose package used for decision support. Its features include query, data retrieval, and report generation.

Pendock Mallorn's *Pro-Forma Plus* is a financial forecasting model for preparing financial projections. "What-if" analysis for alternative assumptions is provided. It does variance, ratio, and break-even analysis.

General purpose statistical software include such packages as Statistical Package for Social Scientists (SPSS), Systat, Statgraphics, Statistical Analysis System (SAS), Statpack, and Minitab.

PROJECT PLANNING AND EVALUATION

Deltek Systems' *Costpoint* does project and activity accounting. It tracks by project costs and hours, compares estimates to actual for each task level, allocates costs, computes project revenue and profitability, tracks backlogs and purchase commitments, manages material, plans procurements, and fosters inventory control.

Concepts Dynamic's *CDI Project Control System* keeps track, manages, and reports revenue, cost, and time by major project.

Power Cerv's *INTERGY* software has features for order processing, purchasing, and project management.

Ross Systems' *The Renaissance CS Financials* monitors, projects and controls financial results. It includes features of purchase order, currency management, inventory control, budgeting, and bid tracking.

ProSoft Corporation's *Carpe Diem* software generates electronic timesheets and cost reports.

Marsh Software Systems' *Axiom Project Manager* tracks projects and performs job costing functions. There is an interface to financial software.

GBA Systems' *Pedigree Software* has modules for project accounting management and for preventive maintenance control.

Design Data Systems' *DDS Work Order Management* is for order entry and project reporting.

Design Data's *SQL*TIME* is software for project scheduling including scheduling for personnel and capital resources. It also resolves scheduling conflicts.

Open Systems' *Traverse* is an international accounting business software.

Proposed projects may be evaluated using the *Project Evaluation Toolkit* template. It uses various capital budgeting methods such as discounted cash flow analysis. Alternative scenarios may be appraised by changing variables such as cost or revenue projections, changes in timing of cash flows, and changes in beginning or interim dates.

CapPlans is a template appraising a proposed project using capital budgeting techniques such as payback period, internal rate of return, and net present value. It can forecast cash flows for up to 15 years. It prepares graphs and managerial reports. Sensitivity analysis routines are also included.

Computer Associates' *CA Masterpiece* performs job and project costing, inventory control, and time recording.

JBA International's *System 21* does costing by project and job, warehousing, work order processing, production control, manufacturing routing and scheduling, capacity planning, and analysis of material requirements.

J.D. Edward's *One World* does job- and project-cost accounting, time recording, warehouse management, production control, master production scheduling, routing, materials requirements planning, capacity requirements planning, and manufacturing control.

Oracle's *Financials* includes applications for job and project costing, work-order processing, production control and scheduling, bills of materials routing, plant capacity, and appraisals of materials.

FTP Software's *Group Works* enables efficient project organization, management, and execution. It performs scheduling assignments, tracks deadlines, assigns tasks, sets priorities, and monitors project status. The software also makes problem-solving suggestions.

CAPITAL BUDGETING

Worth It Software's *Worth It* does capital budgeting and analysis. It aids in the capital expenditure management process. The software is used to budget acquisitions by business units, project future operating changes, highlight negative trends, and appraise alternative investment plans and compare relative costs.

RISK ANALYSIS

Corporate risk may be analyzed using the spreadsheet add-in *@Risk*. It examines the effect of changing circumstances on the company's profitability, competitive reaction, and market position. Sampling methods are used for "what-if" analysis. The software indicates the degree of acceptability of the particular risk and recommends ways to reduce such risk including contingency plans.

Business Foundations' *Internal Operations Risk Analysis* appraises a company's areas of risk. It is an expert system developed around more than 150 interview questions. Based on the answers to the questions, the software prepares analytical and management reports summarizing the strengths and weaknesses in the company's operations. A risk rating (high, medium, low) is assigned to risk categories. It recommends for problem areas corrective steps. There is an upgrade for industry-specific situations.

Pleier and Associates' *ADM Plus* also performs risk management.

COST ACCOUNTING SYSTEMS

Maxwell Business Systems' *Job Cost Accounting and Management Information System* (JAMIS) is a job costing system. The software keeps track of employee hours worked, distributes (allocates) labor cost to the responsible unit, keeps track of department or product costs, distinguishes between direct labor and indirect labor, and manages inventory. Job costs are broken down into 100 different transactions. Since the software tracks all costs, it can also perform activity-based accounting because the jobs can be expressed in terms of activities or tasks. The activities can further be divided into subactivities or subtasks. Costs may be broken down by operation or function (e.g., buying materials). Costs may also be identified by division or department. JAMIS can also be used to budget by cost type (e.g., labor, materials and supplies). Costs may be tracked by project or contract for multiple years. It has time-based budgeting. It makes automated retroactive rate adjustments. The system supports contract types, cost classes, and job budgeting.

SouthWare Innovations' *Excellence Series* has features for job costing, contract management, service management and wholesale distribution.

Manufacturing Management Systems' *Quite-A-Profit* performs competitive pricing, target costing, and earnings appraisal by product or service.

Peachtree Accounting has a module for *Job Costing* to track and report the revenue, cost, and profit for individual jobs and projects.

Macola Software's *Progression Series Accounting and Distribution Software* has modules for job costing, inventory management, and shop floor control. It prepares many management reports, including those analyzing inventory and manufacturing operations.

Lawson Software's *Activity Manager* performs activity-based management and costing. It performs multi-dimensional data analysis, offers "what-if" scenarios, does cost allocations, performs inventory control, and aids in warehousing.

Abacus Data Systems' *ADAMS 4GL* aids in warehousing, shop-floor control, inventory control and management, work-order management, and customer analysis.

Prosoft's Inc's *Contractor Cost Accounting Package* offers speed and flexibility. The system is fully integrated and each module interacts with others. It offers modules for General Ledger, Accounts Payable, Job Costing, Payroll, Accounts Receivable, and Purchase Orders. Accounts are user-defined and can be referenced and accessed by name or by number. You can customize the program and its reports to suit your needs.

3C Software's *Impact* allows you to set up the system to use any cost accounting method—ABC, Traditional, Machine Based, Job, Direct, Japanese, JIT, or your own hybrid—so you can control how costs are calculated. It allows you to define the methodology, calculations, variables, products, processes, and reports. *Impact* contains an integrated, full-featured query and report writer which allows reports to be generated quickly and easily. Typical reports include: Product Cost Sheets, Product Pricing Sheets, Variance Reports, Inventory Valuations, Budgets and Forecasts, Profitability Reports, and other customized reports to meet cost reporting requirements.

ACTIVITY-BASED COSTING (ABC)

Activity-Based Costing (ABC) records cost based on manufacturing or service activities. Costs are assigned by activity and linked to the related products and services. Besides using spreadsheets for this purpose, there exists specialized software unique to ABC.

Price Waterhouse's *Activa* is activity-based software providing cost management for manufacturing and service companies. It does forecasting and simulation, product and service costing, activity-based budgeting, performance measurement reporting, profitability analysis, and valuing products and processes. It can manage information across multiple periods for multiple locations. For multinational companies, it can provide information in multiple currencies.

Armstrong Laing's *Hyper ABC* provides ABC costing information. It provides multidimensional cost object analysis which allows the user to evaluate business across customers, products, services, and distribution channels. It compares budget to actual figures for variance determination. "What-if" analysis is performed such as for the effects of changing variables on volume.

Sapling Software's *Net Prophet* does activity-based costing, constraint checking, capacity planning, "what-if" evaluation, scenario playing, and process analysis. It has flexible reporting, model validation, and graphic features.

ABC Technologies' *Oros EIS With Power Play* and *Oros 3.0* provide data warehousing, target costing, and process yield. They provide a picture of activity-based information through active charts, graphs, and crosstable formats. *Oros* does analysis of profitability and performance.

ICMS Software's *CMS-PC* software has spreadsheet-style screens for activity-based product costing. There is an activity dictionary database. The project manager helps with activity interview questions.

Syspro Impact Software's *IMPACT* ABC module appraises pre-production manufacturing and sales costs. There is online cost inquiry and simulated cost recovery.

Applied Computer Services' *PROFILE* ABC software performs analysis of activity data, profitability evaluation, appraisal of staffing requirements, reengineering, and makes activity-based management decisions.

Deloitte and Touche's *Strategic Cost Management* software assigns costs to activities, operations, products, and services. It manages cross-functional processes and involves "what-if" decision making.

Com MIT Systems' *Com MIT-ABC* tracks, collects, and allocates costs based on activities and cost drivers. "What-if" alternatives are evaluated.

Lead Software's *Activity Analyzer* involves product costing by activity and process. It tracks cycle time, capacity, cost drivers, rates, and manpower.

Automatic Consulting's *Cost Accounting System for Service Organizations* (CASSO) evaluates costs at the activity, work group and product levels.

There are many other software packages that may be used in activity-based costing including KPMG Peat Marwick's *Profit Manager,* Deloitte and Touche's *TR/ACM,* Coopers and Lybrand's *AB Cost Manager,* VanDeMark Products' *Alpha Cost,* Polaris Systems' *e3 System,* ABC Technologies' *Easy ABC,* and Marcam Corporation's *Prism.*

APPRAISAL OF INVENTORY

SQL Financials International's *Purchasing Control* is used to control the purchasing processes. It provides information about purchase orders, items, vendors, receipts, invoices, and payments.

Computer Associates' *ACCPAC* is a financial management software including order entry, inventory control, and job costing.

Lawson Software's *Insight Business Management System* includes supply chain and procurement, materials distribution, and audit controls.

Inventory Analyst is a template for computing economic order quantity, reorder point, and optimal inventory levels. Inventory history is depicted as a basis to predict future trends. It incorporates such forecasting techniques as moving average, exponential smoothing, and time series. Seasonal factors are incorporated.

Computron Software's *Computron Financials* does inventory stock control and time recording.

Dun & Bradstreet's *Smart Stream* does inventory stock control, warehousing, accounting for manufacturing processes, production scheduling and routing, and materials requirements planning.

Syspro Impact Software's *Impact Encore* does materials and resource planning to aid in cutting costs and improving delivery and quality. It has a purchase order system and can handle activity-based costing. It aids in tracking items through the production process.

Open Systems' *Accounting Software* inventory module features alternative costing and pricing methods including matrix pricing for customers. It can perform physical and cycle counts based on specified criteria. It also determines the level of inventory requiring a reorder. The package also has sales order functions.

Fourth Shift Corporation's *Manufacturing Software System* keeps track of inventory and manufacturing.

Best Ware's *MYOB* software's inventory module provides a listing of items, restocking information, and backorder listing.

EXECUTIVE MANAGEMENT GAMES

Computerized management games provide an excellent learning tool in making financial and managerial decisions so as to develop analytical and strategic abilities. The management game is a type of mathematical model and simulation. Simulation is designed to simulate a system and to generate a series of quantitative and financial results regarding system operations. In management games, participants make decisions at various stages in an attempt to better comprehend the external simulated environment. The games allow for a better understanding of the interrelationships of the various functions within the business and how such interactions affect overall performance. Some good management games are *PERT-SIM* for project planning and control, *Westinghouse Simulation Exercise* for distribution and logistics, *IBM Production Manpower Decision Model* for production and manpower scheduling, *MARKSIM* for marketing decision making, *X-Otol* for distribution analysis, Green and Sisson's *Materials Inventory Management Game* for inventory planning, and *FINASIM* for financial management simulation. (PERT stands for Program Evaluation and Review Technique which refers to the sequence of steps to complete a long-term project in the minimum time.) Other executive management games are Harvard University's *Harvard Business Game,* K. Goosen's *Management Accounting Game,* R. Schrieber's *Top Management Decision Game,* Carnegie Mellon's *COGITATE,* and R. Barton's *IMAGINIT Management Game.*

LINEAR PROGRAMMING

Linear programming is the allocation of limited capital and human resources to maximize gain or minimize cost. *Linear Interactive and Discrete Optimization* (LINDO) can be used to obtain optimal solutions.

What's Best! is a linear programming software aiding in determining the optimal allocation of limited capital, human, and financial resources. It considers time constraints and is ideal for management decision making. The objective of the software is to maximize revenue or minimize cost.

FLOWCHARTING

Flowcharts are diagrams that use standardized symbols, interconnected with flow lines, to visually represent complex procedures and data flow. People generally understand pictures better than words, and visual representation of data can often enhance understanding. Accountants can use flowcharts to document and understand the processing of information through the accounting system. Flowcharting software allows users to illustrate policies, processes, and procedures with diagrams. Typical flowcharting packages allow users to create diagrams for process and data flows, hierarchy charts, fishbone diagrams, structure charts, cause and effect diagrams, and organizational charts. Most packages contain templates or specialized libraries for symbols typically used by accountants and other professionals. It is also possible to create a custom library composed of frequently used shapes.

Micrografx Inc's *ABC FlowCharter* is a powerful and easy-to-use package. You can "drag and drop" hundreds of shapes from its extensive template library.

HavenTree Software Ltd.'s *EasyFlow* is a specialized drawing program. It uses the "drag and drop" approach to flowcharting. The user selects shapes from a palette and drops them into the appropriate place in the work area. *EasyFlow* comes with excellent documentation and tutorials.

Clear Software's *allCLEAR* takes a unique approach to flowcharting. To create a flowchart in *allCLEAR,* you write a script in the form of an outline. The punctuation in the script determines how the flowchart will look. The script approach makes it easy to create and modify even complicated flowcharts. However, the script approach greatly restricts the user's ability to customize flowcharts.

Patton & Patton Software Corp's *Flow Charting* is a good choice for the flowcharting beginner. It is a specialized drawing program and utilizes the drag and drop approach to flow charting. It comes with an excellent tutorial.

Aldus Corp.'s *IntelliDraw* is a powerful diagramming and illustration package. It is not exclusively a flowcharting package. *IntelliDraw* is ideal if you work with many types of drawings, and flowcharting is just one of your many needs.

Micrografx Inc.'s *ABC SnapGraphics* is a general purpose drawing and illustration package. It offers an easy-to-use interface and makes extensive use of drag and drop capabilities. It is ideal for an individual that prefers ease of use over esoteric features.

Shapeware Corp's *Visio* offers users a choice of drag and drop or script approach. Drawing flowcharts with *Visio* is very similar to manually drawing flowcharts. *Visio* works with computerized versions of plastic stencils that include cutouts for various symbols.

CORPORATE VALUATIONS

There are many reasons for determining the value of a company. The reason for the valuation might be for the purchase or sale of the business, mergers and acquisitions, buy-back agreements, expanding the credit line, or tax matter (see Table 1).

For buying or selling a business, a valuation might be important for establishing an asking or offering price. But what is the value of the business? Is it the value of the company's assets? Is it the value of the company's earnings? Is it the value of the company's loyal customers and good reputation? Is it something else? The answer is that it might be any of the above, or all of the above. Further, you must consider the type of business and its major activities, industry conditions, competition, marketing requirements, management possibilities, risk factors, earning potential, and financial health of the business.

Usually, *value* is determined by an interested party. Although there is usually no single value (or "worth") that can be associated with a business in all situations, there is usually a defendable value that can be assigned to a business in most situations. To be a proficient valuation analyst, a CFO requires analytical and writing skills. More specifically, one must be adept at financial analysis, economic forecasts, accounting and audit fundamentals, income taxes, and legal and economic research.

The valuation process is an art and not a science because everyone's perception is slightly different. This chapter provides basic steps involved in valuation and various ways to determine what a business is worth. Further, various Internal Revenue Service Revenue Rulings are presented, recommending specific valuation measures especially with regard to income tax issues.

To determine a company's value, the purpose of the valuation and an appropriate perspective must be specified. The perspective might be that

Table 1 Business Valuation Opportunities

- Buy-sell agreements
- Mergers, acquisitions, and spinoffs
- Liquidation or reorganization of a business
- Initial public offering
- Minority shareholder interests
- Employee stock ownership plans
- Financing
- Return on investment analysis
- Government actions
- Allocation of acquisition price
- Adequacy of life insurance
- Litigation
- Divorce action
- Compensatory damage cases
- Insurance claims
- Estate and gift taxes
- Incentive stock options
- Charitable contributions

Source: National Association of Certified Valuation Analysts

of a buyer, a seller, the IRS, or a court. When these are known, a business appraisal can be performed. Generally, the appraisal process determines the value of the business based on an asset, earnings (or cash flows), and/or market approach. In valuing the business, the following factors should be considered:

- History of the business
- Nature of the company
- Economic and political conditions
- Health of the industry
- Distribution channels and marketing factors
- Financial position
- Degree of risk
- Growth potential
- Trend and stability of earnings
- Competition
- Employee relationships
- Location
- Customer base

Corporate Valuations

- Quality of management
- Ease of transferability of ownership

STEPS IN VALUATION

As an initial step in valuation, the key financial information must be accumulated and analyzed including historical financial statements, projected financial statements, and tax returns. There must be familiarity with the business, including the company's strategic position in the industry. Further, the major assumptions of the valuation must be clearly spelled out. A variety of "what-if" scenarios must be investigated to reduce valuation errors. Figure 1 summarizes the basic steps in business valuations.

DEFINITIONS OF "VALUE"

Various individuals will have different ideas of how much a business is worth and how its value should be determined. Various individuals and groups might define 'value' differently.

FAIR MARKET VALUE

Fair market value is generally defined as the price at which property would change hands between a willing buyer and a willing seller, when neither is compelled to act and both have a reasonable knowledge of the relevant facts. With the asset approach, assets are valued at fair (i.e., appraised) market value.

Fair market value is often an important valuation definition in estate, gift, and other Federal tax related valuations. It is a well-accepted IRS and tax court concept. Generally, these groups will consider that a company's value is equivalent to its fair market value. Accordingly, a financial manager will need to consider this definition when performing valuations that may have the IRS as an interested party.

REPLACEMENT VALUE

Replacement value is the cost of replacing something. The use of the definition might be applicable for establishing "damages" in antitrust suits, in condemnation proceedings, and in similar situations. At times, the definition could be used in a Federal or state court. In some situations, replacement value might be determined to be a company's fair market value.

Figure 1 Steps in a Valuation

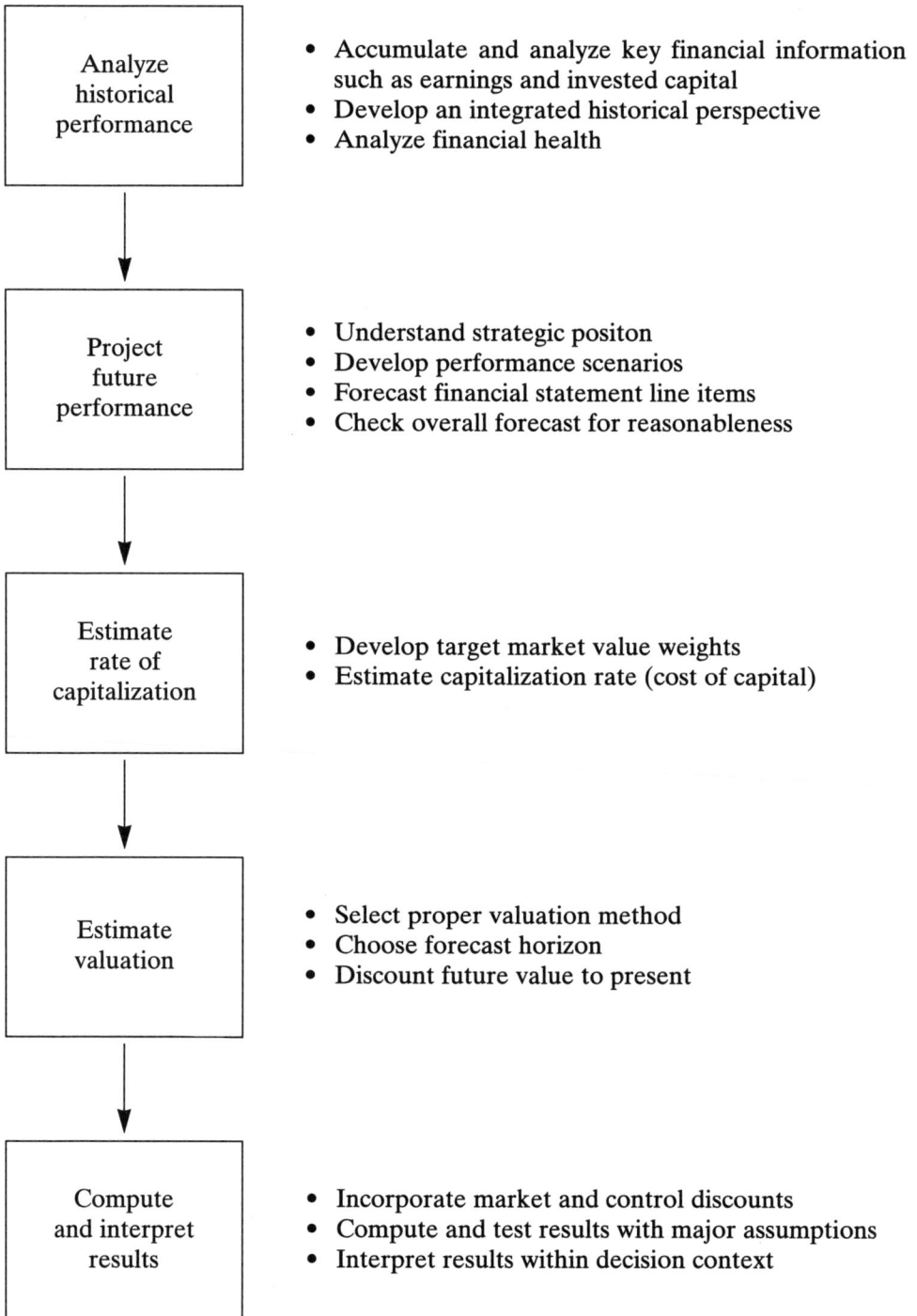

Analyze historical performance	• Accumulate and analyze key financial information such as earnings and invested capital • Develop an integrated historical perspective • Analyze financial health
Project future performance	• Understand strategic positon • Develop performance scenarios • Forecast financial statement line items • Check overall forecast for reasonableness
Estimate rate of capitalization	• Develop target market value weights • Estimate capitalization rate (cost of capital)
Estimate valuation	• Select proper valuation method • Choose forecast horizon • Discount future value to present
Compute and interpret results	• Incorporate market and control discounts • Compute and test results with major assumptions • Interpret results within decision context

LIQUIDATION VALUE

The lowest value associated with a business is its liquidation value. Liquidation value is, in effect, the value of an item (a business) sold to the highest available bidder. Typically, the seller is compelled to sell and the buyer knows of the seller's need to sell. Liquidation value is a depressed value. For a business, assets might be sold piecemeal. Usually, liquidation value is defined as the amount received by the seller after selling and administrative expenses are paid. At times, a company's liquidation value could be its fair market value.

"GOING CONCERN" VALUE

"Going concern" value is the opposite of liquidation value. Going concern value is the value of a business based on the presumption that the business will continue as an operating entity. That is, the company will not be liquidated. A company's going concern value will usually be its fair market value.

MATCHING VALUE DEFINITIONS AND VALUATION REASONS

An initial step in the business valuation process is to match the reason and perspective of the valuation with an appropriate definition of value. Note that each definition of "value" is not mutually exclusive. In a given situation, several definitions might concurrently apply. Table 2 shows valuation reasons and value definitions that might be connected with them.

GENERAL APPROACHES TO BUSINESS VALUATION

When a company is not publicly traded, willing buyers and willing sellers capable of establishing an independent and objective value for a business won't exist at most times when the valuation is needed. Accordingly, an

Table 2 Definition of Value

Valuation Reason	FMV	Liq. Value	Repl. Value	Going Concern Value
Purchase of Business	x		x	x
Sale of Business	x			x
Shareholder Litigation	x			x
Bankruptcy, Dissolution		x		
Recapitalization	x			x

estimate of the price at which the company might change hands between a willing buyer and a willing seller must be made. To do this, one or more of three approaches to valuation might be used.

Market Comparison

Values of comparable companies in the industry may provide useful norms. The idea is to establish the company's value based on actual sales that are indicative of the company's current value.

A basic requirement for using prior sales of a firm's ownership interests in the appraisal of its current value is that each prior sale be indicative of the existing circumstances of the company. If prior sales were made in the too distant past, or were of a form or substance not indicative of the subject company's current situation, the use of the sale(s) may not be appropriate for establishing the company's current worth. In particular, small sales of non-controlling interests and sales between related parties might not indicate the value of the company and its related ownership interests at the time of the sale. They would not be indicative of the company's current value either.

When comparable company sales are evaluated, the requirements are greater. Comparable company sales should only be used when the sales have occurred in the recent past and are of a sufficient size to appropriately establish a supportable value. They should be in the same industry. The companies should be similar in products and services offered, competitive positions, financial structures, and historical financial performance. Unfortunately, finding comparable companies is difficult because closely held company operating performance and sale information are frequently unavailable. *Note:* Refer to Sanders, John, *Biz-Comps Business Sale Statistics* published by BizComps (P.O. Box 711777, San Diego, CA 92171, www.bizcomps.com). This is the annual report compiling information for 1,600 businesses in many industries.

Earnings (or Cash Flows)

A second approach for business valuations is based on earnings. The earnings approach considers a company's value to be equivalent to its ability to create income (or cash flow). The concept is to associate the firm's income with a rate of return commensurate with the company's investment risk.

Assets

A third approach for establishing the value of a business is to consider the company's value to be equivalent to the value of its net tangible assets. For the dissolution of the business, the company's value might be based on the liquidated value of the company's assets. If the company is to be "duplicated," the company's value might be based on asset replacement values. If the company will continue as a going concern, the company's value might be based on the fair market value of the company's assets.

PERFORMING A GENERAL ANALYSIS OF THE COMPANY BEING VALUED

For appraisal purposes, the determination of a company's value is usually based on a market, earnings, and/or assets approach to value. There are various business valuation methods associated with each. To understand and apply the methods, one needs to understand various attributes about the company being valued. Especially, an understanding is necessary of the company's:

- industry
- customers and markets
- products and services
- employees and management
- assets, and
- historical and projected financial performance

Each of these areas will significantly affect the valuation of the business and the use of various valuation methods.

Industry Outlook

In assessing a company's industry, a CFO should evaluate the economic outlook for the industry, barriers to entry, government controls, and similar items. If the industry is expected to grow, firms in the industry might be perceived as being increasingly valuable. Further, you will need to consider competition. In a highly competitive industry, companies might be reduced in value because of competitive pressures, price discounting, etc.

Customers and Markets

In assessing a company's customers and markets, you should evaluate the company's key customers and the strength of the customers. If the company has many customers, and none of the customers represent a significant percentage of the sales of the company, the company might be increasingly stable. The company may have a lower associated investment risk. If a company has only a few large customers, you will need to weigh carefully the implications and the likelihood of its losing the customers.

Products and Services

In evaluating a company's products and services, you should look at their quality. You should compare the company's products and services with competitive products and services. Evaluate the company's investments in research and development and historical trends in sales and expenses of important products and services. Consider the number of products and services the company offers and the extent to which the company relies on one or several products or services for most of its sales and profits. When a company has only one or a few products or services, the competitive risks associated with the products and services become a factor. Generally, diverse and stable product lines might be associated with a stable company. Limited product lines might imply an increased investment risk.

Employees and Management

Qualified management usually means that the company is stable. Qualified management might enhance the value of the company. To the extent that a firm has had significant turnover in its management (and/or employees), the company might be considered a risky investment. In general, inexperienced management and a high turnover rate are indicative of a high-risk company.

Assets

Typically, the value of a company's tangible assets is a minimum value associated with the business. For valuation purposes, judge a company's assets to ensure that the assets are indeed valuable. Scrutinize in detail such items as obsolete inventory, old fixed assets, bad debts in accounts receivable, and capitalized expenses. For some assets, specific evaluations may be necessary.

Historical and Projected Financial Performance

Evaluating a company's historical and projected financial performance can be time consuming and complex. A CFO needs to establish the reliability of the company's historical financial statements and assess the implications of sales, expenses, and profits. Typically, for determining the value of a company, you evaluate the company's operating performance. Accordingly, you may have to remove the implications of non-typical and non-operating transactions included in the company's financial statements.

A company's historical financial statements might include excess compensation and significant perks to owners. Frequently, the CFO will need to add excess compensation paid to owners back to the company's income to fully understand the profitability of the company. Adjustments might also be made to the financial statements to convert cash basis statements to accrual basis statements. In particular, cash basis statements might not display accounts receivable, accounts payable, and accrued liabilities.

In evaluating a company's financial performance, the CFO will want to review various expense ratios as a percent of sales and various sales, income, and expense trends. In particular, the CFO would assess the financial statements for purposes of making assumptions about the future profitability of the company. Evaluate various company ratios and compare them with other companies in the industry. You might also develop projected financial statements for the company for three or more years.

BUSINESS VALUATION METHODS

There are numerous ways of determining the value of the business. Further, there are many possible combinations of various methods. Nine popular valuation methods are illustrated below.

1. Adjusted Net Assets Method

The adjusted net assets valuation method presumes the value of a company is equivalent to the value of its net tangible assets. Asset values are often based on fair market values when the company is expected to continue as a going concern, liquidated values when the company is not expected to continue as a going concern, and replacement values when the costs of duplicating the company are being assessed.

The fair market value of the net tangible assets of the company may be based on independent appraisal. An addition is made for goodwill. An investment banking firm, who handles the purchase and sale of businesses, may be hired to appraise the tangible property. Usually, the fair market value of the assets exceeds their book value.

An advantage of the adjusted net assets valuation method is that it is frequently easy to determine the value of a company's tangible net assets. A disadvantage of the method is that it ignores the important implications of company earnings. In many instances, an adjusted net assets valuation is a conservative valuation. It might be a minimum value associated with a business.

Example 1.

Net Tangible Assets (at Fair Market Value)	$12,000,000
Plus Goodwill	6,000,000
Valuation	$18,000,000

2. Gross Revenue Multiplier Method

The value of the company may be determined based on the revenue generating capacity of the company. For example, many Internet stocks that lose money in the short run and yet have great future earnings potential tend to derive their value from their revenue-generating capacity or registered member subscriptions. The formula for this method is as follows:

Value of the Business = Revenue x Gross Revenue Multiplier

The gross revenue multiplier used is the one customary in the industry. The industry norm gross multiplier is based on the average ratio of market price to sales typical in the industry.

If reported earnings are suspect, this method may also be advisable.

Example 2.

Gross revenue	$32,500,000
x Gross revenue multiplier	.4
Valuation	$13,000,000

3. Capitalization of Earnings Method

The capitalization of earnings valuation method is in many ways the opposite of the adjusted net assets valuation method. It uses income, as opposed to assets, to value the business. A variation of the method incorporates *cash flows* as opposed to earnings.

The capitalization of earnings valuation method is based on the notion that the investors will only acquire stock in a company if they can earn a rate of return that is high enough to offset the risks associated with the investment. The trade-off is the risk of the loss of the investment with the rate of return that might be realized. In general, high-risk companies need to yield high rates of return to stimulate equity investments. Low risk companies can produce lower rates of return and still attract equity investors.

The formula for the capitalization of earnings method follows:

Value of the Business = Earnings (or Cash Flow)/Capitalization Rate

Frequently, earnings or cash flow for this method is the current year's earnings (or cash flow), a simple average of two to five prior years, a weighted-average adjusted historical earnings, or the company's projected profit for the following year. The method presumes the earnings value used in the method is indicative of future earnings expectations on an ongoing basis. In this method, earnings can be any one of the following:

- Before-tax earnings
- After-tax earnings
- Earnings before interest and taxes (EBIT)

The capitalization rate is the rate of return an investor would expect to receive for investing in the company based on the company's perceived risk. It is typically a weighted cost of capital, weights being target mix of different sources of financing, equity or nonequity.

Two examples for this method are presented below.

Example 3.

Earnings (Simple Average)	$1,250,000
/Capitalization rate	10%
Valuation	$12,500,000

The following example uses weighted-average historical earnings, in which more weight is given to the most recent years. This is more representative than a simple average. Weighted-average makes sense because current earnings reflect current prices and recent business activity. In the case of a five-year weighted average, the current year is assigned a weight of 5 while the initial year is assigned a weight of 1. The multiplier is then applied to the weighted-average five-year adjusted historical earnings to derive a valuation.

Example 4.

Year	Historical Earnings	Weight	Total
20x0	$2,780,000	5	$13,900,000
20x1	$1,670,000	4	$6,680,000
20x2	$1,350,000	3	$4,050,000
20x3	$1,780,000	2	$3,560,000
20x4	$2,100,000	1	$2,100,000
		15	$30,290,000

Weighted average 5 year earnings:

$30,290,000/15 = $2,019,333

Weighted average 5 year earnings	$2,019,333
/Capitalization Rate (20%)	20%
Valuation	$10,096,667

4. Price-Earnings Ratio Method

For publicly traded stocks, stock trading prices are often directly proportional to earnings. Often, within industries, there is a consistency between companies. The price-earnings ratio method is predicated on the notion that price-earnings ratios (P/Es) of publicly traded stocks might be indicative of a closely held company's value. The notion is this: if the closely held company were publicly traded, it would trade at a price similar to the price at which comparable companies trade.

The formula for this method is as follows:

Value of the Business = Earnings per share (EPS)/Price-Earnings Multiplier (P/E)

Typically, earnings for this method is the most recent year's earnings per share (EPS) or an average of two to five prior years. The P/E multiplier is usually an historical average based on comparable, actively traded stocks. Some use a P/E ratio based on the most current period rather than an average of prior years.

Example 5.

Earnings after taxes	$1,000,000
Outstanding shares	250,000
Earnings per share (EPS)	$4
P/E ratio	15
Estimated market price per share	$60
x Number of shares outstanding	250,000
Valuation	$15,000,000

5. Dividend Payout (or Dividend Paying Capacity) Method

The dividend payout (or dividend paying capacity) valuation method presumes that the "compensation" for stock ownership is dividends. The method is based on the notion that a stock's value is related to the company's ability to pay dividends and the yield investors expect.

The dividend payout method involves the following steps:

1. Company's Dividend Paying Capacity = Earnings x Dividend Payout Percentage
2. Value of Business = Company's Dividend Paying Capacity/Dividend Yield Rate

Typically, earnings for this method is an average of two to five prior years. Some use before-tax profits. Others use after-tax profits. The dividend payout percentage and dividend yield rate are established with reference to comparable, publicly traded stocks. A variation of the method would establish the company's dividend paying capacity to be monies received by the owners of the closely held company as dividends, excess compensation, and perks.

Although the method is in infrequent use, the method incorporates some of the most defendable valuation principles of all methods.

Example 6.

Earnings after taxes	$1,000,000
Dividend payout percentage	40%
Dividend paying capacity	$400,000
/Dividend Yield Rate	4%
Valuation	$10,000,000

6. Excess Earnings Return on Assets Method

The excess earnings return on assets valuation method implies that within an industry, a given level of company assets will generate a particular level of earnings. To the extent a company has earnings above the expected level of earnings, the company is presumed to have an enhanced value. The enhanced value is attributed to goodwill (or intangible assets). The addition of the value of the goodwill and the fair market value of the net tangible assets equals the total valuation.

The excess earnings return on assets method involves the following steps:

1. Industry Expected Earnings = Company Assets x Industry Expected Return on Assets
2. Excess Earnings = Company Earnings – Industry Expected Earnings
3. Goodwill (intangible assets) = Excess Earnings/Capitalization Rate
4. Value of the Business = Goodwill + Fair Market Value of Net Tangible Assets

This method has several variations. Gross assets or net assets and book values or fair market values might be used to calculate industry earnings and excess earnings.

As per IRS Revenue Ruling 59-60 (to be discussed later), the IRS recommends this method to value a business for tax purposes.

Example 7.

Year	Net Tangible Assets	Assets	Weight Total
20x0	$10,000,000	1	$10,000,000
20x1	$14,000,000	2	$28,000,000
20x2	$18,000,000	3	$54,000,000
20x3	$19,000,000	4	$76,000,000
20x4	$18,500,000	5	$92,500,000
		15	$260,500,000

Weighted Average Net Tangible Assets	
$260,500,000/15 = $17,366,667	
Weighted Average Earnings (5 years)—Assumed	$1,800,000
Minus Industry Rate of Return on Weighted-Average	
Net Tangible Assets ($17,366,667 x 10%)	1,736,667
Excess Earnings	$63,333
/Capitalization Factor (20%)	0.2
Plus Goodwill (Intangibles)	$316,667
Plus Fair Market Value of Net Tangible Assets	$16,000,000
Valuation	$16,316,667

7. Excess Earnings Return on Sales Method

The excess earnings return on sales valuation method values a company based on sales, earnings, and assets. Generally, the method implies that within an industry, a given level of sales will generate a given level of earnings. When a company has earnings above the industry's expected level of earnings, the company is considered to have goodwill (or intangible assets). The value of goodwill plus the fair market value of the net tangible assets is considered to be the value of the company.

The excess earnings return on sales method involves the following steps:

1. Industry Expected Earnings = Company Sales x Industry Expected Return on Sales

2. Excess Earnings = Company Earnings – Industry Expected Earnings
3. Goodwill (Intangible Assets) = Excess Earnings/Capitalization Rate
4. Value of the Business = Goodwill + Fair Market Value of Net Tangible Assets

Variations in this method include the use of the Company's current year's sales or a two to five year average for computing the industry expected profits.

Example 8.

Year	Sales	Weight	Total
20x0	$11,100,000	1	$11,100,000
20x1	$12,500,000	2	$25,000,000
20x2	$20,000,000	3	$60,000,000
20x3	$21,000,000	4	$84,000,000
20x4	$24,200,000	5	$121,000,000
		15	$301,100,000

Weighted Average Sales
    $301,100,000/15 = $802,933

Weighted Average Earnings (5 years)—Assumed	$1,800,000
Minus Industry Rate of Return on Weighted-Average	
Sales ($20,073,333 x 4%)	802,933
Excess Earnings	$ 997,067
/Capitalization Factor (20%)	0.2
Valuation of Goodwill (Intangibles)	$4,985,333
Plus Fair Market Value of Net Tangible Assets	$16,000,000
Valuation	$20,985,333

8. Discounted Cash Flow Method

The discounted cash flow (DCF) method equates the value of a business with the cash flows the business is expected to create.

The discounted cash flow method presumes that the purpose of a company is to generate cash flow (or earnings) and therefore, assets, distribution channels, etc., have a value related to the cash flows they are able to create. Conceptually, the method is similar to the capitalization of earnings valuation method except that in the discounted cash flow method projected earnings (or cash flows) as opposed to historical earnings (or cash flows) are assessed. If the growth rate is used to project future earnings, the rate may be based on prior growth rate, future expectations, and the inflation rate. The discount rate may be based on the market interest rate of a low risk asset investment.

The formula for the discounted cash flow method follows:

Value of the Business =
Present Value of the Earnings (or Cash Flow) Projection
+ Present Value of Terminal Value (Selling Price)

Typically, cash flows are projected for at least five years and a terminal value (or selling price) is established for the value of the business at the end of the term.

Example 9.

Year	Cash Flows (7% growth rate)	Present Value (PV) Factor at a 10% discount rate	Total PV
20x0	$500,000	0.909	$454,500
20x1	$535,000	0.826	$441,910
20x2	$572,450	0.751	$429,910
20x3	$612,522	0.683	$418,352
20x4	$655,398	0.621	$407,002
Present Value of Future Earnings			$2,151,674

If the anticipated selling price at the end of
    year 20x4 is $15,000,000, the valuation
    of the business equals:

Present value of future earnings	$2,151,674
Present value of selling price $18,000,000 × .621	$11,178,000
Valuation	$13,329,674

9. Combination Valuation Method

The combination valuation method is not really a method; it's a combination of other methods. Often, the use of a combination method establishes a more reasonable value for a business than any single method. In particular, in a combination method earnings, assets, comparable companies, prior sales of company stock, and other important valuation concepts might be accounted for.

Further, the valuation of the company may be estimated based on a weighted-average value of several methods. The most weight should typically be placed on the earnings method and the least on the asset approaches.

Example 10.

Method	Valuation Amount	Weight	Total
Adjusted Net Assets	$18,000,000	1	$18,000,000
Excess Earnings on Rate of Return	$20,985,333	2	$41,970,666
		3	$59,970,666
Total/3 = $69,970,666/3 = $19,990,222			
Valuation			$19,990,222

Generally, before a combination method should be used, it should be established that the combination method results in a better valuation than any method individually, and that the use of each method in the combination supports the final valuation.

MARKETABILITY DISCOUNTS

Generally, a business ownership interest that can be sold quickly will be worth more than a similar ownership interest that cannot be sold quickly. In various business valuation methods, this implication may or may not be considered. When it is not, a marketability discount might be associated with the value of the ownership interest otherwise determined. A marketability discount is the reduction in the value of a company (or ownership interest) because the company (or ownership interest) might take considerable time to sell.

There are differences of opinion about marketability discounts. The IRS objects to them and will argue that the implications of marketability will have been accounted for elsewhere in the valuation process. Many believe that statistics prove there is in fact a depressed value for closely held company ownership interests, and they might assign discounts as high as 25% to 45% to account for this.

In assigning a marketability discount, some analysts compute the cost of taking the company public and deduct the amount from the value of the company otherwise determined. The presumption is that if the company is taken public, its ownership interests will be marketable.

CONTROL PREMIUMS AND DISCOUNTS

A business valuation does not have to be restricted to the valuation of an entire company. Frequently, partial ownership interests are valued for purchase or sale, divorce proceedings, estate planning, and other reasons.

When a partial ownership interest is appraised, it is not necessarily true that its value is equivalent to its ownership percentage times the value of the company. Generally, to the extent the ownership interest can control the activities of the business, the ownership interest may have an enhanced value. To the extent the ownership interest has little control over the operations of the company, the ownership interest might have a reduced value. Practitioners frequently account for this with control premiums and lack of control discounts.

For closely held companies, noncontrolling ownership interests can have a depressed value. The company might not be particularly marketable, and the noncontrolling interests might have an even greater lack of appeal because of their inability to influence the payment of dividends and the general operations of the company.

In developing control premiums and lack of control discounts, the circumstances of the ownership interests must be considered. Before a discount or premium is assigned, it should be determined that in fact an ownership interest has an increased or decreased value based on control/lack of control implications. For example, in a company where the father is the controlling owner and two children are the noncontrolling owners, circumstances might indicate that the noncontrolling owners are in fact receiving dividends, etc., commensurate with the value of their ownership percentages. Accordingly, depending on the purpose of the valuation, the assignment of a discount to the non-controlling interests might not be appropriate. Before assigning premiums or discounts, it is very important to ensure that the control/lack of control implications were not accounted for in some other way in the valuation process.

SUMMARY

Performing a business valuation is not a simple task. Although a business valuation might seem overwhelming at first, valuation concepts are in fact very logical and intuitive. The major issue is to clearly understand the concepts of valuation and how the concepts are used by the interested party. The next step is to fully investigate the company being valued, its industry, and various implications that might affect its value. Financial forecasting, analytical reviews, sales forecasting, financial analysis, and various planning activities are an important part of the business valuation process.

REVENUE RULING 59–60

In valuing the stock of closely held corporations, or the stock of corporations where market quotations are not available, all other available financial data, as well as all relevant factors affecting the fair market value must be considered for estate tax and gift tax purposes. No general formula may be given that is applicable to the many different valuation situations arising in the valuation of such stock. However, the general approach, methods, and factors which must be considered in valuing such securities are outlined.

Section 1. Purpose

The purpose of this Revenue Ruling is to outline and review the approach, methods and factors to be considered in valuing shares of the capital stock of closely held corporations for estate tax and gift tax purposes. The methods discussed herein will apply likewise to the valuation of corporate stocks on which market quotations are either unavailable or are of such scarcity that they do not reflect the fair market value.

Section 2. Background and Definitions

01. All valuations must be made in accordance with the applicable provisions of the Internal Revenue Code of 1954 and the Federal Estate Tax & Gift Tax Regulations. Sections 2031(a), 2032 and 2512(a) of the 1954 Code (Sections 811 and 1005 of the 1939 Code) require that the property to be included in the gross estate, or made the subject of a gift, shall be taxed on the basis of the value of the property at the time of death of the decedent, the alternative date if so elected, or the date of gift.

02. Section 20.2031-1(b) of the Estate Tax Regulations (Section 81.10 of the Estate Tax Regulations 105) and Section 25.2512-1 of the Gift Tax Regulations (Section 86.19 of Gift Tax Regulations 108) define fair market value, in effect, as the price at which the property would change hands between a willing buyer and a willing seller when the former is not under any compulsion to buy and the latter is not under any compulsion to sell, both parties having reasonable knowledge of relevant facts. Court decisions frequently state in addition that the hypothetical buyer and seller are assumed to be able, as well as willing, to trade and to be well informed about the market for the property.

03. Closely held corporations are those company shares owned by a relatively limited number of stockholders. Often the entire stock issue is held by one family. The result of this situation is that little, if any, trading in the shares takes place. There is, therefore, no established market for the stock and such sales as occur at irregular intervals seldom reflect all of the elements of a representative transaction as defined by the term "fair market value."

Section 3. Approach To Valuation

01. A determination of fair market value, being a question of fact, will depend upon the circumstances in each case. No formula can be devised that will be generally applicable to the multitude of different valuation issues arising in estate and gift tax cases. Often, an appraiser will find wide differences of opinion as to the fair market value of a particular stock. In resolving such differences, he or she should maintain a reasonable attitude in recognition of the fact that valuation is not an exact science. A sound valuation will be based upon all the relevant facts, but the elements of common sense, informed judgment, and reasonableness must enter into the process of weighing those facts and determining their aggregate significance.

02. The fair market value of specific shares of stock will vary as general economic conditions change from "normal" to "boom" or "depression," that is, according to the degree of optimism or pessimism with which the investing public regards the future at the required date of appraisal. Uncertainty as to the stability or continuity of the future income from a property decreases its value by increasing the risk of loss of earnings and value in the future. The value of shares of stock of a company with very uncertain future prospects is highly speculative. The appraiser must exercise his judgment as to the degree of risk attaching to the business of the corporation which issued the stock, but that judgment must be related to all of the other factors affecting value.

03. Valuation of securities is, in essence, a prophecy as to the future and must be based on facts available at the required date of appraisal. As a generalization, the prices of stocks which are traded in volume in a free and active market by informed persons best reflect the consensus of the investing public as to what the future holds for the corporations and industries represented. When a stock is closely held, is traded infrequently, or is traded in an erratic market, some other measure of value must be used. In many instances, the next best measure may be found in the prices at which the stocks of companies engaged in the same or a similar line of business are selling in a free and open market.

Section 4. Factors To Consider

01. It is advisable to emphasize that in the valuation of the stock of closely held corporations or the stock of corporations where market quotations are either lacking or too scarce to be recognized, all available financial data, as well as all relevant factors affecting the fair market value, should be considered. The following factors, although not all inclusive are fundamental and require careful analysis in each case:

(a) Nature of the business and the history of the enterprise from its inception.

(b) Economic outlook in general and the condition and outlook of the specific industry in particular.

(c) Book value of the stock and the financial condition of the business.

(d) Earning capacity.

(e) Dividend-paying capacity.

(f) Whether or not the enterprise has goodwill or other intangible value.

(g) Sales of the stock and the size of the block of stock to be valued.

(h) Market price of stocks of corporations engaged in the same or a similar line of business having their stocks actively traded in a free and open market, either on an exchange or over-the-counter.

02. The following is a brief discussion of each of the foregoing factors.

(a) The history of a corporate enterprise will show its past stability or instability, its growth or lack of growth, the diversity or lack of diversity of its operations, and other facts to form an opinion of the degree of business risk. For an enterprise which changed its form of organization but carried on the same or closely similar operations of its predecessor, the history of the former enterprise should be considered. The detail considered should increase with the date of appraisal, since recent events are of greatest help in predicting the future—but a study of gross and net income, and of dividends covering a long prior period, is highly desirable. The history to be studied should include, but need not be limited to, the nature of the business, its products or services, its operating and investment assets, capital structure, plant facilities, sales records and management, all of which should be considered as of the date of the appraisal, with due regard for recent significant changes. Events of the past that are unlikely to recur in the future should be discounted, since value has a close relation to future expectancy.

(b) A sound appraisal of a closely held stock must consider current and prospective economic conditions as of the date of appraisal, both in the national economy and in the industry or industries with which the corporation is allied. It is important to know that the company is more or less successful than its competitors in the same industry, or that it is maintaining a stable position with respect to competitors. Equal or even greater significance may attach to the ability of the industry with which the company is allied to compete with other industries. Prospective competition which has not been a factor in prior years should be given careful attention. For example, high profits due to the novelty of its product and the lack of competition often lead to increasing competition. The public's appraisal of the future prospects of competitive industries or of competitors within an industry may be indicated by price trends in the markets for commodities and for securities. The loss of the manager of a so-called 'one-man' business may have a depressing effect upon the value of the stock of such business, particularly if there is a lack of trained personnel capable of succeeding to the management of the enterprise. In valuing the stock of this type of business, therefore, the effect of the loss of the manager on the future expectancy of the business, and the absence of management-succession potentialities are pertinent factors to be taken into consideration. On the other hand, there may be factors which offset, in whole or in part, the loss of the manager's services. For instance, the nature of the business and of its assets may be such that, they will not be impaired by the loss of the manager. Furthermore, the loss may be adequately covered by life insurance, or competent management might be employed on the basis of the consideration paid for the former manager's services. These, or other offsetting factors, if found to exist, should be carefully weighed against the loss of the manager's services in valuing the stock of the enterprise.

(c) Balance sheets should be obtained, preferably in the form of comparative annual statements for two or more years immediately preceding the date of appraisal, together with a balance sheet at the end of the month preceding that date, if corporate accounting will permit. Any balance sheet descriptions that are not self-explanatory, and balance sheet items comprehending diverse assets or liabilities, should be clarified in essential detail by supporting supplemental schedules. These statements usually will disclose to the appraiser:

- liquid position (ratio of current assets to current liabilities);
- gross and net book value of principal classes of fixed assets;
- working capital;
- long-term indebtedness;
- capital structure;
- net worth

Consideration should be given to any assets not essential to the operation of the business, such as investments in securities, real estate, etc. In general, such nonoperating assets will command a lower rate of return than do the operating assets, although in exceptional cases the reverse may be true. In computing the book value per share of stock, assets of the investment type should be revalued on the basis of their market price and the book value adjusted accordingly. Comparison of the company's balance sheets over several years may reveal, among other facts, such developments as the acquisition of additional production facilities or subsidiary companies, improvement in financial position, and details as to recapitalizations and other changes in the capital structure of the corporation. If the corporation has more than one class of stock outstanding, the charter or certificate of incorporation should be examined to ascertain the explicit rights and privileges of the various stock issues including:

- voting powers,
- preference as to dividends, and
- preference as to assets in the event of liquidation

(d) Detailed profit-and-loss statements should be obtained and considered for a representative period immediately prior to the required date of appraisal, preferably five or more years.

Such statements should show

- gross income by principal items;
- principal deductions from gross income including major prior items of operating expenses, interest and other expense on each item of long-term debt, depreciation and depletion if such deductions are made, officers' salaries, in total if they appear to be reasonable or in detail if they seem to be excessive, contributions (whether or not deductible for tax purposes) that the nature of its business and its community position require the corporation to make, and taxes by principal items, including income and excess profits taxes;
- net income available for dividends;

- rates and amounts of dividends paid on each class of stock,
- remaining amount carried to surplus; and
- adjustments to, and reconciliation with, surplus as stated on the balance sheet. With profit and loss statements of this character available, the appraiser should be able to separate recurrent from nonrecurrent items of income and expense, to distinguish between operating income and investment income, and to ascertain whether or not any line of business in which the company is engaged is operated consistently at a loss and might be abandoned with benefit to the company. The percentage of earnings retained for business expansion should be noted when dividend paying capacity is considered. Potential future income is a major factor in many valuations of closely-held stocks, and all information concerning past income which will be helpful in predicting the future should be secured. Prior earnings records usually are the most reliable guide as to the future expectancy, but resort to arbitrary five-or-ten-year averages without regard to current trends or future prospects will not produce a realistic valuation. If, for instance, a record of progressively increasing or decreasing net income is found, then greater weight may be accorded the most recent years' profits in estimating earning power. It will be helpful, in judging risk and the extent to which a business is a marginal operator, to consider deductions from income and net income in terms of percentage of sales. Major categories of cost and expense to be so analyzed include the consumption of raw materials and supplies in the case of manufacturers, processors and fabricators; the cost of purchased merchandise in the case of merchants; utility services; insurance; taxes; depletion or depreciation; and interest

(e) Primary consideration should be given to the dividend-paying capacity of the company rather than to dividends actually paid in the past. Recognition must be given to the necessity of retaining a reasonable portion of profits in a company to meet competition. Dividend-paying capacity is a factor that must be considered in an appraisal, but dividends actually paid in the past may not have any relation to dividend paying capacity. Specifically, the dividends paid by a closely held family company may be measured by the income needs of the stockholders or by their desire to avoid taxes on dividend receipts, instead of by the ability of the company to pay dividends. Where an actual or effective controlling interest in a corporation is to be valued, the dividend factor is not a material element, since the payment of such dividends is discretionary with the controlling stockholders. The individual or group in control can substitute salaries and bonuses for dividends, thus reducing net income and understating the dividend-paying capacity of the company. It follows, therefore, that dividends are a less reliable criteria of fair market value than other applicable factors.

(f) In the final analysis, goodwill is based upon earning capacity. The presence of goodwill and its value, therefore, rests upon the excess of net earnings over and above a fair return on the net, tangible assets. While the element of goodwill may be based primarily on earnings, such factors as the prestige and renown of the business, the ownership of a trade or brand name, and a record of successful operation over a prolonged period in a particular locality, also may furnish support for the inclusion of intangible value. In some instances, it may not be possible to make a separate appraisal of the tangible and intangible assets of the business. The enterprise has a value as an entity. Whatever intangible value there is, which is supportable by the facts, may be measured by the amount by which the appraised value of the tangible assets exceeds the net book value of such assets.

(g) Sales of stock of a closely held corporation should be carefully investigated to determine whether they represent transactions at arm's length. Forced or distress sales do not ordinarily reflect fair market value nor do isolated sales in small amounts necessarily control as the measure of value. This is especially true in the valuation of a controlling interest in a corporation. Since, in the case of closely held stocks, no prevailing market prices are available, there is no basis for making an adjustment for blockage. It follows, therefore, that such stocks should be valued upon a consideration of all the evidence affecting fair market value. Although it is true that a minority interest in an unlisted corporation's stock is more difficult to sell than a similar block of listed stock, it is equally true that control of a corporation, either actual or in effect, representing as it does an added element of value, may justify a higher value for a specific block of stock.

(h) Section 2031(b) of the Code states, in effect, that in valuing unlisted securities the value of stock or securities of corporations engaged in the same or a similar line of business which are listed on an exchange should be taken into consideration along with all other factors. An important consideration is that the corporations to be used for comparisons have capital stocks which are actively traded by the public. In accordance with Section 2031(b) of the Code, stocks listed on an exchange are to be considered first. However, if sufficient comparable companies whose stocks are listed on an exchange cannot be found, other comparable companies which have stocks actively traded on the over-the-counter market also may be used. The essential factor is that whether the stocks are sold on an exchange or over-the-counter there is evidence of an active, free public market for the stock as of the valuation date. In selecting corporations for comparative purposes, care should be taken to use only comparable companies (corporations specified in the statute have similar lines of business). However, consideration must be given to other relevant factors in order that the most valid comparison possible be obtained. For example, a corporation having one or more issues of preferred stock, bonds or debentures in addition to its common stock should not be considered to be directly comparable to one having only common stock outstanding. In like manner, a company with a declining business and decreasing markets is not comparable to one with a record of current progress and market expansion.

Section 5. Weight To Be Accorded Various Factors

The valuation of closely held corporate stock entails the consideration of all relevant factors as stated in Section 4. Depending upon the circumstances in each case, certain factors may carry more weight than others because of the nature of the company's business. To illustrate:

- Earnings may be the most important criterion of value in some cases whereas asset value will receive primary consideration in others. In general, the appraiser will accord primary consideration to earnings when valuing stocks of companies which sell products or services to the public; conversely, in the investment or holding type of company, the appraiser may accord the greater weight to the assets underlying the security to be valued.

- The value of the stock of a closely held investment or real estate holding company, whether or not family owned, is closely related to the value of the assets underlying the stock. For companies of this type the appraiser should determine the fair market values of the assets of the company. Operating expenses of such a company and the cost of liquidating it, if any, merit consideration when appraising the relative values of the stock and the underlying assets. The market values of the underlying assets give due weight to potential earnings and dividends of the particular items of property underlying the stock, capitalized at rates deemed proper by the investing public at the date of appraisal. A current appraisal by the investing public should be superior to the retrospective opinion of an individual. For these reasons, adjusted net worth should be accorded greater weight in valuing the stock of a closely held investment or real estate holding company, whether or not family owned, than any of the other customary yardsticks of appraisal, such as earnings and dividend paying capacity.

Section 6. Capitalization Rates

In the application of certain fundamental valuation factors, such as earnings and dividends, it is necessary to capitalize the average, or current, results at some appropriate rate. A determination of the proper capitalization rate presents one of the most difficult problems in valuation. That there is no ready or simple solution will become apparent by a cursory check of the rates of return and dividend yields in terms of the selling prices of corporate shares listed on the major exchanges of the country. Wide variations will be found even for companies in the same industry. Moreover, the ratio will fluctuate from year to year depending upon economic conditions. Thus, no standard tables of capitalization rates applicable to closely held corporations can be formulated. Among the more important factors to be taken into consideration in deciding upon a capitalization rate in a particular case are:

- Nature of the business
- Risk
- Stability or irregularity of earnings

Section 7. Average of Factors

Because valuations cannot be made on the basis of a prescribed formula, there is no means whereby the various applicable factors in a particular case can be assigned mathematical weights in deriving the fair market value. For this reason, no useful purpose is served by taking an average of several factors (for example, book value, capitalized earnings, and capitalized dividends) and basing the valuation on the result. Such a process excludes active consideration of other pertinent factors, and the end result cannot be supported by a realistic application of the significant facts in the case except by mere chance.

Section 8. Restrictive Agreements

Frequently, in the valuation of closely held stock for estate and gift tax purposes, it will be found that the stock is subject to an agreement restricting its sale or transfer. Where shares of stock were acquired by a decedent subject to an option reserved by the issuing corporation to repurchase at a certain price, the option price is usually accepted as the fair market value for estate tax purposes. See Rev. Rule. 54-76 C.B. 1954-1, 194. However, in such a case the option price is not determinative of fair market value for gift tax purposes. Where the option, or buy and sell agreement, is the result of voluntary action by the stockholders and is binding during the life as well as at the death of the stockholders, such agreement may or may not, depending upon the circumstances of each case, fix the value for estate tax purposes. However, such agreement is a factor to be considered, with other relevant factors, in determining fair market value. Where the stockholder is free to dispose of shares during life and the option is to become effective only upon death, the fair market value is not limited to the option price. It is always necessary to consider the relationship of the parties, the relative number of shares held by the decedent, and other material facts, to determine whether the agreement represents a bona fide business arrangement or is a device to pass the decedent's shares to the natural objects of his bounty for less than an adequate and full consideration in money or money's worth. In this connection see Rev. Rul. 157 C.B. 1953-2, 255, and Rev. Rul. 189, C.B. 1953-2, 294.

Section 9. Effect On Other Documents

Revenue Ruling 54-77, C.B. 1954-1, 187, is hereby superseded.

MANAGEMENT ANALYSIS OF OPERATIONS

This chapter discusses the analysis of a company's profit including the revenue and cost components. Means to control costs are included. There is a discussion of the cost of quality (COQ) and the cost of prediction errors. The chapter presents performance measures, productivity concerns, monitoring of sales efforts, appraising personnel, evaluating the efficiency of space utilization, and analysis of business processes. The corporate controller must also take into account life cycles and time considerations. Divestitures may be necessary to get rid of operations draining the firm such as those losing money and generating excessive risk levels.

ANALYSIS OF PROFIT

Profit margin (net income/net sales) measures the profitability of each sales dollar. Profitability should be determined by source (product, service, customer (including customer profiles), age group, industry segment, geographic area, channel of distribution, type of marketing effort, market segment, and responsibility center (division, plant, department, and units within the department). Profit variance analysis should be performed to identify causes for actual profit being less than expected. Problems should be immediately identified and corrected. Profit maximization strategies should be formulated. Reports should be prepared by profit-generating source (e.g., market, client). Profit planning including strategic pricing and volume plans should be undertaken.

ANALYSIS OF REVENUE

An analysis should be made of sales mix, product demand, order quantities, product obsolescence, manufacturing schedules, storage space, and competition. Appraise sales generated by different types of selling efforts (direct mail, television, newspaper). Also, compare sales and profit before and after product refinement. The amount of sales returns and allowances is a good indicator of the quality of merchandise. If returns and allowances are high relative to sales, buyer dissatisfaction exists having a negative effect on the company's reputation. Further, the company may have to pay the freight for returned goods.

Sales ratios include:

- Quality of sales = cash sales/total sales
- Days of sales backlog = backlog balance/sales volume divided by sales in period. This ratio helps to monitor sales status and planning.
- Sales per customer = net sales/average number of customers
- Order response rate = average number of transactions/average number of solicitations
- Sales response rate = average dollar sales/average solicitations
- Customer contact ratio = calls to customers/total calls

The ratio of sales to current debt looks at the degree to which short-term liabilities finances sales growth.

Determine the variability in volume, price, and cost of each major product or service.

Questions to be asked and answered are:

- Should products or services be more personalized?
- Which services or products are ineffective and/or excessively costly?
- How can products, services, manufacturing, or distribution be redesigned to make them more profitable?

A "close to the customer" strategy assures more useful customer information and improved sales, and lower distribution costs.

COST ANALYSIS AND CONTROL

Cost Analysis

A company's costs should be compared over the years to determine if there is a problem in cost incurrence. The reasons for unusual changes in costs should be noted and corrective steps taken when warranted.

Direct cost ratios may be used in analyzing operating costs such as (1) direct labor/sales, (2) direct travel/sales, and (3) computer usage/sales.

Determine if costs are excessive relative to production volume. The ratio of selling expenses to net sales reflects the cost of selling the product. Is such cost excessive?

Locked-in (designed) costs will be incurred in the "future" based on decisions already made. It is difficult to reduce locked-in costs. "Cost down" is reducing product costs but still fulfill customer expectations. Also, compare the number of project rejections due to high initial costs to total projects available.

Proper cost allocation should be made to responsibility centers, geographic areas, products, services, and customers.

Cost Control

Recommendations should be made on improving quality control. Expenses are often related to sales to determine if proper controls exist and if the expenditures are resulting in improved revenue and/or profitability. Examine the following ratios:

- Total operating expenses/net sales
- Specific expense/net sales
- Utilities expense/net sales
- Selling expenses/net sales

A cost-benefit analysis is crucial. Costs should be controlled by major type (e.g., manufacturing, selling, administrative, legal, insurance). Cost control reports should be prepared. Cost control may be evaluated by doing the following:

- Undertake a cost reduction program for projects, products, and services. Such a program may eliminate waste and inefficiency resulting in improved profitability. However, cost reductions must make sense.
- Evaluate leased premises to reduce rental charges.
- Consider joint ventures to reduce cost.
- Eliminate duplicate facilities and activities by streamlining operations.
- Implement an energy conservation program.
- Place "caps" on expense categories (e.g., telephone, travel and entertainment). Pinpoint those responsible for excessive costs (e.g., excessive telephone calls). Authorization will be needed on an employee basis for amounts exceeding ceiling levels.

- Assign each employee an identification number for xerox, fax, and computer use.
- Substitute cheaper sources of supply or self-manufacture the part.
- Undertake an engineering study to see if manufactured goods can be redesigned to save costs.
- Perform inspection at key points in the manufacturing cycle to correct problems early.
- Adjust output levels as needed.
- Contract for long-term purchase agreements.
- Obtain competitive bids and change suppliers, insurance companies, consultants, etc. when lower fees are obtained assuming similar levels of quality.
- Redesign the delivery system to reduce fuel costs.
- Tie salary increments to increased productivity.
- Subcontract work if lower costs arise.

COST OF QUALITY (COQ)

The cost of quality (COQ) is defined as any costs to correct poor quality or to enhance good quality. It takes into account the costs to "prevent" product defects (e.g., employee training, machine maintenance), appraisal costs (e.g., testing, inspecting), and the cost of the failure to control (e.g., scrap, rework, warranties). Problems must be detected and corrected in a timely fashion. There is also an opportunity cost of foregone earnings arising from customers switching to other suppliers because of the company's poor quality products or services. The following ratios may be enlightening: (1) cost of quality/total operating costs and (2) cost of quality/sales. The manager's objective is to minimize COQ subject to the constraints of corporate policy, customer requirements, and manufacturing limitations. Ultimately, the overall quality of the company's goods benefit.

COST OF PREDICTION ERRORS

The failure to accurately project sales could result in poor production planning, improper labor levels, etc. causing potentially huge financial losses. The cost of the prediction error is the profit lost because of the inaccurate prediction. It can be measured in lost sales, disgruntled customers, and idle machinery. It is important to determine the cost of the prediction error so as to minimize the potential negative affect on the business. Prediction relates to sales, expenses, and purchases.

PERFORMANCE MEASURES

Performance evaluation must consider the trend in a measure over time within the company, to competing companies, and to industry norms. Index numbers may be used to compare current-year figures to base-year (representative, typical year) figures. Revenue, cost, and profit may be tracked by division, department, product, service, process, contract, job, sales territory, and customer. Measures of performance include:

- Repeat sales to customers
- Backup of orders
- Number of skills per worker
- Number of complaints and warranty required services
- Rework costs relative to cost of goods manufactured
- Setup time relative to total manufacturing time
- Number and length of equipment breakdowns
- Number and duration of manufacturing delays
- Output per manhour
- Manufacturing costs to total costs
- Manufacturing costs to revenue
- Lead time
- Time per business process
- Time between receipt of an order and delivery
- Time between order placement and receipt
- Non-value added cost to total cost
- Percentage of declining and developmental products to total products

"Production run size" is an optimum production run quantity which minimizes the sum of carrying and setup costs.

STUDYING PRODUCTIVITY

Productivity is enhanced by minimizing direct labor cost. Also, an attempt should be made to reduce indirect costs relative to direct labor costs. Management might consolidate facilities and equipment to achieve a more efficient productivity level. A measure of productivity is the relationship between the cost, time, and quality of an "input" to the quality and units generated for the "output." A proper input-output balance is needed. Resources should be utilized in an optimum fashion.

SALES EFFORTS

An appraisal should be made of salesperson effectiveness (e.g., income generated by salesperson, cost per salesperson, salesperson incentives, call frequency, dollar value of orders obtained per hour spent), promotional and advertising effectiveness (marketing costs to sales, dollar expenditure by media compared to sales generated, media measures, comparison of profit before and after promotion), test market analysis (consumer vs. industry), and activity analysis (sales and marketing, customer support, order management). An analysis should also be made of product/service warranties and complaints.

LOOKING AT PERSONNEL

The ratio of sales to personnel represents a comparison of sales dollars and/or sales volume generated relative to the number of employees. It provides insight into levels of employee productivity. The following ratios should be computed: (1) sales/number of employees, (2) sales volume/number of employees, (3) sales/salaries expense. Other useful ratios are: (1) net income/manpower, (2) number of transactions/average number of employees, (3) total tangible assets/number of workers, (4) labor costs/total costs, (5) labor costs/sales, and (6) labor costs/net income. Another consideration as to employee efficiency and morale is employee turnover (number of employees leaving/average number of employees).

The ratio of indirect labor to direct labor monitors indirect labor planning and control. Labor planning and control are crucial at all supervisory levels to produce competitive products and/or to perform profitable services. Management uses this ratio to appraise indirect personnel requirements through the impact of these requirements on operations, earnings, and overhead costs. A declining ratio is unfavorable because it shows management has not maintained a desirable relationship.

Consider automation and up-to-date technology to decrease labor costs.

EFFICIENCY OF SPACE USE

The usefulness of space may be computed as follows:

- Revenue per square foot = net sales/square feet of space.
- Sales per square foot of machinery = net sales/square feet of space for machinery.

- Production per square foot = total units produced/square feet of space for machinery.
- Profit per square foot = net income/square feet of space.
- Customer space = number of customers/square feet of space
- Employee space = square feet of space/number of employees
- Parking lot space = square feet of parking lot space/number of customers.
- Rent per square foot = rent expense/square feet of space.
- Expenses per square foot for owned property = expenses of owning property/square feet of space.

BUSINESS PROCESSES

A business process is an operation, function, or activity that crosses among divisions or departments of a company to manufacture the product or render the service. By concentrating on the process itself (rather than each department separately) operations and product/service quality may be improved, costs slashed, and processing time reduced.

By analyzing a process itself it is easier to understand the complexities and interrelationships among units of the organization, and aid in better communication as to where each responsibility unit fits in. Concentrating on and improving the business process (as distinct from individual departments) results in greater efficiency and effectiveness. In appraising business processes, consider:

- What does the process cost and how long does it take?
- Does the process involve irrelevant and unneeded steps that can be cut?
- What is the quality associated with the process?
- What problems or bottlenecks exist?
- What is the work flow?

The financial manager should identify cases in which work performed at the client is redundant or unnecessary, or where such work is too costly or time consuming. Further, procedures, activities or policies may be unjustifiably complex and can be simplified. A process needs to be revamped when its cost or time does not add value to the customer. Therefore, a customer survey may be warranted. The CPA may decide to recommend modifying, adding, or dropping a process.

The business process might be improved by doing the following: reduce the number of employees involved or functions required, reduce cycle time, reduce the number of individuals required to approve the process or modification thereto, reorganize the procedures, eliminate illogical administrative steps, improve the sequence of the operation, prioritize strategies, cut out excessive paper work, improve training, clarify job descriptions and instructions, upgrade equipment, and use up-to-date technology.

Cycle time should be expressed as average and maximum. An example of cycle time is how long it takes to process a bill to a customer. The efficiency to which a cycle is performed may be expressed by the ratio of total processing time divided by total processing plus non-processing time. A lower ratio is unfavorable and requires corrective action.

"A value-added evaluation" should be conducted for each operation, function, or responsibility unit. How much is the value-added? Is it sufficient to justify that activity or business segment? If not, what should be done (e.g., improvements made, disbandonment)? Work improvement teams can be used in production, material handling, shipping, and accounting. Such teams should document the process flows, layouts, etc. and find ways to reorganize the process to make it better.

A business process analysis may be undertaken as a pre-emptive troubleshooter and should be on an ongoing basis. Examples of situations to which a business process analysis is crucial are when profit margins for a product line are shrinking, market share is dramatically declining, service quality is deteriorating, and customer response time is becoming prohibitive.

Operational audits should be performed examining corporate policies and procedures to assure that they are functioning properly.

LIFE CYCLES

There are different types of life cycles affecting a business. "Product-life cycle" is the time from the start of the R&D effort to the ending of customer support for the product. A "life cycle budget" of costs is for this time period and aids in formulating selling prices. Many costs occur even before production starts. The development product period may range from short to long. "Product life-cycle reporting" is not on a calendar year basis but rather tracks the revenue and costs for each product over several calendar years. Product cost analysis is done by product over each major stage in their life cycle (early, middle, late). There is a highlighting of cost interrelationships among major business functions. "Life-cycle costing" organizes costs based on the product or service life cycle. It monitors and computes the actual total costs of the product or service from beginning to end. Decisions are then made about the good or service based on its profile. "Customer life-cycle costs" concentrate on the total costs to a customer of buying and using a product over its life.

TIME CONSIDERATIONS

Time-based competition stresses the customer and considers product quality, timing, and cost/pricing. An example is how long it takes to design a new product model to meet customer demand. Another example is how long it takes to fill a customer's order. Such analysis strives to enhance productivity, improve market position, raise selling prices, and reduce risk. Efforts should be made to streamline operations.

The time between developing and marketing a product or service should be minimized to lower up-front costs (e.g., design, process, and promotion). Revenue must be generated as quickly as possible to recoup such costs.

DIVESTITURES

Divestitures may be made of unprofitable and/or risky business segments. Divestiture involves the complete or partial conversion, sale, or reallocation of capital or human resources as well as product/service lines. Freed resources may be used for some more productive business purpose. A business segment may qualify for divestiture if it is providing a poor rate of return, does not generate adequate cash flow, does not mesh with overall company strategy, has excessive risk (e.g., vulnerable to lawsuits), is in a state of decline, or where the pieces are worth more than the whole. The objectives of divestiture include repositioning the company in the industry, getting out of an industry, meeting market changes, obtaining needed funds, and cutting losses. Before a divestiture is made, a joint venture may be considered with another company.

ECONOMIC INDICATORS

ECONOMIC INDICATORS AND BOND YIELDS

The bond investor makes an analysis of the economy primarily to determine his or her investment strategy. It is not necessary for the investor to formulate his or her own economic forecasts. The investor can rely on published forecasts in an effort to identify the trends in the economy and adjust his/her investment position accordingly.

The investor must keep abreast of the economic trend and direction and attempt to see how they affect bond yields and bond prices. Unfortunately, there are too many economic indicators and variables to be analyzed. Each has its own significance. In many cases, these variables could give mixed signals about the future of the economy and therefore mislead the investor.

Various government agencies and private firms tabulate the appropriate economic data and calculate various indices. Sources for these indicators are available at an affordable price or can be found in your local public and college libraries. They include daily local newspapers and national newspapers such as *USA Today, the Wall Street Journal, Investor's Business Daily, Chicago Tribune* and *New York Times* or periodicals, such as *Business Week, Forbes, Fortune, Money, Kiplinger's Personal Finance Magazine, Worth, Barron's, Smart Money, Nation's Business,* and *U.S. News and World Report.* Internet users can view the semiannual *Livingston Survey,* started in 1946 by the late economist Joseph A. Livingston. It is the oldest continuous survey of economists' expectations. The Federal Reserve Bank of Philadelphia took responsibility for the survey in 1990 and it can be found at the bank's Web site at http://www.phil.frb.org/econ/liv/welcome.html.

Figure 1 Probable Effects of Economic Variables on Bond Yields

Indicators**	*Effects on Bond Yields***	*Reasons*
Business Activity		
GNP and industrial production falls	Fall	As economy slows, Fed may ease credit by allowing rates to fall
Unemployment rises	Fall	High unemployment indicates lack of economic expansion; Fed may loosen credit
Inventories rise	Fall	Inventory levels are good indicators of duration of economic slowdown
Trade deficit rises	Fall	Dollar weakens; That's inflationary
Leading indicators	Rise	Advance signals about economic rise health; Fed may tighten credit
Housing starts rise	Rise	Growing economy due to increased new housing demand; Fed may tighten; mortgage rates rise
Personal income rises	Rise	Higher income means higher consumer spending, thus inflationary; Fed may tighten
Inflation		
Consumer Price Index	Rise	Inflationary rises
Producer Price Index	Rise	Early signal for inflation increase
Monetary Policy		
Money supply rises	Rise	Excess growth in money supply is inflationary; Fed may tighten
Fed funds rate rises	Rise	Increase in business and consumer loan rates; used by Fed to slow economic growth and inflation
Fed buys (sells) bills	Rise (fall)	Adds (deduct) money to the economy; interest rates may go down (up)
Required reserve rises	Rise	Depresses banks' lending

*This table merely serves as a handy guide and should not be construed as accurate at all times.
** Fall in any of these indicators will have the opposite effect on bond yields.
***Note: The effects are based on yield and are therefore opposite of how bond prices will be affected.

The accompanying chart provides a concise list of the significant economic indicators and how they affect bond yields. Remember, bond yields and bond prices act conversely, so a rise in yields means a fall in prices and vice versa. The accompanying chart, however, merely serves as a handy guide and should not be construed as an accurate predictor in all cases. Many times the anticipation of good or bad news is built into the market and when the news comes out, the reverse move happens. That's because traders are unwinding the positions they took to profit from that news.

ECONOMIC INDICATORS AND STOCKS

As with bonds, the investor makes an analysis of the economy primarily to determine his/her investment strategy. It is not necessary for him/her to formulate his/her own economic forecasts. Here too the investor can rely on published forecasts in an effort to identify the trends in the economy and adjust his/her investment position accordingly. The investor must keep abreast of the economic trend and direction and attempt to see how they affect the security market.

Various government agencies and private firms tabulate the appropriate economic data and calculate various indices. Sources for these indicators are easily subscribed at an affordable price or can be found in your local public and college libraries. See previous discussion on sources.

The accompanying chart summarizes the types of economic variables and their probable effect on the security market and the economy in general. The accompanying chart, however, merely serves as a handy guide and should not be construed as an accurate predictor in all cases. Many times the anticipation of good or bad news is built into the market and when the news comes out, the reverse move happens. That's because traders are unwinding the positions they took to profit from that news.

FACTORY ORDERS AND PURCHASING MANAGER'S INDEX

The factory order series presents new orders received by manufacturers of durable goods other than military equipment. (Durable goods are defined as those having a useful life of more than three years.) Non-defense equipment represents about one-fifth to one-third of all durable goods production. The series includes engines, construction, mining, and materials handling equipment; office and store machinery; electrical transmission and distribution equipment and other electrical machinery (excluding household appliances

Figure 2 Economic Variables and Their Impacts on the Economy and Stocks

Economic Variables	Impact on Security Market
Real growth in GNP	Positive (without inflation) for stocks.
Industrial production	Consecutive drops are a sign of recession. Bad for stocks.
Inflation	Detrimental to stocks.
Capacity utilization	A high percentage is positive, but full capacity is inflationary.
Durable goods orders	Consecutive drops are a sign of recession. Very bad for stocks in cyclical industries.
Increase in business investment, consumer confidence, personal income, etc.	Positive for stocks, especially retailing. Worrisome for utility shares.
Leading indicators	Rise is bullish for the economy and stocks; drops are a sign of bad times ahead.
Housing starts	Rise is positive for housing stocks.
Corporate profits	Strong corporate earnings are positive for stocks; Corporate bonds also fare well.
Unemployment	Upward trend unfavorable for stocks and economy.
Increase in business inventories	Positive for those fearful of inflationary; Negative for those looking for growing economy.
Lower federal deficit	Lowers interest rates, good for many stocks. Potential negative for depressed economy.
Deficit in trade and balance of payments	Negative for economy and stocks of companies facing stiff import competition.
Weak dollar	Negative for economy; good for companies with stiff foreign competition.
Interest rates	Rising rates can choke off investment in new plants and lure skittish investors from stocks.

and electronic equipment); and railroad, ship and aircraft transportation equipment. Military equipment is excluded because new orders for such items do not respond directly to the business cycle. The National Association of Purchasing Management releases its monthly *Purchasing Index* which tells you about buying intentions of corporate purchasing agents.

The factory order series is released by the Department of Commerce. Each month, more than 2,000 companies are asked to file a report covering orders, inventories and shipments. As for the Purchasing Index, the

National Association of Purchasing Agents conducts a survey that polls purchasing managers from key industries. They are reported in daily newspapers and business dailies. Commerce Department statistics can be found at www.census.gov/econ/ on the Internet.

Economists typically count on factory production, particularly of "big ticket" durable goods ranging from airplanes to home appliances, to help lift the economy from downturn. A decline in this series suggests that factories are unlikely to hire new workers. A drop in the backlog of unfilled orders is also an indication of possible production cutbacks and layoffs. The wider dispersal of gains in many types of goods is looked upon as a favorable sign for the economic recovery. The broader the dispersal of order increases, the broader the rehiring.

The purchasing managers are responsible for buying the raw materials that feed the nation's factories. Their buying patterns are considered a good indication of the direction of the economy. A reading of 50 or more percent indicates that the manufacturing economy is generally expanding. A reading above 44.5 percent over a period of time indicates that the overall economy is augmenting.

A Word of Caution: Again, in order to make an overall assessment of the economy, the investor must look to other important economic indicators.

GROSS DOMESTIC PRODUCT (GDP)

Gross Domestic Product (GDP) measures the value of all goods and services produced by the economy within its boundaries and is the nation's broadest gauge of economic health. GDP is normally stated in annual terms, though data are compiled and released quarterly. The Department of Commerce compiles GDP. It is reported as a "real" figure, that is, economic growth minus the impact of inflation. The figure is tabulated on a quarterly basis, coming out in the month after a quarter has ended. It is then revised at least twice, with those revisions being reported once in each of the months following the original release.

GDP reports appear in most daily newspapers and online at services such as America Online. Also visit the Federal Government Statistics Web site on the Internet at http://www.fedstats.gov/ GDP is often a measure of the state of the economy. For example, many economists speak of recession when there has been a decline in GDP for two consecutive quarters. The GDP in dollar and real terms is a useful economic indicator. An expected growth rate of 3 percent in real terms would be very attractive for long-term investment and would affect the stock market positively. Since inflation and price increases are detrimental to equity prices, a real growth of GDP without inflation is favorable and desirable.

The following diagram charts a series of events leading from a rising GDP to higher security prices.

GDP up—> Corporate profits up—> Dividends up—> Stock prices up.

Generally speaking, too much growth is inflationary and thus negative for the stock and bond markets. When companies are producing "flat out," they need workers desperately and are willing to pay big wage increases to attract new workers and keep them. But these wage increases raise business costs and lead firms to raise prices and must be avoided. Too little production is undesirable as well. Low levels of production mean layoffs, unemployment, low incomes for workers, and tend to depress the stock market.

Investors watching for signs of inflation should check the "deflator" portion of the GDP report. That contains what some experts feel is the most detailed tracking of price pressures from the government.

A Word of Caution: GDP fails the timely release criterion for useful economic indicators. Unfortunately, there is no way of measuring whether we are in a recession or prosperity currently, based on the GDP measure. Only after the quarter is over can it be determined if there was growth or decline. Experts look upon other measures such as unemployment rate, industrial production, durable orders, corporate profits, retail sales, and housing activity to look for a sign of recession.

HOUSING STARTS AND CONSTRUCTION SPENDING

Housing starts is an important economic indicator followed by investors and economists. It offers an estimate of the number of dwelling units on which construction has begun during a stated period. It covers construction of new homes and apartments. When an economy is going to take a downturn, the housing sector is the first to decline. This indicates the future strength of the housing sector of the economy. At the same time, it is closely related to interest rates and other basic economic factors.

The statistics for construction spending covers homes, office buildings and other construction projects. Both housing starts and construction spending figures are issued monthly by the Department of Commerce. Visit the Federal Government Statistics Web site: http://www.fedstats.gov/ National business daily newspapers and many local newspaper report on these property-related figures as do many reliable Internet-based financial news services.

Housing is a key interest-sensitive sector that usually leads the rest of the economy out of the recession. Also, housing is vital to a broader economic revival, not only because of its benefits for other industries but also because it signals consumer's confidence about making long-term financial commitments.

A Word of Caution: For the housing sector to be sustained, housing start figures need to be backed by building permits. Permits are considered a leading indicator of housing starts.

INDEX OF LEADING INDICATORS

The Index of Leading Indicators is the economic series of indicators that tends to predict future changes in economic activity. This index was designed to reveal the direction of the economy in the next six to nine months. By melding 10 economic yardsticks, an index is created that has shown a tendency to change before the economy makes a major turn. Hence, the term "leading indicators." The index is designed to forecast economic activity six to nine months ahead.

This series is calculated and published monthly by the Conference Board, consisting of:

- Average weekly hours for U.S. manufacturing workers. Employers find it a lot easier to increase the number of hours worked in a week than to hire more employees.

- Average weekly initial claims for unemployment insurance. The number of people who sign up for unemployment benefits signals changes in present and future economic activity.

- Manufacturers' new orders, consumer goods and materials. New orders mean more workers hired, more materials and supplies purchased, and increased output. Gains in this series usually lead recoveries by as much as four months.

- Vendor performance, slower deliveries diffusion index. Represents the percentage of companies reporting slower deliveries. As the economy grows, firms have more trouble filling orders.

- Manufacturers' new orders, non-defense capital goods. Factories will employ more as demand for big-ticket items, especially those not bought by the government, stay strong.

- Building permits, new private housing units. Optimistic builders often a good sign for the economy.

- Stock prices, 500 common stocks. Stock market advances usually precede business upturns by three to eight months.

- Money supply, M2. A rising money supply means easy money that sparks brisk economic activity. This usually leads recoveries by as much as fourteen months.

- Interest rate spread, 10-year Treasury bonds minus federal funds rate. Steep yield curve, when long rates are much higher than short ones, is sign of healthy economic outlook.

Consumer expectations index. Consumer spending buys two-thirds of GNP (all goods and services produced in the economy), so any sharp change could be an important factor in an overall turnaround.

The monthly report is well covered by daily business publications, major newspapers, business TV shows and on the Internet. You can also check the Conference Board's Web site at www.conference-board.com. If the index is consistently rising, even only slightly, the economy is chugging along and a setback is unlikely. If the indicator drops for three or more consecutive months, look for an economic slowdown and possibly a recession in the next year or so.

A rising (consecutive percentage increases in) indicator is bullish for the economy and the stock market, and vice versa. Falling index results could be good news for bondholders looking to make capital gains from falling interest rates.

Now the Conference Board points out that while it is often stated in the press that three consecutive downward movements in the leading index signal a recession, they do not endorse the use of such a simple, inflexible rule. Their studies show that a 1 percent decline (2 percent when annualized) in the leading index, coupled with declines in a majority of the 10 components, provides a reliable, but not perfect, recession signal.

A Word of Caution: The composite figure is designed to tell only in which direction business will go. It is not intended to forecast the magnitude of future ups and downs. The index has also given some false warning signals in recent years.

INDUSTRIAL PRODUCTION AND CAPACITY UTILIZATION

The index of industrial production, more precisely Federal Reserve Board Index of Industrial Production, measures changes in the output of the mining, manufacturing, and gas and electric utilities sectors of the economy. Detailed breakdowns of the index provide a reading on how individual industries are faring. Industrial production is narrower than gross domestic product (GDP) since it omits agriculture, construction, wholesale and retail trade, transportation, communications, services, finance, and government.

Another way to view the performance of the real economy is to look at industrial production relative to the production capacity of the industrial sector. The actual production level as a percent of the full capacity level is called the rate of capacity utilization. This monthly rate is limited to manufacturing industries.

Data for the index is drawn from 250 data series obtained from private trade associations and internal estimates. This monthly Index of Industrial Production is released only two weeks into the next month is published by the Federal Reserve Board. The rate of capacity utilization is announced every month by the Fed, one day after the Index of Industrial Production. Both are published in the *Federal Reserve Bulletin* and appear in major daily newspapers and on online computer news services such as America Online.

As the index rises, this is a sign that the economy will strengthen and that the stock market should turn up. A falling industrial production should be a concern for the economy and the investor. Regardless of the state of the economy, however, detailed breakdowns of the index provide a reading on how individual industries are faring and on what industries should be attended by investors.

A rising rate of capacity utilization is positive for the economy and the stock market; a falling rate is an indication of a sinking economy and thus negative for the stock market.

A Word of Caution: Industrial production is more volatile that GDP, because GDP, unlike industrial production, includes activities that are largely spared cyclical fluctuations, such as services, finance, and government.

INFLATION

Inflation is the general rise in prices of consumer goods and services. The federal government measures inflation with four key indices: Consumer Price Index (CPI), Producer Price Index (PPI), Gross Domestic Product (GDP) Deflator and Employment Cost Index (ECI)

Price indices are designed to measure the rate of inflation of the economy. Various price indices are used to measure living costs, price level changes, and inflation. They are:

- *Consumer Price Index:* The Consumer Price Index (CPI), the most well-known inflation gauge, is used as the cost-of-living index, which labor contracts and social security are tied to. The CPI measures the cost of buying a fixed bundle of goods (some 400 consumer goods and services), representative of the purchase of the typical working-class urban family. The fixed basket is divided into the following categories:

food and beverages, housing, apparel, transportation, medical care, entertainment, and other. Generally referred to as a "cost-of-living index," it is published by the Bureau of Labor Statistics of the U.S. Department of Labor. The CPI is widely used for escalation clauses. The base year for the CPI index was 1982-84 at which time it was assigned 100.

- *Producer Price Index:* Like the CPI, the PPI is a measure of the cost of a given basket of goods priced in wholesale markets, including raw materials, semifinished goods, and finished goods at the early stage of the distribution system. The PPI is published monthly by the Bureau of Labor Statistics of the Department of Commerce. The PPI signals changes in the general price level, or the CPI, some time before they actually materialize. (Since the PPI does not include services, caution should be exercised when the principal cause of inflation is service prices). For this reason, the PPI and especially some of its subindexes, such as the index of sensitive materials, serve as one of the leading indicators that are closely watched by policy makers. It is the one that signals changes in the general price level, or the CPI, some time before they actually materialize.

- *GDP Deflator:* The index of inflation used to separate price changes in GDP calculations from real changes in economic activity. The Deflator is a weighted average of the price indexes used to deflate GDP so true economic growth can be separated from inflationary growth. Thus, it reflects price changes for goods and services bought by consumers, businesses, and governments. Because it covers a broader group of goods and services than the CPI and PPI, the GDP Deflator is a very widely used price index that is frequently used to measure inflation. The GDP deflator, unlike the CPI and PPI, is available only quarterly—not monthly. It is published by the U.S. Department of Commerce.

- *Employment Cost Index:* The most comprehensive and refined measure of underlying trends in employee compensation as a cost of production. Measures the cost of labor and includes changes in wages and salaries and employer costs for employee benefits. ECI tracks wages and bonuses, sick and vacation pay plus benefits such as insurance, pension and Social Security and unemployment taxes from a survey of 18,300 occupations at 4,500 sample establishments in private industry and 4,200 occupations within about 800 state and local governments.

Price indices get major coverage, appear in daily newspapers and business dailies, on business TV programs like *CNNfn* and *CNBC,* and on Internet financial news services. Government Internet Web sites www.stats.bls.gov and www.census.gov/econ/www/ also provide this data.

Check to see whether the inflation rate has been rising—a negative, or bearish, sign for stock and bond investors—or falling, which is bullish.

Rising prices is public enemy No. 1 for stocks and bonds. Inflation usually hurts stock prices since higher consumer prices lessen the value of future corporate earnings, which make shares of those companies less appealing to investors. By contrast, when prices rocket ahead, investors often flock to long-term inflation hedges such as real estate.

See how a chain of events leading from lower rates of inflation to increased consumer spending and possibly, an up stock market:

Inflation is down *so* real personal income up *so* consumer confidence jumps *so* consumer spending up *so* retail sales surge *as* housing starts rise *as* auto sales jump *so* the stock market goes up.

Do note that Federal Reserve Chairman Alan Greenspan is a big fan of the ECI as a good measure to see if wage pressures are sparking inflation.

A Word of Caution: Of course, if inflation disappears, that's no good in the long run, too. Deflation, that is, sharp falling prices is a disastrous event. Think of Texas real estate in the 1980s or California's property woes of the early 1990s. A broader example is the Great Depression of the 1930s.

When demand for goods is so weak that merchants have to brutally slash prices just to stay in business, that's deflation. It leads to layoffs and recession. That bad for stock investors as profits shrink, but it is good for bond holders—as long as they own a bond backed by an issuer who can pay it back.

MONEY SUPPLY

This is the level of funds available at a given time for conducting transactions in an economy, as reported by the Federal Reserve. The Federal Reserve System can influence money supply through its monetary policy measures. There are several definitions of the money supply: M1 (which is currency in circulation, demand deposits, traveler's checks, and those in interest-bearing accounts), M2 (the most widely followed measure, it equals M1 plus savings deposits, money market deposit accounts, and money market funds), and M3 (which is M2 plus large CDs).

The Federal Reserve System computes these measures. The weekly money supply figures are released on Thursday afternoons by the Federal Reserve Board and reported in daily newspapers and the *Wall Street Journal* and *Barron's*.

A rapid growth is viewed as inflationary; in contrast, a sharp drop in the money supply is considered to be recessionary. Moderate growth is thought to have a positive impact on the economy. Economists attempt to compare with targets proposed by the Fed.

The Fed affects money supply through its monetary policy such as open market operations. The following summarizes its possible impact on the economy and the stock market.

- *Easy Money Policy:* Fed buys securities *so* bank reserves rise *so* bank lending is up *so* money supply is up *so* interest rates are down *as* bond prices rise *so* loan demand goes up *so* the stock market rises.
- *Tight Money Policy:* Fed sells securities *so* bank reserves fall *so* bank lending is down *so* money supply is down *so* interest rates are up *as* bond prices fall *so* loan demand is down *so* the stock market falls.

A Word of Caution: A rapid growth (excessively easy monetary policy) is viewed as inflationary and could impact the economy adversely. In contrast, a sharp drop in the money supply is considered to be recessionary and can hurt the economy and the stock market. Moderate growth is thought to have a positive impact on the economy.

PERSONAL INCOME AND CONFIDENCE INDICES

Personal income shows the before-tax income received by individuals and unincorporated businesses such as wages and salaries, rents, and interest and dividends, and other payments such as unemployment and Social Security.

There are two popular indices that track the level of consumer confidence: one is the Conference Board of New York, an industry-sponsored, non-profit economic research institute and the other is the University of Michigan's index. The Consumer Confidence Index measures consumer optimism and pessimism about general business conditions, jobs, and total family income. The University of Michigan Survey Research Center is another research organization that compiles its own index called the Index of Consumer Sentiment. It measures consumers' personal financial circumstances and their outlook for the future.

Personal income data are released monthly by the Commerce Department. The Conference Board's index is derived from a survey of 5,000 households nationwide, covering questions that range from home-buying plans to the outlook for jobs, both presently and during the next six months.

The University of Michigan's index is compiled through a telephone survey of 500 households. Daily newspapers, financial television and online business news services cover these releases.

Personal income represents consumers' spending power. When personal income rises, it usually means that consumers will increase their purchases, which will in turn affect favorably the investment climate.

The Conference Board's index is considered a useful economic barometer because it provides insight into consumer spending, which is critical to any sustainable economic upswing. Many economists pay close attention to the index, which provides insight into consumer attitudes toward spending and borrowing. Consumers account for two-thirds of the nation's economic activity (i.e., national gross domestic product) and thus drive recovery and expansion.

A low or decreased level of consumer confidence indicates concern about their employment prospects and their earnings in the months ahead. Uncertainty requires cautions in investing. On the other hand, an increased level of consumer confidence spells economic recovery and expansion, thus presenting an investment opportunity. In summary, an increase in personal income, coupled with substantial consumer confidence, is bullish for the economy and the stock market.

A Word of Caution: One must look carefully at how consumers are staying confident. The Personal income figures, when measured against spending and borrowing patterns, may show that consumers are dipping into savings or even running up big debt to pay for buying sprees. That's an expansion that is rarely sustainable. To formulate the future prospects about the economy, investors must weigh various economic indicators such as inflation measures.

PRODUCTIVITY

Productivity measures the relationship between real output and the labor time involved in its production, or output per hour of work. The Labor Department compiles productivity figures from its own job surveys that produce unemployment reports and the Commerce Department's work that creates gross domestic product figures. Only business sector output—GDP minus government and not-for-profit organizations—is used in the productivity calculation.

Productivity measures reflect the joint effects of many influences, including changes in technology; capital investment; level of output; utilization of capacity, energy, and materials; the organization of production; managerial skill; and the characteristics and effort of the work force.

Daily newspapers, financial television and online business news services such as America Online cover these releases. The ECI is provided quarterly by the Bureau of Labor Statistics in the U.S. Department of Labor. The data are published in a press release and in BLS journals and computer users can visit www.stats.bls.gov on the Internet for this data.

Economists consider productivity the key to prosperity. Sizable gains mean companies can pay workers more, hold the line on prices and still earn the kind of profits that keep stock prices rising. Increased productivity, or getting more worker output per hour on the job, is considered vital to increasing the nation's standard of living without inflation.

A Word of Caution: The productivity statistics mainly covers the manufacturing sector of the economy and does not deal substantively with the large service sector.

And, note that high productivity may be good for stocks but low productivity is just a mixed bag. Consider that productivity grew at a brisk 2.9 percent annual rate in the 1960s and early 1970s, relatively good times for stock investors. Productivity then slowed to a paltry 1 percent from 1974 through 1995, both horribly weak and extremely strong stock periods. From 1995 through 1998, good times for stocks, productivity grew at around a 2 percent rate, seemingly a new era of productivity driven by computers and other high-tech innovations.

RECESSION

Recession means a sinking economy. Unfortunately, there is no consensus definition and measure of recession. In general, it means that the economy is shrinking in size and the number of jobs being lost outnumbers jobs being created. Here are three primary ways economists define a recession:

1. Three or more straight monthly drops of the Index of Leading Economic Indicators are generally considered a sign of recession.
2. Two consecutive quarterly drops of Gross Domestic Product (GDP) signals recession.
3. Consecutive monthly drops of durable goods orders which most likely results in less production and increasing layoffs in the factory sector.

Newspapers, TV shows and online services all try to guess when recessions start—and end. Recession tends to dampen the spirits of consumers and investors and thus depress prices of various investment vehicles including securities and real estate.

A Word of Caution: Not all industries in the economy during recession go bad. Some industrial sectors (for example, consumer products industry) are recession resistant or defensive. Investors need to analyze industry by industry.

Also, remember that recessions (or depressions) have political impact for the nation. Political analysts say that President Bush lost the 1992 presidential election—just a year after his leadership of victorious Allied forces in the Persian Gulf War—because the U.S. economy grudgingly recovered from a recession throughout the campaign.

In fact, there is so much political power in defining when the country is actually in recession, that a nonpartisan group of economists known as the National Bureau of Economic Research are the official arbiters of a recession's start and end.

Unfortunately for investors, they act so slowly that it is of little use. And unfortunately for Bush and his recession, the bureau announced one month after Bill Clinton's victory in November 1992 that the nation's ninth post World War II recession officially began in July 1990 and ended in March 1991.

RETAIL SALES

This figure is the estimate of total sales at the retail level. It includes everything from bags of groceries to durable goods such as automobiles. It is used as a measure of future economic conditions: A long slowdown in sales could spell cuts in production. Data is issued monthly by the Commerce Department which conducts a mail survey of about 4,100 merchants. That previous month's sales figure is an estimate of sales activity based on percentage changes by industry aggregates from older, revised and more reliable data that is derived from larger samplings. The median revision is a change of two-tenths of a percentage point in sales.

Commerce Department statistics can be found at www.census.gov/econ/www/ on the Internet.

Retail sales are a major concern of analysts because they represent about half of overall consumer spending. Consumer spending, in turn, accounts for about two-thirds of the nation's Gross Domestic Product (GDP). The amount of retail sales depends heavily on consumer confidence about the economy.

A Word of Caution: This number is volatile and subject to occasionally steep revisions. Remember, too, that strong retail sales could spurt fears of inflation. It could hurt stock and bond markets.

UNEMPLOYMENT RATE, INITIAL JOBLESS CLAIMS, AND HELP-WANTED INDEX

Unemployment is the nonavailability of jobs for people able and willing to work at the prevailing wage rate. It is an important measure of economic health, since full employment is generally construed as a desired goal. When the various economic indicators are mixed, many analysts look to the unemployment rate as being the most important. Weekly initial claims for unemployment benefits are another closely watched indicator along with the unemployment rate to judge the jobless situation in the economy. The help-wanted advertising index tracks employers' advertisements for job openings in the classified section of newspapers in 50 or so labor market areas. The index represents job vacancies resulting from turnover in exiting positions such as workers changing jobs or retiring and from the creation of new jobs. The help-wanted figures are seasonally adjusted.

The unemployment rate is the number of unemployed workers divided by total employed and unemployed who constitute the labor force. Both statistics are released by the Department of Labor. The help-wanted advertising figures are obtained from classified advertisements in newspapers in major labor markets.

They are frequently reported in daily newspapers, business dailies, business TV shows and through online services. Labor Department releases can be found at www.stats.bls.gov for computer users.

An increase in employment, a decrease in initial jobless claims, and a decrease in unemployment are favorable for the economy and the stock market; the opposite situation is unfavorable. The help-wanted index is inversely related to *unemployment*. When help-wanted advertisements increase, unemployment declines, while a decline in help-wanted advertisements is accompanied by a rise in unemployment.

The effect of unemployment on the economy is summarized in Figure 3.

A Word of Caution: No one economic indicator is able to point to the direction to which an economy is heading. It is common that many indicators give mixed signals regarding, for example, the possibility of a recession.

Figure 3 Unemployment's Effects

1. **Less Tax Revenue:** Fewer jobs means less income tax to the state and nation, which means a bigger U.S. government deficit and forces states to make cuts in programs to balance their budgets.
2. **Higher Government Costs:** When people lose jobs they often must turn to the government for benefits.
3. **Less Consumer Spending:** Without a job, individuals can't afford to buy cars, computers, houses, or vacations.
4. **Empty Stores:** Retailers and homebuilders can't absorb lower sales for long. Soon they have to lay off workers and, in more serious shortfalls, file for bankruptcy.
5. **Manufacturing Cuts:** The companies that make consumer products or housing materials are forced to cut jobs, too, as sales of their goods fall.
6. **Real Estate Pain:** As companies fall and as individuals struggle, mortgages and other bank loans go unpaid. That causes real estate values to go down and pummels lenders. One reason for the S&L crisis is the high number of defaulted loans.

But perhaps the best example of economic theory being turned on its head is the low unemployment figures in 1998 not creating inflationary pressures. Investors, and shoppers, can thank increased productivity and cheap foreign goods for that change.

U.S. BALANCE OF PAYMENTS AND THE VALUE OF THE DOLLAR

A balance of payments is a systematic record of a country's receipts from, or payments to, other countries. In a way, it is like the balance sheets for businesses, only on a national level. The references you see in the media to the "balance of trade" usually refer to goods within the goods and services category of the current account. It's also known as merchandise or "visible" trade because it consists of tangibles like foodstuffs, manufactured goods, and raw materials. "Services," the other part of the category, is known as "invisible" trade and consists of intangibles such as interest or dividends, technology transfers, services (like insurance, transportation, financial), and so forth.

When the net result of both the current account and the capital account yields more credits than debits, the country is said to have a surplus in its balance of payments. When there are more debits than credits, the country has a deficit in the balance of payments.

When deficits in the balance of payments persist, this generally depresses the value of the dollar and can boost inflation. The reason is a weak dollar makes foreign goods relatively expensive, often allowing U.S. makers of similar products to raise prices as well.

Trade data is collected by the U.S. Customs Service. Figures are reported in seasonally adjusted volumes and dollar amounts. It is the only non-survey, non-judgmental report produced by the Department of Commerce. Foreign exchange rates are compiled from trading activity both in bulk transactions among dealers and in commodity markets trading forward contracts.

Trade figures and foreign exchange rates are quoted daily.

It is necessary for an investor to know the condition of a country's balance of payments, since resulting inflation will affect the market.

What is better, a strong dollar or a weak dollar? The answer is, unfortunately, it depends. A strong dollar makes Americans' cash go further overseas and reduces import prices—generally good for U.S. consumers and for foreign manufacturers. If the dollar is overvalued, U.S. products are harder to sell abroad and at home, where they compete with low-cost imports. This helps give the U.S. its huge trade deficit.

A weak dollar can restore competitiveness to American products by making foreign goods comparatively more expensive. But too weak a dollar can spawn inflation, first through higher import prices and then through spiraling prices for all goods. Even worse, a falling dollar can drive foreign investors away from U.S. securities, which lose value along with the dollar. A strong dollar can be induced by interest rates. Relatively higher interest rates abroad will attract money dollar-denominated investments which will raise the value of the dollar.

Those Americans owning foreign investments must watch the dollar carefully. A weak dollar makes overseas investments more valuable since assets sold in the foreign currency will yield more dollars. Conversely, a strong dollar will hurt the values of an American's overseas holdings.

A Word of Caution: Unfortunately, it is difficult to establish a good correlation between the dollar's value and the U.S. stock market's performance. Attention should be focused on the domestic scene as well as international economic developments.

LEGAL AND REGULATORY ENVIRONMENT OF THE FIRM

An important element of the competitive environment is the growing importance of government involvement in the market economy. Recent changes in the method and scope of government regulation, including moves toward deregulation, affect the entire spectrum of economic activity, from industrials, to financial institutions (banks, savings and loans, insurance, etc.), to power and transportation utilities. Both state and federal regulation and antitrust policy constitute important constraints on many managerial decisions. As a result, their analysis constitutes an important aspect of managerial economics. This chapter presents the role of government in the market economy, including:

(a) economic and political rationale for regulation,

(b) direct regulation of firms possessing substantial market power,

(c) antitrust policy designed to maintain a "workable" level of competition in the economy, and

(d) public expenditure decisions and cost-benefit analysis

THE RATIONALE FOR REGULATION

Government regulation is sometimes justified on the basis of its ability to correct various market imperfections or market failures which lead to inefficiency and waste. Most often, market failure is thought to be caused by:

(a) Structural problems: too few buyers or sellers.

(b) Incentive problems: externalities such as pollution.

Government regulation is sometimes justified on the basis of political considerations. Primary among such considerations are desires to:

(a) Preserve Consumer Choice: A wide variety of production enhances personal freedom.

(b) Limit Economic and Political Power: Unchecked economic and political power could threaten basic liberties.

ANTITRUST POLICY: GOVERNMENT REGULATION OF MARKET CONDUCT AND STRUCTURE

Antitrust policy is a set of legislations aimed at prohibiting monopolies, restraints of trade, price fixing and discrimination, exorbitant quantity discounts to large buyers, and conspiracies to suppress competition. Federal statutes include the Sherman Antitrust Act, Clayton Antitrust Act, Robinson-Patman Act, and Celler-Kefauver Act.

Sherman Antitrust Act (1890)

The cornerstone of U.S. antitrust policy is contained in Sections 1 and 2 of the *Sherman Antitrust Act* of 1890:

Section 1: Every contract, combination in the form of trust or otherwise, or conspiracy, in restraint of trade or commerce among the several states, or with foreign nations, is hereby declared to be illegal. Every person who shall make any such contract or engage in any such combination or conspiracy shall be deemed guilty of a felony, and, on conviction thereof shall be punished by a fine not exceeding five thousand dollars (one million dollars if a corporation, or, if any other person, one hundred thousand dollars) or by imprisonment not exceeding one (three) years, or by both said punishments, in the discretion of the court.

Section 2: Every person who shall monopolize, or attempt to monopolize, or combine or conspire with any person or persons, to monopolize any part of the trade or commerce among the several States, or with foreign nations, shall be deemed guilty of a felony, and, on conviction thereof, shall be punished by a fine not exceeding five thousand dollars (one million dollars if a corporation, or, if any other person, one hundred thousand dollars) or by imprisonment not exceeding one (three) years, or by both said punishments, in the discretion of the court.

Clayton Act (1914)

The Clayton Act was designed to overcome some of the ambiguity of the Sherman Act by explicitly prohibiting certain behavior. The Clayton Antitrust Act is one of three major antitrust laws, passed as an amendment to the Sherman Antitrust Act in 1914. The Act listed four illegal practices in restraint of competition. It outlawed price discrimination, tying contracts and exclusive dealerships, and horizontal mergers. It also outlawed *interlocking directorates* (the practice of having the same people serve as directors of two or more competing firms).

> *Section 2:* Forbade price discrimination between firms which tended to lessen competition. This section was later amended by the Robinson-Patman Act (1936). It is important to remember that price discrimination between consumers, such as senior citizen discounts for bus service, is legal.
>
> *Section 3:* Made leases or any sales contracts which lessened competition illegal. This provision was aimed at so-called tying contracts.
>
> *Section 7:* Forbade stock mergers for monopoly purposes.

Robinson-Patman Act (1936)

The *Robinson Patman Act* (1936) is an amendment to strengthen Section 2 of the Clayton Act regarding price discrimination. For example, Section 2(a) of the Robinson Patman Act amends Section 2 of the Clayton Act and makes price discrimination illegal if it is designed to lessen competition or create a monopoly:

> *Section 2(a):* That it shall be unlawful for any person engaged in commerce, in the course of such commerce, either directly or indirectly, to discriminate in price between different purchasers of commodities of like grade and quality, . . . where such discrimination may be substantially to lessen competition or tend to create a monopoly in line of commerce, or to injure, destroy, or prevent competition.

Price discrimination that arises because of cost or quality differences is permitted under the act, as is price discrimination when it is necessary to meet a competitor's price in a market. Still, there is considerable ambiguity regarding whether a particular type of price discrimination is illegal under the law.

Celler-Kefauver Act (1950)

The *Cellar-Kefauver Act* (1950) strengthened Section 7 of the Clayton Act by making it more difficult for firms to engage in mergers and acquisitions without violating the law:

> *Section 7:* That no corporation engaged in commerce shall acquire, directly or indirectly, the whole or any part of the stock or other share capital and no corporation subject to the jurisdiction of the Federal Trade Commission shall acquire the whole or any part of the assets of another corporation engaged also in commerce, where in any line of commerce in any section of the country, the effect of such acquisition may be substantially to lessen competition, or to tend to create a monopoly.

Enforcement

The *Antitrust Division of the Department of Justice (DOJ)* and the *Federal Trade Commission (FTC)* are charged with the task of enforcing antitrust regulations. The FTC has limited judicial power; taking violators to court falls almost exclusively on the Antitrust Division of the DOJ. Instead, the FTC issues cease-and-desist orders based on information gathered in a specific case. If the cease-and-desist order is not followed, the FTC may levy a fine of up to $10,000 on the guilty party. If further noncompliance occurs, the FTC usually enjoins the DOJ for further prosecution.

RESOURCE ALLOCATION AND THE SUPPLY OF PUBLIC GOODS

The resource allocation question applies both to privately produced goods and to public sector output. In theory the amount of any good that should be supplied at a point in time is that quantity which equates the marginal social cost (MSC) of the good with its marginal social benefit (MSB).

First, the marginal *private* economic cost of a good includes all explicit and implicit costs of its production that are borne by the producer. A product's marginal *social* cost differs from its marginal private cost by the amount of external costs (third-party costs) that accompany the production of an incremental unit of output. This cost includes the value to consumers of any alternative product or products whose production is reduced or eliminated.

In a similar fashion, we can define marginal social benefit as the sum of marginal private benefits and marginal external, or third-party, benefits. The private benefits accrue to those who directly pay a price for the good, while the external benefits are enjoyed by either the purchaser or the nonpurchasers but are not accounted for in the product's market price.

A good should be provided up to the quantity where MSC = MSB. A theoretically optimal allocation of society's resources exists when for all goods the condition that MSB = MSC is attained.

Example 1. Assume a two-good case, where a and b are the goods, where both costs and benefits are measured in dollars, and where initially we have

$$MSB_a = MSC_a = 20$$
$$MSB_b = MSC_b = 40$$

Thus, the social cost of producing the marginal or last unit of a is $20, while that of producing the marginal unit of b is $40. Obviously, it is also true that

$$\frac{MSB_a}{MSC_a} = \frac{MSB_b}{MSC_b} = 1$$

First, for a given income distribution, efficient resource allocation will take place when, for n goods,

$$\frac{MSB_a}{MSC_a} = \frac{MSB_b}{MSC_b} = \ldots \ldots \frac{MSB_n}{MSC_n} = 1$$

This condition simply means that a dollar's worth of social benefit is received for an additional dollar spent on the production of each good. Any deviation from this condition would result in a situation where too much of some good (or goods) and too little of some other good (or goods) is produced.

PUBLIC PROJECT ANALYSIS AND COST-BENEFIT ANALYSIS

In public project analysis, we seek to evaluate investments from the point of view of society as a whole. This means that we need to determine social benefits deriving from public projects and social costs incurred to launch those projects. A social benefit is any gain in utility and a social cost is any loss of utility as measured by the opportunity cost of the project.

We use *cost-benefit analysis*, which is simply the extension of capital project analysis to public sector microeconomic decisions. The steps taken in the construction of a cost-benefit analysis for a public-sector undertaking are as follows:

1. Specify objectives and identify constraints.
2. Formulate alternative means of meeting objectives.
3. Estimate costs of each alternative.
4. Estimate benefits attributable to each alternative.
5. Select the best alternative.

The *benefit-cost (B/C) ratio* or *profitability index* is widely used for public expenditure decisions.

CLASSIFICATION OF GOODS

Most goods originate with private sectors. They are categorized as private goods, and those that are governmental in origin are public goods. Public goods are *nonrival* and nonexclusionary in consumption and therefore benefit persons other than those who buy the goods. A good is *nonrival* in consumption if the consumption of the good by one person does not preclude other people from also consuming the good. A good is *nonexclusionary* if, once provided, no one can be excluded from consuming it. Examples of public goods are radio signals, lighthouses, national defense, and clean air.

In order to determine which public goods or projects are worthwhile, and their optimal magnitude, we have to quantify the expected stream of costs and the value of the benefits, and whether revenues can be collected or not. Since any public project involves expected future flows of costs and benefits, we need to deal with the issue of appropriate discounting. What is a proper *social discount rate?*

SOCIAL GOODS AND EXTERNALITIES

When goods are public or social goods, there are always nonmarket interactions in which people are forced to provide resources to others while receiving full compensation or in which people receive benefits without having to make appropriate payments. These nonmarket flows of burdens and benefits are known as *externalities.* Externalities are the positive (beneficial) or negative (harmful) effects that market exchanges have on people who do not participate directly in those exchanges. Externalities are third-party *spillover,* or *neighborhood,* effects. Positive externalities include the social benefits conferred by a firm in training workers who become available to work for other firms that incur no training costs. Negative externalities include traffic congestion and environmental pollution created by a manufacturing plant. The term *technological* externalities is often used and is distinguished from *pecuniary* externalities. Quantifying these externalities and including in estimates of social benefits and social costs may not be an easy task.

Example 2. State Senator Dan Smith has proposed a new state supported convention facility in the state's capitol. The convention facility would provide the state with annual social benefits $500,000 (in lease receipts and in positive externalities) and would cost $4,000,000. The project has a 15 year life. The state planning board normally uses a 9% discount rate when evaluating capital projects. To determine if the state legislature should adopt Smith's proposal, we can calculate the benefit-cost (B/C) ratio. The present value of the benefit is: $500,000 at 9% for 15 years = $500,000 × 8.061= $4,030,500. B/C = 4,030,500/4,000,000 = 1.008, thus the state should accept Smith's proposal because it has a B/C ratio greater than 1.

MANAGEMENT OF ACCOUNTS RECEIVABLES

CASH DISBURSEMENT

The disbursement of cash is improved if based on controlled disbursement when the amount of money to be deposited on a daily basis to pay checks clearing that day is determined. Other effective means to disburse cash are using a positive pay service to reduce the incidence of fraud, and an accounts receivable reconcilement service.

Export receivables and foreign risk may be managed better by taking out export credit insurance coverage to assure payment for shipped goods. Credit coverage may be obtained via the U.S. Export-Import Bank or a letter of credit from a U.S. or foreign bank. Even though a letter of credit guards against customer default, it needs to be secured before each export transaction. In emerging markets, the multinational company should consider the following as part of its accounts receivable management program:

- Stability of the foreign country's banking system.
- Variability in foreign exchange rates.
- Variance in foreign payment schedules.
- Stability of political, economic and financial conditions.
- Astuteness of financial management by the country's trade representatives and other government officials.

Financial Derivative Products and Financial Engineering

FINANCIAL DERIVATIVES

A derivative is simply a transaction, or contract, whose value depends on (or, as the name implies, derives from) the value of underlying assets such as stocks, bonds, mortgages, market indexes, or foreign currencies. One party with exposure to unwanted risk can pass some or all of that risk to a second party. The first party can assume a different risk from the second party, pay the second party to assume the risk, or, as is often the case, create a combination.

The participants in derivatives activity can be divided into two broad types—dealers and end-users. Dealers, few in numbers, include investment banks, commercial banks, merchant banks, and independent brokers. In contrast, the number of end-users is large and growing as more organizations are involved in international financial transactions. End-users include business, banks, securities firms, insurance companies, governmental units at the local, state, and federal levels, "supernational" organizations such as the World Bank, mutual funds, and both private and public pension funds.

The objectives of end-users may vary. A common reason to use derivatives is so that the risk of financial operations can be controlled. Derivatives can be used to manage foreign exchange exposure, especially unfavorable exchange rate movements. Speculators and arbitrageurs can seek profits from general price changes or simultaneous price differences in different markets, respectively. Others use derivatives to *hedge* their position; that is, to set up two financial assets so that any unfavorable price movement in one asset is offset by favorable price movement in the other asset.

There are five common types of derivatives: options, futures, forward contracts, asset swaps, and hybrid. The general characteristics of each are summarized in Figure 1, although only two most common types—options and futures—are covered in detail in this chapter.

An important feature of derivatives is that the types of risk are not unique to derivatives and can be found in many other financial activities. The risks for derivatives are especially difficult to manage for two principal reasons: (1) the derivative products are complex, and (2) there are very real difficulties in measuring the risks associated derivatives. It is imperative for financial officers of a firm to know how to manage the risks from the use of derivatives.

Figure 1   General Characteristics of Major Types of Financial Derivatives

Type	*Market*	*Contract*	*Definition*
Option	OTC or Organized Exchange	Custom* or Standard	Gives the buyer the right but *not* obligation to buy or sell a specific amount at a specified price within a specified period.
Futures	Organized Exchange	Standard	*Obligates* the holder to buy or sell at a specified price on a specified date.
Forward	OTC	Custom	Same as futures
Swap	OTC	Custom	Agreement between the parties to make periodic payments to each other during the swap period.
Hybrid	OTC	Custom	Incorporates various provisions of other types of derivatives.

*Custom contracts vary and are negotiated between the parties with respect to their value, period, and other terms.

OPTIONS

An option is a contract to give the investor the right—but *not an obligation*—to buy or sell something. It has three main features. It allows you, as an investor to "lock in":

1. a specified number of shares of stock
2. at a fixed price per share, called strike or exercise price
3. for a limited length of time.

For example, if you have purchased an option on a stock, you have the right to "exercise" the option at any time during the life of the option. This means that, regardless of the current market price of the stock, you have the right to buy or sell a specified number of shares of the stock at the strike price (rather than the current market price).

Options possess their own inherent value and are traded in *secondary markets*. You may want to acquire an option so that you can take advantage of an expected rise in the price of the underlying stock. Option prices are directly related to the prices of the common stock they apply to. Investing in options is very risky and requires specialized knowledge.

KINDS OF OPTIONS

All options are divided into two broad categories: calls and puts. A call option gives you the right (but not the obligation) to buy:

1. 100 shares of a specific stock
2. at a fixed price per share, called the "strike or exercise price"
3. for up to 9 months, depending on the expiration date of the option

When you purchase a call, you are buying the right to purchase stock at a set price. You expect price appreciation to occur. You can make a sizable gain from a minimal investment, but you may lose all your money if stock price does not go up.

Example 1. You purchase a 3-month call option on Dow Chemical stock for $4 1/2 at an exercise price of $50 when the stock price is $53.

On the other hand, a single put option gives you the right (but not the obligation) to sell:

1. 100 shares of a specific stock
2. at a fixed price, the strike price
3. for up to 9 months, depending on the expiration date of the option

Purchasing a put gives you the right to sell stock at a set price. You buy a put if you expect a stock price to fall. You have the chance to earn a considerable gain from a minimal investment, but you lose the whole investment if price depreciation does not materialize.

The buyer of the contract (called the "holder") pays the seller (called the "writer") a premium for the contract. In return for the premium, the buyer obtains the right to buy securities from the writer or sell securities to the writer at a fixed price over a stated period of time.

Option Holder = Option Buyer = Long Position

Option Writer = Option Seller = Short Position

	Call Option	*Put Option*
Buy (long)	The right to call (buy) from the writer	The right to put (sell) from the writer
Sell (short)	Known as *writing a call,* being obligated to sell if called	Known as *writing a put,* if the stock or contract is put

Calls and puts are typically for widely held and actively traded securities on organized exchanges. With calls there are no voting privileges, ownership interest, or dividend income. However, option contracts are adjusted for stock splits and stock dividends.

Calls and puts are not issued by the company with the common stock but rather by option makers or option writers. The maker of the option receives the price paid for the call or put minus commission costs. The option trades on the open market. Calls and puts are written and can be acquired through brokers and dealers. The writer is required to purchase or deliver the stock when requested.

Holders of calls and puts do not have to exercise them to earn a return. They can trade them in the secondary market for whatever their value is. The value of a call increases as the underlying common stock goes up in price. The call can be sold on the market before its expiration date.

WHY INVESTORS USE OPTIONS

Why use options? Reasons can vary from the conservative to the speculative. The most common reasons are:

1. You can earn large profits with *leverage,* that is, without having to tie up a lot of your own money. The leverage you can have with options typically runs 20:1 (each investor dollar controls the profit on twenty dollars of stock) as contrasted with the 2:1 leverage with stocks bought on margin or the 1:1 leverage with stocks bought outright with cash. *Note:* Leverage is a two-edge sword. It works both ways. You can lose a lot, too. That is why it is a risk, derivative instrument.

2. Options may be purchased as "insurance or hedge" against large price drops in underlying stocks already held by the investor.

3. If you are neutral or slightly bullish in the short term on stocks you own you can sell (or write) options on those stocks and realize extra profit.

4. Options offer a range of strategies that cannot be obtained with stocks. Thus, options are a flexible and complementary investment vehicle to stocks and bonds.

HOW OPTIONS ARE TRADED

Options are traded on listed option exchanges (secondary markets) such as *the Chicago Board Options Exchange, American Stock Exchange, Philadelphia Stock Exchange, and Pacific Stock Exchange.* They may also be exchanged in the *over-the counter (OTC)* market. Option exchanges are only for buying and selling call and put options. Listed options are traded on organized exchanges. Conventional options are traded in the OTC market.

The *Options Clearing Corporation (OCC)* acts as principal in every options transaction for listed options contracts. As principal it issues all listed options, guarantees the contracts, and is the legal entity on the other side of every transaction. Orders are placed with this corporation, which then issues the calls or closes the position. Since certificates are not issued for options, a brokerage account is required. When an investor exercises a call, he goes through the Clearing Corporation, which randomly selects a writer from a member list. A call writer is obligated to sell 100 shares at the exercise price.

Exchanges permit general orders (i.e., limit) and orders applicable only to the option (i.e., spread order).

TERMS OF AN OPTION

There are three key terms you need to be familiar with in connection with options: the exercise or strike price, expiration date, and option premium. The *exercise price* is the price per share for 100 shares, which you may buy at (call). For a put, it is the price at which the stock may be sold. The purchase or sale of the stock is to the writer of the option. The striking price is set for the life of the option on the options exchange. When stock price changes, new exercise prices are introduced for trading purposes reflecting the new value.

In case of conventional calls, restrictions do not exist on what the striking price should be. However, it is usually close to the market price of the stock it relates to. But in the case of listed calls, stocks having a price lower than $50 a share must have striking prices in $5 increments. Stocks between $50 and $100 have striking prices in $20 increments. Striking prices are adjusted for material stock splits and stock dividends.

The *expiration date* of an option is the last day it can be exercised. For conventional options, the expiration date can be any business day; for a listed option there is a standardized expiration date.

The cost of an option is referred to as a *premium.* It is the price the buyer of the call or put has to pay the seller (writer). In other words, the option premium is what an option costs to you as a buyer. *Note:* With other securities, the premium is the excess of the purchase price over a determined theoretical value.

USING PROFIT DIAGRAMS

In order to understand the risks and rewards associated with various option strategies, it is very helpful to understand how the profit diagram works. In fact, it is essential to understanding how an option works. The profit diagram is a visual portrayal of your profit in relation to the price of a stock at a single point in time.

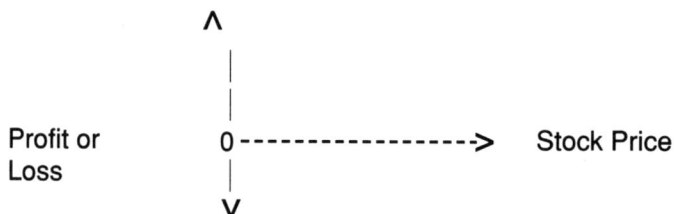

```
                         ^
                         |
                         |
Profit or            0 ----------------->    Stock Price
Loss                     |
                         v
```

Example 2.

IBM Stock Price in 3 months	Profit (Loss)
$ 60	-$2000
$ 70	-$1000
$ 80	$ 0
$ 90	$1000
$ 100	$2000

The following shows the profit diagram for 100 shares of IBM stock if you bought them today at $80 per share and sold them in 3 months. (Commissions are ignored in this example.)

Financial Derivative Products and Financial Engineering

```
$2000  -  |                                      +
$1500  -  |                                  +
$1000  -  |                              +
$ 500  -  |                          +
Profit or Loss      0 ------+------+----*----+-----+-->   Stock Price
-$ 500  -  |   $60        + |              $100
-$1000  -  |           +   $80
-$1500  -  |        +
-$2000  -  |     +
              V
```

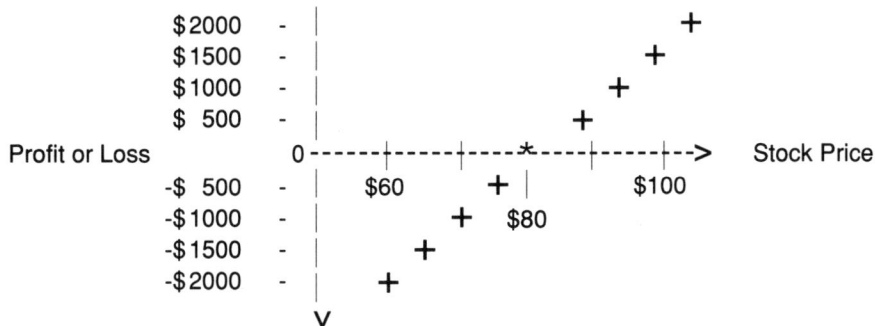

Note that all stocks have the same shape on the profit diagram at any point in the future. You will later see that this is *not* the case with options.

Example 3. Assume that on April 7, you become convinced that IBM stock which is trading at $80 a share will move considerably higher in the next few months. So, you buy one call option on IBM stock with a premium of $2 a share. Since the call option involves a block of 100 shares of stock, it costs you a total of $2 times 100 shares or $200. Assume further that this call option has a striking price of $85 and an expiration date near the end of September. What this means is that for $200 you have the right to buy:

1. 100 shares of IBM stock
2. at $85 a share
3. until near the end of September

This may not sound like you're getting much for $200, but if IBM stock goes up to $95 a share by the end of September, you'd have the right to purchase 100 shares of IBM stock for $8500 ($85 times 100 shares) and to turn right around and sell them for $9500, keeping the difference of $1000, an $800 profit. That works out to 400% profit in less than five months.

However, if you are wrong and IBM stock goes down in price, the most you could lose would be the price of the option, $200. The following displays the profit table for this example.

If the IBM stock price in Sep. turns out to be:		The value of the call option would be:		And your profit would be:
$ 75	---->	$ 0	---->	-$ 200
$ 80		$ 0		-$ 200
$ 85		$ 0		-$ 200
$ 87		$ 200		$ 0
$ 90		$ 500		$ 300
$ 95		$1000		$ 800

The profit diagram will look like this:

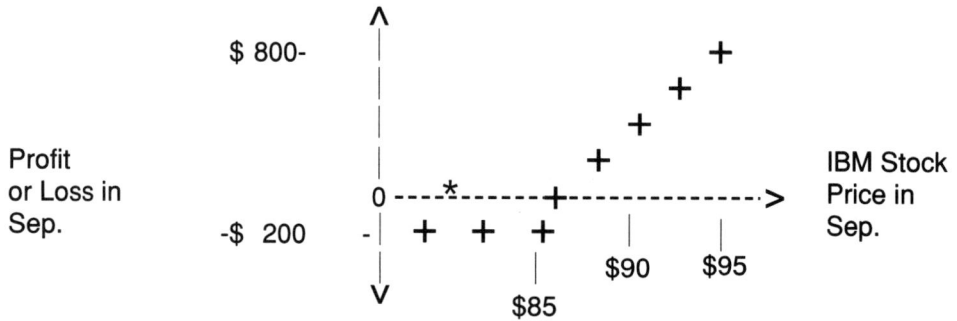

```
                            ^
        $ 800-              |                           +
                            |                        +
                            |                     +
    Profit                  |                  +            IBM Stock
    or Loss in            0 ----*------+--------------->   Price in
    Sep.                    |                            Sep.
            -$ 200        - |  +   +   +      |      |
                            |               $90    $95
                            V
                                   $85
```

You are "long 1 IBM Sep 85 call" option.

Notice where the profit line bends—at $85, unlike stocks that have the same shape on the profit diagram at any point in the future. This is *not* the case with options. You start making money after the price of IBM stock goes higher than the $85 striking price of the call option. When this happens, the option is called "in-the-money."

On the other hand, the profit diagram for a put option looks like this:

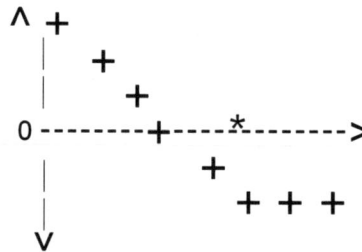

```
        ^ +
        |    +
        |      +
      0 --------+----*-------->
        |            +
        |              + + +
        V
```

So, a put is typically used by an investor who is bearish on that particular stock. The put option can also be used as "insurance" against price drops for the investor with a long stock position.

OPTION COSTS

The premium for an option (or cost of an option) depends primarily on:

- Fluctuation in price of the underlying security. (A higher variability means a higher premium because of the greater speculative appeal of the option.)
- Time period remaining before the option's expiration. (The more time there is until the expiration, the greater the premium you must pay the seller.)

- Price spread between the stock compared to the option's strike price. (A wider difference translates to a higher price.)

Example 4. ABC stock is selling at $32 a share today. Consider two options:

1. Option X gives you the right to buy the stock at $25 per share.

2. Option Y gives you the right to buy the stock at $40 per share.

Since you would rather have an option to pay $25 for a $32 stock instead of $32, Option X is more valuable than Option Y. Thus, it will cost you more to buy Option X than to buy Option Y.

Other factors that determine the cost of an option are:

- The dividend trend of the underlying security
- The volume of trading in the option
- The exchange the option is listed on
- "Going" interest rates
- The market price of the underlying stock

In-the-Money and Out-of-the-Money Call Options

Options may or may not be exercised, depending on the difference between the market price of the stock and the exercise price.

Let P = the price of the underlying stock

and S = the exercise price

There are three possible situations:

1. If $P > X$ or $P - X > 0$, then the call option is said to be *in the money.* (By exercising the call option, you, as a holder, realize a positive profit, $P–X$)

The value of the call in this case is:

Value of call = (market price of stock – exercise price of call) $\times 100$

Example 5. Assume that the market price of a stock is $90, with a strike price of $80. The call has a value of $1,000.

2. If $P - X = 0$, then the option is said to be *at the money.*

3. If $P - X < 0$, then the option is said to be *out of the money.* It is unprofitable. The option holder can purchase the stock at the cheaper price in the market rather than exercising the option and thus the option is thrown away. Out-of-the-money call options have no intrinsic value.

If the total premium (option price) of an option is $14 and the intrinsic value is $6, there is an additional premium of $8 arising from other factors.

Total premium is comprised of the intrinsic value and speculative premium (time value) based on variables like risk, expected future prices, maturity, leverage, dividend, and fluctuation in price.

$$\text{Total premium} = \text{intrinsic value} + \text{speculative premium (time value)}$$

1. Intrinsic value = In the money option
i.e., $P - S > 0$ for a call and $S - P > 0$ for a put option
2. Time value—For in the money options, time value is the difference between premium and intrinsic value. For other options all value is time value.

Call option   Put option

In-the-Money and Out-of-the-Money Put Options

A put option on a common stock allows the holder of the option to sell ("put") a share of the underlying stock at an exercise price until an expiration date. The definition of in-the-money and out-of-the-money are different for puts since the owner may sell stock at the strike price. For a put option, the option is in the money if $P - X < 0$.

Its value is determined as follows:

$$\text{Value of put} = (\text{exercise price of put} - \text{market price of stock}) \times 100$$

And the option is out of the money when $P - X > 0$ and has no value.

Example 6. Assume a stock has a market price of $100 and a strike price of the put is $116. The value of the put is $1,600.

If market price of stock exceeds strike price, an out-of-the money put exists. Because a stock owner can sell it for a greater amount in the market relative to exercising the put, no intrinsic value exists of the out-of-money put.

	ABC Calls at 60 Strike Price Stock Price	ABC Puts at 60 Strike Price Stock Price
In-the-money	Over 60	Under 60
At-the-money	60	60
Out-of-the-money	Under 60	Over 60

The theoretical value for calls and puts reflects the price the options should be traded. But usually they are traded at prices exceeding true value when options have a long period to go. This difference is referred to as investment premium.

$$\text{Investment premium} = \frac{\text{option premium} - \text{option value}}{\text{option value}}$$

Example 7. Assume a put with a theoretical value of $2,500 and a price of $3,000. It is therefore traded at an investment premium of 20% [($3,000 − $2,500)/$2,500].

THE RISKS AND REWARDS OF OPTIONS

Your risk in buying options is limited to the premium you paid. That is the downside risk for option investing. For example, assume you own a two-month call option to acquire 500 shares of ABC Company at $20 per share. Within that time period, you exercise the option when the market price is $38. You make a gain of $9,000 ($18 × 500 shares) except for the brokerage commission. Of course, the higher the stock's price goes, the more you can profit. However, if the market price had declined from $20 you would not have exercised the call option, and you would have lost the cost of the option. *Note:* If you owned the stock whose price fell $10 per share, you would have lost $10 a share. But if you had an option to buy that stock, you could have lost only the cost (premium) of that option, no matter how far the stock price fell.

How Do Calls Work?

By buying a call you can own common stock for a low percentage of the cost of buying regular shares. Leverage is obtained since a small change in common stock price can magnify a major move in the call option's price. An element of the percentage gain in the price of the call is the speculative premium related to the remaining time left on the call. Calls can also be viewed as a way of controlling 100 shares of stock without a large monetary commitment.

Example 8. Assume that a security has a present market price of $70. A call can be bought for $600 permitting the purchase of 100 shares at $70 per share. If stock price goes up, the call increases in value. Assume the stock goes to $95 at the call's expiration date. The profit is $25 per share in the call, or a total of $2,500 on an investment of $600. There is a return of 417%. When you exercise the call for 100 shares at $70 each, you can immediately sell them at $95 per share.

Note: You could have earned the same amount by investing directly in the common stock. However, you would have needed to invest $7,000 resulting in a much lower return rate.

How Do Puts Work?

The put holder may sell 100 shares at the exercise price for a specified time period to a put writer. A put is bought when a price decline is expected. Like a call option, the entire premium cost (investment) would be lost if the price does not drop.

Example 9. Assume that a stock has a market price of $80. You buy a put to sell 100 shares of stock at $80 per share. The put cost is $500. At the exercise date, the price of the stock goes to $70 a share. The profit is $10 per share, or $1,000. You just buy on the market 100 shares at $70 each and then sell them to the writer of the put for $80 each. The net gain is $500 ($1,000 − $500).

The following tables summarize payoffs, risks, and breakeven stock prices for various option participants.

Option Payoffs and Risks

	Call buyer	Call seller (writer)
Pay-off	$-c + (P - S)$ where c = the call premium For a break-even, $-c + (P - S) = 0$ or $P = S + c$.	$+c - (P - S)$
Risk	Maximum risk is to lose the premium because investor	No risk limit as the stock price rises above

	throws away the out-of-money option	the exercise price— Uncovered (naked) option
		To be covered, investor should own the underlying stock or hold a long call on the same stock

	Put buyer	*Put seller (writer)*
Pay-off	$-c + (S - P)$ where c = the put premium For a breakeven, $-c + (S - P)$ $= 0$ or $P = S - c$	$+c - (S - P)$
Risk	Maximum risk is to lose the premium	Maximum risk is the strike price when the stock price is zero— Uncovered (naked) To be covered, investor should sell the underlying stock short or hold a long put on the same stock

Breakeven Points for Option Parties

Option parties	*Breakeven market price*
A call-holder	the strike price + the premium
A put-holder	the strike price – the premium
A call-writer	the strike price + the premium
A put-writer	the strike price – the premium
A covered call-writer	the original cost of the security – the premium
A covered put-writer	the strike price + the premium (short the stock)

CALL AND PUT INVESTMENT STRATEGIES YOU MAY USE

Investment possibilities with calls and puts include (1) hedging, (2) speculation, (3) straddles, and (4) spreads. If you own call and put options, you can *hedge* by holding two or more securities to reduce risk and earn a profit. You may purchase a stock and subsequently buy an option on it. For instance, you may buy a stock and write a call on it. Further, if you own a stock that has appreciated you may buy a put to insulate from downside risk.

Example 10. You bought 100 shares of XYZ at $52 per share and a put for $300 on the 100 shares at an exercise price of $52. If the stock does not move, you lose $300 on the put. If the price falls, your loss offsets your gain on the put. If stock price goes up, you have a capital gain on the stock but lose your investment in the put. To obtain the advantage of a hedge, you incur a loss on the put. Note that at the expiration date, you have a loss with no hedge any longer.

You may employ calls and puts to *speculate*. You may buy options when you believe you will make a higher return compared to investing in the underlying stock. You can earn a higher return at lower risk with out-of-the-money options. However, with such an option, the price is composed just of the investment premium, which may be lost if the stock does not increase in price.

Here is an example of this kind of speculation.

Example 11. You speculate by buying an option contract to purchase 100 shares at $55 a share. The option costs $250. The stock price increases to $63 a share. You exercise the option and sell the shares in the market, recognizing a gain of $550 ($63 − $55 − $2.50 = $5.50 × 100 shares). You, as a speculator, can sell the option and earn a profit due to the appreciated value. But if stock price drops, your loss is limited to $250 (the option's cost). Obviously, there will also be commissions. In sum, this call option allowed you to buy 100 shares worth $5,500 for $250 up to the option's expiration date.

Straddling combines a put and call on the identical security with the same strike price and expiration date. It allows you to trade on both sides of the market. You hope for a substantial change in stock price either way so as to earn a gain exceeding the cost of both options. If the price change does materialize, the loss is the cost of the both options. You may increase risk and earning potential by closing one option prior to the other.

Example 12. You buy a call and put for $8 each on October 31 when the stock price is $82. There is a three-month expiration date. Your investment is $16, or $1,600 in total. If the stock increases to $150 at expiration of the options, the call generates a profit of $60 ($68 − $8) and the loss on the put is $8. Your net gain is $52, or $5,200 in total.

In a *spread,* you buy a call option (long position) and write a call option (short position) in the identical stock. A sophisticated investor may write many spreads to profit from the spread in option premiums. There is substantial return potential but high risk. Different kinds of spreads exist such as a *bull call spread* (two call's having the same expiration date) and *horizontal spread* (initiated with either two call options or two put options on the identical underlying stock). These two options must be with the same strike price but different expiration dates.

You may purchase straddles and spreads to maximize return or reduce risk. You may buy them through dealers belonging to the *Put and Call Brokers and Dealers Association.*

HOW OPTION WRITING WORKS

The writer of a call contracts to sell shares at the strike price for the price incurred for the call option. Call option writers do the opposite of buyers. Investors write options expecting price appreciation in the stock to be less than what the call buyer anticipates. They may even anticipate the price of the stock to be stable or decrease. Option writers receive the option premium less applied transaction costs. If the option is not exercised, the writer earns the price he paid for it. If the option is exercised, the writer incurs a loss, possibly significant.

If the writer of an option elects to sell, he must give the stock at the contracted price if the option is exercised. In either instance, the option writer receives income from the premium. (Shares are in denominations of 100.) An investor typically sells an option when he anticipates it not to be exercised. The risk of option writing is that the writer, if uncovered, must purchase stock or, if covered, loses the gain. As the writer, you can purchase back an option to end your exposure.

Example 13. Assume a strike price of $50 and a premium for the call option of $7. If the stock is below $50, the call would not be exercised, and you earn the $7 premium. If the stock is above $50, the call may be exercised, and you must furnish 100 shares at $50. But the call writer loses money if the stock price was above $57.

SELLING AN OPTION ON SOMETHING YOU DON'T OWN

Naked (uncovered) and *covered* options exist. Naked options are on stock the writer does not own. There is much risk because you have to buy the stock and then immediately sell it to the option buyer on demand, irrespective of how much you lose. The investor writes the call or put for the premium and will retain it if the price change is beneficial to him or insignificant. The writer has unlimited loss possibilities.

To eliminate this risk, you may write *covered options* (options written on stocks you own). For instance, a call can be written for stock the writer owns or a put can be written for stock sold short. This is a conservative strategy to generate positive returns. The objective is to write an out-of-the-money option, retain the premium paid, and have the stock price equal but not exceed the option exercise price. The writing of a covered call option is like hedging a position because if stock price drops, the writer's loss on the security is partly offset against the option premium.

OPTION STRATEGIES

Currently, about 90% of the option strategies implemented by investors are long call's and long put's only. These are the most basic strategies and are the easiest to implement. However, they are usually the riskiest in terms of a traditional measure of risk: variability (uncertainty) of outcomes. A variety of other strategies can offer better returns at less risk.

(1) *Long Call*
   This strategy is implemented simply by purchasing a call option on a stock. This strategy is good for a very bullish stock assessment.

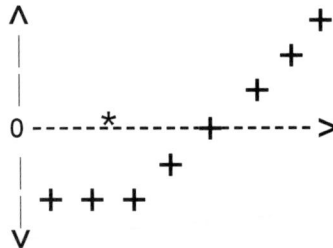

```
      ^                        +
      |                      +
      |                    +
    0 -----*------+------>
      |          +
      | + + +  +
      v
```

(2) *Bull Call Spread*
   This strategy requires two call's, both with the same expiration date. It is good for a mildly bullish assessment of the underlying stock.

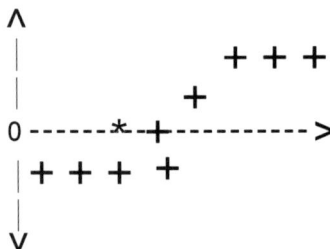

```
      ^
      |              + + +
      |            +
    0 ------*-+----------->
      |+ + + +
      |
      v
```

(3) *Naked Put Write*
   This strategy is implemented by writing a put and is appropriate for a neutral or mildly bullish projection on the underlying stock.

```
      ^
      |              + + + +
      |           +
    0 -----+-----*------>
      |       +
      |+
      V
```

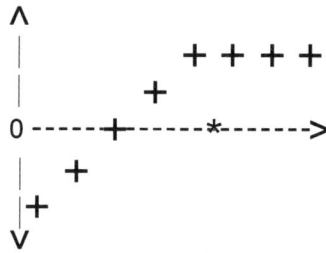

(4) Covered Call Write

This strategy is equivalent to the *naked put write.* This strategy is good as a neutral or mildly bullish assessment of the underlying stock.

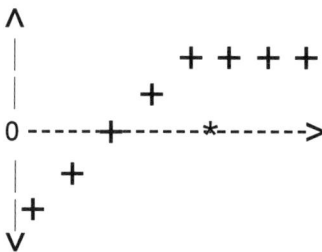

```
      ^
      |              + + + +
      |           +
    0 -----+------*----->
      |        +
      |+
      V
```

(5) Straddle

This strategy is implemented by purchasing both a call and a put option on the same underlying stock. This strategy is good when the underlying stock is likely to make a big move but there is uncertainty as to its direction.

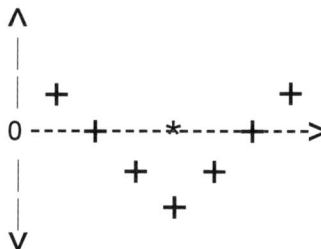

```
      ^
      |
      |   +              +
    0 ----+----*----+--->
      |         +    +
      |            +
      |
      V
```

(6) Inverse Straddle

This strategy is implemented by writing both a call and a put on the same underlying stock. This strategy is appropriate for a neutral assessment of the underlying stock. A substantial amount of collateral is required for this strategy due to the open-ended risk should the underlying stock make a big move.

```
      ^
      |         +
      |      +     +
    0 ----+----*----+--->
      |  +            +
      |
      v
```

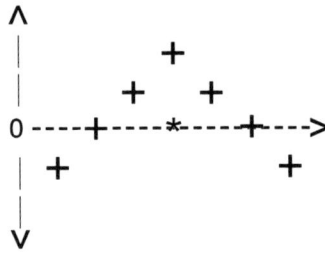

(7) Horizontal Spread

This strategy is implemented with either two call options or two put options on the same underlying stock. These two options must have the same striking price but have different expiration dates.

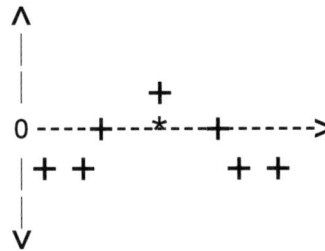

```
        ^
        |
        |          +
      0 ----+---*--+------>
        |++        + +
        |
        v
```

(8) Naked Call Write

This strategy is implemented by writing a call and is appropriate for a neutral or mildly bearish assessment on the underlying stock. A substantial amount of collateral is required for this strategy due to the open-ended risk should the underlying stock rise in value.

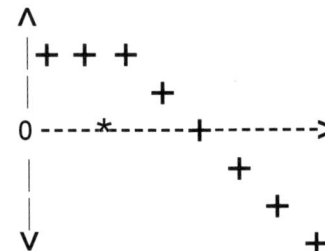

```
      ^
      |+ + +
      |       +
    0 ----*------+-------->
      |        +
      |          +
      v            +
```

(9) Bear Put Spread

This strategy is the opposite of the bull call spread. It is implemented with two put's, both with the same expiration date. This strategy is appropriate for a mildly bearish assessment of the underlying stock.

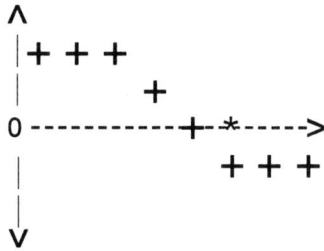

```
     ^
     |+ + +
     |       +
   0 ----------+-*----->
     |           + + +
     |
     |
     V
```

(10) *Long Put*

This strategy is implemented simply by purchasing a put option on a stock. It is good for a very bearish stock assessment.

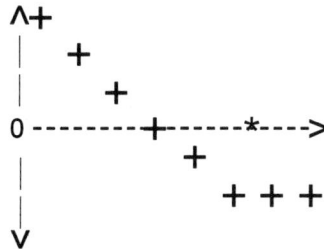

```
     ^+
     |    +
     |      +
   0 --------+------*---->
     |          +
     |            + + +
     |
     V
```

Note: Computer software such as *OptionVue* plots profit tables and diagrams and helps you evaluate large numbers of options for minimum risk and maximum reward.

HOW TO CHOOSE AN OPTION STRATEGY

The key question remains: Which option strategy should you choose? What factors should you consider? What would be a typical decision process? There are three major steps in the decision process:

(1) *Select the underlying stock*

First, you should decide which stock to consider and do a thorough analysis on the stock, including the effects of current market trends.

(2) *Choose the strategy*

You then determine the risk involved in the stock based on its volatility. Computer software can be of great help. Based on the assessment on the stock (bullish or bearish) and its volatility, a strategy is chosen. For example, a strongly bullish, high volatility stock would indicate a long call strategy since the underlying stock is likely to rise a substantial amount.

The ranking of strategies so far discussed, from bullish to bearish, is as follows:

Bullish	• Long Call
	• Bull Call Spread
	• Naked Put Write (Covered Call Write)
Neutral	• Straddle
	• Inverse Straddle
	• Horizontal Spread
Bearish	• Naked Call Write
	• Bear Put Spread
	• Long Put

Note: The key to choosing the specific option contracts to implement a strategy is to accurately forecast both the price of the underlying stock and the amount of time it will take to get to that price. This will facilitate choosing the striking price and expiration date of the options to be used.

(3) *Assess the risk*

Option strategies have some interesting risk/reward tradeoffs. Some strategies have a small chance of a very large profit while other strategies have a large chance of making a small profit.

You have to decide exactly how much to risk for how much reward.

INDEX OPTIONS

Options on stock indexes rather than on individual stocks have been popular among investors. Index options include ones on S&P 100, S&P OTC 250, S&P 500, Gold/Silver Index, and Computer Technology Index.

Index options offer advantages over stock options in several ways:

1. There is greater stability in a stock index due to *diversification*. Since an index is a composite of stocks, the effects of mergers, announcements, and reports are much milder in an index than with an individual stock.

2. Index options provide a wider selection of striking prices and expiration dates than stock options.

3. It appears easier to predict the behavior of the market than an individual stock.

4. More liquidity exists with index options. Due to the high volume of activity, it is easier to buy and sell index options for the price you want. This is especially helpful for far out-of-the-money or deep in-the-money options.

5. Index options are always settled in cash, never in shares of the underlying stock. This settlement is automatic at expiration and the cash settlement prevents unintended stock assignment.

A disadvantage of index options is that no covered writing is possible on index options.

SOFTWARE FOR OPTIONS ANALYSIS

The Value Line Options Survey (800-535-9643 ext. 2854-Dept. 414M10) recommends the few dozen buying and covered writing candidates (out of more than 10,000 options listed on the several exchanges), based on their computerized model.

The following is a list of popular options software:

Stock Option Analysis Program and Stock Options Scanner (DOS)
H&H Scientific, (301) 292-2958

An Option Valuator/An Option Writer (DOS)
Revenge Software, (516) 271-9556

Strategist (DOS)
Iotinomics Corp., (800) 255-3374 or (801) 466-2111

Advanced Stock Option Analyzer (DOS, Mac)
Option-80, (508) 369-1589

Optionvue IV (DOS)
Optionvue Systems International, Inc.,
(800) 733-6610 or (708) 816-6610

Option Pro (Windows)
Essex Trading Co., (800) 726-2140 or (708) 416-3530

Options and Arbitrage Software Package (DOS)
Programmed Press, (516) 599-6527

THE BLACK-SCHOLES OPTION PRICING MODEL (OPM)

The model provides the relationship between call option value and the five factors that determine the premium of an option's market value over its expiration value:

1. **Time to maturity.** The longer the option period, the greater the value of the option.
2. **Stock price volatility.** The greater the volatility of the underlying stock's price, the greater its value.
3. **Exercise price.** The lower the exercise price, the greater the value.
4. **Stock price.** The higher the price of the underlying stock, the greater the value.
5. **Risk-free rate.** The higher the risk-free rate, the higher the value.

The formula is:

$$V = P[N(d_1)] - Xe^{-rt}[N(d_2)]$$

where

> V = current value of a call option
>
> P = current price of the underlying stock
>
> $N(d)$ = cumulative normal probability density function = probability that a deviation less than d will occur in a standard normal distribution.
>
> X = exercise or strike price of the option
>
> t = time to exercise date (For example, 3 months means $t = 3/12 = 1/4 = 0.25$)
>
> r = (continuously compounded) risk-free rate of interest
>
> e = 2.71828
>
> $$d_1 = \frac{\ln(P/X) + [r + s^2/2]t}{s\sqrt{t}}$$
>
> $$d_2 = \frac{\ln(P/X) + [r + s^2/2]t}{s\sqrt{t}} \text{ or } = d_1 - s\sqrt{t}$$
>
> s^2 = variance per period of (continuously compounded) rate of return on the stock

The formula, while somewhat imposing, actually requires readily available input data, with the exception of s^2, or volatility. P, X, r, and t are easily obtained. The implications of the option model are the following:

1. The value of the option increases with the level of stock price relative to the exercise price (P/X), the time to expiration times the interest rate (rt), and the time to expiration times the stock's variability (s^2t).
2. Other properties:

a. The option price is always less than the stock price.
b. The optional price never falls below the payoff to immediate exercise (P − EX or zero, whichever is larger).
c. If the stock is worthless, the option is worthless.
d. As the stock price becomes very large, the option price approaches the stock price less the present value of the exercise price.

Example 14. You are evaluating a call option which has a $20 exercise price and sells for $1.60. It has three months to expiration. The underlying stock price is also $20 and its variance is 0.16. The risk-free rate is 12 percent. The option's value is:

First, calculate d_1 and d_2:

$$d_1 = \frac{\ln(P/X) + [r + s^2/2]t}{s\sqrt{t}}$$

$$= \frac{\ln(\$20/\$20) + [0.12 + (0.16/2)](0.25)}{(0.40)\sqrt{0.25}}$$

$$= \frac{0 + 0.05}{0.20} = 0.25$$

$$d_2 = d_1 - s\sqrt{t} = 0.25 - 0.20 = 0.05$$

Next, look up the values for $N(d_1)$ and $N(d_2)$:

$$N(d_1) = N(0.25) = 1 - 0.4013 = 0.5987$$
$$N(d_2) = N(0.05) = 1 - 0.4801 = 0.5199$$

Finally, use those values to find the option's value:

$$V = P[N(d_1)] - Xe^{-rt}[N(d_2)]$$
$$= \$20[0.5987] - \$20e^{(-0.12)(0.25)}[0.5199]$$
$$= \$11.97 - \$19.41(0.5199)$$
$$= \$11.97 - \$10.09 = \$1.88$$

At $1.60, the option is undervalued according to the Black-Scholes model. The rational investor would buy one option and sell .5987 shares of stock short.

Note: Under FASB Statement No. 123, *Accounting for Stock-Based Compensation,* companies are required to provide new footnote disclosures about employee stock options based on their fair value at the date of the grant. Since options granted to employees generally are not traded on an organized exchange, Statement No. 123 requires companies to use recognized option pricing models such as the Black-Scholes model to estimate the fair values.

FUTURES CONTRACTS

Futures is another derivative instrument. A futures is a contract to purchase or sell a given amount of an item for a given price by a certain date in the future (thus the name "futures market"). The seller of a futures contract agrees to deliver the item to the buyer of the contract, who agrees to purchase the item. The contract specifies the amount, valuation, method, quality, month, and means of delivery, and exchange to be traded in. The month of delivery is the expiration date; in other words, the date on which the commodity or financial instrument must be delivered.

Commodity contracts are guarantees by a seller to deliver a commodity (e.g., cocoa or cotton). Financial contracts are a commitment by the seller to deliver a financial instrument (e.g., a Treasury bill) or a specific amount of foreign currency.

What Is the Difference Between a Long and Short Position?

A long position is the purchase of a contract expecting the price to increase. A short position is selling expecting price to decrease. The position may be terminated by reversing the transaction. For example, the long buyer can subsequently engage in a short position of the commodity or financial instrument. Mostly all futures are offset (canceled out) prior to delivery. It is unusual for delivery to settle the futures contract.

How Are Futures Contracts Traded?

A futures contract is traded in the futures market. Trading is performed by specialized brokers. Some commodity firms deal exclusively in futures. The fee for a futures contract is tied to the amount of the contract and the item's price. Commissions vary depending on the amount and nature of the contract. The trading in futures is basically the same as with stocks, except the investor needs a commodity trading account. However, the margin buying and the types of orders are the same. You buy or sell contracts with desired terms.

FUTURES TRADING AND RISK

Futures trading may assist an investor handling inflation but is specialized with much risk. Your loss may be magnified due to *leverage*. Leverage (using of other people's money) means with minimal down payment you control something of much greater value. For instance, you can put down $2,000 to control a futures contract valued at $40,000. Each time the price of a commodity increases $1 you could earn or lose $20. With an *option,* you just lose the money invested. With a futures contract, you lose a lot more. Further, futures contract prices may be very unstable. However, many exchanges place per day price limits on each contract trading to insulate traders from huge losses.

COMMODITIES FUTURES

A commodity contract involves a seller who contracts to deliver a commodity by a specified date at a set price. The contract stipulates the item, price, expiration date, and standardized unit to be traded (e.g., 100,000 pounds). Commodity contracts may last up to one year. You must always appraise the impact of market activity on the contract's value.

Assume that you purchase a futures contract for the delivery of 2,000 units of a commodity six months from now at $5.00 per unit. The seller of the contract does not have to have physical custody of the item, and the contract buyer does not have to take possession of the commodity at the "deliver" date. Commodity contracts are typically reversed, or terminated, before consummation. For example, as the initial buyer of 5,000 bushels of wheat, you may engage in a similar contract to sell the same amount, in effect closing your position.

You may enter into commodity trading to achieve high return rates and hedge inflation. In times of increasing prices, commodities react favorably because they are tied to economic trends. However, there is high risk and uncertainty since commodity prices fluctuate and there is a lot of low-margin investing. You need a lot of cash in case of a margin call to cover losses. To minimize risk, hold a diversified portfolio. Futures contracts are only for knowledgeable and experienced investors.

The buyer of a commodity can opt to terminate the contract or continue holding on expectation of higher profits. Conversely, the investor may use the earnings to furnish margin on another futures contract (called an inverse pyramid in a futures contract).

Commodity futures enable buyers and sellers to negotiate cash (spot) prices. Cash is paid to immediately obtain custody of a commodity. Prices in the cash market depend partly upon prices in the futures market. There may be higher prices for the commodity over time, taking into account carrying costs and expected inflation.

Commodity futures are traded in the *Chicago Board of Trade (CBOT),* the largest exchange. There are other exchanges specializing in particular commodities such as *the New York Cotton Exchange (NCTN), Chicago Mercantile Exchange (CME)*, and *Kansas City Board of Trade (KBOT)*. Because of the possibility of substantial gains and losses in commodities, exchanges have caps on the highest daily price changes for a commodity. *The Federal Commodity Futures Trading Commission* regulates commodities exchanges. Commodity futures trading is accomplished through open outcry auction.

RETURNS AND RISKS FOR FUTURES CONTRACTS

The return on a futures contract stems from capital appreciation (selling price less acquisition cost) because no current income is earned. Significant capital gain may arise from price fluctuation in the commodity and the impact of leverage due to low margin. If things go against you, much of your investment may be lost. The return on investment in commodities (a long or short position) equals:

$$\text{Return on investment} = \frac{\text{Selling price} - \text{purchase price}}{\text{Margin deposit}}$$

Example 15. Assume you buy a contract on a commodity for $80,000, with a deposit of $10,000. Subsequently, you sell the contract for $85,000. The return is:

$$\frac{\$85,000 - \$80,000}{\$10,000} = 50\%$$

The margin requirement for commodity contracts is small, typically from 3% to 6% of the contract's value. (For stocks, recall that the margin requirement was 50%). Because in commodities trading there is no loan involved, there is no interest.

An *initial margin deposit* must be made on a futures contract so as to cover a drop in market price on the contract. Such deposit varies with the type of contract and the particular commodity exchange.

A *maintenance deposit* may also be required, which is lower than the initial deposit. It furnishes the minimum margin that must be kept in the account. It is typically about 80% of the initial margin.

Example 16. On September 1, you contract to purchase 50,000 pounds of sugar at $2 a pound to be delivered by December 31. The value of the total contract is $100,000. The initial margin requirement is 15%, or $15,000. The margin maintenance requirement is 80%, or $12,000. Assuming a contract loss of $2,500, you must pay $2,500 to cover the margin position. If not, the contract will be terminated with the ensuing loss.

WHO USES FUTURES?

Trading in futures is performed by hedgers and speculators. Investors employ hedging to protect their position in a commodity. For instance, a farmer (the seller) may hedge to obtain a higher price for his goods while a processor (or buyer) of the product will hedge to get a lower price. By hedging you reduce the risk of loss but forego earning a sizable profit.

Example 17. A commodity is presently selling at $160 a pound. The potential buyer (assume a manufacturer) anticipates the price to increase. To protect against higher prices, the purchaser buys a futures contract selling at $175 a pound. Five months later, the commodity price is $225. The futures contract price will similarly increase to say, $250. The buyer's profit is $75 a pound. If 10,000 pounds are involved, the total profit is $750,000. However, the cost on the market rose by only $65 pound, or $650,000. The producer has hedged his position, deriving a profit of $100,000, and has put a tip on the rising commodity costs.

Commodities may also be used for speculation in the market. Speculators engage in futures contracts to obtain capital gain on price increases of the commodity, currency, or financial instrument.

Example 18. You buy a September futures contract for 20,000 pounds of wheat at $2 a pound. If the price rises to $2.20, you'll gain $.20 a pound for a total gain of $4,000. The percent gain, assuming an initial margin requirement of 5%, is 200% ($.2/$.1). Assuming transactions occur over a three-month period, the annual gain would be 800% (200% × 12 months/3 months). This resulted from a mere 10% ($.2/$2.00) gain in the price of a pound of wheat.

HOW TO MINIMIZE RISKS

Spreading capitalizes on wide swings in price and at the same time limits loss exposure. Spreading is like stock option trading. You engage in at least two contracts to earn some profit while capping loss potential. You buy one contract and sell the other expecting to achieve a reasonable profit. If the worst occurs, the spread aids in minimizing the investor's loss.

Example 19. You buy Contract A for 20,000 pounds of commodity T at $300 a pound. Simultaneously, you sell short Contract B for 20,000 pounds of the identical commodity at $325 per pound. Later, you sell Contract A for $325 a pound and buy Contract B for $345 a pound. Contract A earns a profit of $25 a pound while Contract B has a loss of $20 a pound. The net effect is a profit of $5 a pound, or a total gain of $100,000.

FINANCIAL FUTURES

Financial futures include: (1) interest rate; (2) foreign currency; and (3) stock-index. Financial futures trading is similar to commodity trading. It represents about 70 percent of all contracts. Due to fluctuation in interest and exchange rates, financial futures can be used as a hedge. They may also be used to speculate having potential for wide price swings. Financial futures have a *lower* margin requirement than commodities do. For instance, the margin on a U.S. Treasury bill might be as low as 2%.

Financial futures are traded in the *New York Futures Exchange, Amex Commodities Exchange, International Monetary Market* (part of *Chicago Mercantile Exchange*), and *the Chicago Board of Trade.*

How Do Interest Rate Futures Work?

An interest rate futures contract gives the holder the right to a specified amount of the underlying debt security at a later date (typically not exceeding three years). They may be in such forms as Treasury bills, notes, and bonds, paper, "Ginnie Mae (GNMA)" certificates, CRB Index, Eurodollars, and U.S. Dollar Index.

Interest rate futures are expressed as a percentage of the face value of the applicable debt security. The value of interest rate futures contracts is linked to interest rates. For instance, as interest rates drop, the contract's value rises. If the price or quote of the contract increases, the buyer gains but the seller loses. A change of one basis point in interest rates causes a price change. A basis point equals 1/100 of 1%.

Those trading in interest rate futures do not typically take custody of the financial instrument. The contract is employed either to hedge or to speculate on future interest rates and security prices.

How Do Currency Futures Work?

A *currency futures contract* provides the right to a stipulated amount of foreign currency at a later date. The contracts are standardized, and secondary markets exist. Currency futures are stated in dollars per unit of the underlying foreign currency. They usually have a delivery not exceeding one year.

Currency futures may be used to either hedge or speculate. Hedging in a currency may lock you into the best possible money exchange.

WHAT IS A STOCK INDEX FUTURE?

A *stock-index futures contract* is linked to a stock market index (e.g., *the S & P 500 Stock Index, New York Stock Exchange Composite Stock Index*). But smaller investors can use the *S & P 100* futures contract which has a lower margin deposit. Stock-index futures allow you to participate in the overall stock market. You can buy and sell the "market as a whole" instead of one security. If you expect a bull market but are not certain which stock will increase, you should purchase (long position) a stock-index future. Since there is a lot of risk, trade in stock-index futures only to hedge.

TRANSACTING IN FUTURES

You may invest directly in a commodity or indirectly through a *mutual fund*. A third way is to buy a *limited partnership* involved with commodity invest-ments. The mutual fund and partnership approaches are more conservative, because risk is spread and there is professional management.

Futures may be directly invested in as follows:

1. *Commodity pools.* Professional traders manage a pool. A filing is made with the *Commodity Futures Trading Commission (CFTC)*.
2. *Full service brokers.* They may recommend something, when attractive.
3. *Discount brokers.* You must decide on your own when and if.
4. *Managed futures.* You deposit funds in an individual managed account and choose a *commodity trading advisor (CTA)* to trade it.

To obtain information on managed futures, refer to:

1. *ATA Research Inc.* provides information on trading advisors and man-ages individuals accounts via private pools and funds.
2. *Barclay Trading Group* publishes quarterly reports on trading advisers.
3. *CMA Reports* monitors the performance of trading advisers and pri-vate pools.
4. *Management Account Reports,* monthly newsletters, tracking the funds and furnishes information on their fees and track records.
5. *Trading Advisor* follows more than 100 trading advisers.

There are several drawbacks to managed futures, including:

1. High cost of a futures program, ranging from 15 to 20 percent of the funds invested.

2. Substantial risk and inconsistent performance of fund advisors. *Note:* Despite its recent popularity, management futures is still a risky choice and should not be done apart from a well-diversified portfolio.

PRINTED CHART SERVICE AND SOFTWARE FOR FUTURES

There are many printed chart services such as *Future Charts* (Commodity Trend Service, (800) 331-1069 or (407) 694-0960). Also, there are many computer software for futures analysis and charting services, including:

Strategist (DOS)
Iotinomics Corp., (800) 255-3374 or (801) 466-2111

Futures Pro (Windows)
Essex Trading Co., (800) 726-2140 or (708) 416-3530

Futures Markets Analyzer (DOS)
Investment Tools, Inc., (702) 851-1157

Commodities and Futures Software Package, Foreign Exchange Software Package (DOS)
Programmed Press, (516) 599-6527

FINANCIAL ENGINEERING

Closely related to the use of financial derivatives for risk management is *financial engineering.* Financial engineering, an obscure term in finance and investments, is based on financial economics, or the application of economic principles to the dynamics of securities markets, especially for the purpose of structuring, pricing, and managing the risk of financial contracts. In designing a risk-management strategy, the financial engineer, like the civil engineer designing a bridge, works within budgetary and physical restrictions. How much will it cost? How will it perform under present and future tax and accounting regulations and rules? Will it survive a financial earthquake, such as an opposite party's default? Will the strategy perform even if the market moves abruptly and severely? Basically, to be successful, the financial engineer must seek optimal solutions within many diverse and often conflicting constraints.

These varied restrictions lead to different solutions. Financial engineers can design different types of financial instruments or strategies to produce a desired outcome. Robert C. Merton has presented a concrete example of the financial engineer's ability to develop alternative routes to the same end, all basically similar but each with its pros and cons (*Journal of Banking and Finance,* June 1995). For instance, assume a corporate investor wishes to take a leveraged position in the S&P 500 basket of American stocks. Merton lists and dwells on eleven ways of accomplishing that goal. The first three are conventional ways: borrowing to buy stocks.

1. Buying each stock individually on the margin
2. Borrowing to buy shares in a S&P 500 index fund
3. Borrowing to purchase a basket of stocks such as AMEX's SPDR product

The next three are products in which traditional financial intermediaries act as principals and offer payoffs that closely emulate the leveraged stock position; the actual products are structured as bank CDs, indexed notes, or variable rate annuities. The last five categories of alternatives deal with buying so-called financial derivatives, such as futures, forwards, swaps, or one of two options on the S&P index. They are so called in that their payoffs are a function (or are derived from) the value of an underlying index.

Each of the eleven instruments or strategies can give the investor exposure to the stock market, and each produces functionally similar payoffs. The multitude of solutions exist due to the differing constraints facing the financial engineer. It is important to realize that as bridges often collapse, financial engineered products can fail and examining their wreckage to determine culpability is equally difficult.

Nevertheless, financial managers need to benchmark and keep abreast of their rivals' successful uses of financial engineering. CPAs need to be familiar with financial derivative products. The issuance of FASB 123, *Accounting for Stock-Based Compensation,* means CPAs who prepare and audit the financial statements of the companies that issue employee stock options will need to become familiar with option pricing models—including the Black-Scholes model. The new standard says the fair value of options at the date of the grant must be disclosed in a footnote.

Option theory has many applications addressed to CFOs and other financial officers. Besides the Black-Scholes solution for a relatively simple option, many capital budgeting projects have option components, corporate debt is callable or convertible, the decision to prepay a mortgage, labor contracts may endow options on workers (e.g., the choice of early retirement), real estate leases can be renewed, a mine can be opened or closed, and bank line of credits often contain contingent elements. The correct valuations of so many interest rate-contingent securities depend on a satisfactory dynamic model of the interest rate process.

GOING PUBLIC—ABOUT AN INITIAL PUBLIC OFFERING (IPO)

Going public, or an initial public offering (IPO) refers to selling formerly privately held shares to new investors on the organized exchange (New York Stock Exchange) or the over-the-counter market for the first time. For the individual company, going public is often the springboard for greater growth and success.

The public sale of ownership interests can generate funds for business expansion, working capital, repayment of debt, diversification, acquisitions, marketing, and other uses. In addition, a successful IPO increases the visibility and appeal of your company, thereby escalating the demand and value for shares. Investors can benefit from an IPO not only because of the potential increase in market value for their stock, but also because publicly held stock is more liquid and can be readily sold if the business appears to falter or if the investor needs quick cash. The availability of a public market for shares will also help determine the taxable values of the shares and assist in estate transfers.

HOW DOES GOING PUBLIC WORK?

A company considering *going public* will typically work with an underwriter (an investment bank) who, either singly, or as part of a group (syndicate), purchase the stock from the company (the issuer) at a discount from the public offering price. The underwriter or syndicate then sells the shares to the public through brokerage firms and other institutions. Creation of a syndicate pools the risk for underwriters and widens distribution channels for the new issue.

The underwriter advises the company on the marketability of, and demand for, its shares. Estimating the demand for the new stock issue is as much art as science. To estimate the demand, the underwriter and any dealers will collect *indications of interest* from their investors as to how many shares each would like to purchase.

Often, some IPOs may be oversubscribed, implying the demand for shares is larger than the number of shares to be issued. In the case of oversubscription, the underwriters determine who will get the shares at the public offering price. After the underwriter issues the shares, the shares begin trading on the open market. The laws of demand and supply take over. The price of IPO shares can increase or decrease substantially in a short time. For example, a company could have an IPO price of $15 per share, with the first trade in the open market executed at $80. Most of the players in the IPO market are fund managers from big institutions.

THE PROS OF GOING PUBLIC

- Going public raises money—if it is common stock, it does not have to be repaid. The typical IPO raises $20–40 million, but offerings of $100 million are not unusual. This will vary widely by industry. Once public, companies can easily go back to the public market to raise more money. Typically, one third of all IPO issuers return to the public market within five years to issue a "seasoned equity offering." For example, in 1995 General Motors raised $1.14 billion by issuing new common stock. Since the shares sold were newly created, GM's issue was defined as a primary market offering, but since the firm was already publicly held, the offering was not an IPO. Firms generally prefer to obtain equity by retained earnings because of the flotation costs and market pressure involved with the sale of new common stock. However, if a firm needs more money than can be generated from retained earnings, a common stock offering may be necessary.

- As a company expands and becomes more valuable, its owners usually have most of their wealth tied up in the company. By selling some of their stock in a public offering, they can reduce the riskiness of their personal portfolios through this diversification of their holdings.

- Management often experiences an increase in prestige and reputation. Public firms have higher profiles than private firms. This is important in industries where success requires suppliers and consumers to make long-term investments. For example, software requires training and no manager wants to buy software from a firm that may not be around for future improvements, upgrades, bug fixes, etc. The suppliers' and consumers' perception of company success is a self fulfilling prophecy. However, public firms are usually bigger to begin with, and this may explain why public firms have a better image, on average. Going public will not increase its sales. The important question is if gong public improves the company's stakeholders' perception of success.

- Publicly traded stock can make a business more attractive to prospective and existing employees if stock option and other stock compensation plans are offered. Employee stock-based programs are worth more if transfer restrictions, such as those normally accompanying private company stock, are not placed on the stock.

- Mergers and Acquisitions—many private companies do not just appear on the "radar screen" of potential acquirers. Being public makes it much easier for other firms to notice and analyze the company for synergy.

- The use of proceeds from the sale of the issue is generally unrestricted.

- Public companies can acquire other businesses with stock, without depleting cash reserves.

- Other financing alternatives may improve.

THE CONS OF GOING PUBLIC

- Much jealously-guarded information must be disclosed. The guarded items include management salaries, competitive position, transactions between the company and its management, and the identity of significant customers and suppliers. In addition to the required disclosure of results of operations and financial condition, public companies must be prepared to disclose information about the company, officers, directors and certain shareholders. This information might include company sales and profits by product line, salaries and other compensation of officers and directors, data about major customers, competitive position, pending litigation, and related party transactions. By releasing the information it will become available to competitors, customers, employees and the general public. The information is required in the initial registration statement and updated annually through annual reports, proxies and other public disclosure documents. The company's IPO filings are with the Securities and Exchange Commission (on the Internet, www.sec.gov).

- In addition to the time and effort required to prepare for the filing and offering, a company must be prepared to incur the cost of going public. The principal costs include the underwriter's compensation, legal and accounting fees, printing charges, and transfer agent and filing fees. A company expecting to go public with a high-quality offering should anticipate spending approximately $200,000, excluding underwriter's commissions. The magnitude of these costs usually make public offerings grossing less than $5 million impractical. Furthermore, principals must remember that there is no guarantee that the offering will be a success. With the exception of underwriter's compensation, the costs are incurred regardless of the outcome. The cost of going public does not stop with the initial offering. Other costs associated with being a public company are ongoing. Management must devote time and money to such new areas as shareholder relations, public relations, public disclosures, periodic filings with the SEC, and reviewing stock activity. All of this time, and the time of the personnel hired to handle these functions, would be spent on other management tasks in a privately held company. There are other out-of-pocket expenses. Shareholder meetings, annual and quarterly reports, public relations efforts and legal, accounting and auditing fees must be paid. The total cost of these expenses vary from company to company, but in most cases they range from $50,000 to $150,000 annually.

- Corporate decision making becomes more cumbersome as the company attempts to move from a tightly controlled, entrepreneurially oriented company to a professionally managed one where ownership and management are divorced. Any decision, long-term or short-term, may be manifested promptly in the company's stock price. The company may worry constantly about improving quarterly earnings (and stock prices) instead of trying to take a longer perspective in developing its strategy.

- All IPO participants in the coalition are jointly liable for each others' actions. In practice, they were routinely sued for various omissions in the IPO prospectus when the public market valuation fell below the IPO offering price. Congress recently passed *The Private Securities Litigation Reform Act of 1995*. This act protects the disclosure of firm projections and forced the suing shareholders to have substantial participation in the firm. Although nothing can eliminate lawsuits, this act reduces the likelihood of successful suits and therefore encourages settlement terms.

- Since the number of shares outstanding increases when the company goes public, greater earnings must be achieved to avoid reducing earnings per share.

- If the market price declines, many problems may result: management is usually personally blamed; the flexibility of issuing stock to make acquisitions may be hampered; if the decline occurs soon after the offering, litigation against everyone involved may take place; and other financing alternatives may evaporate.

- If the company is sitting on a gold mine, future earnings have to be shared with outsiders. After a typical IPO, about 40% of the company remains with insiders, but this can vary from 1%–88%, with 20%–60% being the comfortable norm.

- Outsiders can take control and even fire the entrepreneur. There is pressure on the managers to produce annual earnings gains, even when it may be in the shareholders' best long-term interests to adopt a strategy that reduces short-term earnings but raises them in the future years. These factors have led a number of newly public firms to go private in leveraged buyout deals where the managers borrow the money to buy out the nonmanagement stockholders. The use of IPOs is limited primarily because:

  (1) There is a very high cost and much complexity in complying with federal and state laws governing the sale of business securities (the cost for a small business can run from $50,000 to $500,000);

  (2) Offering your business's ownership for public sale does little good unless your company has sufficient investor awareness and appeal to make the IPO worthwhile; and

  (3) Management must be ready to handle the administrative and legal demands of widespread public ownership. Of course, an IPO also means a dilution of the existing shareholders' interests, and the possibility of takeovers or adjustments in management control are present.

HOW TO AVOID THE DRAWBACKS OF GOING PUBLIC

Here are some tips for avoiding the pitfalls of going public.

- Assemble the proper team. This involves selecting an underwriter, accountant, counsel, and perhaps some new directors.
- When choosing an underwriter, distribution capacity is important.
- An underwriter appropriate for one company or one industry may be inappropriate for another. In addition to technical ability, personalities and confidence should be considered.
- The selection of accountants and lawyers need careful examination.
- The registration process is complex, coupled with absolute liability for the company for material misstatements or ommissions—regardless of good faith or motive. It is important to remember that malpractice insurance in the securities field is the most expensive of any specialty. That carries a message. It is good to hire a "Big Five" or nationally prominent accounting firm because it enhances marketability and confidence. The use of large accounting and legal firms may be viewed by the underwriter as insurance in the event of litigation.

- Securities laws are complicated. The sale of "securities" to the public is regulated by federal and state laws that have two primary objectives:

    (1) Require businesses to disclose material information about the company to investors, and

    (2) Prohibit misrepresentation and fraud in the sale of securities. Under federal law, a "security" is broadly defined and would include stocks, notes, bonds, evidence of indebtedness, and most ownership interests. The law defines a "public offering" of a security not by the number of investors to whom the stock is offered, but by the classification of whether the investors are considered "sophisticated" or not. However, state law definitions of a "security" and of a "public offering" can vary from the federal law.

WHAT SHOULD THE OFFER PRICE BE?

The offer price is of great concern to issuers. How much should be charged for giving away a part of the firm? There are two methods that can be used:

- Net Present Value (NPV)—This method relies on discounted cash flow (DCF) methodology. The rationale for NPV is straightforward. An NPV of zero signifies that the IPOs cash flows are exactly sufficient to repay the invested capital and to provide the required rate of return on that capital. If an IPO has a positive NPV, then its cash flows are generating more than the required rate of return on that capital.

- Price/Earnings or Cash Flow Ratios—This shows how much investors are willing to pay per dollar of reported (expected) profits. P/E ratios are higher for firms with higher growth expectations, other things held constant, and lower for riskier companies, suggesting lower growth prospects.

The part of an IPO which every company wants to know is how much money are they going to get. After all, that's what this is all about. Keep in mind that pricing an IPO is more of an art than a science. Also keep in mind that your IPO is going to be underpriced.

The company, its advisors, and the underwriter, will determine the amount of money which can be raised. Don't expect to raise all the money you need at the time of the IPO. What you need to get is enough money to put your expansion plans into place and to clean up your debt. Once the amount of money that needs to be raised is determined, the price per share is going to determine the amount of shares which will be offered to the public. Look to price the issue anywhere from $10 to $20 per share. Generally, one million shares is the low end of the amount of shares which should be issued. Never let an issue go for less than 500,000 shares. There won't be enough liquidity to stabilize the share price. Try not to let the initial share price go for less than $6 per share. Remember that $5 is the minimum price a stock can trade for and still be marginal, while pricing below $3 is considered a penny stock. A company is much better served by issuing one million shares at $10 than 500,000 shares at $20. The problem is that mutual funds, pension funds, and other institutional funds, need good liquidity to purchase the stock. Otherwise, their purchases (10,000 shares and on up) will account for too much ownership in the company. Many of these institutional accounts are prohibited by policy from owning more than 5% of a company. If the company only has 500,000 shares issued, 25,000 shares is the most many institutional accounts can purchase. So make sure you have a good "float" which is the amount of shares in circulation not owned by insiders.

The first part of the pricing analysis includes comparing the company with other companies which are similar in the same industry. The impact of the added capital from the IPO also needs to be evaluated with respect to its impact on the financial condition of the company and operating results. The company's financial projections need to be weighed against comparable companies with similar assets, earnings, and revenue.

Other factors need to be evaluated. These include the current trends in the investment community as to what is selling and what isn't selling right now. Timing of the issue involves determining how backed up the SEC is in reviewing other applications. Investor confidence levels are evaluated as well as Federal Reserve policy, industry trends, and national/international developments. (Equity Analytics, 1998).

WHAT IS THE PROCESS OF GOING PUBLIC?

A company that is thinking of going public should start acting like a public company as much as two years in advance. Several "to do's" include developing a business plan and preparing detailed financial results on a regular basis. Once a company decides to go public, it needs to choose its IPO team consisting of a lead investment bank, accountant, lawyer, etc. The IPO process officially begins with an "all hands" meeting. This meeting usually takes place six to eight weeks before a company officially registers with the SEC. At this meeting all members of the IPO team assign certain duties to each individual and plan a timetable for going public.

The most important and time consuming task facing the IPO team is the development of the prospectus, which is a business document that basically serves as a brochure for the company. Since the SEC requires a "quiet period" on firms once they file an IPO until 25 days after a stock starts trading, the prospectus will have to do most of the talking and selling for the team. The prospectus includes all financial data for a company for the past five years. It also includes information on the management team and a description of a company's target market, competitors, and growth strategy. There is much more information in the prospectus, and the underwriting team goes to great efforts to make sure that it is all accurate.

The next step in the IPO process is the grueling tour, also known as the road show. The road show usually lasts a week, with company management going to a new city every day to meet with prospective investors and show off their business plan. The typical stops generally include the larger cities such as Los Angeles, San Francisco, Boston, and Chicago. If necessary, international cities such as London and Hong Kong are included. The management team's performance on the road show is crucial. It helps determine the success of the IPO. The team has to impress institutional investors and influence them to make significant long-term investments.

Once the road show ends and the final prospectus is distributed to investors, management officials meet with their investment bank to decide on the final offering size and price. Investment banks generally suggest an appropriate price based on expected demand for the deal and other market conditions. The pricing of an IPO is a delicate balancing act. Investment firms have to be concerned with two different sets of customers, the company going public, which wants to raise as much money as possible, and the investors buying the shares of stock, who expect to see immediate gains from their investment. If public interest appears to be slowing it is common for the offering price and number of shares to decrease from expected ranges. Sometimes, a company even has to postpone an offering due to insufficient demand. If a deal is especially hot, the offering size and/or price can be raised from initial projections.

Once the offering price has been agreed to, an IPO is declared effective. This is generally done after a market closes, with the trading of the new stock beginning the next day. In the meantime, the chief underwriter works to confirm its buy orders. The chief underwriter is responsible for ensuring smooth trading during the first crucial days. This underwriter is legally allowed to support the price of a newly issued stock through buying shares in the market or selling them short. They can also impose penalty bids on brokers to discourage "flipping," which is when investors sell shares of an IPO soon after the stock starts trading. An IPO is not declared final until seven days after the firm's initial market appearance. On rare occasions, an IPO can be cancelled even after the stock begins trading (Chervitz, 1998).

ALTERNATIVES TO GOING PUBLIC

Many businesses can sell stock to insiders or to a small group of investors without being subject to securities laws; in effect, they can take advantage of alternatives to going public. However, it's not always clear where the exemptions end, so you should always consult a knowledgeable attorney before selling any stock in your company. The process of soliciting money from the public through the issuance and sale of securities requires a working knowledge of the state and federal registration statements concerning the securities to be sold, complex disclosure documents about the company with detailed information for potential investors, and financial statements. Employing professionals (attorney, accountant, and sometimes a stock underwriter) to assist in the process is a practical necessity.

While many small businesses sell interests in their companies that are "securities," as defined by federal or state laws, the transactions are often exempt from registration regulations because the offerings are sufficiently small in dollar amount, and they are restricted to a limited number and/or type of investor. These exempt offers of securities are called "limited private offerings" and they can avoid much of the cost and delay of a public offering. Unfortunately, to qualify for any of the exemptions, you must fit the criteria for both federal and state security laws. Limited private offerings can be either debt or equity instruments, or a hybrid of both. For instance, a convertible debt warrant would be a debt instrument that allowed the holder to convert the debt into an equity interest at a certain time. These alternative offerings allow the business to tailor the amount of immediate equity (ownership and control) that it relinquishes, and the amount of debt (cash outflow) that it can safely assume. In this module, discussion of the use of limited private offerings is largely confined to equity financing.

Federal exemptions. At the federal level, the most popular exemption from registration requirements for small businesses is Rule 504, commonly known as "Regulation D." Under this provision, private companies that are selling less than $1 million worth of securities to any number of investors within a 12-month period are exempt from federal registration requirements. Solicitations of investors by a private business may be made through almost any means, including advertisements and seminars, and no specific disclosure requirements regarding the stock or the company are required. Most startups and smaller businesses would fall within this exemption.

Even if a securities offer is exempt from the registration requirements of federal or state law, the anti-fraud provisions of those laws may still apply. Therefore, you must take care to prevent misrepresentations or omissions in the offering that create an overly optimistic picture of the investment. The investor should be provided with sufficient information to make an informed decision regarding the investment.

Another exemption may be available to either private or publicly held companies that sell less than $5 million within a 12-month period, if the sales are made only to "accredited investors" and no more than 35 such investors are involved. Accredited investors include institutional investors (e.g., banks, brokers and dealers, insurance companies), company insiders (e.g., officers and directors), and wealthy investors ("wealthy" meaning they have more than $200,000 individual annual income or, individually or jointly with their spouse, have a net worth of over $1 million).

A lesser degree of exemption from regulation exists for a private or publicly-held company that sells an unlimited issuance of securities to an unlimited number of accredited investors, or to no more than 35 nonaccredited but "sophisticated investors" (sophisticated investors have sufficient knowledge and experience so that they understand the risks of the sale, or the issuer reasonably believes the investors have these qualifications). Finally, an exemption exists for private offerings of stock that is sold only to persons living in the same state where the company is both incorporated and does significant business, although reliance upon this intra-state exemption is subject to continual policing because the securities must remain within the state.

State exemptions. Because each state has securities regulations, the local exemptions must be checked. Just because a sale may be exempt from federal registration does not mean state registration is not required. State securities laws are commonly referred to as "blue sky" laws because the regulations were originally enacted to prevent unscrupulous issuers from selling "speculative schemes that have no more basis than so many feet of blue sky." The state laws need not match the federal regulatory exemptions and even though a Uniform Securities Act exists for states to follow, that Act has not been adopted by each state nor is it consistently interpreted in those states which claim to follow it. The result is that consultation with a qualified professional is a practical necessity before soliciting investors for sales of securities.

Forty-seven states currently have relaxed their securities regulations for small business by offering a Small Company Offering Registration (SCOR) procedure. Even if your business is not based in one of these states, you may still register and sell your securities in the states, which have adopted SCOR. For a current list of eligible states, contact the North American Securities Administrators Association at 202-737-0900, or at http://www.nasaa.org.

DIFFERENT MEANS OF OBTAINING FUNDS

- Venture Capital—Some IPO issuers are financed by venture capital (VC) before they go public. This varies by industry, but tends to be higher for firms in industries such as biotechnology. In general, venture capital provides financing for firms that are smaller and at an earlier stage than IPO firms. Venture capitalists prefer high risk, high return investments. In addition, venture capitalists take an active interest in the firm's management. On the positive side, this provides the firm with additional management experience and financing expertise. Many of the successful hi-tech firms would not exist without venture capital. On the negative side, venture capital is expensive. Venture capitalists take a large portion of the firm and often acquire control. See chapter on Venture Capital Financing for more information.

- Private Placements and Limited Offerings—If a firm or its financial advisor have access to interested high net worth individuals and the publicity of an IPO is not important, then this is an excellent alternative. Unlike venture capitalists, private investors typically play a smaller role in the management of the firm. This can be both good or bad, depending on the firm.

- Banks and Finance Companies—This is a better choice than IPOs for stable, non-growth, profitable companies that can provide collateral. One alternative source of financing can be collateralization of receivables.

- Leases—This option avoids initial outlays. Small growth companies often do not have the profits to get immediate use of the tax depreciation laws. Leasing firms can use these tax advantages and will pass on this benefit through lower lease rates.

- Government Loans—Recently the Small Business Administration (SBA) has experienced a reawakening. If the company and its advisors have the appropriate connections and the experience for governmental red tape, then this is a great way to get some tax dollars back.

- Funds from Partners—The company's consumers and suppliers know the company's potential better than unaffiliated investors, and therefore, may be amenable to become investors. Because they have better information than outside investors, they should be willing to provide the company with funds on better terms (Welch, 1996).

PRIVATE PLACEMENT

In a private placement, a company issues equity and debt securities directly to either one or a few large investors. The large investors are financial institutions such as insurance companies, pension plans, and commercial banks.

Advantages of Private Placement Versus Public Issuance

- The flotation cost is less. Flotation cost is the expense of registering and selling the stock issue. Examples are brokerage commissions and underwriting fees. The flotation cost for common stock exceeds that for preferred stock. Flotation cost expressed as a percentage of gross proceeds is higher for smaller issues than for larger ones.

- It avoids SEC filing requirements.

- It avoids the disclosure of information to the public at large.
- There is less time involved to obtain funds.
- It may not be practical to issue securities in the public market when a company is so small that an investment banker would not find it profitable.
- The company's credit rating may be low and as a consequence, investors may not be interested in buying securities when the money supply is limited.

Disadvantages of Private Placement Versus Public Issuance

- It is more difficult to obtain significant amounts of money privately.
- Large investors usually employ stringent credit standards requiring the company to be in a strong financial position.
- Large institutional investors may watch more closely the company's activities.
- Large institutional investors are more capable of obtaining voting control of the company.

Additional Readings

A. G. Edwards & Sons, Inc. *Initial Public Offerings,* 1996–1998. (http://www.agedwards.com/invbank/ipo.shtml).

Arkebauer, James B. *Going Public/Initial Public Offerings (IPOs),* 1997. (http://www.venturea.com/public.htm).

Chervitz, Darren. *CBS Marketwatch: IPO Investing,* Sept. 9, 1998.

Equity Analytics, Ltd. *Equity Analytics Academic Quality Information on Investing,* 1998. (http://www.e-analytics.com/ipo.bplan6.htm).

Fraser, Andrew. *Don't Get Burned Playing the IPO Game,* 1998. (http://biz.yahoo.com/).

Peterson, John. *Initial Public Offerings,* 1998. (http://www.ipo-law.com/ipo.html).

Rini, Bill. *The Investment Faq—Stocks: IPOs,* 1995. (http://www.invest-faq.com/articles/stock-ipo.html).

Welch, Ivo. *IPO—The Initial Public Offerings (IPOs) Resource Page,* 1996. (http://linux.agsm.ucla.edu/ipo/).

VENTURE CAPITAL FINANCING

INTRODUCTION

Venture capital firms supply funding from private sources for investing in select companies that have a high, rapid growth potential and a need for large amounts of capital. Venture capital (VC) firms speculate on certain high-risk businesses producing a very high rate of return in a very short time. The firms typically invest for periods of three to seven years and expect at least a 20 percent to 40 percent annual return on their investment.

When dealing with venture capital firms, keep in mind that they are under great pressure to identify and exploit fast growth opportunities before more conventional financing alternatives become available to the target companies. Venture capital firms have a reputation for negotiating tough financing terms and setting high demands on target companies. Three bottom-line suggestions:

- Make sure to read the fine print.
- Watch for delay maneuvers (they may be waiting for your financial position to weaken further).
- Guard your trade secrets and other proprietary information zealously.

TARGET FIRMS

Venture capital financing may not be available, nor a good choice of financing, for many small businesses. Usually, venture capital firms favor existing businesses that have a minimal operating history of several years; financing of startups is limited to situations where the high risk is tempered by special circumstances, such as a company with extremely experienced management and a very marketable product or service. In 1995, venture capital firms invested in less than 2000 companies. The target companies often have revenues in excess of two million dollars and a preexisting capital investment of at least one million.

VCs research target companies and markets more vigorously than conventional lenders, although the ultimate investment decision is often influenced by the market speculations of the particular venture capitalists. Due to the amount of money that venture capital firms spend in examining and researching businesses before they invest, they will usually want to invest at least a quarter of a million dollars to justify their costs.

DEALING WITH VENTURE CAPITAL FIRMS

Be wary of "shopping" innovative ideas to multiple venture capitalists or private investors. Use caution in revealing any information you consider proprietary. Even if you already have intellectual property protection (e.g., a patent, trademark, or copyright), you don't want to be forced to police your rights. Do your best to limit the details of your particular innovation and seek confidentiality arrangements for additional protection of any preexisting legal rights you may have. The price of financing through venture capital firms is high. Ownership demands for an equity interest in 30 percent to 50 percent of the company are not uncommon even for established businesses, and a startup or higher risk venture could easily require transfer of a greater interest. Although the investing company will not typically get involved in the ongoing management of the company, it will usually want at least one seat on the target company's board of directors and involvement, for better or worse, in the major decisions affecting the direction of the company.

The ownership interest of the VC firm is usually a straight equity interest or an ownership option in the target company through either a convertible debt (where the debt holder has the option to convert the loan instrument into stock of the borrower) or a debt with warrants to a straight equity investment (where the warrant holder has the right to buy shares of common stock at a fixed price within a specified time period). An arrangement that eventually calls for an initial public offering is also possible. Despite the high costs of financing through venture capital companies, they offer tremendous potential for obtaining a very large amount of equity financing and they usually provide qualified business advice in addition to capital.

Venture capital firms are located nationwide, and a directory is available for $25 through the National Association of Venture Capital, 1655 N. Fort Meyer Dr., Arlington, VA 22209, (703 351-5269). In addition, other sources for venture capital can be found through bankers, insurance companies, and business associations.

HOW TAXES AFFECT BUSINESS DECISIONS

DIVIDENDS-RECEIVED DEDUCTION

The application of the general rule may be illustrated as follows:

Sales	$300,000
Dividend income received from a less than 20%-owned corporation	100,000
	400,000
Operating expenses	310,000
Tentative taxable income	90,000
Dividends-received deduction; limited to 70% of $90,000	63,000
Taxable income	$ 27,000

On the other hand, had the corporation sustained an operating loss of $90,000, the "70% of tentative taxable income limitation" would not be applicable; accordingly, the dividends-received deduction would be 70% of $100,000, or $70,000, effectively increasing the net operating loss to $160,000.

Further, the following example illustrates that the "70% of tentative taxable income limitation" does not apply if the corporation sustains a net operating loss after the dividends-received deduction:

Sales	$300,000
Dividend income received from a less than 20%-owned corporation	100,000
	400,000
Operating expenses	390,000
Tentative taxable income	10,000
Dividends-received deduction; 70% of $100,000	70,000
Net operating loss	$ (60,000)

Investment strategies should be carefully monitored in order to secure the benefits of the dividends-received deduction. The wrong investment vehicles could easily result in the loss of the desired tax benefit. For example, the following dividends are not eligible for the dividends-received deduction:

1. Dividends from mutual savings banks, which in essence represent interest on bank accounts.
2. Dividends derived from real estate investment trusts.
3. Capital gains dividends passed through from mutual funds.
4. Dividends from money market funds which invest solely in interest-paying securities.

It should also be noted that the dividends-received deduction is allowed only if the dividend-paying stock is held at least 46 days during the 90-day period that commences 45 days before the stock became ex-dividend with respect to the dividend.

CHARITABLE CONTRIBUTIONS

There is a typographical error in the next to the last sentence of the first paragraph on page 909 of the main text. The sentence should read as follows: "Corporations using the accrual method of accounting may deduct charitable contributions authorized by the board of directors but paid after year-end as long as payment is made within *2 1/2* months after year-end."

NET OPERATING LOSS DEDUCTIONS

Under the Taxpayer Relief Act of 1997 (TRA), with respect to net operating losses arising in tax years beginning after August 5, 1997, the carryback period is reduced to two years and the carryforward period is increased to twenty years.

DEPRECIATION

As indicated on page 911 of the main text, automobiles are included in a special category of property referred to as "listed property." It should be noted that the annual deduction for such autos is dependent upon the year in which the auto was placed into service, since the Internal Revenue Services issues applicable tables annually. The annual deduction for autos placed into service in 1997 are as follows:

Year	Allowable Deduction
1	$3,160
2	5,000
3	3,050
Each Year Thereafter	1,775

The annual deduction for autos places into service in 1998 are as follows:

Year	Allowable Deduction
1	$3,160
2	5,000
3	2,950
Each Year Thereafter	1,775

The annual deduction for an automobile placed into service in 1999 is as follows:

Year	Allowable Deduction
1	$3,060
2	5,000
3	2,950
Each Year Thereafter	1,775

It should be noted that if a business leases an automobile that is used 100% for business purposes, the full lease cost will generally be deductible. However, in order to prevent the avoidance of the "listed property" limitations, the IRS requires that an "add-back" be included in income each year of the automobile's use. The inclusion, which is based on the initial fair market value of the vehicle and the year in which the lease was effected, is adjusted annually for inflation.

THE ALTERNATIVE MINIMUM TAX

If a corporation is deemed to be a small corporation, then it may not be subject to the alternative minimum tax. To be treated initially as a small corporation, the corporation's average annual gross receipts for the most recent three-year period beginning after 1994 must be less than $5,000,000. Treatment as a small corporation will be lost in a particular year if the entity's average gross receipts for the preceding three years is in excess of $7,500,000.

THE PERSONAL HOLDING COMPANY TAX

The personal holding company tax is imposed on "undistributed personal holding company income," which is taxable income with the following adjustments, minus the dividends paid deduction:

1. Deduction is allowed for federal and foreign income and excess profits taxes.
2. Deduction is allowed for excess charitable contributions; in lieu of the normal 10% limit, the deduction may be as high as 50% of taxable income.
3. Deduction is allowed for net long-term capital gain less related federal income taxes.
4. The dividends-received deduction is not allowed.
5. Other than a special one-year net operating loss carryover deduction, no deduction is allowed for a net operating loss.

As indicated in the main text (page 915), corporations may plan to mitigate the personal holding company tax by paying sufficient dividends to their stockholders. It should be noted that the deduction for dividends paid includes the following:

1. Dividends actually paid during the tax year.
2. Consent dividends, which represent amounts not actually paid out as dividends but that are includible in the shareholder's income because such an election was made by consenting shareholders on the last day of the corporation's tax year.
3. With certain limitations, "late paid" dividends. "Late paid" dividends are dividends paid after year-end, but no later than the 15th day of the

third month of the following year. In order to claim the deduction for "late paid" dividends, a proper election must be made.

On page 914 of the main text, reference is made to the stock ownership test. It should be noted that for purposes of determining the five individuals, the rules of constructive ownership are applicable. Pursuant to the constructive ownership rules, stock owned, directly or indirectly, by or for a corporation, partnership, estate, or trust shall be considered as being owned proportionately by its shareholders, partners, or beneficiaries. Additionally, an individual shall be considered as owning the stock owned, directly, or indirectly, by or for his or her family or by or for his or her partner. Family, for this purpose, is limited to brothers, sisters, spouse, ancestors (i.e., grandparents) and lineal descendants (i.e., children and grandchildren).

CORPORATE REORGANIZATIONS

It is important to note that a stock redemption (which occurs when a corporation cancels or redeems its own stock) is *not* a corporate reorganization.

STOCK REDEMPTIONS

A stock redemption, which occurs when a corporation cancels or redeems its own stock, may afford shareholders beneficial tax treatment.

In general, a stockholder will recognize capital gain or loss in connection with a stock redemption if one of the following conditions is satisfied:

1. The redemption is not essentially equivalent to a dividend; i.e., the redemption results in a meaningful reduction in the shareholder's voting power, interest in the earnings and assets of the corporation, etc.
2. The redemption is substantially disproportionate; i.e., immediately after the redemption (a) the ratio of the shareholder's voting stock to the total outstanding voting stock is less than 80% of that ratio immediately before the redemption, and (b) the shareholder owns less than 50% of the corporation's outstanding voting stock.
3. The redemption results in the complete termination of the shareholder's interest.
4. The redemption is a redemption of a noncorporate shareholder's stock in partial liquidation of the corporation.
5. The redemption occurred in order to pay a decedent's death taxes and administrative expenses.

Distributions received in connection with redemptions not meeting one of the conditions above will be treated as dividends; accordingly, such distributions will be taxed as ordinary income.

CONTROLLED GROUP OF CORPORATIONS

There are two types of controlled groups of corporations.

The first type is known as a brother-sister controlled group. A brother-sister controlled group exists when (1) five or fewer persons (which may be individuals, estates or trusts) own at least 80% of the total voting stock (or value of shares) of each of two or more corporations, and (2) these same persons own more than 50% of the total voting power (or value of shares) of each corporation. It should be observed that a particular person's stock is to be considered only to the extent that it is owned identically with respect to each corporation.

The second type of controlled group is known as the parent-subsidiary group. (See the discussion on affiliated corporations.)

It is important to recognize the existence of either type of controlled groups of corporations. A controlled group of corporations must generally apportion the preferential tax bracket amounts (on page 912 of the main text) equally among all members of the group. However, a valid election may be made by all members of the group to an apportionment plan. For example, assuming Corporation A and Corporation B are brother-sister corporations. Corporations A and B may (1) apportion the first $50,000 of taxable income (subject to the preferential 15% tax rate) equally between themselves or (2) apportion the first $50,000 of taxable income between themselves in any manner that is most beneficial to the group. Under the latter election, if Company A sustained a net operating loss of $50,000 and Company B generated a $50,000 profit, it would probably by prudent to allocate the entire $50,000 tax bracket (subject to the preferential tax rate of 15%) to Company B.

Further, a controlled group of corporations must apportion other tax attributes. For example, the annual Section 179 election must be apportioned amongst the corporations in the controlled group. In this case, if the apportionment rules were not applicable, establishing multiple corporations could easily enable the intent of the law's annual limit to be overridden.

AFFILIATED CORPORATIONS

An affiliated group of corporations is created when one or more chains of includible corporations is connected through stock ownership with a common parent corporation which is an includible corporation, but only if (1) the common parent corporation owns at least 80% of the total voting power and at least 80% of the total value of the stock of at least one includible corporation, and (2) stock meeting the 80% requirement in each of the includible corporations (but not the common parent corporation) is owned directly by one or more of the other includible corporations.

An includible corporation is defined as any corporation other than the following:

1. An exempt corporation.
2. A life insurance or mutual insurance company.
3. A foreign corporation.
4. A corporation deriving at least 80% of its income from possessions of the United States.
5. A regulated investment company.
6. A real estate investment trust.
7. Certain domestic international sales corporations.

If all of the corporations that were members of the affiliated group at any time during the tax year consent before the last day for filing the return, an election may be made to file consolidated tax returns for the period that they are affiliated. Accordingly, net operating losses of some members of the group may be used to offset taxable income of other group members; the net effect obviously results in a decrease in tax liability.

TAX-FREE EXCHANGE OF PROPERTY FOR STOCK

Under Internal Revenue Code Section 351, if property is transferred to a corporation by one or more persons (which includes individuals, trusts, estates, partnerships and corporations) solely in exchange for stock in that corporation, and immediately after the exchange such person or persons are in control of the corporation to which the property was transferred, then no gain or loss will generally be recognized by the transferor or transferee.

For purposes of this Code section, control means that the person or persons making the transfer (i.e., transferor(s)) must own, immediately after the exchange, 80% or more of the total combined voting power of all classes of voting stock and 80% or more of the total number of outstanding non-voting shares.

It should be noted that "property" includes cash or other property, but does not include services rendered to the corporation. If stock is received for services rendered, then a taxable event has occurred. The recipient will be required to recognize ordinary income measured by the fair market value of the stock.

In the event that a transferor receives cash or other property in addition to stock, then gain will be recognized by the transferor, but only to the extent of the cash and/or fair market value of the other property received in the exchange. However, a loss on the transaction may never be recognized.

If property encumbered by debt (e.g., a mortgage) is transferred to a corporation, gain will only be recognized to the extent that the debt assumed by the corporation is in excess of the adjusted basis of the property transferred.

The stockholder's basis in stock received is equal to the cash plus the adjusted basis of any property transferred to the corporation, increased by any gain to be recognized. The stockholder's basis is reduced by the cash and the fair market value of any property received by the shareholder as part of the exchange. Further, since debt assumed by the corporation is treated as cash, the shareholder's basis in the stock is reduced by any debt assumed by the corporation.

From the corporation's point of view, the basis of property it receives is generally equal to the shareholder's basis immediately prior to the transfer, increased by any gain recognized by the shareholder in connection with the transfer.

To illustrate the major points above, assume that on July 1 of the current year, Moose Inc. is formed by Katie and Michael. Katie transfers $200,000 in cash to Moose and Michael transfers land and a building that originally cost him 180,000, but have a fair market value of $250,000 on July 1. The building is subject to a $150,000 mortgage, which is assumed by Moose. Based on these facts, the following should be noted:

1. No gain or loss is to be recognized by Katie, Michael, or Moose Inc.
2. Katie's basis in her Moose stock is $200,000.
3. Michael's basis in his Moose stock is $180,000 less $150,000, or $30,000.
4. Moose's basis in the land and building received from Michael is $180,000.

S CORPORATIONS

As discussed on page 917 of the main text, Form 2553 must be filed on time in order to make the proper S election. A copy of Form 2553, along with realted instructions, follows.

Form **2553**

(Rev. September 1997)

Department of the Treasury
Internal Revenue Service

Election by a Small Business Corporation

(Under section 1362 of the Internal Revenue Code)
▶ **For Paperwork Reduction Act Notice, see page 2 of instructions.**
▶ **See separate instructions.**

OMB No. 1545-0146

Notes:

1. This election, to be an S corporation can be accepted only if all the tests are met under **Who May Elect** on page 1 of the instructions; all signatures in Parts I and III are originals (no photocopies); and the exact name and address of the corporation and other required form information are provided.

2. Do not file Form **1120S**, U.S. Income Tax Return for an S Corporation, for any tax year before the year the election takes effect.

3. If the corporation was in existence before the effective date of this election, see **Taxes an S Corporation May Owe** on page 1 of the instructions.

Part I **Election Information**

Please Type or Print	Name of corporation (see instructions)	A Employer identification number
	Number, street, and room or suite no. (If a P.O. box, see instructions.)	B Date incorporated
	City or town, state, and ZIP code	C State of incorporation

D Election is to be effective for tax year beginning (month, day, year) . . . . ▶

E Name and title of officer or legal representative who the IRS may call for more information	**F** Telephone number of officer or legal representative

G If the corporation changed its name or address after applying for the EIN shown in A, check this box . . . . ▶ ☐

H If this election takes effect for the first tax year the corporation exists, enter month, day, and year of the **earliest** of the following: (1) date the corporation first had shareholders, (2) date the corporation first had assets, or (3) date the corporation began doing business. . . ▶

I Selected tax year: Annual return will be filed for tax year ending (month and day) ▶ . . . .
If the tax year ends on any date other than December 31, except for an automatic 52-53-week tax year ending with reference to the month of December, you **must** complete Part II on the back. If the date you enter is the ending date of an automatic 52-53 week tax year, write "52-53-week year" to the right of the date. See Temporary Regulations section 1.441-2T(e)(3).

J Name and address of each shareholder, shareholder's spouse having a community property interest in the corporation's stock, and each tenant in common, joint tenant, and tenant by the entirely. (A husband and wife (and their estates) are counted as one shareholder in determining the number of shareholders without regard to the manner in which the stock is owned.)	**K** Shareholders' Consent Statement. Under penalties of perjury, we declare that we consent to the election of the above-named corporation to be an S corporation under section 1362(a) and that we have examined this consent statement, including accompanying schedules and statements, and to the best of our knowledge and belief, it is true, correct, and complete. We understand our consent is binding and may not be withdrawn after the corporation has made a valid election. (Shareholders sign and date below.)		**L** Stock owned		**M** Social security number or employer identification number (see instructions)	**N** Share-holder's tax year ends (month and day)
	Signature	Date	Number of shares	Dates acquired		

Under penalties of perjury, I declare that I have examined this election, including accompanying schedules and statements, and to the best of my knowledge and belief, it is true, correct, and complete.

Signature of officer ▶ _____ Title ▶ _____ Date ▶ _____

See Parts II and III on back.

DXA

Form **2553** (Rev. 9-97)

Corporation: ID number:

Form 2553 (Rev. 9-97)   **Page 2**

Selection of Fiscal Tax Year (All corporations using this part must complete item O and item P, Q, or R.)

O   Check the applicable box below to indicate whether the corporation is:
  1. ☐ A new corporation adopting the tax year entered in Item I, Part I.
  2. ☐ An existing corporation retaining the tax year entered in Item I, Part I.
  3. ☐ An existing corporation changing to the tax year entered in item I, Part I.

P   Complete item P if the corporation is using the expeditious approval provisions of Rev. Proc. 87-32, 1987-2, C.B. 396, to request **(1)** a natural business year (as defined in section 4.01(1) of Rev. Proc. 87-32) or **(2)** a year that satisfies the ownership tax year test in section 4.01(2) of Rev. Proc. 87-32. Check the applicable box below to indicate the representation statement the corporation is making as required under section 4 of Rev. Proc. 87-32.

  1. Natural Business Year ▶ ☐ I represent that the corporation is retaining or changing to a tax year that coincides with its natural business year as defined in section 4.01(1) or Rev. Proc. 87-32 and as verified by its satisfaction of the requirements of section 4.02(1) of Rev. Proc. 87-32. In addition, if the corporation is changing to a natural business year as defined in section 4.01(1), I further represent that such tax year results in less deferral of income to the owners than the corporation's present tax year. I also represent that the corporation is not described in section 3.01(2) of Rev. Proc. 87-32. (See instructions for additional information that must be attached.)

  2. Ownership Tax Year ▶ ☐ I represent that shareholders holding more than half of the shares of the stock (as of the first day of the tax year to which the request relates) of the corporation have the same tax year or are concurrently changing to the tax year that the corporation adopts, retains, or changes to per item I, Part I. I also represent that the corporation is not described in section 3.01(2) of Rev. Proc. 87-32.

Note: If you do not use item P and the corporation wants a fiscal tax year, complete either item Q or R below. Item Q is used to request a fiscal tax year based on a business purpose. Item R is used to make a regular section 444 election.

Q   Business Purpose-To request a fiscal year based on a business purpose, you must check box Q1 and pay a user fee. See instructions for details. You may also check box Q2 and/or box Q3.

  1. Check here ▶ ☐ if the fiscal year entered in item I, Part I, is requested under the provisions of section 6.03 of Rev. Proc. 87-32. Attach to Form 2553 a statement showing the business purpose for the requested fiscal year. See instructions for additional information that must be attached.

  2. Check here ▶ ☐ to show that the corporation intends to make a back-up section 444 election in the event the corporation's business purpose request is not approved by the IRS. (See instructions for more information.)

  3. Check here ▶ ☐ to show that the corporation agrees to adopt or change to a tax year ending December 31 if necessary for the IRS to accept this election for S corporation status in the event (1) the corporation's business purpose request is not approved and the corporation makes a back-up section 444 election, but is ultimately not qualified to make a section 444 election, or (2) the corporation's business purpose request is not approved and the corporation did not make a back-up section 444 election.

R   Section 444 Election-To make a section 444 election, you must check box R1 and you may also check box R2. To make the election, you must complete **Form 8716**, Election To Have a Tax Year Other Than a Required Tax Year, and either attach it to Form 2553 or file it separately.

  1. Check here ▶ ☐ to show the corporation will make, if qualified, a section 444 election to have the fiscal tax year shown in item I, Part I. To make the election, you must complete **Form 8716**, Election To Have a Tax Year Other Than a Required Tax Year, and either attach it to Form 2553 or file it separately.

  2. Check here ▶ ☐ to show that the corporation agrees to adopt or change to a tax year ending December 31 if necessary for the IRS to accept this election for S corporation status in the event the corporation is ultimately not qualified to make a section 444 election.

Part III

Qualified Subchapter S Trust (QSST) Election Under Section 1361(d) (2)*

Income beneficiary's name and address	Social security number
Trust's name and address	Employer identification number

Date on which stock of the corporation was transferred to the trust (month, day, year) . . . . ▶

In order for the trust named above to be a QSST and thus a qualifying shareholder of the S corporation for which this Form 2553 is filed, I hereby make the election under section 1361(d)(2). Under penalties of perjury, I certify that the trust meets the definitional requirements of section 1361(d)(3) and that all other information provided in Part III is true, correct, and complete.

_____   _____
Signature of income beneficiary or signature and title of legal representative or other qualified person making the election   Date

* Use Part III to make the QSST election only if stock of the corporation has been transferred to the trust on or before the date on which the corporation makes its election to be an S corporation. The QSST election must be made and filed separately if stock of the corporation is transferred to the trust after the date on which the corporation makes the S election.

Instructions for Form 2553

(Revised September 1997)

Department of the Treasury
Internal Revenue Service

Election by a Small Business Corporation

Section references are to the Internal Revenue Code unless otherwise noted.

General Instructions

Purpose.— To elect to be an S corporation, a corporation must file Form 2553. The election permits the income of the S corporation to be taxed to the shareholders of the corporation rather than to the corporation itself, except as noted below under **Taxes an S Corporation May Owe.**

Who May Elect.— A corporation may elect to be an S corporation only if it meets all of the following tests:

1. It is a domestic corporation.

2. It has no more than 75 shareholders. A husband and wife (and their estates) are treated as one shareholder for this requirement. All other persons are treated as separate shareholders.

3. Its only shareholders are individuals, estates, certain trusts described in section 1361(c)(2)(A), or, for tax years beginning after 1997, exempt organizations described in section 401(a) or 501(c)(3). Trustees of trusts that want to make the election under section 1361(e)(3) to be an electing small business trust should see Notice 97-12, 1997-3 I.R.B. 11.

Note: *See the instructions for Part III regarding qualified subchapter S trusts.*

4. It has no nonresident alien shareholders.

5. It has only one class of stock (disregarding differences in voting rights). Generally, a corporation is treated as having only one class of stock if all outstanding shares of the corporation's stock confer identical rights to distribution and liquidation proceeds. See Regulations section 1.1361-1(1) for more details.

6. It is not one of the following ineligible corporations:

a. A bank or thrift institution that uses the reserve method of accounting for bad debts under section 585;

b. An insurance company subject to tax under the rules of subchapter L of the Code;

c. A corporation that has elected to be treated as a possessions corporation under section 936; or

d. A domestic international sales corporation (DISC) or former DISC.

7. It has a permitted tax year as required by section 1378 or makes a section 444 election to have a tax year other than a permitted tax year. Section 1378 defines a permitted tax year as a tax year ending December 31, or any other tax year for which the corporation establishes a business purpose to the satisfaction of the IRS. See Part II for details on requesting a fiscal year based on a business purpose or on making a section 444 election.

8. Each shareholder consents as explained in the instructions for column K.

See sections 1361, 1362, and 1378 for additional information on the above tests.

An election can be made by a parent S corporation to treat the assets, liabilities, and items of income, deduction, and credit of an eligible wholly-owned subsidiary as those of the parent. For details, see Notice 97-4, 1997-2 I.R.B. 24.

Taxes an S Corporation May Owe.— An S corporation may owe income tax in the following instances:

1. If, at the end of any tax year, the corporation had accumulated earnings and profits, and its passive investment income under section 1362(d)(3) is more than 25% of its gross receipts, the corporation may owe tax on its excess net passive income.

2. A corporation with net recognized built-in gain (as defined in section 1374(d)(2)) may owe tax on its built-in gains.

3. A corporation that claimed investment credit before its first year as an S corporation will be liable for any investment credit recapture tax.

4. A corporation that used the LIFO inventory method for the year immediately preceding its first year as an S corporation may owe an additional tax due to LIFO recapture.

For more details on these taxes, see the Instructions for Form 1120S.

Where To File.— File this election with the Internal Revenue Service Center listed below.

If the corporation's principal business, office, or agency is located in	Use the following Internal Revenue Service Center address
New Jersey, New York (New York City and counties of Nassau, Rockland, Suffolk, and Westchester)	Holtsville, NY 00501
New York (all other counties), Connecticut, Maine, Massachusetts, New Hampshire, Rhode Island, Vermont	Andover, MA 05501
Florida, Georgia, South Carolina	Atlanta, GA 39901
Indiana, Kentucky, Michigan, Ohio, West Virginia	Cincinnati, OH 45999
Kansas, New Mexico, Oklahoma, Texas	Austin, TX 73301
Alaska, Arizona, California (counties of Alpine, Amador, Butte, Calaveras, Colusa, Contra Costa, Del Norte, El Dorado, Glenn, Humboldt, Lake, Lassen, Marin, Mendocino, Modoc, Napa, Nevada, Placer, Plumas, Sacramento, San Joaquin, Shasta, Sierra, Siskiyou, Solano, Sonoma, Sutter, Tehama, Trinity, Yolo, and Yuba), Colorado, Idaho, Montana, Nebraska, Nevada, North Dakota, Oregon, South Dakota, Utah, Washington, Wyoming	Ogden, UT 84201
California (all other counties), Hawaii	Fresno, CA 93888
Illinois, Iowa, Minnesota, Missouri, Wisconsin	Kansas City, MO 64999
Alabama, Arkansas, Louisiana, Mississippi, North Carolina, Tennessee	Memphis, TN 37501
Delaware, District of Columbia, Maryland, Pennsylvania, Virginia	Philadelphia, PA 19255

When To Make the Election.— Complete and file Form 2553 **(a)** at any time before the 16th day of the 3rd month of the tax year, if filed during the tax year the election is to take effect, or **(b)** at any time during the preceding tax year. An election made no later than 2 months and 15 days after the beginning of a tax year that is less than 2½ months long is treated as timely made for that tax year. An election made after the 15th day of the 3rd month but before the end of the tax year is effective for the next year. For example, if a calendar tax year

corporation makes the election in April 1998, it is effective for the corporation's 1999 calendar tax year.

However, an election made after the due date will be accepted as timely filed if the corporation can show that the failure to file on time was due to reasonable cause. To request relief for a late election, the corporation generally must request a private letter ruling and pay a user fee in accordance with Rev. Proc. 97-1, 1997-1 I.R.B. 11 (or its successor). But if the election is filed within 6 months of its due date and the original due date for filing the corporation's initial Form 1120S has not passed, the ruling and user fee requirements do not apply. To request relief in this case, write "FILED PURSUANT TO REV. PROC. 97-40" at the top of page 1 of Form 2553, attach a statement explaining the reason for failing to file the election on time, and file Form 2553 as otherwise instructed. See Rev. Proc. 97-40, 1997-33 I.R.B. 50, for more details.

See Regulations section 1.1362-6(b)(3)(iii) for how to obtain relief for an inadvertent invalid election if the corporation filed a timely election, but one or more shareholders did not file a timely consent.

Acceptance or Nonacceptance of Election.— The service center will notify the corporation if its election is accepted and when it will take effect. The corporation will also be notified if its election is not accepted. The corporation should generally receive a determination on its election within 60 days after it has filed Form 2553. If box Q1 in Part II is checked on page 2, the corporation will receive a ruling letter from the IRS in Washington, DC, that either approves or denies the selected tax year. When box Q1 is checked, it will generally take an additional 90 days for the Form 2553 to be accepted.

Do not file Form 1120S for any tax year before the year the election takes effect. If the corporation is now required to file **Form 1120,** U.S. Corporation Income Tax Return, or any other applicable tax return, continue filing it until the election takes effect.

Care should be exercised to ensure that the IRS receives the election. If the corporation is not notified of acceptance or nonacceptance of its election within 3 months of date of filing (date mailed), or within 6 months if box Q1 is checked, take follow-up action by corresponding with the service center where the corporation filed the election. If the IRS questions whether Form 2553 was filed, an acceptable proof of filing is **(a)** certified or registered mail receipt (timely filed) from the U.S. Postal Service or its equivalent from a designated private delivery service (see Notice 97-26, 1997-17 I.R.B. 6); **(b)** Form 2553 with accepted stamp; **(c)** Form 2553 with stamped IRS received date; or **(d)** IRS letter stating that Form 2553 has been accepted.

End of Election.— Once the election is made, it stays in effect until it is terminated. If the election is terminated in a tax year beginning after 1996, the corporation (or a successor corporation) can make another election on Form 2553 only with IRS consent for any tax year before the 5th tax year after the first tax year in which the termination took effect. See Regulations section 1.1362-5 for more details.

Cat. No. 49978N

Specific Instructions

Part I

Note: *All corporations must complete Part I.*

Name and Address of Corporation.— Enter the true corporate name as stated in the corporate charter or other legal document creating it. If the corporation's mailing address is the same as someone else's, such as a shareholder's, enter "c/o" and this person's name following the name of the corporation. Include the suite, room, or other unit number after the street address. If the Post Office does not deliver to the street address and the corporation has a P.O. box, show the box number instead of the street address. If the corporation changed its name or address after applying for its employer identification number, be sure to check the box in item G of Part I.

Item A. Employer Identification Number (EIN).— If the corporation has applied for an EIN but has not received it, enter "applied for." If the corporation does not have an EIN, it should apply for one on **Form SS-4,** Application for Employer Identification Number. You can order Form SS-4 by calling 1-800-TAX-FORM (1-800-829-3676).

Item D. Effective Date of Election.— Enter the beginning effective date (month, day, year) of the tax year requested for the S corporation. Generally, this will be the beginning date of the tax year for which the ending effective date is required to be shown in item I, Part I. For a new corporation (first year the corporation exists) it will generally be the date required to be shown in item H, Part I. The tax year of a new corporation starts on the date that it has shareholders, acquires assets, or begins doing business, whichever happens first. If the effective date for item D for a newly formed corporation is later than the date in item H, the corporation should file Form 1120 or Form 1120-A for the tax period between these dates.

Column K. Shareholders' Consent Statement.— Each shareholder who owns (or is deemed to own) stock at the time the election is made must consent to the election. If the election is made during the corporation's tax year for which it first takes effect, any person who held stock at any time during the part of that year that occurs before the election is made, must consent to the election, even though the person may have sold or transferred his or her stock before the election is made.

An election made during the first 2½ months of the tax year is effective for the following tax year if any person who held stock in the corporation during the part of the tax year before the election was made, and who did not hold stock at the time the election was made, did not consent to the election.

Each shareholder consents by signing and dating in column K or signing and dating a separate consent statement described below. The following special rules apply in determining who must sign the consent statement.

• If a husband and wife have a community interest in the stock or in the income from it, both must consent.

• Each tenant in common, joint tenant, and tenant by the entirety must consent.

• A minor's consent is made by the minor, legal representative of the minor, or a natural or adoptive parent of the minor if no legal representative has been appointed.

• The consent of an estate is made by the executor or administrator.

• The consent of an electing small business trust is made by the trustee.

• If the stock is owned by a trust (other than an electing small business trust), the deemed owner of the trust must consent. See section 1361(c)(2) for details regarding trusts that are permitted to be shareholders and rules for determining who is the deemed owner.

Continuation sheet or separate consent statement.— If you need a continuation sheet or use a separate consent statement, attach it to Form 2553. The separate consent statement must contain the name, address, and EIN of the corporation and the shareholder information requested in columns J through N of Part I. If you want, you may combine all the shareholders' consents in one statement.

Column L.— Enter the number of shares of stock each shareholder owns and the dates the stock was acquired. If the election is made during the corporation's tax year for which it first takes effect, do not list the shares of stock for those shareholders who sold or transferred all of their stock before the election was made. However, these shareholders must still consent to the election for it to be effective for the tax year.

Column M.— Enter the social security number of each shareholder who is an individual. Enter the EIN of each shareholder that is an estate, a qualified trust, or an exempt organization.

Column N.— Enter the month and day that each shareholder's tax year ends. If a shareholder is changing his or her tax year, enter the tax year the shareholder is changing to, and attach an explanation indicating the present tax year and the basis for the change (e.g., automatic revenue procedure or letter ruling request).

Signature.— Form 2553 must be signed by the president, treasurer, assistant treasurer, chief accounting officer, or other corporate officer (such as tax officer) authorized to sign.

Part II

Complete Part II if you selected a tax year ending on any date other than December 31 (other than a 52-53-week tax year ending with reference to the month of December).

Box P1.— Attach a statement showing separately for each month the amount of gross receipts for the most recent 47 months as required by section 4.03(3) of Rev. Proc. 87-32, 1987-2 C.B. 396. A corporation that does not have a 47-month period of gross receipts cannot establish a natural business year under section 4.01(1).

Box Q1.— For examples of an acceptable business purpose for requesting a fiscal tax year, see Rev. Rul. 87-57, 1987-2 C.B. 117.

In addition to a statement showing the business purpose for the requested fiscal year, you must attach the other information necessary to meet the ruling request requirements of Rev. Proc. 97-1 (or its successor). Also attach a statement that shows separately the amount of gross receipts from sales or services (and inventory costs, if applicable) for each of the 36 months preceding the effective date of the election to be an S corporation. If the corporation has been in existence for fewer than 36 months, submit figures for the period of existence.

If you check box Q1, you will be charged a $250 user fee (subject to change). Do not pay the fee when filing Form 2553. The service center will send Form 2553 to the IRS in Washington, DC, who, in turn, will notify the corporation that the fee is due.

Box Q2.— If the corporation makes a back-up section 444 election for which it is qualified, then the election will take effect in the event the business purpose request is not approved. In some cases, the tax year requested under the back-up section 444 election may be different than the tax year requested under business purpose. See **Form 8716,** Election To Have a Tax Year Other Than a Required Tax Year, for details on making a back-up section 444 election.

Boxes Q2 and R2.— If the corporation is not qualified to make the section 444 election after making the item Q2 back-up section 444 election or indicating its intention to make the election in item R1, and therefore it later files a calendar year return, it should write "Section 444 Election Not Made" in the top left corner of the first calendar year Form 1120S it files.

Part III

Certain qualified subchapter S trusts (QSSTs) may make the QSST election required by section 1361(d)(2) in Part III. Part III may be used to make the QSST election only if corporate stock has been transferred to the trust on or before the date on which the corporation makes its election to be an S corporation. However, a statement can be used instead of Part III to make the election.

Note: *Use Part III only if you make the election in Part I (i.e., Form 2553 cannot be filed with only Part III completed).*

The deemed owner of the QSST must also consent to the S corporation election in column K, page 1, of Form 2553. See section 1361(c)(2).

Paperwork Reduction Act Notice.— We ask for the information on this form to carry out the Internal Revenue laws of the United States. You are required to give us the information. We need it to ensure that you are complying with these laws and to allow us to figure and collect the right amount of tax.

You are not required to provide the information requested on a form that is subject to the Paperwork Reduction Act unless the form displays a valid OMB control number. Books or records relating to a form or its instructions must be retained as long as their contents may become material in the administration of any Internal Revenue law. Generally, tax returns and return information are confidential, as required by section 6103.

The time needed to complete and file this form will depend on individual circumstances. The estimated average time is:

Recordkeeping .... 6 hr., 28 min.

Learning about the law or the form .... 3 hr., 41 min.

Preparing, copying, assembling, and sending the form to the IRS .... 3 hr., 56 min.

If you have comments concerning the accuracy of these time estimates or suggestions for making this form simpler, we would be happy to hear from you. You can write to the Tax Forms Committee, Western Area Distribution Center, Rancho Cordova, CA 95743-0001. **DO NOT** send the form to this address. Instead, see **Where To File** on page 1.

SAMPLE FILLED-IN TAX FORMS

Presented below are (1) the adjusted trial balance and (2) filled-in Form 1120, U.S. Corporation Income Tax Return, for Karen, Katie and Michael Corp. for the year ended December 31, 1998 (i.e., the initial year of the corporation). In this example, the corporation is a C corporation, as opposed to an S corporation.

```
         KAREN, KATIE AND MICHAEL CORP.      Prepared by_____

                 Adjusted Trial Balance      Reviewed by_____
         For the  1 period(s) ended December 31, 1998       Page    1


Account #       Account Name                        Current
-------------------------------------------------------------------

      1001 CASH IN BANK-CHECKING                     144,209

      1031 ACCOUNTS RECEIVABLE                        41,460

      1051 INVENTORY                                   6,830

      1521 MACHINERY                                 135,101

      1621 ACCUM DEPRECIATION                        (35,162)

      1801 DEPOSITS                                      150

      1821 PREPAID EXPENSES                           45,294

      1851 PREPAID FEDERAL INC TAX                    21,336

      2200 PAYROLL TAXES PAYABLE                     (23,236)

      2205 NOTE PAYABLE-LONG TERM                   (126,803)

      2207 NOTE PAYABLE-SHAREHOLDER                  (82,630)

      2208 NOTE PAYABLE-CURRENT                       (8,749)

      2216 ACCRUED EXPENSES & TAXES                  (21,661)

      2218 ACCOUNTS PAYABLE                          (15,374)

      3000 CAPITAL STOCK                              (6,000)

      4001 SALES                                    (645,675)

      5001 PURCHASES                                 107,538

      5021 INVENTORY, ENDING                          (6,830)

      6001 SALARIES - OFFICER                        128,435

      6021 SALARIES - OTHERS                         119,080

      6031 PAYROLL TAXES                              15,890
```

Account #	Account Name	Current
6041	ADVERTISING	3,336
6051	AUTO EXPENSES	26,883
6071	COMPUTER EXPENSES	4,879
6091	DEPRECIATION/AMORTIZATION	35,162
6101	DUES AND SUBSCRIPTIONS	462
6121	EMPLOYEE BENEFITS	3,525
6131	HOSPITALIZATION INSURANCE	2,586
6141	INSURANCE - GENERAL	11,545
6161	INTEREST	2,659
6171	OFFICE EXPENSES	8,504
6181	PROFESSIONAL FEES	7,990
6201	REPAIRS AND MAINTENANCE	22,275
6211	POSTAGE AND SHIPPING	7,477
6221	STORAGE	2,700
6241	STATE FRANCHISE TAX	1,325
6251	MISCELLANEOUS TAXES	1,315
6261	TELEPHONE	9,547
6271	TRAVEL AND ENTERTAINMENT	1,882
6281	UTILITIES	5,940
6311	FINES AND PENALTIES	269
6331	ROYALTIES	25,200
8031	FEDERAL INCOME TAX	21,336

```
                              ---------------- ----------------
                                             0                0
                              ================ ================
```

Form 1120

Department of the Treasury
Internal Revenue Service

U.S. Corporation Income Tax Return

For calendar year 1998 or tax year beginning _____, 1998, end. _____, 19 ___

▶ Instructions are separate. See page 1 for Paperwork Reduction Act Notice.

1998

A Check if a:
1 Consolidated return (attach Form 851) ☐
2 Personal holding co. (attach Sch. PH) ☐
3 Personal service corp. (as defined in Temporary Regs. sec. 1.441-4T -- see instructions) ☐

Use IRS label. Otherwise, print or type.

Name   No., street, and room or suite no.   City/town, state, and ZIP code

KAREN, KATIE & MICHAEL CORP.
123 ANY STREET
ANY CITY, NY 99999

B Employer identification no.
99-9999999

C Date incorporated
01/01/1998

D Total assets (see page 5 of Inst.)
$ 359,218

E Check applicable boxes: (1) ☒ Initial return   (2) ☐ Final return   (3) ☐ Change of address

Income	**1a** Gross receipts/sales	645,675 **b** Less returns and allowances _____ C Bal▶	**1c**	645,675
	2 Cost of goods sold (Schedule A, line 8)		**2**	100,708
	3 Gross profit. Subtract line 2 from line 1c		**3**	544,967
	4 Dividends (Schedule C, line 19)		**4**	
	5 Interest		**5**	
	6 Gross rents		**6**	
	7 Gross royalties		**7**	
	8 Capital gain net income (attach Schedule D (Form 1120))		**8**	
	9 Net gain or (loss) from Form 4797, Part II, line 18 (attach Form 4797)		**9**	
	10 Other income (see page 6 of instructions -- attach schedule)		**10**	
	11 Total income. Add lines 3 through 10 ▶		**11**	544,967
Deductions (See instructions for limitations on deductions.)	**12** Compensation of officers (Schedule E, line 4)		**12**	128,435
	13 Salaries and wages (less employment credits)		**13**	119,080
	14 Repairs and maintenance		**14**	22,275
	15 Bad debts		**15**	
	16 Rents		**16**	
	17 Taxes and licenses		**17**	18,530
	18 Interest		**18**	2,659
	19 Charitable contributions (see page 8 of instructions for 10% limitation)		**19**	
	20 Depreciation (attach Form 4562) **20** 35,162			
	21 Less depreciation claimed on Schedule A and elsewhere on return **21a**		**21b**	35,162
	22 Depletion		**22**	
	23 Advertising		**23**	3,336
	24 Pension, profit-sharing, etc., plans		**24**	
	25 Employee benefit programs		**25**	3,525
	26 Other deductions (attach schedule)		**26**	114,654
	27 Total deductions. Add lines 12 through 26 ▶		**27**	447,656
	28 Taxable income before net operating loss deduction and special deductions. Subtract line 27 from line 11		**28**	97,311
	29 Less: **a** Net operating loss deduction (see page 9 of instructions) **29a**			
	b Special deductions (Schedule C, line 20) **29b**		**29c**	
Tax and Payments	**30** Taxable income. Subtract line 29c from line 28		**30**	97,311
	31 Total tax (Schedule J, line 12)		**31**	21,336
	32 Payments: **a** 1997 overpayment credited to 1998 ..... **32a**			
	b 1998 estimated tax payments **32b** 21,336			
	c Less 1998 refund applied for on Form 4466 **32c** (_____) **d** Bal ▶ **32d** 21,336			
	e Tax deposited with Form 7004 ..... **32e**			
	f Credit for tax paid on undistributed capital gains (attach Form 2439) **32f**			
	g Credit for Federal tax on fuels (attach Form 4136). See instructions **32g**		**32h**	21,336
	33 Estimated tax penalty (see page 10 of instructions). Check if Form 2220 is attached ..... ▶ ☐		**33**	
	34 Tax due. If line 32h is smaller than the total of lines 31 and 33, enter amount owed		**34**	0
	35 Overpayment. If line 32h is larger than the total of lines 31 and 33, enter amount overpaid		**35**	
	36 Enter amount of line 35 you want: **Credited to 1999 estimated tax** ▶ _____ **Refunded** ▶		**36**	

Sign Here

Under penalties of perjury, I declare that I have examined this return, including accompanying schedules and statements, and to the best of my knowledge and belief, it is true, correct, and complete. Declaration of preparer (other than taxpayer) is based on all information of which preparer has any knowledge.

▶ Signature of officer _____ Date _____ ▶ Title _____

Paid Preparer's Use Only

Preparer's signature ▶	Date	Check if self-employed ☐	Preparer's SSN
Firm's name (or yours if self-employed) and address ▶		EIN ▶	
		ZIP code ▶	

Schedule A Cost of Goods Sold (See page 10 of instructions.)

1	Inventory at beginning of year	1	
2	Purchases	2	107,538
3	Cost of labor	3	
4	Additional section 263A costs (attach schedule)	4	
5	Other costs (attach schedule)	5	
6	**Total.** Add lines 1 through 5	6	107,538
7	Inventory at end of year	7	6,830
8	**Cost of goods sold.** Subtract line 7 from line 6. Enter here and on page 1, line 2	8	100,708

9a Check all methods used for valuing closing inventory:

(i) ☐ Cost as described in Regulations section 1.471-3

(ii) ☒ Lower of cost or market as described in Regulations section 1.471-4

(iii) ☐ Other (Specify method used and attach explanation.) ▶

b Check if there was a writedown of subnormal goods as described in Regulations section 1.471-2(c) . . . . ▶ ☐

c Check if the LIFO inventory method was adopted this tax year for any goods (if checked, attach Form 970) . . . . ▶ ☐

d If the LIFO inventory method was used for this tax year, enter percentage (or amounts) of closing inventory computed under LIFO **9d**

e If property is produced or acquired for resale, do the rules of section 263A apply to the corporation? . . . . ☐ Yes ☒ No

f Was there any change in determining quantities, cost, or valuations between opening and closing inventory? If "Yes," attach explanation . . . . ☐ Yes ☒ No

Schedule C Dividends and Special Deductions (See page 11 of instructions.)

		(a) Dividends received	(b) %	(c) Special deductions (a) x (b)
1	Dividends from less-than-20%-owned domestic corporations that are subject to the 70% deduction (other than debt-financed stock)		70	
2	Dividends from 20%-or-more-owned domestic corporations that are subject to the 80% deduction (other than debt-financed stock)		80	
3	Dividends on debt-financed stock of domestic and foreign corps. (sec. 246A)		see instructions	
4	Dividends on certain preferred stock of less-than-20%-owned public utilities		42	
5	Dividends on certain preferred stock of 20%-or-more-owned public utilities		48	
6	Dividends from less-than-20%-owned foreign corporations and certain FSCs that are subject to the 70% deduction		70	
7	Dividends from 20%-or-more-owned foreign corporations and certain FSCs that are subject to the 80% deduction		80	
8	Dividends from wholly owned foreign subsidiaries subject to 100% deduction (section 245(b))		100	
9	**Total.** Add lines 1 through 8. See page 12 of instructions for limitation			
10	Dividends from domestic corporations received by a small business investment company operating under the Small Business Investment Act of 1958		100	
11	Dividends from certain FSCs that are subject to 100% deduction (sec. 245(c)(1))		100	
12	Dividends from affiliated group members subject to 100% ded. (sec. 243(a)(3))		100	
13	Other dividends from foreign corporations not included on lines 3, 6, 7, 8, or 11			
14	Income from controlled foreign corps. under subpart F (attach Form(s) 5471)			
15	Foreign dividend gross-up (section 78)			
16	IC-DISC & former DISC dividends not included on lines 1, 2, or 3 (sec. 246(d))			
17	Other dividends			
18	Deduction for dividends paid on certain preferred stock of public utilities			
19	**Total dividends.** Add lines 1 through 17. Enter here and on line 4, page 1 . . ▶			
20	**Total special deductions.** Add lines 9, 10, 11, 12, and 18. Enter here and on line 29b, page 1 . . . . ▶			

Schedule E Compensation of Officers (See instructions for line 12, page 1.)

Complete Schedule E only if total receipts (line 1a plus lines 4 through 10 on page 1, Form 1120) are $500,000 or more.

1	(a) Name of officer	(b) Social security number	(c) Percent of time devoted to business	(d) Common	(e) Preferred	(f) Amount of compensation
	MICHAEL LIGHTYEAR	999-99-9999	100.00%	%	%	128,435
			%	%	%	
			%	%	%	
			%	%	%	
			%	%	%	

2	Total compensation of officers	128,435
3	Compensation of officers claimed on Schedule A and elsewhere on return	
4	Subtract line 3 from line 2. Enter the result here and on line 12, page 1	128,435

Schedule J   Tax Computation (See page 13 of instructions.)

1 Check if the corporation is a member of a controlled group (see sections 1561 and 1563) . . . . ▶ ☐

   Important: Members of a controlled group, see instructions on page 13.

2a If the box on line 1 is checked, enter the corporation's share of the $50,000, $25,000, and $9,925,000 taxable income brackets (in that order):

   (1) |$ | **(2)** |$ | **(3)** |$ |

  b Enter the corporation's share of: **(1)** Additional 5% tax (not more than $11,750) |$ |

                       (2) Additional 3% tax (not more than $100,000) |$ |

3 Income tax. Check if a qualified personal service corporation under section 448(d)(2) (see page 13) . . . . ▶ ☐	**3**	21,336
4a Foreign tax credit (attach Form 1118). **4a**		
b Possessions tax credit (attach Form 5735) **4b**		
c Check: ☐ Nonconventional source fuel credit ☐ QEV credit (attach Form 8834) **4c**		
d General business credit. Enter here & check which forms are attached: ☐ 3800		
☐ 3468 ☐ 5884 ☐ 6478 ☐ 6765 ☐ 8586 ☐ 8830 ☐ 8826		
☐ 8835 ☐ 8844 ☐ 8845 ☐ 8846 ☐ 8820 ☐ 8847 ☐ 8861 **4d**		
e Credit for prior year minimum tax (attach Form 8827) **4e**		
5 Total credits. Add lines 4a through 4e.	**5**	0
6 Subtract line 5 from line 3	**6**	21,336
7 Personal holding company tax (attach Schedule PH (Form 1120)).	**7**	
8 Recapture taxes. Check if from: . . . ☐ Form 4255 ☐ Form 8611	**8**	
9 Alternative minimum tax (attach Form 4626).	**9**	
10 Add lines 6 through 9.	**10**	21,336
11 Qualified zone academy bond credit (attach Form 8860).	**11**	
12 Total tax. Subtract line 11 from line 10. Enter here and on line 31, page 1	**12**	21,336

Schedule K   Other Information (See page 15 of instructions.)

	Yes	No
1 Check method of accounting: **a** ☐ Cash		
b ☒ Accrual **c** ☐ Other (specify) ▶		

2 See page 17 of the instructions and state the:

a Business activity code no. (**NEW**) ▶ 334110

b Business activity ▶ MANUFACTURING

c Product or service ▶ COMPUTERS

	Yes	No
3 At the end of the tax year, did the corporation own, directly or indirectly, 50% or more of the voting stock of a domestic corporation? (For rules of attribution, see section 267(c).)		X

If "Yes," attach a schedule showing: (**a**) name and identifying number, (**b**) percentage owned, and (**c**) taxable income or (loss) before NOL and special deductions of such corporation for the tax year ending with or within your tax year.

	Yes	No
4 Is the corporation a subsidiary in an affiliated group or a parent-subsidiary controlled group?		X

If "Yes," enter employer identification number and name of the parent corporation ▶

	Yes	No
5 At the end of the tax year, did any individual, partnership, corporation, estate or trust own, directly or indirectly, 50% or more of the corporation's voting stock? (For rules of attribution, see section 267(c).)		X

If "Yes," attach a schedule showing name and identifying no. (Do not include any info. already entered in **4** above.) Enter percentage owned ▶

	Yes	No
6 During this tax year, did the corporation pay dividends (other than stock dividends & distributions in exchange for stock) in excess of the corporation's current and accumulated earnings & profits? (See secs. 301 & 316.) . .		X

If "Yes," file Form 5452. If this is a consolidated return, answer here for the parent corporation and on **Form 851**, Affiliations Schedule, for each subsidiary.

	Yes	No
7 Was the corporation a U.S. shareholder of any controlled foreign corporation? (See sections 951 and 957.).		X
If "Yes," attach Form 5471 for each such corporation. Enter number of Forms 5471 attached ▶		
8 At any time during the 1998 calendar year, did the corp. have an interest in or a signature or other authority over a financial account (such as a bank account, securities account, or other financial account) in a foreign country?. .		X
If "Yes," the corp. may have to file Form TD F 90-22.1. If "Yes," enter name of foreign country ▶		
9 During the tax year, did corporation receive a distribution from, or was it the grantor of, or transferor to, a foreign trust? If "Yes," the corporation may have to file Form 3520 . .		X
10 At any time during 1998 did one foreign person own, directly or indirectly, at least 25% of: (**a**) total voting power of all classes of stock of the corp. entitled to vote, or (**b**) the total value of all classes of stock of corp.? If "Yes,"		X

a Enter percentage owned ▶

b Enter owner's country ▶

c The corporation may have to file Form 5472. Enter number of Forms 5472 attached ▶

11 Check this box if the corporation issued publicly offered debt instruments with original issue discount . . . . . . ▶ ☐

If so, the corporation may have to file Form 8281.

12 Enter the amount of tax-exempt interest received or accrued during the tax year ▶ $

13 If there were 35 or fewer shareholders at the end of the tax year, enter the number ▶ 3

14 If the corporation has an NOL for the tax year and is electing to forego the carryback period, check here . . ▶ ☐

15 Enter the available NOL carryover from prior tax years (Do not reduce it by any deduction on line 29a.)
▶ $

Schedule L	Balance Sheets per Books	Beginning of tax year		End of tax year	
	Assets	(a)	(b)	(c)	(d)
1	Cash				144,209
2a	Trade notes and accounts receivable			41,460	
b	Less allowance for bad debts	( )		( )	41,460
3	Inventories				6,830
4	U.S. government obligations				
5	Tax-exempt securities (see instructions)				
6	Other current assets (attach schedule)				66,630
7	Loans to stockholders				
8	Mortgage and real estate loans				
9	Other investments (attach schedule)				
10a	Buildings and other depreciable assets			135,101	
b	Less accumulated depreciation	( )		(35,162)	99,939
11a	Depletable assets				
b	Less accumulated depletion	( )		( )	
12	Land (net of any amortization)				
13a	Intangible assets (amortizable only)				
b	Less accumulated amortization	( )		( )	
14	Other assets (attach schedule)				150
15	Total assets		0		359,218
	Liabilities and Stockholders' Equity				
16	Accounts payable				15,374
17	Mortgages, notes, bonds payable in less than 1 year				8,749
18	Other current liabilities (attach schedule)				
19	Loans from stockholders				82,630
20	Mortgages, notes, bonds payable in 1 year or more				126,803
21	Other liabilities (attach schedule)				44,897
22	Capital stock: **a** Preferred stock				
	b Common stock			6,000	6,000
23	Additional paid-in capital				
24	Retained earnings -- Appropriated (attach sch.)				
25	Retained earnings -- Unappropriated				74,765
26	Adjustments to shareholders' equity (attach sch.)				
27	Less cost of treasury stock		( )		( )
28	Total liabilities and stockholders' equity		0		359,218

Note: You are not required to complete Schedules M-1 & M-2 below if the total assets on line 15, column (d) of Schedule L are less than $25,000.

Schedule M-1	Reconciliation of Income (Loss) per Books With Income per Return (See page 16 of instructions.)

1	Net income (loss) per books	74,765	7	Income recorded on books this year not included on this return (itemize):	
2	Federal income tax	21,336			
3	Excess of capital losses over capital gains			Tax-exempt interest .... $	
4	Income subject to tax not recorded on books this year:				
			8	Deductions on this return not charged against book income this year (itemize):	
5	Expenses recorded on books this year not deducted on this return (itemize):			**a** Depreciation .. $	
	a Depreciation.... $			**b** Contributions carryover ...... $	
	b Contributions carryover .... $				
	c Travel and entertainment .... $ 941				
	See Sch. 269				
		1,210	9	Add lines 7 and 8	
6	Add lines 1 through 5	97,311	10	Income (line 28, pg. 1) - line 6 less line 9	97,311

Schedule M-2	Analysis of Unappropriated Retained Earnings per Books (Line 25, Schedule L)

1	Balance at beginning of year		5	Distributions: **a** Cash	
2	Net income (loss) per books	74,765		**b** Stock	
3	Other increases:			**c** Property	
			6	Other decreases:	
			7	Add lines 5 and 6	
4	Add lines 1, 2, and 3	74,765	8	Balance at end of year (line 4 less line 7)	74,765

Form **4562**	**Depreciation and Amortization**		OMB No. 1545-0172
	(Including Information on Listed Property)		**1998**
Department of the Treasury Internal Revenue Service (99)	▶ **See separate instructions.** ▶ **Attach this form to your return.**		Attachment Sequence No. **67**

Name(s) shown on return	Business or activity to which this form relates	Identifying number
KAREN, KATIE & MICHAEL CORP.		99-9999999

Part I Election To Expense Certain Tangible Property (Section 179) (Note: If you have any "listed property," complete Part V before you complete Part I.)

1 Maximum dollar limitation. If an enterprise zone business, see page 2 of the instructions	**1**	$18,500
2 Total cost of section 179 property placed in service. See page 2 of the instructions	**2**	135,101
3 Threshold cost of section 179 property before reduction in limitation	**3**	$200,000
4 Reduction in limitation. Subtract line 3 from line 2. If zero or less, enter -0-	**4**	
5 Dollar limitation for tax year. Subtract line 4 from line 1. If zero or less, enter -0-. If married filing separately, see page 2 of the instructions	**5**	18,500

6 (a) Description of property	(b) Cost (business use only)	(c) Elected cost	
MACHINERY	135,101	18,500	

7 Listed property. Enter amount from line 27	**7**		
8 Total elected cost of section 179 property. Add amounts in column (c), lines 6 and 7	**8**	18,500
9 Tentative deduction. Enter the smaller of line 5 or line 8	**9**	18,500
10 Carryover of disallowed deduction from 1997. See page 3 of the instructions.	**10**	
11 Business income limitation. Enter smaller of business income (not less than zero) or line 5 (see instructions). .	**11**	18,500
12 Section 179 expense deduction. Add lines 9 and 10, but do not enter more than line 11	**12**	18,500
13 Carryover of disallowed deduction to 1999. Add lines 9 and 10, less line 12 . . . . . ▶	**13**		

Note: Do not use Part II or Part III below for listed property (automobiles, certain other vehicles, cellular telephones, certain computers, or property used for entertainment, recreation, or amusement). Instead, use Part V for listed property.

Part II MACRS Depreciation For Assets Placed in Service ONLY During Your 1998 Tax Year (Do Not Include Listed Property.)

Section A -- General Asset Account Election

14 If you are making the election under section 168(i)(4) to group any assets placed in service during the tax year into one or more general asset accounts, check this box. See page 3 of the instructions. . . . . ▶ ☐

Section B -- General Depreciation System (GDS) (See page 3 of the instructions.)

(a) Classification of property	(b) Month and year placed in service	(c) Basis for depr. (business/investment use only -- see instructions)	(d) Recovery period	(e) Convention	(f) Method	(g) Depreciation deduction
15a 3-year property						
b 5-year property						
c 7-year property		116,601	7. yr	HY	200DB	16,662
d 10-year property						
e 15-year property						
f 20-year property						
g 25-year property			25 yrs.		S/L	
h Residential rental			27.5 yrs.	MM	S/L	
property			27.5 yrs.	MM	S/L	
i Nonresidential real			39 yrs.	MM	S/L	
property				MM	S/L	

Section C -- Alternative Depreciation System (ADS) (See page 5 of the instructions.)

16a Class life					S/L	
b 12-year			12 yrs.		S/L	
c 40-year			40 yrs.	MM	S/L	

Part III Other Depreciation (Do Not Include Listed Property.) (See page 6 of the instructions.)

17 GDS and ADS deductions for assets placed in service in tax years beginning before 1998.	**17**	
18 Property subject to section 168(f)(1) election.	**18**	
19 ACRS and other depreciation	**19**	

Part IV Summary (See page 6 of the instructions.)

20 Listed property. Enter amount from line 26	**20**	
21 Total. Add deductions on line 12, lines 15 and 16 in column (g), and lines 17 through 20. Enter here and on the appropriate lines of your return. Partnerships and S corporations -- see instructions.	**21**	35,162
22 For assets shown above and placed in service during the current year, enter the portion of the basis attributable to section 263A costs	**22**		

For Paperwork Reduction Act Notice, see the separate instructions. Form **4562** (1998)

Form **4626**

Department of the Treasury
Internal Revenue Service

Alternative Minimum Tax -- Corporations

▶ See separate instructions.
▶ Attach to the corporation's tax return.

OMB No. 1545-0175

1998

Name	Employer identification number
KAREN, KATIE & MICHAEL CORP.	99-9999999

1	Taxable income or (loss) before net operating loss deduction	**1**		97,311
2	**Adjustments and preferences:**			
a	Depreciation of post-1986 property	**2a**	10,832	
b	Amortization of certified pollution control facilities	**2b**		
c	Amortization of mining exploration and development costs	**2c**		
d	Amortization of circulation expenditures (personal holding companies only) . .	**2d**		
e	Adjusted gain or loss	**2e**		
f	Long-term contracts	**2f**		
g	Installment sales	**2g**		
h	Merchant marine capital construction funds	**2h**		
i	Section 833(b) deduction (Blue Cross, Blue Shield, and similar type organizations only)	**2i**		
j	Tax shelter farm activities (personal service corporations only)	**2j**		
k	Passive activities (closely held corporations and personal service corporations only)	**2k**		
l	Loss limitations	**2l**		
m	Depletion	**2m**		
n	Tax-exempt interest from specified private activity bonds	**2n**		
o	Intangible drilling costs	**2o**		
p	Accelerated depreciation of real property (pre-1987)	**2p**		
q	Accelerated depreciation of leased personal property (pre-1987) (personal holding companies only)	**2q**		
r	Other adjustments	**2r**		
s	Combine lines 2a through 2r	**2s**		10,832
3	Preadjustment alternative minimum taxable income (AMTI). Combine lines 1 and 2s	**3**		108,143
4	**Adjusted current earnings (ACE) adjustment:**			
a	Enter the corporation's ACE from line 10 of the worksheet on page 11 of the instructions	**4a**	108,143	
b	Subtract line 3 from line 4a. If line 3 exceeds line 4a, enter the difference as a negative amount (see examples beginning on page 5 of the instructions)	**4b**	0	
c	Multiply line 4b by 75% (.75). Enter the result as a positive amount	**4c**		
d	Enter the excess, if any, of the corporation's total increases in AMTI from prior year ACE adjustments over its total reductions in AMTI from prior year ACE adjustments (see page 6 of the instructions). **Note:** You **must** enter an amount on line 4d (even if line 4b is positive)	**4d**		
e	ACE adjustment: • If you entered a positive number or zero on line 4b, enter the amount from line 4c here as a positive amount. • If you entered a negative number on line 4b, enter the smaller of line 4c or line 4d here as a negative amount.	**4e**		
5	Combine lines 3 and 4e. If zero or less, stop here; the corporation does not owe alternative minimum tax	**5**		108,143
6	Alternative tax net operating loss deduction (see page 6 of the instructions)	**6**		
7	**Alternative minimum taxable income.** Subtract line 6 from line 5. If the corporation held a residual interest in a REMIC, see page 6 of the instructions	**7**		108,143

For Paperwork Reduction Act Notice, see separate instructions.

Form **4626** (1998)

8	Enter the amount from line 7 (alternative minimum taxable income)	**8**	108,143

9   **Exemption phase-out computation** (if line 8 is $310,000 or more, skip lines 9a and 9b and enter –0– on line 9c):

a   Subtract $150,000 from line 8 (if you are completing this line for a member of a controlled group, see page 7 of instructions). If zero or less, enter –0– . .   **9a** | 0 |

b   Multiply line 9a by 25% (.25) **9b**

c	Exemption. Subtract line 9b from $40,000 (if you are completing this line for a member of a controlled group, see page 7 of the instructions). If zero or less, enter –0–	**9c**	40,000
10	Subtract line 9c from line 8. If zero or less, enter –0–	**10**	68,143
11	Multiply line 10 by 20% (.20)	**11**	13,629
12	Alternative minimum tax foreign tax credit. See page 7 of the instructions	**12**	
13	Tentative minimum tax. Subtract line 12 from line 11	**13**	13,629
14	Regular tax liability before all credits except the foreign tax credit and possessions tax credit.	**14**	21,336
15	**Alternative minimum tax.** Subtract line 14 from line 13. Enter the result on the appropriate line of the corporation's income tax return (e.g., Form 1120, Schedule J, line 9). If zero or less, enter –0–	**15**	0

How Taxes Affect Business Decisions

Adjusted Current Earnings Worksheet

▶ See ACE Worksheet Instructions (which begin on page 7).

1	Pre-adjustment AMTI. Enter the amount from line 3 of Form 4626			**1**	108,143
2	ACE depreciation adjustment:				
a	AMT depreciation	**2a**	5,830		
b	ACE depreciation:				
	(1) Post-1993 property	**2b**(1)	5,830		
	(2) Post-1989, pre-1994 property	**2b**(2)			
	(3) Pre-1990 MACRS property	**2b**(3)			
	(4) Pre-1990 original ACRS property	**2b**(4)			
	(5) Property described in sections 168(f)(1) through (4)	**2b**(5)			
	(6) Other property	**2b**(6)			
	(7) Total ACE depreciation. Add lines 2b(1) through 2b(6)	**2b**(7)	5,830		
c	ACE depreciation adjustment. Subtract line 2b(7) from line 2a			**2c**	
3	Inclusion in ACE of items included in earnings and profits (E&P):				
a	Tax-exempt interest income	**3a**			
b	Death benefits from life insurance contracts	**3b**			
c	All other distributions from life insurance contracts (including surrenders)	**3c**			
d	Inside buildup of undistributed income in life insurance contracts	**3d**			
e	Other items (see Regulations sections 1.56(g)-1(c)(6)(iii) through (ix) for a partial list)	**3e**			
f	Total increase to ACE from inclusion in ACE of items included in E&P. Add lines 3a through 3e			**3f**	
4	Disallowance of items not deductible from E&P:				
a	Certain dividends received	**4a**			
b	Dividends paid on certain preferred stock of public utilities that are deductible under section 247	**4b**			
c	Dividends paid to an ESOP that are deductible under section 404(k)	**4c**			
d	Nonpatronage dividends that are paid and deductible under section 1382(c)	**4d**			
e	Other items (see Regulations sections 1.56(g)-1(d)(3)(i) and (ii) for a partial list)	**4e**			
f	Total increase to ACE because of disallowance of items not deductible from E&P. Add lines 4a through 4e			**4f**	
5	Other adjustments based on rules for figuring E&P:				
a	Intangible drilling costs	**5a**			
b	Circulation expenditures	**5b**			
c	Organizational expenditures	**5c**			
d	LIFO inventory adjustments	**5d**			
e	Installment sales	**5e**			
f	Total other E&P adjustments. Combine lines 5a through 5e			**5f**	
6	Disallowance of loss on exchange of debt pools			**6**	
7	Acquisition expenses of life insurance companies for qualified foreign contracts			**7**	
8	Depletion			**8**	
9	Basis adjustments in determining gain or loss from sale or exchange of pre-1994 property			**9**	
10	**Adjusted current earnings.** Combine lines 1, 2c, 3f, 4f, and 5f through 9. Enter the result here and on line 4a of Form 4626			**10**	108,143

Form **Corp**	SUPPLEMENTAL SCHEDULE FORM 1120 PAGES 1-4	For Tax Year **1998**
Name KAREN, KATIE & MICHAEL CORP.		Employer ID Number 99-9999999

Form 1120, Taxes (Line 17)

Description	Amount
PAYROLL	15,890
STATE FRANCHISE TAX	1,325
MISCELLANEOUS TAXES	1,315
Total	18,530

Form 1120, Other Deductions (Line 26)

Description	Amount
AUTOMOBILE EXPENSES	26,883
COMPUTER EXPENSES	4,879
DUES AND SUBSCRIPTIONS	462
HOSPITALIZATION INSURANCE	2,586
GENERAL INSURANCE	11,545
OFFICE EXPENSES	8,504
PROFESSIONAL FEES	7,990
POSTAGE & SHIPPING	7,477
STORAGE	2,700
TELEPHONE	9,547
UTILITIES	5,940
ROYALTIES	25,200
Meals/Entertainment (1882 * .5)	941
Total	114,654

Form **Corp**	SUPPLEMENTAL SCHEDULE FORM 1120 PAGES 1-4	For Tax Year **1998**
Name KAREN, KATIE & MICHAEL CORP.		Employer ID Number 99-9999999

Schedule L, Other Current Assets (Line 6)

Description	Year Beginning	Year End
PREPAID EXPENSES		45,294
PREPAID FEDERAL INCOME TAXES		21,336
Total		66,630

Schedule L, Other Assets (Line 14)

Description	Year Beginning	Year End
DEPOSITS		150
Total		150

Schedule L, Other Liabilities (Line 21)

Description	Year Beginning	Year End
PAYROLL TAXES PAYABLE		23,236
ACCRUED EXPENSES AND TAXES		21,661
Total		44,897

Schedule M-1, Other Expenses Recorded and Not Deducted (Line 5)

Description	Amount
FINES AND PENALTIES	269
Total	269

How Taxes Affect Business Decisions

Presented below are (1) the adjusted trial balance and (2) filled-in Form 1120S, U.S. Income Tax Return for an S Corporation, for Karen, Katie and Michael Corp. for the year ended December 31, 1998 (i.e., the initial year of the corporation). In this example, the corporation is an S corporation, as opposed to a C corporation. It should be noted that the trial balance in this example has been modified to eliminate any items specific to a C corporation.

```
            KAREN, KATIE AND MICHAEL CORP.     Prepared by_____

                  Adjusted Trial Balance       Reviewed by_____
            For the  1 period(s) ended December 31, 1998      Page    1

Account #        Account Name                         Current
-------------------------------------------------------------------------

     1001 CASH IN BANK-CHECKING                       144,209

     1031 ACCOUNTS RECEIVABLE                          41,460

     1051 INVENTORY                                     6,830

     1521 MACHINERY                                   135,101

     1621 ACCUM DEPRECIATION                          (35,162)

     1801 DEPOSITS                                        150

     1821 PREPAID EXPENSES                             66,630

     2200 PAYROLL TAXES PAYABLE                       (23,236)

     2205 NOTE PAYABLE-LONG TERM                     (126,803)

     2207 NOTE PAYABLE-SHAREHOLDER                    (82,630)

     2208 NOTE PAYABLE-CURRENT                         (8,749)

     2216 ACCRUED EXPENSES & TAXES                    (21,661)

     2218 ACCOUNTS PAYABLE                            (15,374)

     3000 CAPITAL STOCK                                (6,000)

     4001 SALES                                      (645,675)

     5001 PURCHASES                                   107,538

     5021 INVENTORY, ENDING                            (6,830)

     6001 SALARIES - OFFICER                          128,435

     6021 SALARIES - OTHERS                           119,080

     6031 PAYROLL TAXES                                15,890

     6041 ADVERTISING                                   3,336
```

```
         KAREN, KATIE AND MICHAEL CORP.        Prepared by_____

                  Adjusted Trial Balance        Reviewed by_____
             For the  1 period(s) ended December 31, 1998        Page    2


    Account #       Account Name                        Current
    ------------------------------------------------------------------------

        6051  AUTO EXPENSES                            26,883

        6071  COMPUTER EXPENSES                         4,879

        6091  DEPRECIATION/AMORTIZATION                35,162

        6101  DUES AND SUBSCRIPTIONS                      462

        6121  EMPLOYEE BENEFITS                         3,525

        6131  HOSPITALIZATION INSURANCE                 2,586

        6141  INSURANCE - GENERAL                      32,881

        6161  INTEREST                                  2,659

        6171  OFFICE EXPENSES                           8,504

        6181  PROFESSIONAL FEES                         7,990

        6201  REPAIRS AND MAINTENANCE                  22,275

        6211  POSTAGE AND SHIPPING                      7,477

        6221  STORAGE                                   2,700

        6241  STATE FRANCHISE TAX                       1,325

        6251  MISCELLANEOUS TAXES                       1,315

        6261  TELEPHONE                                 9,547

        6271  TRAVEL AND ENTERTAINMENT                  1,882

        6281  UTILITIES                                 5,940

        6311  FINES AND PENALTIES                         269

        6331  ROYALTIES                                25,200

                                        ---------------- ----------------
                                                       0                0
                                        ================ ================
```

410   *How Taxes Affect Business Decisions*

Form **1120S**

Department of the Treasury
Internal Revenue Service

U.S. Income Tax Return for an S Corporation

▶ Do not file this form unless the corporation has timely filed
Form 2553 to elect to be an S corporation.

▶ See separate instructions.

OMB No. 1545-0130

1998

For calendar year 1998, or tax year beginning _____ , 1998, & ending _____ , 19 ___

A Effective date of election as S corp.	Use IRS label. Other-wise, please print or type.	Name Number, street, & room/suite no. City/town, state, & ZIP code	**C** Employer identification no.
01/01/1998		KAREN, KATIE & MICHAEL CORP.	99-9999999
B NEW bus. code no. (see pages 26-28)		123 ANY STREET	**D** Date incorporated
		ANY CITY, NY 99999	01/01/1998
334110			**E** Total assets (see page 10)
			$ 359,218

F Check applicable boxes: (1) ☒ Initial return   (2) ☐ Final return   (3) ☐ Change in address   (4) ☐ Amended return

G Enter number of shareholders in the corporation at end of the tax year .... ▶ 3

Caution: Include **only** trade or business income and expenses on lines 1a through 21. See the instructions for more information.

Income	**1a** Gross receipts or sales	645,675	**b** Less returns and allowances		C Bal ▶	**1c**	645,675
	2 Cost of goods sold (Schedule A, line 8)		**2**	100,708
	3 Gross profit. Subtract line 2 from line 1c		**3**	544,967
	4 Net gain (loss) from Form 4797, Part II, line 18 (attach Form 4797)		**4**	
	5 Other income (loss) (attach schedule)		**5**	
	6 **Total income (loss).** Combine lines 3 through 5 .... ▶		**6**	544,967

Deduc-tions (see page 11 of the instruc-tions for limita-tions)	**7** Compensation of officers		**7**	128,435
	8 Salaries and wages (less employment credits)		**8**	119,080
	9 Repairs and maintenance		**9**	22,275
	10 Bad debts		**10**	
	11 Rents		**11**	
	12 Taxes and licenses		**12**	18,530
	13 Interest		**13**	2,659
	14a Depreciation (if required, attach Form 4562)	**14a**	16,662		
	b Depreciation claimed on Schedule A and elsewhere on return	**14b**			
	c Subtract line 14b from line 14a		**14c**	16,662
	15 Depletion (**Do not deduct oil and gas depletion.**)		**15**	
	16 Advertising		**16**	3,336
	17 Pension, profit-sharing, etc., plans		**17**	
	18 Employee benefit programs		**18**	3,525
	19 Other deductions (attach schedule)		**19**	135,990
	20 **Total deductions.** Add the amounts shown in the far right column for lines 7 through 19. .... ▶		**20**	450,492
	21 Ordinary income (loss) from trade or business activities. Subtract line 20 from line 6		**21**	94,475

Tax and Payments	**22** **Tax: a** Excess net passive income tax (attach schedule)	**22a**			
	b Tax from Schedule D (Form 1120S)	**22b**			
	c Add lines 22a and 22b (see page 14 of the instructions for additional taxes)		**22c**	
	23 **Payments: a** 1998 estimated tax payments and amount applied from 1997 return.	**23a**			
	b Tax deposited with Form 7004	**23b**			
	c Credit for Federal tax paid on fuels (attach Form 4136)	**23c**			
	d Add lines 23a through 23c		**23d**	
	24 Estimated tax penalty. Check if Form 2220 is attached .... ▶ ☐		**24**	
	25 **Tax due.** If the total of lines 22c and 24 is larger than line 23d, enter amount owed. See page 4 of the instructions for depository method of payment. .... ▶		**25**	
	26 **Overpayment.** If line 23d is larger than the total of lines 22c and 24, enter amount overpaid .... ▶		**26**	
	27 Enter amount of line 26 you want: **Credited to 1999 est. tax** ▶ _____ **Refunded** ▶		**27**	

Please Sign Here	Under penalties of perjury, I declare that I have examined this return, including accompanying schedules and statements, and to the best of my knowledge and belief, it is true, correct, and complete. Declaration of preparer (other than taxpayer) is based on all information of which preparer has any knowledge.
	▶ _____ _____ ▶ _____
	Signature of officer Date Title

Paid Preparer's Use Only	Preparer's signature ▶		Date	Check if self-employed ▶ ☐	Preparer's SSN
	Firm's name (or yours if self-employed) and address ▶			EIN ▶	
				ZIP code ▶	

For Paperwork Reduction Act Notice, see the separate instructions.

Form **1120S** (1998)

Schedule A Cost of Goods Sold (see page 15 of the instructions)

1	Inventory at beginning of year	1	
2	Purchases	2	107,538
3	Cost of labor	3	
4	Additional section 263A costs (attach schedule)	4	
5	Other costs (attach schedule)	5	
6	**Total.** Add lines 1 through 5	6	107,538
7	Inventory at end of year	7	6,830
8	**Cost of goods sold.** Subtract line 7 from line 6. Enter here and on page 1, line 2	8	100,708

9a Check all methods used for valuing closing inventory:

    (i) ☐ Cost as described in Regulations section 1.471-3

    (ii) ☒ Lower of cost or market as described in Regulations section 1.471-4

    (iii) ☐ Other (specify method used and attach explanation) ▶

  b Check if there was a writedown of "subnormal" goods as described in Regulations section 1.471-2(c) .... ▶ ☐

  c Check if the LIFO inventory method was adopted this tax year for any goods (if checked, attach Form 970) .... ▶ ☐

  d If the LIFO inventory method was used for this tax year, enter percentage (or amounts) of closing

    inventory computed under LIFO .... | 9d |

  e Do the rules of section 263A (for property produced or acquired for resale) apply to the corporation? .... ☐ Yes ☒ No

  f Was there any change in determining quantities, cost, or valuations between opening and closing inventory? .... ☐ Yes ☒ No

    If "Yes," attach explanation.

Schedule B Other Information

		Yes	No
1	Check method of accounting: (**a**) ☐ Cash (**b**) ☒ Accrual (**c**) ☐ Other (specify)▶ _____		
2	Refer to the list on pages 26 through 28 of the instructions and state the corporation's principal:		
	(**a**) Business activity ▶ MANUFACTURING (**b**) Product or service ▶ COMPUTERS		
3	Did the corporation at the end of the tax year own, directly or indirectly, 50% or more of the voting stock of a domestic corporation? (For rules of attribution, see section 267(c).) If "Yes," attach a schedule showing: (**a**) name, address, and employer identification number and (**b**) percentage owned		X
4	Was the corporation a member of a controlled group subject to the provisions of section 1561?		X
5	At any time during calendar year 1998, did the corporation have an interest in or a signature or other authority over a financial account in a foreign country (such as a bank account, securities account, or other financial account)? (See page 15 of the instructions for exceptions and filing requirements for Form TD F 90-22.1.)		X
	If "Yes," enter the name of the foreign country ▶ _____		
6	During the tax year, did the corporation receive a distribution from, or was it the grantor of, or transferor to, a foreign trust?		
	If "Yes," the corporation may have to file Form 3520. See page 15 of the instructions		X
7	Check this box if the corporation has filed or is required to file **Form 8264**, Application for Registration of a Tax Shelter. .... ▶ ☐		
8	Check this box if the corporation issued publicly offered debt instruments with original issue discount .... ▶ ☐		
	If so, the corporation may have to file **Form 8281**, Information Return for Publicly Offered Original Issue Discount Instruments.		
9	If the corporation: (**a**) filed its election to be an S corporation after 1986, (**b**) was a C corporation before it elected to be an S corporation **or** the corporation acquired an asset with a basis determined by reference to its basis (or the basis of any other property) in the hands of a C corporation, and (**c**) has net unrealized built-in gain (defined in section 1374(d)(1)) in excess of the net recognized built-in gain from prior years, enter the net unrealized built-in gain reduced by net recognized built-in gain from prior years (see page 16 of the instructions) .... ▶ $ _____		
10	Check this box if the corporation had accumulated earnings and profits at the close of the tax year (see page 16 of the instructions) .... ▶ ☐		

How Taxes Affect Business Decisions

Schedule K	Shareholders' Shares of Income, Credits, Deductions, etc.		
	(a) Pro rata share items		**(b)** Total amount

	1	Ordinary income (loss) from trade or business activities (page 1, line 21)	**1**	94,475
	2	Net income (loss) from rental real estate activities (attach Form 8825)............	**2**	
	3a	Gross income from other rental activities **3a**		
	b	Expenses from other rental activities (attach schedule) **3b**		
	c	Net income (loss) from other rental activities. Subtract line 3b from line 3a	**3c**	
	4	Portfolio income (loss):		
Income (Loss)	**a**	Interest income	**4a**	
	b	Ordinary dividends..	**4b**	
	c	Royalty income	**4c**	
	d	Net short-term capital gain (loss) (attach Schedule D (Form 1120S))	**4d**	
	e	Net long-term capital gain (loss) (attach Schedule D (Form 1120S)):		
		(1) 28% rate gain (loss)▶ _____ **(2)** Total for year ▶	**4e(2)**	
	f	Other portfolio income (loss) (attach schedule)	**4f**	
	5	Net section 1231 gain (loss) (other than due to casualty or theft) (attach Form 4797)	**5**	
	6	Other income (loss) (attach schedule).................................	**6**	
Deduc-tions	**7**	Charitable contributions (attach schedule).............................	**7**	
	8	Section 179 expense deduction (attach Form 4562)	**8**	18,500
	9	Deductions related to portfolio income (loss) (itemize).....................	**9**	
	10	Other deductions (attach schedule)...................................	**10**	
Invest-ment Interest	**11a**	Interest expense on investment debts	**11a**	
	b	**(1)** Investment income included on lines 4a, 4b, 4c, and 4f above	**11b(1)**	
		(2) Investment expenses included on line 9 above	**11b(2)**	
	12a	Credit for alcohol used as a fuel (attach Form 6478)	**12a**	
	b	Low-income housing credit:		
		(1) From partnerships to which sec. 42(j)(5) applies for property placed in service before 1990 .	**12b(1)**	
		(2) Other than on line 12b(1) for property placed in service before 1990	**12b(2)**	
Credits		**(3)** From partnerships to which section 42(j)(5) applies for property placed in service after 1989 .	**12b(3)**	
		(4) Other than on line 12b(3) for property placed in service after 1989	**12b(4)**	
	c	Qualified rehabilitation expenditures related to rental real estate activities (attach Form 3468).....	**12c**	
	d	Credits (other than credits shown on lines 12b and 12c) related to rental real estate activities....	**12d**	
	e	Credits related to other rental activities.............................	**12e**	
	13	Other credits	**13**	
Adjust-ments and Tax Prefer-ence Items	**14a**	Depreciation adjustment on property placed in service after 1986	**14a**	10,832
	b	Adjusted gain or loss	**14b**	
	c	Depletion (other than oil and gas)	**14c**	
	d	**(1)** Gross income from oil, gas, or geothermal properties	**14d(1)**	
		(2) Deductions allocable to oil, gas, or geothermal properties.............	**14d(2)**	
	e	Other adjustments and tax preference items (attach schedule)	**14e**	
Foreign Taxes	**15a**	Type of income ▶ _____		
	b	Name of foreign country or U.S. possession _____		
	c	Total gross income from sources outside the United States (attach schedule)...............	**15c**	
	d	Total applicable deductions and losses (attach schedule)....................	**15d**	
	e	Total foreign taxes (check one): ▶ ☐ Paid ☐ Accrued	**15e**	
	f	Reduction in taxes available for credit (attach schedule)	**15f**	
	g	Other foreign tax information (attach schedule)	**15g**	
Other	**16**	Section 59(e)(2) expenditures: **a** Type ▶ _____ **b** Amount ▶	**16b**	
	17	Tax-exempt interest income......................................	**17**	
	18	Other tax-exempt income	**18**	
	19	Nondeductible expenses	**19**	
	20	Total property distributions (including cash) other than dividends reported on line 22 below.....	**20**	
	21	Other items and amounts required to be reported separately to shareholders (attach schedule)		
	22	Total dividend distributions paid from accumulated earnings and profits.................	**22**	
	23	**Income (loss).** (Required only if Schedule M-1 must be completed.) Combine lines 1 through 6 in column (b). From the result, subtract the sum of lines 7 through 11a, 15e, and 16b	**23**	75,975

Schedule L	**Balance Sheets per Books**	Beginning of tax year		End of tax year	
	Assets	**(a)**	**(b)**	**(c)**	**(d)**
1	Cash				144,209
2a	Trade notes and accounts receivable			41,460	
b	Less allowance for bad debts				41,460
3	Inventories				6,830
4	U.S. Government obligations				
5	Tax-exempt securities				
6	Other current assets (attach schedule)				66,630
7	Loans to shareholders				
8	Mortgage and real estate loans				
9	Other investments (attach schedule)				
10a	Buildings and other depreciable assets			135,101	
b	Less accumulated depreciation			35,162	99,939
11a	Depletable assets				
b	Less accumulated depletion				
12	Land (net of any amortization)				
13a	Intangible assets (amortizable only)				
b	Less accumulated amortization				
14	Other assets (attach schedule)				150
15	Total assets				359,218
	Liabilities and Shareholders' Equity				
16	Accounts payable				15,374
17	Mortgages, notes, bonds payable in less than 1 yr				8,749
18	Other current liabilities (attach schedule)				44,897
19	Loans from shareholders				82,630
20	Mortgages, notes, bonds payable in 1 year or more				126,803
21	Other liabilities (attach schedule)				
22	Capital stock				6,000
23	Additional paid-in capital				
24	Retained earnings				74,765
25	Adjustments to shareholders' equity (attach sch.)				
26	Less cost of treasury stock		( )		( )
27	Total liabilities and shareholders' equity				359,218

Schedule M-1	**Reconciliation of Income (Loss) per Books With Income (Loss) per Return** (You are not required to complete this schedule if the total assets on line 15, column (d), of Schedule L are less than $25,000.)		
1	Net income (loss) per books	74,765	**5** Income recorded on books this year not included on Schedule K, lines 1 through 6 (itemize):
2	Income included on Schedule K, lines 1 through 6, not recorded on books this year		**a** Tax-exempt int. $
3	Expenses recorded on books this year not included on Schedule K, lines 1 through 11a, 15e, and 16b (itemize):		**6** Deductions included on Schedule K, lines 1 through 11a, 15e, and 16b, not charged against book income this year (itemize): **a** Depreciation $
a	Depreciation $		
b	Travel and entertainment $ 941 See Sch. 269	1,210	**7** Add lines 5 and 6 **8** Income (loss) (Schedule K, line 23).
4	Add lines 1 through 3	75,975	Line 4 less line 7 75,975

Schedule M-2	**Analysis of Accumulated Adjustments Account, Other Adjustments Account, and Shareholders' Undistributed Taxable Income Previously Taxed** (see page 24 of the instructions)		
		(a) Accumulated adjustments account	**(b)** Other adjustments account	**(c)** Shareholders' undistributed taxable income previously taxed
1	Balance at beginning of tax year			
2	Ordinary income from page 1, line 21	94,475		
3	Other additions			
4	Loss from page 1, line 21	( )		
5	Other reductions	(19,710)	( )	
6	Combine lines 1 through 5	74,765		
7	Distributions other than dividend distributions			
8	Balance at end of tax year. Subtract line 7 from line 6	74,765		

SCHEDULE K-1	Shareholder's Share of Income, Credits, Deductions, etc.	OMB No. 1545-0130

SCHEDULE K-1
(Form 1120S)

Department of the Treasury
Internal Revenue Service

Shareholder's Share of Income, Credits, Deductions, etc.

▶ See separate instructions.
For calendar year 1998 or tax year
beginning _____ , 1998, and ending _____ , 19 ___

OMB No. 1545-0130

1998

Shareholder's identifying number ▶ 111-11-1111 | Corporation's identifying number ▶ 99-9999999

Shareholder's name, address, and ZIP code

MICHAEL LIGHTYEAR
222 ANY BLVD.
ANY CITY, NY 99999

Corporation's name, address, and ZIP code

KAREN, KATIE & MICHAEL CORP.
123 ANY STREET
ANY CITY, NY 99999

A Shareholder's percentage of stock ownership for tax year (see instructions for Schedule K-1) . . . . ▶ 33.3333%
B Internal Revenue Service Center where corporation filed its return ▶ Holtsville, NY 00501-0013
C Tax shelter registration number (see instructions for Schedule K-1) . . . . ▶ _____
D Check applicable boxes: **(1)** ☐ Final K-1 **(2)** ☐ Amended K-1

		(a) Pro rata share items		(b) Amount	(c) Form 1040 filers enter the amount in col. (b) on:
Income (Loss)	1	Ordinary income (loss) from trade or business activities	1	31,492	See pages 4 and 5 of the Shareholder's Instructions for Schedule K-1 (Form 1120S).
	2	Net income (loss) from rental real estate activities	2		
	3	Net income (loss) from other rental activities	3		
	4	Portfolio income (loss):			
	a	Interest	4a		Sch. B, Part I, line 1
	b	Ordinary dividends	4b		Sch. B, Part II, line 5
	c	Royalties	4c		Sch. E, Part I, line 4
	d	Net short-term capital gain (loss)	4d		Sch. D, line 5, col. (f)
	e	Net long-term capital gain (loss):			
		(1) 28% rate gain (loss)	e(1)		Sch. D, line 12, col. (g)
		(2) Total for year	e(2)		Sch. D, line 12, col. (f)
	f	Other portfolio income (loss) (attach schedule)	4f		(Enter on applicable line of your return.) See Shareholder's Instructions for Schedule K-1 (Form 1120S).
	5	Net section 1231 gain (loss) (other than due to casualty or theft)	5		(Enter on applicable line of your return.)
	6	Other income (loss) (attach schedule)	6		
Deduc-tions	7	Charitable contributions (attach schedule)	7		Sch. A, line 15 or 16
	8	Section 179 expense deduction	8	6,167	See page 6 of the Shareholder's Instructions for Schedule K-1 (Form 1120S).
	9	Deductions related to portfolio income (loss) (attach schedule)	9		
	10	Other deductions (attach schedule)	10		
Invest-ment Interest	11a	Interest expense on investment debts	11a		Form 4952, line 1
	b	**(1)** Investment income included on lines 4a, 4b, 4c, and 4f above . . .	b(1)		See Shareholder's Instructions for Schedule K-1 (Form 1120S).
		(2) Investment expenses included on line 9 above	b(2)		
Credits	12a	Credit for alcohol used as fuel	12a		Form 6478, line 10
	b	Low-income housing credit:			
		(1) From section 42(j)(5) partnerships for property placed in service before 1990	b(1)		Form 8586, line 5
		(2) Other than on line 12b(1) for property placed in service before 1990	b(2)		
		(3) From section 42(j)(5) partnerships for property placed in service after 1989	b(3)		
		(4) Other than on line 12b(3) for property placed in service after 1989	b(4)		
	c	Qualified rehabilitation expenditures related to rental real estate activities	12c		See page 7 of the Shareholder's Instructions for Schedule K-1 (Form 1120S).
	d	Credits (other than credits shown on lines 12b and 12c) related to rental real estate activities	12d		
	e	Credits related to other rental activities	12e		
	13	Other credits	13		

For Paperwork Reduction Act Notice, see the Instructions for Form 1120S.

Schedule K-1 (Form 1120S) 1998

How Taxes Affect Business Decisions

415

	(a) Pro rata share items		(b) Amount	(c) Form 1040 filers enter the amount in column (b) on:
Adjust-ments and Tax Preference Items	**14a** Depreciation adjustment on property placed in service after 1986	**14a**	3,611	See page 7 of the Shareholder's Instructions for Schedule K-1 (Form 1120S) and Instructions for Form 6251
	b Adjusted gain or loss	**14b**		
	c Depletion (other than oil and gas).	**14c**		
	d (1) Gross income from oil, gas, or geothermal properties	**d(1)**		
	(2) Deductions allocable to oil, gas, or geothermal properties	**d(2)**		
	e Other adjustments and tax preference items (attach schedule).	**14e**		
Foreign Taxes	**15a** Type of income ▶ _____			Form 1116, Check boxes
	b Name of foreign country or U.S. possession ▶ _____			
	c Total gross income from sources outside the United States (attach schedule).	**15c**		▶ Form 1116, Part I
	d Total applicable deductions and losses (attach schedule)	**15d**		
	e Total foreign taxes (check one): . . ▶ ☐ Paid ☐ Accrued	**15e**		Form 1116, Part II
	f Reduction in taxes available for credit (attach schedule).	**15f**		Form 1116, Part III
	g Other foreign tax information (attach schedule)	**15g**		See Inst. for Form 1116
Other	**16** Section 59(e)(2) expenditures: **a** Type ▶ _____			See Shareholder's Instructions for Schedule K-1 (Form 1120S).
	b Amount	**16b**		
	17 Tax-exempt interest income	**17**		Form 1040, line 8b
	18 Other tax-exempt income.	**18**		
	19 Nondeductible expenses	**19**		See pages 7 and 8 of the Shareholder's Instructions for Schedule K-1 (Form 1120S).
	20 Property distributions (including cash) other than dividend distributions reported to you on Form 1099-DIV.	**20**		
	21 Amount of loan repayments for "Loans From Shareholders".	**21**		
	22 Recapture of low-income housing credit:			
	a From section 42(j)(5) partnerships	**22a**		▶ Form 8611, line 8
	b Other than on line 22a	**22b**		
Supple-mental Information	**23** Supplemental information required to be reported separately to each shareholder (attach additional schedules if more space is needed):			

SCHEDULE K-1
(Form 1120S)

Department of the Treasury
Internal Revenue Service

Shareholder's Share of Income, Credits, Deductions, etc.
▶ See separate instructions.
For calendar year 1998 or tax year
beginning _____ , 1998, and ending _____ , 19 _____

OMB No. 1545-0130

1998

Shareholder's identifying number ▶ 222-22-2222	Corporation's identifying number ▶ 99-9999999
Shareholder's name, address, and ZIP code KAREN LIGHTYEAR 222 ANY BLVD. ANY CITY, NY 99999	Corporation's name, address, and ZIP code KAREN, KATIE & MICHAEL CORP. 123 ANY STREET ANY CITY, NY 99999

A Shareholder's percentage of stock ownership for tax year (see instructions for Schedule K-1) .... ▶ __33.3333%__

B Internal Revenue Service Center where corporation filed its return ▶ Holtsville, NY 00501-0013

C Tax shelter registration number (see instructions for Schedule K-1) .... ▶ _____

D Check applicable boxes: **(1)** ☐ Final K-1 **(2)** ☐ Amended K-1

		(a) Pro rata share items		(b) Amount	(c) Form 1040 filers enter the amount in col. (b) on:
Income (Loss)	1	Ordinary income (loss) from trade or business activities	1	31,492	See pages 4 and 5 of the Shareholder's Instructions for Schedule K-1 (Form 1120S).
	2	Net income (loss) from rental real estate activities.................	2		
	3	Net income (loss) from other rental activities....................	3		
	4	Portfolio income (loss):			
	a	Interest	4a		Sch. B, Part I, line 1
	b	Ordinary dividends	4b		Sch. B, Part II, line 5
	c	Royalties	4c		Sch. E, Part I, line 4
	d	Net short-term capital gain (loss)	4d		Sch. D, line 5, col. (f)
	e	Net long-term capital gain (loss):			
		(1) 28% rate gain (loss)................................	e(1)		Sch. D, line 12, col. (g)
		(2) Total for year.................................	e(2)		Sch. D, line 12, col. (f)
	f	Other portfolio income (loss) (attach schedule)..................	4f		(Enter on applicable line of your return.)
	5	Net section 1231 gain (loss) (other than due to casualty or theft)	5		See Shareholder's Instructions for Schedule K-1 (Form 1120S).
	6	Other income (loss) (attach schedule).........................	6		(Enter on applicable line of your return.)
Deductions	7	Charitable contributions (attach schedule)	7		Sch. A, line 15 or 16
	8	Section 179 expense deduction	8	6,167	See page 6 of the Shareholder's Instructions for Schedule K-1 (Form 1120S).
	9	Deductions related to portfolio income (loss) (attach schedule).......	9		
	10	Other deductions (attach schedule)	10		
Investment Interest	11a	Interest expense on investment debts.........................	11a		Form 4952, line 1
	b	**(1)** Investment income included on lines 4a, 4b, 4c, and 4f above ...	b(1)		See Shareholder's Instructions for Schedule K-1 (Form 1120S).
		(2) Investment expenses included on line 9 above..............	b(2)		
Credits	12a	Credit for alcohol used as fuel............................	12a		Form 6478, line 10
	b	Low-income housing credit:			
		(1) From section 42(j)(5) partnerships for property placed in service before 1990	b(1)		
		(2) Other than on line 12b(1) for property placed in service before 1990	b(2)		
		(3) From section 42(j)(5) partnerships for property placed in service after 1989	b(3)		▶ Form 8586, line 5
		(4) Other than on line 12b(3) for property placed in service after 1989	b(4)		
	c	Qualified rehabilitation expenditures related to rental real estate activities	12c		
	d	Credits (other than credits shown on lines 12b and 12c) related to rental real estate activities	12d		See page 7 of the Shareholder's Instructions for Schedule K-1 (Form 1120S).
	e	Credits related to other rental activities	12e		
	13	Other credits...................................	13		

For Paperwork Reduction Act Notice, see the Instructions for Form 1120S.

Schedule K-1 (Form 1120S) 1998

How Taxes Affect Business Decisions

	(a) Pro rata share items		(b) Amount	(c) Form 1040 filers enter the amount in column (b) on:
Adjust-ments and Tax Preference Items	**14a** Depreciation adjustment on property placed in service after 1986	**14a**	3,611	See page 7 of the Shareholder's Instructions for Schedule K-1 (Form 1120S) and Instructions for Form 6251
	b Adjusted gain or loss	**14b**		
	c Depletion (other than oil and gas).	**14c**		
	d (1) Gross income from oil, gas, or geothermal properties	**d(1)**		
	(2) Deductions allocable to oil, gas, or geothermal properties	**d(2)**		
	e Other adjustments and tax preference items (attach schedule).	**14e**		
Foreign Taxes	**15a** Type of income ▶ _____			Form 1116, Check boxes
	b Name of foreign country or U.S. possession ▶ _____			
	c Total gross income from sources outside the United States (attach schedule)	**15c**		Form 1116, Part I
	d Total applicable deductions and losses (attach schedule)	**15d**		
	e Total foreign taxes (check one): . . ▶ ☐ Paid ☐ Accrued	**15e**		Form 1116, Part II
	f Reduction in taxes available for credit (attach schedule).	**15f**		Form 1116, Part III
	g Other foreign tax information (attach schedule)	**15g**		See Inst. for Form 1116
Other	**16** Section 59(e)(2) expenditures: **a** Type ▶ _____			See Shareholder's Instructions for Schedule K-1 (Form 1120S)
	b Amount.	**16b**		
	17 Tax-exempt interest income	**17**		Form 1040, line 8b
	18 Other tax-exempt income.	**18**		
	19 Nondeductible expenses	**19**		See pages 7 and 8 of the Shareholder's Instructions for Schedule K-1 (Form 1120S).
	20 Property distributions (including cash) other than dividend distributions reported to you on Form 1099-DIV.	**20**		
	21 Amount of loan repayments for "Loans From Shareholders".	**21**		
	22 Recapture of low-income housing credit:			
	a From section 42(j)(5) partnerships	**22a**		Form 8611, line 8
	b Other than on line 22a	**22b**		
Supple-mental Information	**23** Supplemental information required to be reported separately to each shareholder (attach additional schedules if more space is needed):			

Shareholder's Share of Income, Credits, Deductions, etc.

▶ See separate instructions.

For calendar year 1998 or tax year
beginning _____ , 1998, and ending _____ , 19 ___

OMB No. 1545-0130

1998

Shareholder's identifying number ▶ 333-33-3333	Corporation's identifying number ▶ 99-9999999
Shareholder's name, address, and ZIP code KATIE LIGHTYEAR 222 ANY BLVD. ANY CITY, NY 99999	Corporation's name, address, and ZIP code KAREN, KATIE & MICHAEL CORP. 123 ANY STREET ANY CITY, NY 99999

A Shareholder's percentage of stock ownership for tax year (see instructions for Schedule K-1) .... ▶ 33.3334%

B Internal Revenue Service Center where corporation filed its return ▶ Holtsville, NY 00501-0013

C Tax shelter registration number (see instructions for Schedule K-1). .... ▶ _____

D Check applicable boxes: **(1)** ☐ Final K-1   **(2)** ☐ Amended K-1

		(a) Pro rata share items		(b) Amount	(c) Form 1040 filers enter the amount in col. (b) on:
Income (Loss)	1	Ordinary income (loss) from trade or business activities	1	31,491	See pages 4 and 5 of the Shareholder's Instructions for Schedule K-1 (Form 1120S)
	2	Net income (loss) from rental real estate activities	2		
	3	Net income (loss) from other rental activities	3		
	4	Portfolio income (loss):			
	a	Interest	4a		Sch. B, Part I, line 1
	b	Ordinary dividends	4b		Sch. B, Part II, line 5
	c	Royalties	4c		Sch. E, Part I, line 4
	d	Net short-term capital gain (loss)	4d		Sch. D, line 5, col. (f)
	e	Net long-term capital gain (loss):			
		(1) 28% rate gain (loss).	e(1)		Sch. D, line 12, col. (g)
		(2) Total for year.	e(2)		Sch. D, line 12, col. (f)
	f	Other portfolio income (loss) (attach schedule).	4f		(Enter on applicable line of your return.)
	5	Net section 1231 gain (loss) (other than due to casualty or theft)	5		See Shareholder's Instructions for Schedule K-1 (Form 1120S).
	6	Other income (loss) (attach schedule).	6		(Enter on applicable line of your return.)
Deductions	7	Charitable contributions (attach schedule)	7		Sch. A, line 15 or 16
	8	Section 179 expense deduction	8	6,166	See page 6 of the Shareholder's Instructions for Schedule K-1 (Form 1120S).
	9	Deductions related to portfolio income (loss) (attach schedule).	9		
	10	Other deductions (attach schedule)	10		
Investment Interest	11a	Interest expense on investment debts	11a		Form 4952, line 1
	b (1)	Investment income included on lines 4a, 4b, 4c, and 4f above ...	b(1)		See Shareholder's Instructions for Schedule K-1 (Form 1120S).
	(2)	Investment expenses included on line 9 above.	b(2)		
Credits	12a	Credit for alcohol used as fuel.	12a		Form 6478, line 10
	b	Low-income housing credit:			
		(1) From section 42(j)(5) partnerships for property placed in service before 1990.	b(1)		
		(2) Other than on line 12b(1) for property placed in service before 1990	b(2)		
		(3) From section 42(j)(5) partnerships for property placed in service after 1989.	b(3)		Form 8586, line 5
		(4) Other than on line 12b(3) for property placed in service after 1989	b(4)		
	c	Qualified rehabilitation expenditures related to rental real estate activities	12c		
	d	Credits (other than credits shown on lines 12b and 12c) related to rental real estate activities	12d		See page 7 of the Shareholder's Instructions for Schedule K-1 (Form 1120S).
	e	Credits related to other rental activities	12e		
	13	Other credits.	13		

For Paperwork Reduction Act Notice, see the Instructions for Form 1120S.

Schedule K-1 (Form 1120S) 1998

(a) Pro rata share items		(b) Amount	(c) Form 1040 filers enter the amount in column (b) on:
Adjustments and Tax Preference Items	**14a** Depreciation adjustment on property placed in service after 1986 ..... **14a**	3,610	See page 7 of the Shareholder's Instructions for Schedule K-1 (Form 1120S) and Instructions for Form 6251
	b Adjusted gain or loss **14b**		
	c Depletion (other than oil and gas)............................ **14c**		
	d (1) Gross income from oil, gas, or geothermal properties .... **d(1)**		
	(2) Deductions allocable to oil, gas, or geothermal properties .... **d(2)**		
	e Other adjustments and tax preference items (attach schedule)........ **14e**		
Foreign Taxes	**15a** Type of income ▶ _____		Form 1116, Check boxes
	b Name of foreign country or U.S. possession ▶ _____		
	c Total gross income from sources outside the United States (attach schedule).. **15c**		▶ Form 1116, Part I
	d Total applicable deductions and losses (attach schedule) **15d**		
	e Total foreign taxes (check one): .. ▶ ☐ Paid ☐ Accrued **15e**		Form 1116, Part II
	f Reduction in taxes available for credit (attach schedule)............. **15f**		Form 1116, Part III
	g Other foreign tax information (attach schedule) **15g**		See Inst. for Form 1116
Other	**16** Section 59(e)(2) expenditures: **a** Type ▶ _____		See Shareholder's Instructions for Schedule K-1 (Form 1120S).
	b Amount.. **16b**		
	17 Tax-exempt interest income **17**		Form 1040, line 8b
	18 Other tax-exempt income.................................... **18**		
	19 Nondeductible expenses **19**		See pages 7 and 8 of the Shareholder's Instructions for Schedule K-1 (Form 1120S).
	20 Property distributions (including cash) other than dividend distributions reported to you on Form 1099-DIV................... **20**		
	21 Amount of loan repayments for "Loans From Shareholders"......... **21**		
	22 Recapture of low-income housing credit:		
	a From section 42(j)(5) partnerships **22a**		▶ Form 8611, line 8
	b Other than on line 22a **22b**		

23 Supplemental information required to be reported separately to each shareholder (attach additional schedules if more space is needed):

Supplemental Information

_____

_____

_____

_____

_____

_____

_____

_____

_____

_____

_____

_____

_____

_____

_____

_____

_____

_____

_____

_____

_____

_____

420   *How Taxes Affect Business Decisions*

Form **4562**

Department of the Treasury
Internal Revenue Service (99)

Depreciation and Amortization

(Including Information on Listed Property)

▶ See separate instructions.   ▶ Attach this form to your return.

OMB No. 1545-0172

1998

Attachment
Sequence No. **67**

Name(s) shown on return	Business or activity to which this form relates	Identifying number
KAREN, KATIE & MICHAEL CORP.		99-9999999

Part I Election To Expense Certain Tangible Property (Section 179) (Note: If you have any "listed property," complete Part V before you complete Part I.)

1 Maximum dollar limitation. If an enterprise zone business, see page 2 of the instructions	**1**	$18,500
2 Total cost of section 179 property placed in service. See page 2 of the instructions	**2**	135,101
3 Threshold cost of section 179 property before reduction in limitation	**3**	$200,000
4 Reduction in limitation. Subtract line 3 from line 2. If zero or less, enter -0-	**4**	
5 Dollar limitation for tax year. Subtract line 4 from line 1. If zero or less, enter -0-. If married filing separately, see page 2 of the instructions	**5**	18,500

6	(a) Description of property	(b) Cost (business use only)	(c) Elected cost	
	MACHINERY	135,101	18,500	

7 Listed property. Enter amount from line 27	**7**	
8 Total elected cost of section 179 property. Add amounts in column (c), lines 6 and 7	**8**	18,500
9 Tentative deduction. Enter the smaller of line 5 or line 8	**9**	18,500
10 Carryover of disallowed deduction from 1997. See page 3 of the instructions	**10**	
11 Business income limitation. Enter smaller of business income (not less than zero) or line 5 (see instructions) . .	**11**	18,500
12 Section 179 expense deduction. Add lines 9 and 10, but do not enter more than line 11	**12**	18,500
13 Carryover of disallowed deduction to 1999. Add lines 9 and 10, less line 12 . . . . . ▶	**13**	

Note: Do not use Part II or Part III below for listed property (automobiles, certain other vehicles, cellular telephones, certain computers, or property used for entertainment, recreation, or amusement). Instead, use Part V for listed property.

Part II MACRS Depreciation For Assets Placed in Service ONLY During Your 1998 Tax Year (Do Not Include Listed Property.)

Section A -- General Asset Account Election

14 If you are making the election under section 168(i)(4) to group any assets placed in service during the tax year into one or more general asset accounts, check this box. See page 3 of the instructions . . . . ▶ ☐

Section B -- General Depreciation System (GDS) (See page 3 of the instructions.)

(a) Classification of property	(b) Month and year placed in service	(c) Basis for depr. (business/investment use only -- see instructions)	(d) Recovery period	(e) Convention	(f) Method	(g) Depreciation deduction
15a 3-year property						
b 5-year property						
c 7-year property		116,601	7. yr	HY	200DB	16,662
d 10-year property						
e 15-year property						
f 20-year property						
g 25-year property			25 yrs.		S/L	
h Residential rental property			27.5 yrs.	MM	S/L	
			27.5 yrs.	MM	S/L	
i Nonresidential real property			39 yrs.	MM	S/L	
				MM	S/L	

Section C -- Alternative Depreciation System (ADS) (See page 5 of the instructions.)

16a Class life					S/L	
b 12-year			12 yrs.		S/L	
c 40-year			40 yrs.	MM	S/L	

Part III Other Depreciation (Do Not Include Listed Property.) (See page 6 of the instructions.)

17 GDS and ADS deductions for assets placed in service in tax years beginning before 1998	**17**	
18 Property subject to section 168(f)(1) election	**18**	
19 ACRS and other depreciation	**19**	

Part IV Summary (See page 6 of the instructions.)

20 Listed property. Enter amount from line 26	**20**	
21 **Total.** Add deductions on line 12, lines 15 and 16 in column (g), and lines 17 through 20. Enter here and on the appropriate lines of your return. Partnerships and S corporations -- see instructions	**21**	16,662
22 For assets shown above and placed in service during the current year, enter the portion of the basis attributable to section 263A costs	**22**	

For Paperwork Reduction Act Notice, see the separate instructions.   Form **4562** (1998)

How Taxes Affect Business Decisions   **421**

Name	Employer ID Number
KAREN, KATIE & MICHAEL CORP.	99-9999999

Form 1120S, Taxes (Line 12)

Description	Amount
PAYROLL	15,890
STATE FRANCHISE TAX	1,325
MISCELLANEOUS TAXES	1,315
Total	18,530

Form 1120S, Other Deductions (Line 19)

Description	Amount
AUTOMOBILE EXPENSES	26,883
COMPUTER EXPENSES	4,879
DUES AND SUBSCRIPTIONS	462
GENERAL INSURANCE	32,881
HOSPITALIZATION INSURANCE	2,586
OFFICE EXPENSES	8,504
POSTAGE & SHIPPING	7,477
PROFESSIONAL FEES	7,990
ROYALTIES	25,200
STORAGE	2,700
TELEPHONE	9,547
UTILITIES	5,940
Meals/Entertainment (1882 * .5)	941
Total	135,990

```
┌─────────────────────┬──────────────────────────────────┬────────────────────┐
│                     │      SUPPLEMENTAL SCHEDULE       │     For Tax Year   │
│   Form Corp         │                                  │       1998         │
│                     │      FORM 1120S PAGES 1-4        │                    │
├─────────────────────┴──────────────────────────────────┼────────────────────┤
│ Name                                                    │ Employer ID Number │
│   KAREN, KATIE & MICHAEL CORP.                          │ 99-9999999         │
└─────────────────────────────────────────────────────────┴───────────────────┘
```

Schedule L, Other Current Assets (Line 6)

Description	Year Beginning	Year End
PREPAID EXPENSES		66,630
Total		66,630

Schedule L, Other Assets (Line 14)

Description	Year Beginning	Year End
DEPOSITS		150
Total		150

Schedule L, Other Current Liabilities (Line 18)

Description	Year Beginning	Year End
ACCRUED EXPENSES AND TAXES		21,661
PAYROLL TAXES PAYABLE		23,236
Total		44,897

Schedule M-1
Other Expenses Recorded Not Included on Schedule K (Line 3)

Description	Amount
FINES AND PENALTIES	269
Total	269

Name
KAREN, KATIE & MICHAEL CORP.

Employer ID Number
99-9999999

Schedule M-2, Other Reductions (Line 5)

Description	Accumulated Adjustments	Other Adjustments
Section 179 Expense Deduction	18,500	
50% of Meals & Entertainment	941	
FINES AND PENALTIES	269	
Total	19,710	

How Taxes Affect Business Decisions

PAYROLL TAXES

SOCIAL SECURITY AND MEDICARE TAXES

For 1999, social security tax must be withheld from the first $72,600 of employee wages. Accordingly, the maximum amount that can be withheld from an employee's wages during 1999 is $4,240.80.

FEDERAL WITHHOLDING TAXES

An updated blank Form W-4, along with related instructions, follows:

Form W-4 (1999)

Purpose. Complete Form W-4 so your employer can withhold the correct Federal income tax from your pay. Because your tax situation may change, you may want to refigure your withholding each year.

Exemption from withholding. If you are exempt, complete only lines 1, 2, 3, 4, and 7, and sign the form to validate it. Your exemption for 1999 expires February 16, 2000.

Note: *You cannot claim exemption from withholding if (1) your income exceeds $700 and includes more than $250 of unearned income (e.g., interest and dividends) and (2) another person can claim you as a dependent on their tax return.*

Basic instructions. If you are not exempt, complete the Personal Allowances Worksheet. The worksheets on page 2 adjust your withholding allowances based on itemized deductions, adjustments to income, or two-earner/two-job situations. Complete all worksheets that apply. They will help you figure the number of withholding allowances you are entitled to claim. **However, you may claim fewer allowances.**

Child tax and higher education credits. For details on adjusting withholding for these and other credits, see **Pub. 919,** Is My Withholding Correct for 1999?

Head of household. Generally, you may claim head of household filing status on your tax return only if you are unmarried and pay more than 50% of the costs of keeping up a home for yourself and your dependent(s) or other qualifying individuals. See line E below.

Nonwage income. If you have a large amount of nonwage income, such as interest or dividends, you should consider making estimated tax payments using Form 1040-ES. Otherwise, you may owe additional tax.

Two earners/two jobs. If you have a working spouse or more than one job, figure the total number of allowances you are entitled to claim on all jobs using worksheets from only one Form W-4. Your withholding will usually be most accurate when all allowances are claimed on the Form W-4 prepared for the highest paying job and zero allowances are claimed for the others.

Check your withholding. After your Form W-4 takes effect, use Pub. 919 to see how the dollar amount you are having withheld compares to your estimated total annual tax. Get Pub. 919 especially if you used the Two-Earner/Two-Job Worksheet and your earnings exceed $150,000 (Single) or $200,000 (Married).

Recent name change? If your name on line 1 differs from that shown on your social security card, call 1-800-772-1213 for a new social security card.

Personal Allowances Worksheet

A Enter "1" for **yourself** if no one else can claim you as a dependent . . . . **A** _____

B Enter "1" if: { • You are single and have only one job; or
• You are married, have only one job, and your spouse does not work; or
• Your wages from a second job or your spouse's wages (or the total of both) are $1,000 or less. } . . **B** _____

C Enter "1" for your **spouse.** But, you may choose to enter -0- if you are married and have either a working spouse or more than one job. (This may help you avoid having too little tax withheld.). . . . . **C** _____

D Enter number of **dependents** (other than your spouse or yourself) you will claim on your tax return . . . . **D** _____

E Enter "1" if you will file as **head of household** on your tax return (see conditions under **Head of household** above) . **E** _____

F Enter "1" if you have at least $1,500 of **child or dependent care expenses** for which you plan to claim a credit . . **F** _____

G **Child Tax Credit:** • If your total income will be between $20,000 and $50,000 ($23,000 and $63,000 if married), enter "1" for each eligible child. • If your total income will be between $50,000 and $80,000 ($63,000 and $115,000 if married), enter "1" if you have two eligible children, enter "2" if you have three or four eligible children, or enter "3" if you have five or more eligible children . . **G** _____

H Add lines A through G and enter total here. **Note:** This amount may be different from the number of exemptions you claim on your return. ▶ **H** _____

For accuracy, complete all worksheets that apply. {
• If you plan to **itemize or claim adjustments to income** and want to reduce your withholding, see the Deductions and Adjustments Worksheet on page 2.
• If you are **single,** have **more than one job** and your combined earnings from all jobs exceed $32,000, OR if you are **married** and have a **working spouse or more than one job** and the combined earnings from all jobs exceed $55,000, see the Two-Earner/Two-Job Worksheet on page 2 to avoid having too little tax withheld.
• If **neither** of the above situations applies, **stop here** and enter the number from line H on line 5 of Form W-4 below.
}

- **Cut here and give the certificate to your employer. Keep the top part for your records.** - - - - - - - - - - - - - - - -

Form **W-4** Department of the Treasury Internal Revenue Service	**Employee's Withholding Allowance Certificate** ▶ **For Privacy Act and Paperwork Reduction Act Notice, see page 2.**	OMB No. 1545-0010 **1999**

1 Type or print your first name and middle initial	Last name	**2** Your social security number

Home address (number and street or rural route)

3 ☐ Single ☐ Married ☐ Married, but withhold at higher Single rate.
Note: *If married, but legally separated, or spouse is a nonresident alien, check the Single box.*

City or town, state, and ZIP code

4 If your last name differs from that on your social security card, check here. **You must call 1-800-772-1213 for a new card** . . . ▶ ☐

5 Total number of allowances you are claiming (from line H above or from the worksheets on page 2 if they apply) . **5** _____

6 Additional amount, if any, you want withheld from each paycheck . . . . **6** $ _____

7 I claim exemption from withholding for 1999, and I certify that I meet BOTH of the following conditions for exemption:
• Last year I had a right to a refund of **ALL** Federal income tax withheld because I had **NO** tax liability **AND**
• This year I expect a refund of **ALL** Federal income tax withheld because I expect to have **NO** tax liability.
If you meet both conditions, write "EXEMPT" here . . . . ▶ **7** _____

Under penalties of perjury, I certify that I am entitled to the number of withholding allowances claimed on this certificate, or I am entitled to claim exempt status.
Employee's signature
(Form is not valid unless you sign it) ▶ _____ Date ▶ _____

8 Employer's name and address (Employer: Complete 8 and 10 only if sending to the IRS)	**9** Office code (optional)	**10** Employer identification number

Cat. No. 102200

426

Payroll Taxes

Deductions and Adjustments Worksheet

Note: *Use this worksheet only if you plan to itemize deductions or claim adjustments to income on your 1999 tax return.*

1   Enter an estimate of your 1999 itemized deductions. These include qualifying home mortgage interest, charitable contributions, state and local taxes (but not sales taxes), medical expenses in excess of 7.5% of your income, and miscellaneous deductions. (For 1999, you may have to reduce your itemized deductions if your income is over $126,600 ($63,300 if married filing separately). Get Pub. 919 for details.)   **1** $ _____

2   Enter: { $7,200 if married filing jointly or qualifying widow(er) / $6,350 if head of household / $4,300 if single / $3,600 if married filing separately } . . . . **2** $ _____

3   **Subtract** line 2 from line 1. If line 2 is greater than line 1, enter -0- . . . . **3** $ _____

4   Enter an estimate of your 1999 adjustments to income, including alimony, deductible IRA contributions, and student loan interest . **4** $ _____

5   **Add** lines 3 and 4 and enter the total . . . . **5** $ _____

6   Enter an estimate of your 1999 nonwage income (such as dividends or interest) . . . . **6** $ _____

7   **Subtract** line 6 from line 5. Enter the result, but not less than -0- . . . . **7** $ _____

8   **Divide** the amount on line 7 by $3,000 and enter the result here. Drop any fraction . . . . . **8** _____

9   Enter the number from Personal Allowances Worksheet, line H, on page 1 . . . . **9** _____

10   **Add** lines 8 and 9 and enter the total here. If you plan to use the Two-Earner/Two-Job Worksheet, also enter this total on line 1 below. Otherwise, **stop here** and enter this total on Form W-4, line 5, on page 1 . . . . **10** _____

Two-Earner/Two-Job Worksheet

Note: *Use this worksheet only if the instructions for line H on page 1 direct you here.*

1   Enter the number from line H on page 1 (or from line 10 above if you used the Deductions and Adjustments Worksheet) **1** _____

2   Find the number in **Table 1** below that applies to the **LOWEST** paying job and enter it here . . . . **2** _____

3   If line 1 is **GREATER THAN OR EQUAL TO** line 2, subtract line 2 from line 1. Enter the result here (if zero, enter -0-) and on Form W-4, line 5, on page 1. **DO NOT** use the rest of this worksheet . . . . **3** _____

Note: *If line 1 is **LESS THAN** line 2, enter -0- on Form W-4, line 5, on page 1. Complete lines 4–9 to calculate the additional withholding amount necessary to avoid a year end tax bill.*

4   Enter the number from line 2 of this worksheet . . . . **4** _____

5   Enter the number from line 1 of this worksheet . . . . **5** _____

6   **Subtract** line 5 from line 4 . . . . **6** _____

7   Find the amount in **Table 2** below that applies to the HIGHEST paying job and enter it here . . . . **7** $ _____

8   **Multiply** line 7 by line 6 and enter the result here. This is the additional annual withholding amount needed **8** $ _____

9   Divide line 8 by the number of pay periods remaining in 1999. (For example, divide by 26 if you are paid every other week and you complete this form in December 1998.) Enter the result here and on Form W-4, line 6, page 1. This is the additional amount to be withheld from each paycheck . . . . **9** $ _____

Table 1: Two-Earner/Two-Job Worksheet

Married Filing Jointly				All Others			
If wages from **LOWEST** paying job are—	Enter on line 2 above	If wages from **LOWEST** paying job are—	Enter on line 2 above	If wages from **LOWEST** paying job are—	Enter on line 2 above	If wages from **LOWEST** paying job are—	Enter on line 2 above
$0 - $4,000	0	40,001 - 45,000	8	$0 - $5,000	0	65,001 - 80,000	8
4,001 - 7,000	1	45,001 - 54,000	9	5,001 - 11,000	1	80,001 - 100,000	9
7,001 - 12,000	2	54,001 - 62,000	10	11,001 - 16,000	2	100,001 and over	10
12,001 - 18,000	3	62,001 - 70,000	11	16,001 - 21,000	3		
18,001 - 24,000	4	70,001 - 85,000	12	21,001 - 25,000	4		
24,001 - 28,000	5	85,001 - 100,000	13	25,001 - 40,000	5		
28,001 - 35,000	6	100,001 - 110,000	14	40,001 - 50,000	6		
35,001 - 40,000	7	110,001 and over	15	50,001 - 65,000	7		

Table 2: Two-Earner/Two-Job Worksheet

Married Filing Jointly		All Others	
If wages from **HIGHEST** paying job are—	Enter on line 7 above	If wages from **HIGHEST** paying job are—	Enter on line 7 above
$0 - $50,000	$400	$0 - $30,000	$400
50,001 - 100,000	770	30,001 - 60,000	770
100,001 - 130,000	850	60,001 - 120,000	850
130,001 - 240,000	1,000	120,001 - 250,000	1,000
240,001 and over	1,100	250,001 and over	1,100

TAX DEPOSITS

A copy of revised Form 941, Employer's Quarterly Federal Tax Return (along with related instructions) referred to on page 925 of the main text, follows:

Form **941**	Employer's Quarterly Federal Tax Return

Form 941 (Rev. January 1999)
Department of the Treasury
Internal Revenue Service

► See separate instructions for information on completing this return.
Please type or print.

OMB No. 1545-0029

Enter state code for state in which deposits were made ONLY if different from state in address to the right ► (see page 2 of instructions).

Name (as distinguished from trade name)	Date quarter ended
Trade name, if any	Employer identification number
Address (number and street)	City, state, and ZIP code

T
FF
FD
FP
I
T

IRS Use

1 1 1 1 1 1 1 1 . 1 1   2   3 3 3 3 3 3 3 3   4 4 4   5 5 5
6 7   8 8 8 8 8 8 8   9 9 9 9 9   10 10 10 10 10 10 10 10 10 10

If address is different from prior return, check here ►

If you do not have to file returns in the future, check here ► ☐ and enter date final wages paid ►
If you are a seasonal employer, see **Seasonal employers** on page 1 of the instructions and check here ►

1	Number of employees in the pay period that includes March 12th ►	1	
2	Total wages and tips, plus other compensation	2	
3	Total income tax withheld from wages, tips, and sick pay	3	
4	Adjustment of withheld income tax for preceding quarters of calendar year	4	
5	Adjusted total of income tax withheld (line 3 as adjusted by line 4—see instructions) . . .	5	
6	Taxable social security wages	6a	× 12.4% (.124) =	6b
	Taxable social security tips	6c	× 12.4% (.124) =	6d
7	Taxable Medicare wages and tips . . .	7a	× 2.9% (.029) =	7b
8	Total social security and Medicare taxes (add lines 6b, 6d, and 7b). Check here if wages are not subject to social security and/or Medicare tax . . . . ► ☐	8	
9	Adjustment of social security and Medicare taxes (see instructions for required explanation) Sick Pay $ _____ ± Fractions of Cents $ _____ ± Other $ _____ =	9	
10	Adjusted total of social security and Medicare taxes (line 8 as adjusted by line 9—see instructions)	10	
11	**Total taxes** (add lines 5 and 10)	11	
12	Advance earned income credit (EIC) payments made to employees	12	
13	Net taxes (subtract line 12 from line 11). **If $1,000 or more, this must equal line 17, column (d) below (or line D of Schedule B (Form 941))**	13	
14	Total deposits for quarter, including overpayment applied from a prior quarter	14	
15	Balance due (subtract line 14 from line 13). See instructions	15	
16	Overpayment. If line 14 is more than line 13, enter excess here ► $ _____		

and check if to be: ☐ Applied to next return **OR** ☐ Refunded.

- **All filers:** If line 13 is less than $1,000, you need not complete line 17 or Schedule B (Form 941).
- **Semiweekly schedule depositors:** Complete Schedule B (Form 941) and check here . . . . ► ☐
- **Monthly schedule depositors:** Complete line 17, columns (a) through (d), and check here . . . . ► ☐

17	Monthly Summary of Federal Tax Liability. Do not complete if you were a semiweekly schedule depositor.			
	(a) First month liability	**(b)** Second month liability	**(c)** Third month liability	**(d)** Total liability for quarter

Sign Here

Under penalties of perjury, I declare that I have examined this return, including accompanying schedules and statements, and to the best of my knowledge and belief, it is true, correct, and complete.

Signature ► _____ Print Your Name and Title ► _____ Date ► _____

For Privacy Act and Paperwork Reduction Act Notice, see back of form. Cat. No. 17001Z Form **941** (Rev. 1-99)

Where to file. In the list below, find the state where your legal residence, principal place of business, office, or agency is located. Send your return to the **Internal Revenue Service** at the address listed for your location. No street address is needed. **Note:** *Where you file depends on whether or not you are including a payment.*

Florida, Georgia, South Carolina
Return without payment: **Return with payment:**
Atlanta, GA 39901-0005 P.O. Box 105703
Atlanta, GA 30348-5703

New Jersey, New York (New York City and counties of Nassau, Rockland, Suffolk, and Westchester)
Return without payment: **Return with payment:**
Holtsville, NY 00501-0005 P.O. Box 416
Newark, NJ 07101-0416

New York (all other counties), Connecticut, Maine, Massachusetts, New Hampshire, Rhode Island, Vermont
Return without payment: **Return with payment:**
Andover, MA 05501-0005 P.O. Box 371493
Pittsburgh, PA 15250-7493

Illinois, Iowa, Minnesota, Missouri, Wisconsin
Return without payment: **Return with payment:**
Kansas City, MO 64999-0005 P.O. Box 970007
St. Louis, MO 63197-0007

Delaware, District of Columbia, Maryland, Pennsylvania, Virginia
Return without payment: **Return with payment:**
Philadelphia, PA 19255-0005 P.O. Box 8786
Philadelphia, PA 19162-8786

Indiana, Kentucky, Michigan, Ohio, West Virginia
Return without payment: **Return with payment:**
Cincinnati, OH 45999-0005 P.O. Box 7329
Chicago, IL 60680-7329

Kansas, New Mexico, Oklahoma, Texas
Return without payment: **Return with payment:**
Austin, TX 73301-0005 P.O. Box 970013
St. Louis, MO 63197-0013

Alaska, Arizona, California (counties of Alpine, Amador, Butte, Calaveras, Colusa, Contra Costa, Del Norte, El Dorado, Glenn, Humboldt, Lake, Lassen, Marin, Mendocino, Modoc, Napa, Nevada, Placer, Plumas, Sacramento, San Joaquin, Shasta, Sierra, Siskiyou, Solano, Sonoma, Sutter, Tehama, Trinity, Yolo, and Yuba), Colorado, Idaho, Montana, Nebraska, Nevada, North Dakota, Oregon, South Dakota, Utah, Washington, Wyoming
Return without payment: **Return with payment:**
Ogden, UT 84201-0005 P.O. Box 7922
San Francisco, CA 94120-7922

California (all other counties), Hawaii
Return without payment: **Return with payment:**
Fresno, CA 93888-0005 P.O. Box 60407
Los Angeles, CA 90060-0407

Alabama, Arkansas, Louisiana, Mississippi, North Carolina, Tennessee
Return without payment: **Return with payment:**
Memphis, TN 37501-0005 P.O. Box 70503
Charlotte, NC 28272-0503

If you have no legal residence or principal place of business in any state
All returns:
Philadelphia, PA 19255-0005

Privacy Act and Paperwork Reduction Act Notice. We ask for the information on this form to carry out the Internal Revenue laws of the United States. We need it to figure and collect the right amount of tax. Subtitle C, Employment Taxes, of the Internal Revenue Code imposes employment taxes on wages, including income tax withholding. This form is used to determine the amount of the taxes that you owe. Section 6011 requires you to provide the requested information if the tax is applicable to you. Section 6109 requires you to provide your employer identification number (EIN). Routine uses of this information include giving it to the Department of Justice for civil and criminal litigation, and to cities, states, and the District of Columbia for use in administering their tax laws. If you fail to provide this information in a timely manner, you may be subject to penalties and interest.

You are not required to provide the information requested on a form that is subject to the Paperwork Reduction Act unless the form displays a valid OMB control number. Books and records relating to a form or instructions must be retained as long as their contents may become material in the administration of any Internal Revenue law. Generally, tax returns and return information are confidential, as required by section 6103.

The time needed to complete and file this form will vary depending on individual circumstances. The estimated average time is:

For Form 941:
Recordkeeping . . . . 11 hr., 44 min.
Learning about the law or the form . 40 min.
Preparing the form . . . . . . 1 hr., 47 min.
Copying, assembling, and sending the form to the IRS . . . . 16 min.

For Form 941TeleFile:
Recordkeeping . . . . 5 hr., 1 min.
Learning about the law or the Tax Record . . . . 6 min.
Preparing the Tax Record . . . . 11 min.
TeleFile phone call . . . . 11 min.

If you have comments concerning the accuracy of these time estimates or suggestions for making this form simpler, we would be happy to hear from you. You can write to the Tax Forms Committee, Western Area Distribution Center, Rancho Cordova, CA 95743-0001. **DO NOT** send the tax form to this address.

Form 941
Payment Voucher

Purpose of Form

Complete Form 941-V if you are making a payment with **Form 941,** Employer's Quarterly Federal Tax Return. We will use the completed voucher to credit your payment more promptly and accurately, and to improve our service to you.

If you have your return prepared by a third party and make a payment with that return, please provide this payment voucher to the return preparer.

Making Payments With Form 941

Make payments with Form 941 only if:

1. Your net taxes for the quarter (line 13 on Form 941) are less than $1,000 or

2. You are a monthly schedule depositor making a payment in accordance with the **accuracy of deposits** rule. (See section 11 of **Circular E,** Employer's Tax Guide, for details.) This amount may be $1,000 or more.

Otherwise, you must deposit the amount at an authorized financial institution or by electronic funds transfer. (See section 11 of Circular E for deposit instructions.) Do not use the Form 941-V payment voucher to make Federal tax deposits.

Caution: If you pay amounts with Form 941 that should have been deposited, you may be subject to a penalty. See Circular E.

Specific Instructions

Box 1—Amount paid. Enter the amount paid with Form 941.

Box 2. Enter the first four characters of your name as follows:

● **Individuals (sole proprietors, estates).** Use the first four letters of your last name (as shown in box 5).

● **Corporations.** Use the first four characters (letters or numbers) of your business name (as shown in box 5). Omit "The" if followed by more than one word.

● **Partnerships.** Use the first four characters of your trade name. If no trade name, enter the first four letters of the last name of the first listed partner.

Box 3—Employer identification number (EIN). If you do not have an EIN, apply for one on **Form SS-4,** Application for Employer Identification Number, and write "Applied for" and the date you applied in this entry space.

Box 4—Tax period. Darken the capsule identifying the quarter for which the payment is made. Darken only one capsule.

Box 5—Name and address. Enter your name and address as shown on Form 941.

● Make your check or money order payable to the United States Treasury. Be sure to enter your EIN, "Form 941," and the tax period on your check or money order. Do not send cash. Please do not staple this voucher or your payment to the return or to each other.

● Detach the completed voucher and send it with your payment and Form 941 to the address provided on the back of Form 941.

⊛

(Detach here)

Form 941-V Department of the Treasury Internal Revenue Service	**Form 941 Payment Voucher** ▶ Use this voucher when making a payment with your return.	OMB No. 1545-0029 **1999**
1 Enter the amount of the payment you are making ▶ $.	**2** Enter the first four letters of your last name (business name if corporation or partnership)	**3** Enter your employer identification number
4 Tax period	**5** Enter your business name (individual name if sole proprietor)	
⬭ 1st Quarter ⬭ 3rd Quarter	Enter your address	
⬭ 2nd Quarter ⬭ 4th Quarter	Enter your city, state, and ZIP code	

For Privacy Act and Paperwork Reduction Act Notice, see back of Form 941.

Payroll Taxes

Instructions for Form 941

(Revised January 1999)

Department of the Treasury
Internal Revenue Service

Employer's Quarterly Federal Tax Return

Section references are to the Internal Revenue Code unless otherwise noted.

Changes To Note

Social security wage base for 1999. Stop withholding social security tax after an employee reaches **$72,600** in taxable wages.

Threshold for deposit requirement increased from $500 to $1,000. Effective July 1, 1998, if your net taxes for the quarter (line 13) are less than **$1,000,** you are not required to make deposits for that quarter and may pay the taxes with Form 941.

General Instructions

Purpose of Form

Use Form 941 to report:
 • Income tax you withheld from wages, including tips, supplemental unemployment compensation benefits, and third-party payments of sick pay.
 • Social security and Medicare taxes.

Who Must File

Employers who withhold income tax on wages, or who must pay social security or Medicare tax, must file Form 941 each calendar quarter. After you file the first Form 941, you must file a return for each quarter, even if you have no taxes to report (but see the *seasonal employer* and *final return* information below). If you filed Form 941 on magnetic tape or by electronic or TeleFile methods, do not also file a paper Form 941.

Seasonal employers are not required to file for quarters when they regularly have no tax liability because they have paid no wages. To alert the IRS that you will not have to file a return for one or more quarters during the year, check the **Seasonal employer** box above line 1 on Form 941. The IRS will mail two Forms 941 to you once a year after March 1. The preprinted name and address information will not include the date the quarter ended. You must enter the date the quarter ended when you file the return. The IRS generally will not inquire about unfiled returns if at least one return showing tax due is filed each year. However, you must check the **Seasonal employer** box on each quarterly return you file. Otherwise, the IRS will expect a return to be filed for each quarter.

Exception. Employers of the following categories of workers do not usually file Form 941.

Household employees. See **Circular E,** Employer's Tax Guide, and **Pub. 926,** Household Employer's Tax Guide (Pub. 15).

Farm employees. See **Form 943,** Employer's Annual Tax Return for Agricultural Employees, and **Circular A,** Agricultural Employer's Tax Guide (Pub. 51).

Business reorganization or termination. If you sell or transfer your business, you and the new owner must each file a return for the quarter in which the transfer occurred.

Each should report only the wages it paid. A change from one form of business to another, such as from sole proprietorship to partnership or corporation, is considered a transfer and requires a new employer identification number (EIN). See section 1 of Circular E. If a change occurs, please attach a statement to your return that shows: new owner's name (or new name of the business); whether the business is now a sole proprietorship, partnership, or corporation; kind of change (sale or transfer); and date of change.

When a business is merged or consolidated with another, the continuing firm must file the return for the quarter in which the change took place. The return should show all wages paid for that quarter. The other firm should file a final return.

Final return. If you go out of business or stop paying wages, file a final return. Be sure to check the final return box and enter the date final wages were paid above line 1. See the *Instructions for Forms W-2 and W-3* for information on the earlier dates for the expedited furnishing and filing of Form W-2 when a final Form 941 is filed.

Preparing the Form

The following will allow the IRS to process Form 941 faster and more accurately:
 • Make dollar entries without the dollar sign and comma (0000.00).
 • Enter negative amounts in parentheses.
 • File the Form 941 that has your preprinted name and address.

When To File

File starting with the first quarter in which you are required to withhold income tax or pay wages subject to social security and Medicare taxes.

Quarter	Ending	Due Date
Jan.-Feb.-Mar.	March 31	April 30
Apr.-May-June	June 30	July 31
July-Aug.-Sept.	Sept. 30	Oct. 31
Oct.-Nov.-Dec.	Dec. 31	Jan. 31

If you made deposits on time in full payment of the taxes for a quarter, you have 10 more days after the above due date to file. Your return will be considered timely filed if it is properly addressed and mailed First-Class or sent by an IRS designated delivery service on or before the due date. See Circular E for more information on IRS designated delivery services. If the due date for filing a return falls on a Saturday, Sunday, or legal holiday, you may file the return on the next business day.

Where To File

See the back of Form 941 for the mailing address for your return.

Cat. No. 14625L

Depositing Taxes

If your net taxes (line 13) are $1,000 or more for the quarter, you must deposit your tax liabilities at an authorized financial institution with **Form 8109,** Federal Tax Deposit Coupon, or by using the **Electronic Federal Tax Payment System (EFTPS).** See section 11 of Circular E for information and rules concerning Federal tax deposits.

Reconciliation of Forms 941 and W-3

Certain amounts reported on the four quarterly Forms 941 for 1999 should agree with the **Form W-2,** Wage and Tax Statement, totals reported on **Form W-3,** Transmittal of Wage and Tax Statements, or equivalent magnetic media reports filed with the Social Security Administration (SSA) (Form 6559). The amounts that should agree are income tax withholding, social security wages, social security tips, Medicare wages and tips, and the advance earned income credit. If the totals do not agree, the IRS will require you to explain any differences and correct any errors. For more information, see section 12 of Circular E.

Penalties and Interest

There are penalties for filing a return late and paying or depositing taxes late, unless there is reasonable cause. If you are late, please attach an explanation to your return. There are also penalties for failure to (1) furnish Forms W-2 to employees and file copies with the SSA or (2) deposit taxes when required. In addition, there are penalties for willful failure to file returns and pay taxes when due and for filing false returns or submitting bad checks. Interest is charged on taxes paid late at the rate set by law. See Circular E for additional information.

Caution: *A* ***trustfundrecoverypenalty*** *mayapplyif income,socialsecurity,andMedicaretaxesthatmustbe withheldarenotwithheldorarenotpaid. Thepenaltyis thefullamountoftheunpaidtrustfundtax.Thispenalty mayapplywhentheseunpaidtaxescannotbe immediatelycollectedfromtheemployerorbusiness. The trustfundrecoverypenaltymaybeimposedonallpersons whoaredeterminedbythe IRStoberesponsiblefor collecting,accountingfor,andpayingoverthesetaxes, andwhoactedwillfullyinnotdoingso.SeeCircularEfor moreinformation.*

Ordering Forms and Publications

IRS forms and publications are available by calling 1–800–829–3676 or by accessing the IRS's Internet Web Site at **www.irs.ustreas.gov.** See Circular E for additional methods of obtaining forms and publications.

Forms W-4

Each quarter, send with Form 941 copies of any **Forms W-4,** Employee's Withholding Allowance Certificate, received during the quarter from employees claiming (1) more than 10 withholding allowances or (2) exemption from income tax withholding if their wages will normally be more than $200 a week. For details, see section 9 of Circular E.

Forms W-5

Each eligible employee wishing to receive any advance earned income credit (EIC) payments must give you a completed **Form W-5,** Earned Income Credit Advance Payment Certificate. The employer's requirement to notify

certain employees about the EIC can be met by giving each eligible employee **Notice 797,** Possible Federal Tax Refund Due to the Earned Income Credit (EIC). See Circular E and **Pub. 596,** Earned Income Credit, for more information.

Employer Identification Number

If you do not have an EIN, apply for one on **Form SS-4,** Application for Employer Identification Number. Get this form from the IRS or the SSA. If you do not have an EIN by the time a return is due, write "Applied for" and the date you applied in the space shown for the number. Form SS-4 has information on how to apply for an EIN by mail or by telephone.

Note: *AlwaysbesuretheEINontheformyoufile matchestheEINassignedtoyourbusinessbythe IRS. Donotshowyourpersonalsocialsecuritynumberon formscallingforanEIN.FilingaForm941withan incorrectEINorusinganotherbusiness'EINmayresult inpenaltiesanddelaysinprocessingyourreturn.*

Preprinted Name and Address Information

If any of the preprinted name, EIN, or address information on Form 941 is not correct, cross it out and type or print the correct information.

Generally, preprinted address information on Form 941 is from IRS records. However, if you filed a change of address card with the United States Postal Service (USPS), that address information may be preprinted on your Form 941 and 941Telefile Tax Record. If the preprinted address is from the USPS, your IRS address of record will be changed when your return is filed and properly processed.

Specific Instructions

State Code

If you made your deposits in a state other than that shown in your address on Form 941, enter the state code for the state where you made deposits in the box provided in the upper left corner of the form. Use the Postal Service two-letter state abbreviation as the state code. Enter the code "MU" in the state code box if you deposit in more than one state. If you deposit in the same state as shown in your address, do not make an entry in this box.

Line 1—Number of employees

Enter the number of employees on your payroll during the pay period including March 12 (on the January-March calendar quarter return only). Do not include household employees, persons who received no pay during the pay period, pensioners, or members of the Armed Forces. An entry of 250 or more on line 1 indicates a need to file Forms W-2 on magnetic media. Call the SSA at 1–800–772–1213 for more information on magnetic media filing requirements.

Line 2—Total wages and tips, plus other compensation

Enter the total of all wages paid, tips reported, taxable fringe benefits provided, and other compensation paid to your employees, **even if you do not have to withhold income or social security and Medicare taxes on it.** Do not include supplemental unemployment

Page 2

compensation benefits, even if you withheld income tax on them. Do not include contributions to employee plans that are excluded from the employee's wages (e.g., section 401(k) and 125 plans).

If you get timely notice from your insurance carrier concerning the amount of third-party sick pay it paid your employees, include the sick pay on line 2. If you are an insurance company, do not include sick pay you paid policyholders' employees here if you gave the policyholders timely notice of the payments. See **Pub. 15-A,** Employer's Supplemental Tax Guide, for details.

Line 3—Total income tax withheld

Enter the income tax you withheld on wages, tips, taxable fringe benefits, and supplemental unemployment compensation benefits. An insurance company should enter the income tax it withheld on third-party sick pay here.

Line 4—Adjustment of withheld income tax

Use line 4 to correct errors in income tax withheld from wages paid in earlier quarters of the ***samecalendaryear.*** You may not adjust or claim a refund or credit for any overpayment of income tax that you withheld or deducted from an employee in a prior year. This is because the employee uses the amount shown on Form W-2 as a credit when filing his or her income tax return. Because any amount shown on line 4 increases or decreases your tax liability, the adjustment must be taken into account on line 17, Monthly Summary of Federal Tax Liability, or on **Schedule B (Form 941),** Employer's Record of Federal Tax Liability. For details on how to report adjustments on the record of Federal tax liability, see the instructions for line 17 (on page 4) or the instructions for Schedule B (Form 941). Explain any adjustments on **Form 941c,** Supporting Statement To Correct Information, or an equivalent statement. See section 13 of Circular E.

Note: *Donotadjustincometaxwithholdingforquarters inearlieryearsunlessitistocorrectanadministrative error.Anadministrativeerroroccursiftheamountyou enteredonForm941isnottheamountyouactually withheld.Forexample,ifthetotalincometaxactually withheldwasincorrectlyreportedonForm941duetoa mathematicalortranspositionerror,thiswouldbean administrativeerror.Theadministrativeerroradjustment correctstheamountreportedonForm941toagreewith theamountactuallywithheldfromtheemployees.*

Line 5—Adjusted total of income tax withheld

Add line 4 to line 3 if you are reporting additional income tax withheld for an earlier quarter. Subtract line 4 from line 3 if you are reducing the amount of income tax withheld. If there is no entry on line 4, line 5 will be the same as line 3.

Line 6a—Taxable social security wages

Enter the total wages subject to social security taxes that you paid your employees during the quarter. Also include any sick pay and taxable fringe benefits subject to social security taxes. See section 5 of Circular E for information on types of wages subject to social security taxes. Enter the amount before deductions. Do not include tips on this line. Stop reporting an employee's wages (including tips) when they reach $72,600 for 1999. However, continue to withhold income tax for the whole year on wages and tips even when the social security wage base of $72,600 is reached. See the line 7a instructions for Medicare tax. **If**

none of the payments are subject to social security tax, check the box in line 8.

Line 6c—Taxable social security tips

Enter all tips your employees reported during the quarter until tips and wages for an employee reach $72,600 in 1999. Do this even if you were not able to withhold the employee tax (6.2%). However, see the line 9 instructions.

An employee must report to you cash tips, including tips you paid the employee for charge customers, totaling $20 or more in a month by the 10th of the next month. The employee may use **Form 4070,** Employee's Report of Tips to Employer, or a written statement.

Do not include allocated tips on this line. Instead, report them on **Form 8027,** Employer's Annual Information Return of Tip Income and Allocated Tips. Allocated tips are not reportable on Form 941 and are not subject to withholding of income, social security, or Medicare taxes.

Line 7a—Taxable Medicare wages and tips

Report all wages and tips subject to Medicare tax. Also include any sick pay and taxable fringe benefits subject to Medicare tax. See section 5 of Circular E for information on types of wages subject to Medicare tax. There is no limit on the amount of wages subject to Medicare tax. **If none of the payments are subject to Medicare tax, check the box in line 8.**

Include all tips your employees reported during the quarter, even if you were not able to withhold the employee tax (1.45%). However, see the line 9 instructions below.

Line 9—Adjustment of social security and Medicare taxes

Current period adjustments. In certain cases, amounts reported as social security and Medicare taxes on lines 6b, 6d, and 7b must be adjusted to arrive at your correct tax liability. See section 13 of Circular E for information on the following:

● Adjustment for the uncollected employee share of social security and Medicare taxes on tips.

● Adjustment for the employee share of social security and Medicare taxes on group-term life insurance premiums paid for former employees.

● Adjustment for the employee share of social security and Medicare taxes withheld by a third-party sick pay payer.

● Fractions of cents adjustment.

Enter the adjustments for sick pay and fractions of cents in the appropriate line 9 entry spaces. Enter the amount of all other adjustments in the "Other" entry space, and enter the total of the three types of adjustments, including prior period adjustments (discussed on page 4), in the line 9 entry space to the right. Provide a supporting statement explaining any adjustments reported in the "Other" entry space.

Prior period adjustments. Use line 9 to correct errors in social security and Medicare taxes reported on an earlier return. If you report both an underpayment and an overpayment, show only the net difference.

Because any prior period adjustments shown on line 9 increase or decrease your tax liability, the adjustments must be taken into account on line 17, Monthly Summary of Federal Tax Liability, or on Schedule B (Form 941). For details on how to report adjustments on the record of

Page 3

Payroll Taxes

Federal tax liability, see the instructions for line 17 below or the instructions for Schedule B (Form 941).

Explain any prior period adjustments on Form 941c. **Do not** file Form 941c separately from Form 941. Form 941c is not an amended return but is a statement providing necessary information and certifications supporting the adjustments on lines 4 and/or 9 on Form 941. If you do not have a Form 941c, you may file an equivalent supporting statement with the return providing the required information about the adjustment(s). See section 13 of Circular E.

If you are adjusting an employee's social security or Medicare wages or tips for a prior year, you must file **Form W-2c,** Corrected Wage and Tax Statement, with **Form W-3c,** Transmittal of Corrected Wage and Tax Statements.

Line 10—Adjusted total of social security and Medicare taxes

Add line 9 to line 8 if line 9 is positive (e.g., the net adjustment increases your tax liability). Subtract line 9 from line 8 if line 9 is negative.

Line 12—Advance earned income credit (EIC) payments made to employees

Enter advance EIC payments made to employees. Your eligible employees may elect to receive part of the EIC as an advance payment. Eligible employees who have a qualifying child must give you a completed Form W-5 stating that they qualify for the EIC. Once the employee gives you a signed and completed Form W-5, you must make the advance EIC payments. Advance EIC payments are generally made from withheld income tax and employee and employer social security and Medicare taxes. See section 10 of Circular E and Pub. 596.

If the amount of your advance EIC payments exceeds your total taxes (line 11) for the quarter, you may claim a refund of the overpayment or elect to have the credit applied to your return for the next quarter. Provide a statement with your return identifying the amount of excess payment(s) and the pay period(s) in which it was paid. See section 10 of Circular E.

Line 15—Balance due

You do not have to pay if line 15 is under $1.
Generally, you should have a balance due only if your net tax liability for the quarter (line 13) is less than $1,000. (However, see section 11 of Circular E regarding payments made under the *accuracy of deposits rule*). If line 13 is $1,000 or more and you have deposited all taxes when due, the amount shown on line 15 (balance due) should be zero.

Caution: *If you fail to make deposits as required and instead pay the taxes with Form 941, you may be subject to a penalty.*

Line 16—Overpayment

If you deposited more than the correct amount for a quarter, you can have the overpayment refunded or

applied to your next return by checking the appropriate box. If you do not check either box, your overpayment will be applied to your next return. The IRS may apply your overpayment to any past due tax account under your EIN. If line 16 is under $1, we will send a refund or apply it to your next return only on written request.

Line 17—Monthly Summary of Federal Tax Liability

Note: *This is a summary of your monthly tax liability,* **not** *a summary of deposits made. If line 13 is less than $1,000, do not complete line 17 or Schedule B (Form 941).*

Complete line 17 only if you were a monthly schedule depositor for the entire quarter (see section 11 of Circular E for details on the deposit rules). You are a monthly schedule depositor for the calendar year if the amount of your Form 941 taxes reported for the lookback period is not more than $50,000. The lookback period is the four consecutive quarters ending on June 30 of the prior year. For 1999, the lookback period begins July 1, 1997, and ends June 30, 1998.

Caution: *If you were a semiweekly schedule depositor during any part of the quarter,* **do not** *complete columns (a) through (d) of line 17. Instead, complete Schedule B (Form 941).*

Reporting adjustments on line 17. If the net adjustment during a month is negative (e.g., correcting an overreported liability in a prior period) and it exceeds the total liability for the month, do not enter a negative amount for the month. Instead, enter -0- for the month and carry over the unused portion of the adjustment to the next month. For example, Pine Co. discovered on February 6, 1999, that it overreported social security tax on a prior quarter return by $2,500. Its Form 941 taxes for the 1st quarter of 1999 were: January $2,000, February $2,000, March $2,000. Pine Co. should enter $2,000 in column (a), -0- in column (b), $1,500 in column (c), and the total, $3,500, in column (d). The prior period adjustment ($2,500) offsets the $2,000 liability for February and the excess $500 must be used to offset March liabilities. Since the error was not discovered until February, it does not affect January liabilities reported in column (a).

If excess negative adjustments are carried forward to the next quarter, do not show these excess adjustments on lines 4 or 9. Line 17, column (d), must equal line 13.

Who Must Sign

- **Sole proprietorship.** The individual owning the business.
- **Corporation.** The president, vice president, or other principal officer.
- **Partnership or unincorporated organization.** A responsible and duly authorized member or officer having knowledge of its affairs.
- **Trust or estate.** The fiduciary.

The return may also be signed by a duly authorized agent of the taxpayer if a valid power of attorney has been filed.

ELECTRONIC FEDERAL TAX PAYMENT SYSTEM

With respect to EFTPS, as discussed on page 926 of the main text (and page 308 of the 1999 supplement), proposed regulations indicate the Treasury's intention to raise the deposit threshold from $50,000 to $200,000. Pursuant to the proposed regulations, non-employment taxes (e.g., corporate income taxes) will have to be included in the determination of whether the $200,000 threshold has been reached.

UNEMPLOYMENT INSURANCE

Copies of the most recent (i.e., 1998) Forms 940 and 940-EZ (along with related instructions) referred to on page 927 of the main text, follow:

Form 940

Department of the Treasury
Internal Revenue Service (99)

Employer's Annual Federal Unemployment (FUTA) Tax Return

▶ See separate instructions for information on completing this return.

OMB No. 1545-0028

1998

T		
FF		
FD		
FP		
I		
T		

Name (as distinguished from trade name)   Calendar year

Trade name, if any

Address and ZIP code   Employer identification number

A Are you required to pay unemployment contributions to only one state? (If "No," skip questions B and C.) . ☐ Yes ☐ No

B Did you pay all state unemployment contributions by February 1, 1999? ((1) If you deposited your total FUTA tax when due, check "Yes" if you paid all state unemployment contributions by February 10. (2) If a 0% experience rate is granted, check "Yes." (3) If "No," skip question C.) . . . . ☐ Yes ☐ No

C Were all wages that were taxable for FUTA tax also taxable for your state's unemployment tax? . . . . ☐ Yes ☐ No

If you answered "No" to any of these questions, you must file Form 940. If you answered "Yes" to all the questions, you may file Form 940-EZ, which is a simplified version of Form 940. (Successor employers see **Special credit for successor employers** on page 3 of the instructions.) You can get Form 940-EZ by calling 1-800-TAX-FORM (1-800-829-3676) or from the IRS's Internet Web Site at **www.irs.ustreas.gov.**

If you will not have to file returns in the future, check here, and complete and sign the return . . . . ▶ ☐
If this is an Amended Return, check here . . . . ▶ ☐

Part I   Computation of Taxable Wages

1	Total payments (including payments shown on lines 2 and 3) during the calendar year for services of employees	**1**	
2	Exempt payments. (Explain all exempt payments, attaching additional sheets if necessary.) ▶ ------------------------------------ --	**2**	
3	Payments for services of more than $7,000. Enter only amounts over the first $7,000 paid to each employee. Do not include any exempt payments from line 2. The $7,000 amount is the Federal wage base. Your state wage base may be different. **Do not use your state wage limitation** .	**3**	
4	Total exempt payments (add lines 2 and 3)	**4**	
5	**Total taxable wages** (subtract line 4 from line 1) . . . . ▶	**5**	

Be sure to complete both sides of this return, and sign in the space provided on the back.
For Privacy Act and Paperwork Reduction Act Notice, see separate instructions.   Cat. No. 112340   Form **940** (1998)

DETACH HERE

Form 940-V

Department of the Treasury
Internal Revenue Service

Form 940 Payment Voucher

Use this voucher only when making a payment with your return.

OMB No. 1545-0028

1998

Complete boxes 1, 2, 3, and 4. Do not send cash, and do not staple your payment to this voucher. Make your check or money order payable to the "United States Treasury". Be sure to enter your employer identification number, "Form 940", and "1998" on your payment.

1 Enter the amount of the payment you are making	**2** Enter the first four letters of your last name (business name if partnership or corporation)	**3** Enter your employer identification number
▶ $.		

Instructions for Box 2

—Individuals (sole proprietors, trusts, and estates)— Enter the first four letters of your last name.

—Corporations and partnerships—Enter the first four characters of your business name (omit "The" if followed by more than one word).

4 Enter your business name (individual name for sole proprietors)

Enter your address

Enter your city, state, and ZIP code

436   *Payroll Taxes*

Part II	Tax Due or Refund

1	Gross FUTA tax. Multiply the wages in Part I, line 5, by .062	**1**
2	Maximum credit. Multiply the wages in Part I, line 5, by .054 . . . **2**	
3	**Computation of tentative credit** (Note: *All taxpayers must complete the applicable columns.*)	

(a) Name of state	(b) State reporting number(s) as shown on employer's state contribution returns	(c) Taxable payroll (as defined in state act)	(d) State experience rate period		(e) State experience rate	(f) Contributions if rate had been 5.4% (col. (c) x .054)	(g) Contributions payable at experience rate (col. (c) x col. (e))	(h) Additional credit (col. (f) minus col.(g)). If 0 or less, enter -0-.	(i) Contributions paid to state by 940 due date
			From	To					

3a	Totals . . . ▶		
3b	Total tentative credit (add line 3a, columns (h) and (i) only—for late payments also see the instructions for Part II, line 6 . . . . ▶		
4			
5			
6	**Credit:** Enter the smaller of the amount in Part II, line 2 or line 3b; or amount from the worksheet in the line 6 instructions	**6**	
7	**Total FUTA tax** (subtract line 6 from line 1). If the result is over $100, also complete Part III . .	**7**	
8	Total FUTA tax deposited for the year, including any overpayment applied from a prior year . .	**8**	
9	**Balance due** (subtract line 8 from line 7). Pay to the "United States Treasury". If you owe more than $100, see "Depositing FUTA Tax" on page 3 of the instructions . . . . ▶	**9**	
10	**Overpayment** (subtract line 7 from line 8). Check if it is to be: ☐ **Applied to next return** or ☐ **Refunded** . . . . ▶	**10**	

Part III	**Record of Quarterly Federal Unemployment Tax Liability** *(Do not include state liability.)* Complete only if line 7 is over $100. See page 6 of the instructions.

Quarter	First (Jan. 1–Mar. 31)	Second (Apr. 1–June 30)	Third (July 1–Sept. 30)	Fourth (Oct. 1–Dec. 31)	Total for year
Liability for quarter					

Under penalties of perjury, I declare that I have examined this return, including accompanying schedules and statements, and, to the best of my knowledge and belief, it is true, correct, and complete, and that no part of any payment made to a state unemployment fund claimed as a credit was, or is to be, deducted from the payments to employees.

Signature ▶   Title (Owner, etc.) ▶   Date ▶

⊛

19**98**

Department of the Treasury
Internal Revenue Service

Instructions for Form 940

Employer's Annual Federal Unemployment (FUTA) Tax Return

Section references are to the Internal Revenue Code unless otherwise noted.

General Instructions

Items To Note

New worksheet for computing the Part II, line 6 credit if state contributions were paid late. Filers who made contributions to their state unemployment fund after the due date for filing Form 940 should complete the new worksheet provided in the instructions for line 6 on page 5 to compute the allowable credit. **Do not** report such contributions in Part II, line 3, column (i) or on line 3b. Any credit allowed for such state contributions will appear on line 6.

Electronic deposit requirement. If your total deposits of social security, Medicare, railroad retirement, and withheld income taxes were more than $50,000 in 1997, you must make electronic deposits for **all** depository tax liabilities (including FUTA tax) that occur after 1998 using the Electronic Federal Tax Payment System (EFTPS). However, if you were first required to use EFTPS on or after July 1, 1997, no penalties for failure to use EFTPS will be imposed for tax liabilities that occur prior to July 1, 1999. To enroll in EFTPS, call 1-800-945-8400 or 1-800-555-4477. For general information about EFTPS, call 1-800-829-1040.

Preprinted EIN relocated. To ensure privacy, we have relocated the employer identification number on preprinted forms to an area above the envelope window.

State unemployment information. Employers must contact their state unemployment tax offices to receive their state reporting number, state experience rate, and details about their state unemployment tax obligations.

Purpose of Form

Use this form to report your annual Federal Unemployment Tax Act (FUTA) tax. FUTA tax, together with state unemployment systems, provides for payments of unemployment compensation to workers who have lost their jobs. Most employers pay both Federal and state unemployment taxes. Only the employer pays FUTA tax. Do not collect or deduct it from your employees' wages. The tax applies to the first $7,000 you pay each employee in a year. The $7,000 amount is the Federal wage base. Your state wage base may be different.

Form 940-EZ, Employer's Annual Federal Unemployment (FUTA) Tax Return, is a simpler version of Form 940. You may use it instead of Form 940 to report your annual FUTA tax if—

1. You paid unemployment contributions to only one state,

2. You paid all state unemployment contributions by February 1, 1999 (February 10 if you deposited all FUTA tax when due), and

3. All wages that were taxable for FUTA tax were also taxable for your state's unemployment tax. If, for example, you paid wages to corporate officers (these wages are taxable for FUTA tax) in a state that exempts these wages from its unemployment tax, you cannot use Form 940-EZ. **Note:** *A successor employer claiming a credit for state unemployment contributions paid by the prior employer must file Form 940.*

For details, get Form 940-EZ. **Do not file Form 940 if you have already filed Form 940-EZ for 1998.** However, see **Amended returns** on page 4.

When To File

File Form 940 for 1998 by February 1, 1999. However, if you deposited all FUTA tax when due, you may file on or before February 10, 1999. Your return will be considered timely filed if it is properly addressed and mailed First Class or sent by an IRS designated delivery service by the due date. See **Circular E (Pub. 15),** Employer's Tax Guide, for a list of designated delivery services.

Caution: *Private delivery services cannot deliver items to P.O. boxes.*

Who Must File

Except as noted below, you must file if Test 1 **or** Test 2 applies.

Test 1. You paid wages of $1,500 or more in any calendar quarter in 1997 or 1998.

Test 2. You had one or more employees for at least some part of a day in any 20 or more different weeks in 1997 or 20 or more different weeks in 1998.

Count all regular, temporary, and part-time employees. A partnership should not count its partners. If there is a change in ownership or other transfer of business during the year, each employer who meets Test 1 or 2 must file. **Do not** report wages paid by the prior (or subsequent) employer.

Household employers. File a FUTA tax return **ONLY** if you paid total cash wages of $1,000 or more (for all household employees) in any calendar quarter in 1997 or 1998 for household work in a private home, local college club, or local chapter of a college fraternity or sorority. Individuals, estates, and trusts that owe FUTA tax for **household work** in a private home, in most cases, must

Cat. No. 13660I

file **Schedule H (Form 1040),** Household Employment Taxes, instead of Form 940 or 940-EZ. See the instructions for Schedule H (Form 1040).

In some cases, such as when you employ both household employees and other employees, you may have the option to report social security, Medicare, and withheld Federal income taxes for your household employee(s) on **Form 941,** Employer's Quarterly Federal Tax Return, or **Form 943,** Employer's Annual Tax Return for Agricultural Employees, instead of on Schedule H. If you reported your household employee's wages on Form 941 or 943, you must use Form 940 or 940-EZ to report FUTA tax.

Agricultural employers. File a FUTA tax return if either 1 **or** 2 below applies:

1. You paid cash wages of $20,000 or more to farmworkers during any calendar quarter in 1997 or 1998 or

2. You employed 10 or more farmworkers during at least some part of a day (whether or not at the same time) during any 20 or more different weeks in 1997 or 20 or more different weeks in 1998.

Count wages paid to aliens admitted on a temporary basis to the United States to perform farmwork, also known as workers with "H-2(A)" visas, to see if you meet either 1 or 2. However, wages paid to H-2(A) visa workers are not subject to FUTA tax.

Nonprofit organizations. Religious, educational, charitable, etc., organizations described in section 501(c)(3) and exempt from tax under section 501(a) are not subject to FUTA tax and are not required to file.

State and local government employees. Wages paid to state or local government employees are not subject to FUTA tax.

Where To File

In the list below, find the location where your legal residence, principal place of business, office, or agency is located. Send your return to the **Internal Revenue Service** at the address listed for your location. No street address is needed.

Note: *Where you file depends on whether or not you are including a payment.*

Florida, Georgia, South Carolina

Return without payment:	**Return with payment:**
Atlanta, GA 39901-0046	P.O. Box 105887
	Atlanta, GA 30348-5887

New Jersey, New York (New York City and counties of Nassau, Rockland, Suffolk, and Westchester)

Return without payment:	**Return with payment:**
Holtsville, NY 00501-0046	P.O. Box 1365
	Newark, NJ 07101-1365

New York (all other counties), Connecticut, Maine, Massachusetts, New Hampshire, Rhode Island, Vermont

Return without payment:	**Return with payment:**
Andover, MA 05501-0046	P.O. Box 371307
	Pittsburgh, PA 15250-7307

Illinois, Iowa, Minnesota, Missouri, Wisconsin

Return without payment:	**Return with payment:**
Kansas City, MO 64999-0046	P.O. Box 970010
	St. Louis, MO 63197-0010

Delaware, District of Columbia, Maryland, Pennsylvania, Puerto Rico, Virginia, U.S. Virgin Islands

Return without payment:	**Return with payment:**
Philadelphia, PA 19255-0046	P.O. Box 8726
	Philadelphia, PA 19162-8726

Indiana, Kentucky, Michigan, Ohio, West Virginia

Return without payment:	**Return with payment:**
Cincinnati, OH 45999-0046	P.O. Box 6977
	Chicago, IL 60680-6977

Kansas, New Mexico, Oklahoma, Texas

Return without payment:	**Return with payment:**
Austin, TX 73301-0046	P.O. Box 970017
	St. Louis, MO 63197-0017

Alaska, Arizona, California (counties of Alpine, Amador, Butte, Calaveras, Colusa, Contra Costa, Del Norte, El Dorado, Glenn, Humboldt, Lake, Lassen, Marin, Mendocino, Modoc, Napa, Nevada, Placer, Plumas, Sacramento, San Joaquin, Shasta, Sierra, Siskiyou, Solano, Sonoma, Sutter, Tehama, Trinity, Yolo, and Yuba), Colorado, Idaho, Montana, Nebraska, Nevada, North Dakota, Oregon, South Dakota, Utah, Washington, Wyoming

Return without payment:	**Return with payment:**
Ogden, UT 84201-0046	P.O. Box 7024
	San Francisco, CA 94120-7024

California (all other counties), Hawaii

Return without payment:	**Return with payment:**
Fresno, CA 93888-0046	P.O. Box 60378
	Los Angeles, CA 90060-0378

Alabama, Arkansas, Louisiana, Mississippi, North Carolina, Tennessee

Return without payment:	**Return with payment:**
Memphis, TN 37501-0046	P.O. Box 1210
	Charlotte, NC 28201-1210

If the location of your legal residence or principal place of business is not listed above

	All Returns:
	Philadelphia, PA 19255-0046

Magnetic Media Reporting

You may file Form 940 using magnetic media. See Rev. Proc. 96-18, 1996-1 C.B. 637, for the procedures and **Pub. 1314** for the tape specifications.

Penalties and Interest

Avoid penalties and interest by making tax deposits when due, filing a correct return, and paying all taxes when due. There are penalties for late deposits and late filing unless you can show reasonable cause. If you file late, attach an explanation to the return. There are also penalties for willful failure to pay tax, keep records, make returns, and for filing false or fraudulent returns. Get Circular E (Pub. 15), for more information on penalties.

Not Liable for FUTA Tax

If you receive Form 940 and are not liable for FUTA tax for 1998, write "Not Liable" across the front of the form, sign the return, and return it to the IRS.

Credit for Contributions Paid to a State Fund

You get a credit for amounts you pay to a state (including the District of Columbia, Puerto Rico, and the U.S. Virgin Islands) unemployment fund by February 1, 1999 (or February 10, 1999, if that is your Form 940 due date). Your FUTA tax will be higher if you do not pay the state contributions timely. See the line 6 instructions on page 5 if you did not pay state contributions by the due date of Form 940.

"Contributions" are payments that a state requires an employer to make to its unemployment fund for the payment of unemployment benefits. However, contributions do not include:

• Any payments deducted or deductible from your employees' pay.

• Penalties, interest, or special administrative taxes not included in the contribution rate the state assigned to you.

• Voluntary contributions paid to get a lower assigned rate.

You may receive an additional credit if you have a state experience rate lower than 5.4% (.054). This applies even if your rate is different during the year. This **additional** credit is equal to the difference between actual payments and the amount you would have been required to pay at 5.4%.

The total credit allowable may not be more than 5.4% of the total taxable FUTA wages.

Special credit for successor employers. A successor employer is an employer who received a unit of another employer's trade or business or all or most of the property used in the trade or business of another employer. Immediately after the acquisition, the successor employer must employ one or more individuals who were employed by the previous owner.

You may be eligible for a credit based on the state unemployment contributions paid by the previous employer. You may claim these credits if you are a successor employer and acquired a business in 1998 from a previous employer who was not required to file Form 940 or 940-EZ for 1998. **If you are eligible to take this credit, you must file Form 940; you may not use Form 940-EZ.** See section 3302(e). Enter in Part II, line 3, columns (a) through (i) the information of the previous employer as if you paid the amounts.

Successor employers may be able to count the wages that the previous employer paid to their employees to meet the $7,000 wage base. See the instructions for Part I, line 3 on page 4.

Depositing FUTA Tax

When to deposit. Although Form 940 covers a calendar year, you may have to make deposits of the tax before filing the return. Generally, deposit FUTA tax quarterly but only when your liability exceeds $100. Determine your FUTA tax for each of the first three quarters by multiplying by .008 that part of the first $7,000 of each employee's annual wages you paid during the quarter. If any part of the amounts paid are exempt from state unemployment tax, you may be required to deposit an amount greater

than that determined using the .008 rate. For example, in certain states, wages paid to corporate officers, certain payments of sick pay by unions, and certain fringe benefits, are exempt from state unemployment tax.

If your FUTA tax liability for any of the first three quarters of 1998 (plus any undeposited amount of $100 or less from any earlier quarter) is over $100, deposit it by the last day of the month after the end of the quarter. If it is $100 or less, carry it to the next quarter; a deposit is not required. If your liability for the fourth quarter (plus any undeposited amount from any earlier quarter) is over $100, deposit the entire amount by February 1, 1999. If it is $100 or less, you can either make a deposit or pay it with your Form 940 by February 1. (If you deposit it by February 1, you may file Form 940 by February 10, 1999.)

The deposit due dates are shown in the following chart:

If undeposited FUTA tax is over $100 on—	Deposit it by—
March 31	April 30
June 30	July 31
September 30	October 31
December 31	February 1

Note: *If any deposit due date shown falls on a Saturday, Sunday, or legal holiday, you may deposit on the next business day.*

How to deposit. If you are not required to use EFTPS (See **Electronic deposit requirement** on page 1), use **Form 8109,** Federal Tax Deposit Coupon, when you make each tax deposit. The IRS will send you a book of deposit coupons when you apply for an employer identification number (EIN). Follow the instructions in the coupon book. If you do not have coupons, see section 11 in Circular E (Pub. 15).

Make your deposits with an authorized financial institution (e.g., a commercial bank that is qualified to accept Federal tax deposits) or the Federal Reserve bank for your area. To avoid a possible penalty, do not mail deposits directly to the IRS. Records of your deposits will be sent to the IRS for crediting to your business accounts.

Specific Instructions

Employer's name, address, and employer identification number. Use the preaddressed Form 940 mailed to you. If you must use a form that is not preaddressed, type or print your name, trade name, address, and EIN on it. If you do not have an EIN, apply for one on **Form SS-4,** Application for Employer Identification Number. If you do not have your EIN by the time a return is due, write "Applied for" and the date you applied for the number.

Questions A through C. The answers to the questions will direct you to the correct form to file. If you answered "Yes" to all the questions, you may file Form 940-EZ, a simpler version of Form 940. If you answer "No" to any of the questions or you are a successor employer claiming a credit for state unemployment contributions paid by the prior employer, complete and file Form 940.

Final return. If you will not have to file returns in the future, check the box on the line below question C. Then

Page 3

complete and sign the return. If you start paying FUTA wages again, file Form 940 or 940-EZ.

Amended returns. Use a new Form 940 to amend a previously filed Form 940. Check the Amended Return box above Part I. Enter all amounts that should have been on the original return, and sign the form. Attach an explanation of the reasons for the amended return. For example, you are filing to claim the 90% credit for contributions paid to your state unemployment fund after the due date of Form 940. File the amended return with the Internal Revenue Service Center where you filed the original return.

If you were required to file Form 940 but filed Form 940–EZ instead and you must correct an error, file the amended return on Form 940.

If you are filing an amended return after June 30 to claim contributions to your state's unemployment fund that you paid after the due date of Form 940, attach a copy of the certification from the state. This will expedite the processing of the amended return.

Part I — Computation of Taxable Wages

Line 1 — Total payments. Enter the total payments you made during the calendar year for services of employees, even if the payments are not taxable for FUTA tax. Include salaries, wages, commissions, fees, bonuses, vacation allowances, and amounts paid to temporary or part-time employees; the value of goods, lodging, food, clothing, and noncash fringe benefits; contributions to a 401(k) plan, payments to medical savings accounts (MSA), payments under adoption assistance programs, and contributions to SIMPLE retirement accounts (including elective salary reduction contributions); section 125 (cafeteria) plan benefits; and sick pay (including third party sick pay if liability transferred to employer). For details on sick pay, see **Pub. 15-A,** Employer's Supplemental Tax Guide. Include tips of $20 or more in a month reported to you by your employees. Also, include payments made by a previous employer if you are counting those payments for the $7,000 wage base as explained under *Successor employer* in the line 3 instructions below. Enter the amount before any deductions.

How you make the payments is not important to determine if they are wages. Thus, you may pay wages for piecework or as a percentage of profits. You may pay wages hourly, daily, weekly, monthly, or yearly. You may pay wages in cash or some other way, such as goods, lodging, food, or clothing. For items other than cash, use the fair market value when paid.

Line 2 — Exempt payments. The amounts reported on line 2 are exempt from FUTA tax. **Do not** enter payments over $7,000 for each employee. Enter such amounts on line 3. For FUTA purposes, "wages" and "employment" do not include every payment and every kind of service an employee may perform. In general, payments excluded from wages and payments for services excepted from employment are not subject to FUTA tax.

You may deduct exempt payments from total payments only if you explain them on line 2. Amounts that may be exempt from your state's unemployment tax, for example, corporate officers' wages, may not be exempt from FUTA tax.

Enter payments such as the following on line 2 if you included them in total payments on line 1:

1. Agricultural labor if you did not meet either 1 or 2 under **Agricultural employers** on page 2 and **all** payments to H-2(A) visa workers.

2. Benefit payments for sickness or injury under a workers' compensation law.

3. Household services if you did not pay total cash wages of $1,000 or more in any calendar quarter in 1997 or 1998.

4. Certain family employment. (See Cir. E (Pub. 15).)

5. Certain fishing activities. (See **Pub. 595,** Tax Highlights for Commercial Fishermen.)

6. Noncash payments for farmwork or household services in a private home. Only cash wages to these workers are taxable.

7. Value of certain meals and lodging. (See Section 5 in Cir. E (Pub. 15).)

8. Cost of group-term life insurance.

9. Payments attributable to the employee's contributions to a sick-pay plan.

10. Employer contributions to a SIMPLE retirement account (other than elective salary reduction contributions).

11. Employer payments to a medical savings account (MSA).

12. Benefits excludable under a section 125 (cafeteria) plan.

13. Certain statutory employees. (See Pub. 15-A.)

14. Services performed by an inmate of a penal institution.

15. Any other exempt service or pay.

For more information, see **Special Rules for Various Types of Services and Payments** in Circular E (Pub. 15) or **How Do Employment Taxes Apply to Farmwork?** in **Circular A,** Agricultural Employer's Tax Guide (Pub. 51).

Line 3 — Payments for services of more than $7,000. Enter the total amounts over $7,000 you paid each employee. For example, if you have 10 employees and paid each $8,000 during the year, enter $80,000 on line 1 and $10,000 on line 3. **Only the first $7,000 paid to each employee is subject to FUTA tax. Do not use the state wage base for this entry. The state wage base may be different from the Federal wage base of $7,000. Do not include any exempt payments from line 2 in figuring the $7,000.**

Successor employer. If you acquired a business from an employer who was liable for FUTA tax, you may count the wages that employer paid to the employees who continue to work for you when you figure the $7,000 wage base. Include on line 3 the payments made by the previous employer that you included on line 1. If the first employer paid $7,000 or more to the employee, also include on line 3 all the wages you paid to that employee. If the first employer did not pay at least $7,000 to the employee, subtract what the first employer paid from $7,000. Then subtract that result from the wages you paid to the employee, and include any result on line 3. See section 3306(b)(1) and Regulations section 31.3306(b)(1)-1(b).

Page 4

Line 5 — Total taxable wages. This is the total amount subject to FUTA tax. Use this amount in Part II to compute the gross FUTA tax and the maximum credit.

Part II — Tax Due or Refund

Line 1 — Gross FUTA tax. Multiply the total taxable wages in Part I, line 5, by .062. This is the maximum amount of FUTA tax.

Line 2 — Maximum credit. Multiply the total taxable wages in Part I, line 5, by .054. This is the maximum credit against FUTA tax for state contributions.

Line 3 — Computation of tentative credit. You must complete all applicable columns to receive any credit. Your state will provide an experience rate. If you have been assigned an experience rate of 0% or more, but less than 5.4%, for all or part of the year, use columns (a) through (i). If you have **not** been assigned any experience rate, use columns (a), (b), (c), and (i) only. If you have been assigned a rate of 5.4% or higher, use columns (a), (b), (c), (d), (e), and (i) only. If you were assigned an experience rate for only part of the year or the rate was changed during the year, complete a separate line for each rate period.

If you need additional lines, attach a separate statement with a similar format. Also, if you are a successor employer, see **Special credit for successor employers,** on page 3.

Column(a). Enter the two-letter abbreviation for the state(s) to which you were required to pay contributions (including the District of Columbia, Puerto Rico, and the U.S. Virgin Islands).

Column(b). Enter the state reporting number assigned to you when you registered as an employer with each state. Failure to enter the correct number may result in unnecessary correspondence.

Column(c). Enter the state taxable payroll on which you must pay state unemployment taxes for each state shown in column (a). If your experience rate is 0%, enter the wages that would have been subject to state unemployment tax if the 0% rate had not been granted.

Column(d). Enter the beginning and ending dates of the experience rate shown in column (e).

Column(e). Enter your state experience rate—the rate the state assigned to you for paying your state unemployment tax. This rate may change based on your "experience" with the state unemployment fund, for example, because of unemployment compensation paid to your former employees. If you do not know your experience rate, contact your state unemployment insurance service. The state experience rate can be stated as a percent or as a decimal.

Column(f). Multiply the amount in column (c) by .054.

Column(g). Multiply the amount in column (c) by the rate in column (e).

Column(h). Subtract column (g) from column (f). If zero or less, enter -0-. This additional credit is the difference between 5.4% and your state experience rate.

Column(i). Enter the contributions **actually paid** to the state unemployment fund **by the due date** for filing Form 940. Do not include amounts you are required to pay but have not paid by the due date (see **When To File** on

page 1). If you are **filing Form 940 after the due date,** include only payments made by the return due date, and see the instructions and worksheet under line 6 below. If you are **claiming excess credits** as payments of state unemployment contributions, attach a copy of the letter from your state. **Do not** include any penalties, interest, or special administrative taxes (such as surcharges, employment and training taxes, excise tax, and assessments, which are generally listed as a separate item on the state's quarterly wage report) not included in the experience rate assigned to you.

Line 3a — Totals. Enter the totals of columns (c), (h), and (i).

Line 3b — Total tentative credit. Add line 3a, columns (h) and (i) only. As noted above, column (i) includes **only** payments to your state unemployment fund that you made by the due date for filing Form 940. Payments made after the due date are eligible for a reduced credit and will appear on line 6 as described below.

Line 6 — Credit. This is the credit allowable for your payments to state unemployment funds. If you made no late state contributions, enter the smaller of the amount in Part II, line 2 or line 3b. If you do not have to make payments to the state, enter zero on this line.

Note: *If any state contributions were made after the Form 940 due date (see* **When To File** *on page 1), your credit for late contributions is limited to* **90%** *of the amount that would have been allowable as a credit if such contributions were paid on or before the Form 940 due date.*

Only taxpayers who made late contributions should complete the worksheet below.

Worksheet for Credit Computation if Any State Contributions Were Paid After the Due Date for Filing Form 940	
A. Enter the amount from Form 940, Part II, line 2	_____
B. Enter the amount from Form 940, Part II, line 3b, if any.	_____
C. Subtract line B from line A. If less than zero, enter -0-	_____
D. Enter total contributions paid to the states **after** the Form 940 due date.	_____
E. Enter the smaller of lines C or D. .	_____
F. Multiply line E by .90 (90%) . . .	_____
G. Add lines B and F	_____
H. Enter the **smaller** of the amount on line G or A here, **and** on Form 940, Part II, line 6	_____

Example: You paid $1,500 of state contributions by the Form 940 due date and $1,000 after that date. Your maximum credit on Form 940, Part II, line 2 is $2,000; and your tentative credit on line 3b is $1,500. The maximum credit less the tentative credit is $500. If you had paid the $1,000 state contributions on time, you would have been allowed an additional amount of credit of only $500 not the full $1,000. Therefore, the credit for the late contributions is limited to 90% of $500. You complete the worksheet as shown on page 6.

A. Enter the amount from Form 940, Part II, line 2	$2,000	
B. Enter the amount from Form 940, Part II, line 3b, if any.	1,500	
C. Subtract line B from line A. If less than zero, enter -0-	500	
D. Enter total contributions paid to the states **after** the Form 940 due date.	1,000	
E. Enter the smaller of lines C or D . .	500	
F. Multiply line E by .90 (90%) . . .	450	
G. Add lines B and F	1,950	
H. Enter the **smaller** of the amount on line G or A here, **and** on Form 940, Part II, line 6	1,950	

Enter $1,950 from line H of the worksheet on Form 940, Part II, line 6. This is the allowable credit for your contributions to the state unemployment fund.

Line 9 — Balance due. Make your check or money order payable to the "United States Treasury". Write your EIN, "Form 940", and "1998" on your check or money order. Enter the amount of the payment in box 1 on Form 940-V at the bottom of Form 940. If the employer information is not preprinted on the payment voucher, enter the requested information. If the amount on line 9 is under $1, you do not have to pay it. On payments over $100, see **How to deposit** on page 3.

Line 10 — Overpayment. If the amount on line 10 is under $1, we will send a refund or apply it to your next return only on written request.

Part III — Record of Quarterly Federal Unemployment Tax Liability

Complete this part only if your FUTA tax on line 7 is over $100. To figure your FUTA tax liability for each quarter, multiply by .008 that part of the first $7,000 of each employee's annual wages you paid during the quarter. Enter the result in the space for that quarter. Your total liability ("Total for year") must equal your total tax shown in Part II, line 7.

Record your liability based on when you pay wages, not on when you deposit the FUTA tax. For example, if you pay wages on March 29, your FUTA tax liability on those wages is $200, and you deposit the $200 on April 30, you would record that $200 in the first quarter, not in the second.

Privacy Act and Paperwork Reduction Act Notice. We ask for the information on this form to carry out the Internal Revenue laws of the United States. We need it to figure and collect the right amount of tax. Chapter 23, Federal Unemployment Tax Act, of Subtitle C, Employment Taxes, of the Internal Revenue Code imposes a tax on employers with respect to employees. This form is used to determine the amount of the tax that you owe. Section 6011 requires you to provide the requested information if you are liable for FUTA tax under section 3301. Section 6109 requires you to provide your employer identification number (EIN).

Routine uses of this information include giving it to the Department of Justice for civil and criminal litigation, and to cities, states, and the District of Columbia for use in administering their tax laws. If you fail to provide this information in a timely manner, you may be subject to penalties and interest.

You are not required to provide the information requested on a form that is subject to the Paperwork Reduction Act unless the form displays a valid OMB control number. Books or records relating to a form or its instructions must be retained as long as their contents may become material in the administration of any Internal Revenue law. Generally, tax returns and return information are confidential, as required by section 6103.

The time needed to complete and file this form will vary depending on individual circumstances. The estimated average time is: **Recordkeeping,** 11 hr., 29 min.; **Learning about the law or the form,** 1 hr., 5 min.; **Preparing and sending the form to the IRS,** 1 hr., 20 min.

If you have comments concerning the accuracy of these time estimates or suggestions for making this form simpler, we would be happy to hear from you. You can write to the Tax Forms Committee, Western Area Distribution Center, Rancho Cordova, CA 95743-0001. **DO NOT** send the tax form to this office. Instead, see **Where To File** on page 2.

Page 6

Form **940-EZ**

Department of the Treasury
Internal Revenue Service   (99)

Employer's Annual Federal
Unemployment (FUTA) Tax Return

▶ **For Privacy Act and Paperwork Reduction Act Notice, see separate instructions.**

OMB No. 1545-1110

1998

T	
FF	
FD	
FP	
I	
T	

Name (as distinguished from trade name)   Calendar year

Trade name, if any

Address and ZIP code   Employer identification number

*Answer the questions under **Who May Use Form 940-EZ** on page 2. If you cannot use Form 940-EZ, you must use Form 940 instead.*

A Enter the amount of contributions paid to your state unemployment fund. (See separate instructions.) . . . ▶ $ _____

B (1) Enter the name of the state where you have to pay contributions . . . . ▶ _____
     (2) Enter your state reporting number as shown on your state unemployment tax return ▶ _____

If you will not have to file returns in the future, check here (see **Who must file** in separate instructions) **and complete and sign the return.** ▶ ☐

If this is an Amended Return, check here . . . . ▶ ☐

Part I   **Taxable Wages and FUTA Tax**

1	Total payments (including payments shown on lines 2 and 3) during the calendar year for services of employees	**1**	
2	Exempt payments. (Explain all exempt payments, attaching additional sheets if necessary.) ▶ _____	**2**	
3	Payments for services of more than $7,000. Enter only amounts over the first $7,000 paid to each employee. Do not include any exempt payments from line 2. The $7,000 amount is the Federal wage base. Your state wage base may be different. **Do not use your state wage limitation**	**3**	
4	Total exempt payments (add lines 2 and 3)	**4**	
5	**Total taxable wages** (subtract line 4 from line 1) . . . . ▶	**5**	
6	**FUTA tax.** Multiply the wages on line 5 by .008 and enter here. **(If the result is over $100, also complete Part II.)**	**6**	
7	Total FUTA tax deposited for the year, including any overpayment applied from a prior year	**7**	
8	**Balance due** (subtract line 7 from line 6). Pay to the "United States Treasury" . . . . ▶	**8**	
	If you owe more than $100, see **Depositing FUTA tax** in separate instructions.		
9	**Overpayment** (subtract line 6 from line 7). Check if it is to be: ☐ **Applied to next return or** ☐ **Refunded** ▶	**9**	

Part II   **Record of Quarterly Federal Unemployment Tax Liability** (Do not include state liability.) **Complete only if line 6 is over $100.**

Quarter	First (Jan. 1 – Mar. 31)	Second (Apr. 1 – June 30)	Third (July 1 – Sept. 30)	Fourth (Oct. 1 – Dec. 31)	Total for year
Liability for quarter					

Under penalties of perjury, I declare that I have examined this return, including accompanying schedules and statements, and, to the best of my knowledge and belief, it is true, correct, and complete, and that no part of any payment made to a state unemployment fund claimed as a credit was, or is to be, deducted from the payments to employees.

Signature ▶   Title (Owner, etc.) ▶   Date ▶

See separate **Instructions for Form 940-EZ** for information on completing this form.   Cat. No. 10983G   Form **940-EZ** (1998)

DETACH HERE

Form **940-EZ(V)**

Department of the Treasury
Internal Revenue Service

Form 940-EZ Payment Voucher

Use this voucher only when making a payment with your return.

OMB No. 1545-1110

1998

Complete boxes 1, 2, 3, and 4. Do not send cash, and do not staple your payment to this voucher. Make your check or money order payable to the **"United States Treasury."** Be sure to enter your employer identification number, "Form 940-EZ", and "1998" on your payment.

1 Enter the amount of the payment you are making

▶ $ _____ .

2 Enter the first four letters of your last name (business name if partnership or corporation)

3 Enter your employer identification number

Instructions for Box 2

—Individuals (sole proprietors, trusts, and estates)—
Enter the first four letters of your last name.

—Corporations and partnerships—Enter the first four characters of your business name (omit "The" if followed by more than one word).

4 Enter your name (individual name for sole proprietors)

Enter your address

Enter your city, state, and ZIP code

---

444   *Payroll Taxes*

Who May Use Form 940-EZ

The following chart will lead you to the right form to use. However, **do not** file Form 940-EZ if you have already filed Form 940 for 1998.

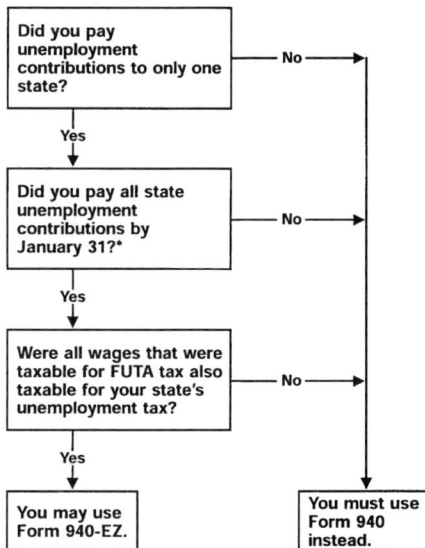

```
┌─────────────────────┐
│ Did you pay         │
│ unemployment        │─── No ──────────┐
│ contributions to    │                 │
│ only one state?     │                 │
└─────────────────────┘                 │
          │                             │
         Yes                            │
          ▼                             │
┌─────────────────────┐                 │
│ Did you pay all     │                 │
│ state unemployment  │─── No ──────────┤
│ contributions by    │                 │
│ January 31?*        │                 │
└─────────────────────┘                 │
          │                             │
         Yes                            │
          ▼                             │
┌─────────────────────┐                 │
│ Were all wages that │                 │
│ were taxable for    │                 │
│ FUTA tax also       │─── No ──────────┤
│ taxable for your    │                 │
│ state's             │                 │
│ unemployment tax?   │                 │
└─────────────────────┘                 │
          │                             │
         Yes                            │
          ▼                             ▼
┌─────────────────┐         ┌──────────────────┐
│ You may use     │         │ You must use     │
│ Form 940-EZ.    │         │ Form 940         │
│                 │         │ instead.         │
└─────────────────┘         └──────────────────┘
```

*If you deposited all FUTA tax when due, you may answer "Yes" if you paid all state unemployment contributions by February 10.

Also, **do not** file Form 940-EZ if–
• You owe FUTA tax **only for** household work in a private home. See **Schedule H (Form 1040).**
• You are a **successor employer** claiming a credit for state unemployment contributions paid by a prior employer. File Form 940.

19**98**

Instructions for Form 940–EZ

Employer's Annual Federal Unemployment (FUTA) Tax Return

Section references are to the Internal Revenue Code unless otherwise noted.

Who May Use Form 940-EZ

The following chart will lead you to the right form to use. However, **do not** file Form 940-EZ if you have already filed Form 940 for 1998.

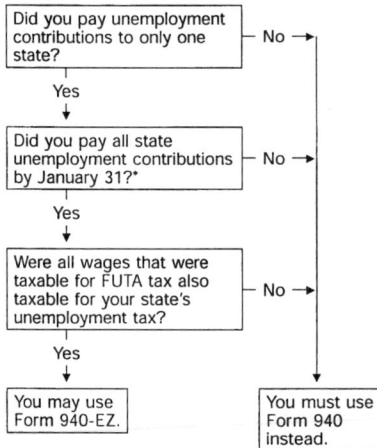

```
┌─────────────────────────────┐
│ Did you pay unemployment    │ ── No ──┐
│ contributions to only one   │         │
│ state?                      │         │
└─────────────────────────────┘         │
           │ Yes                        │
           ▼                            │
┌─────────────────────────────┐         │
│ Did you pay all state       │ ── No ──┤
│ unemployment contributions  │         │
│ by January 31?*             │         │
└─────────────────────────────┘         │
           │ Yes                        │
           ▼                            │
┌─────────────────────────────┐         │
│ Were all wages that were    │         │
│ taxable for FUTA tax also   │ ── No ──┤
│ taxable for your state's    │         │
│ unemployment tax?           │         │
└─────────────────────────────┘         │
           │ Yes                        │
           ▼                            ▼
┌──────────────────┐        ┌──────────────────┐
│ You may use      │        │ You must use     │
│ Form 940-EZ.     │        │ Form 940         │
│                  │        │ instead.         │
└──────────────────┘        └──────────────────┘
```

*If you deposited all FUTA tax when due, you may answer "Yes" if you paid all state unemployment contributions by February 10.

Also, **do not** file Form 940-EZ if—

- You owe FUTA tax **only** for household work in a private home. See **Household employers** on page 2.
- You are a **successor employer** claiming a credit for state unemployment contributions paid by a prior employer. File Form 940.

Items To Note

Preprinted EIN relocated. To ensure privacy, we have relocated the employer identification number on preprinted forms to an area above the envelope window.

FUTA rate. The (net) FUTA rate of .8% (FUTA tax rate of 6.2% less state credit of 5.4%) shown as .008 on line 6 of Form 940–EZ is effective through 2007. If you qualify to file Form 940–EZ, you are entitled to the full 5.4% state credit regardless of your actual experience rate.

Electronic deposit requirement. If your total deposits of social security, Medicare, railroad retirement, and withheld income taxes were more than $50,000 in 1997, you must make electronic deposits for **all** depository tax liabilities (including FUTA tax) that occur after 1998 using the Electronic Federal Tax Payment System (EFTPS). However, if you **were** first required to use EFTPS on or after July 1, 1997, no penalties for failure to use EFTPS will be imposed for tax liabilities that occur prior to January 1, 1999. To enroll in EFTPS, call 1-800-945-8400 or 1-800-555-4477. For general information about EFTPS, call 1-800-829-1040.

General Instructions

Purpose of form. Use this form to report your annual Federal Unemployment Tax Act (FUTA) tax. FUTA tax, together with state unemployment systems, provides for payments of unemployment compensation to workers who have lost their jobs. Most employers pay both Federal and state unemployment taxes. **Only the employer pays this tax.** The tax applies to the first $7,000 you pay each employee in a year. The $7,000 amount is the Federal wage base. Your state wage base may be different.

When to file. File Form 940-EZ for 1998 by February 1, 1999. However, if you deposited all FUTA tax when due, you may file on or before February 10, 1999. Your return will be considered timely filed if it is properly addressed and mailed First Class or sent by an IRS designated delivery service by the due date. See **Circular E,** Employer's Tax Guide (Pub. 15), for a list of designated delivery services. See also, **Where to file** on page 2. **Caution:** *Private delivery services cannot deliver items to P.O. boxes.*

Who must file. Except as noted below, you must file if Test 1 **or** Test 2 below applies.

Test 1. You paid wages of $1,500 or more in any calendar quarter in 1997 or 1998.

Test 2. You had one or more employees for at least some part of a day in any 20 or more different weeks in 1997 or 20 or more different weeks in 1998.

Count all regular, temporary, and part-time employees. A partnership should not count its partners. If a business changes hands during the year, each employer meeting Test 1 or 2 must file. **Do not** report wages paid by the prior (or subsequent) employer.

State and local government employers. Wages paid to state or local government employees are not subject to the FUTA tax.

Cat. No. 25947I

Nonprofit organizations. Religious, educational, charitable, etc., organizations described in section 501(c)(3) and exempt from tax under section 501(a) are not subject to FUTA tax and are not required to file.

Household employers. File a FUTA tax return **ONLY** if you paid total cash wages of $1,000 or more (for all household employees) in any calendar quarter in 1997 or 1998 for household work in a private home, local college club, or local chapter of a college fraternity or sorority. Individuals, estates, and trusts that owe FUTA tax for **household work** in a private home, in most cases, must file **Schedule H (Form 1040),** Household Employment Taxes, instead of Form 940 or 940-EZ. See the instructions for Schedule H (Form 1040). In some cases, such as when you employ both household employees and other employees, you may have the option to report social security, Medicare, and withheld Federal income taxes for your household employee(s) on **Form 941,** Employer's Quarterly Federal Tax Return, or **Form 943,** Employer's Annual Tax Return for Agricultural Employees, instead of on Schedule H (Form 1040). If you choose to report on Form 941 or 943, you must use Form 940 or 940-EZ to report FUTA taxes.

Agricultural employers. File a FUTA tax return if either 1 **or** 2 below applies:

1. You paid cash wages of $20,000 or more to farmworkers during any calendar quarter in 1997 or 1998 or

2. You employed 10 or more farmworkers during some part of a day (whether or not at the same time) during any 20 or more different weeks in 1997 or 20 or more different weeks in 1998.

Count wages paid to aliens admitted on a temporary basis to the United States to perform farmwork, also known as workers with "H-2(A)" visas, to see if you meet either 1 or 2 above. However, wages paid to H-2(A) visa workers are not subject to FUTA tax.

Where to file. In the list below, find the location where your legal residence, principal place of business, office, or agency is located. Send your return to the **Internal Revenue Service** at the address listed for your location. No street address is needed.

Note: Where you file depends on whether or not you are including a payment.

Florida, Georgia, South Carolina

Return without payment:	Return with payment:
	P.O. Box 105659
Atlanta, GA 39901-0047	Atlanta, GA 30348-5659

New Jersey, New York (New York City and counties of Nassau, Rockland, Suffolk, and Westchester)

Return without payment:	Return with payment:
	P.O. Box 210
Holtsville, NY 00501-0047	Newark, NJ 07101-0210

New York (all other counties), Connecticut, Maine, Massachusetts, New Hampshire, Rhode Island, Vermont

Return without payment:	Return with payment:
	P.O. Box 371324
Andover, MA 05501-0047	Pittsburgh, PA 15250-7324

Illinois, Iowa, Minnesota, Missouri, Wisconsin

Return without payment:	Return with payment:
	P.O. Box 970010
Kansas City, MO 64999-0047	St. Louis, MO 63197-0010

Delaware, District of Columbia, Maryland, Pennsylvania, Puerto Rico, Virginia, U.S. Virgin Islands

Return without payment:	Return with payment:
	P.O. Box 8738
Philadelphia, PA 19255-0047	Philadelphia, PA 19162-8738

Indiana, Kentucky, Michigan, Ohio, West Virginia

Return without payment:	Return with payment:
	P.O. Box 6796
Cincinnati, OH 45999-0047	Chicago, IL 60680-6796

Kansas, New Mexico, Oklahoma, Texas

Return without payment:	Return with payment:
	P.O. Box 970017
Austin, TX 73301-0047	St. Louis, MO 63197-0017

Alaska, Arizona, California (counties of Alpine, Amador, Butte, Calaveras, Colusa, Contra Costa, Del Norte, El Dorado, Glenn, Humboldt, Lake, Lassen, Marin, Mendocino, Modoc, Napa, Nevada, Placer, Plumas, Sacramento, San Joaquin, Shasta, Sierra, Siskiyou, Solano, Sonoma, Sutter, Tehama, Trinity, Yolo, and Yuba), Colorado, Idaho, Montana, Nebraska, Nevada, North Dakota, Oregon, South Dakota, Utah, Washington, Wyoming

Return without payment:	Return with payment:
	P.O. Box 7028
Ogden, UT 84201-0047	San Francisco, CA 94120-7028

California (all other counties), Hawaii

Return without payment:	Return with payment:
	P.O. Box 60150
Fresno, CA 93888-0047	Los Angeles, CA 90060-0150

Alabama, Arkansas, Louisiana, Mississippi, North Carolina, Tennessee

Return without payment:	Return with payment:
	P.O. Box 1210
Memphis, TN 37501-0047	Charlotte, NC 28201-1210

If the location of your legal residence or principal place of business is not listed above

	All Returns:
	Philadelphia, PA 19255-0047

Amended returns. Use a new Form 940-EZ to amend a previously filed Form 940-EZ. Check the Amended Return box above Part I, enter all amounts that should have been on the original return, and sign the amended return. Attach an explanation of the reasons for amending the original return.

If you were required to file Form 940 but filed Form 940-EZ instead and you must correct an error on Form 940–EZ, file the amended return on Form 940. See the **Instructions for Form 940.**

Not liable for FUTA tax? If you receive Form 940-EZ and are not liable for FUTA tax for 1998, write "Not Liable" across the front of the form, sign the return, and return it to the IRS.

Note: *If you will not have to file returns in the future, check the box on the line below B(2) and complete and sign the return. See* **Where to file** *above.*

Page 2

Employer's name, address, and employer identification number. If you are not using a preaddressed Form 940–EZ, type or print your name, trade name, address, and employer identification number (EIN) on the form.

If you do not have an EIN, see Circular E (Pub. 15) for instructions on how to obtain make deposits, file a return, etc. Apply for an EIN on **Form SS-4,** Application for Employer Identification Number.

Identifying your payments. When you pay any amount you owe to the United States Treasury (line 8) or make Federal tax deposits, write the following on your check or money order: your EIN, "Form 940–EZ", and the tax year to which the payment applies. This helps us credit your account properly.

Penalties and interest. Avoid penalties and interest by making tax deposits when due, filing a correct return, and paying all taxes when due. There are penalties for late deposits and late filing unless you can show reasonable cause. If you file late, attach an explanation to the return. There are also penalties for willful failure to pay tax, keep records, make returns, and for filing false or fraudulent returns.

Credit for contributions paid to a state fund. You get a credit for amounts you pay to a state (including Puerto Rico and the U.S. Virgin Islands) unemployment fund by February 1, 1999 (or February 10, 1999, if that is your Form 940-EZ due date). This credit is reflected in the FUTA tax rate (.008) shown on line 6. See **FUTA rate** on page 1.

"Contributions" are payments that a state requires an employer to make to its unemployment fund for the payment of unemployment benefits. However, contributions do not include:

• Any payments deducted or deductible from your employees' pay.

• Penalties, interest, or special administrative taxes not included in the contribution rate the state assigned to you.

• Voluntary contributions you paid to get a lower assigned rate.

Note: *Be sure to enter your state reporting number on line B(2) at the top of the form. The IRS needs this to verify your state contributions.*

Depositing FUTA Tax

When to deposit. Although Form 940–EZ covers a calendar year, you may have to make deposits of the tax before filing the return. Generally, deposit FUTA tax quarterly but only when your liability exceeds $100. Determine your FUTA tax for each of the first three quarters by multiplying by .008 that part of the first $7,000 of each employee's annual wages you paid during the quarter. If any part of the amounts paid are exempt from state unemployment tax, you may be required to deposit an amount greater than that determined using the .008 rate. For example, in certain states, wages paid to corporate officers, certain payments of sick pay by unions, and certain fringe benefits, are exempt from state unemployment tax.

If your FUTA tax liability for any of the first three quarters of 1998 (plus any undeposited amount of $100 or less from any earlier quarter) is over $100, deposit it by the last day of the month after the end of the quarter. If it is $100 or less, carry it to the next quarter; a deposit is not required. If your liability for the fourth quarter (plus any undeposited amount from any earlier quarter) is over $100, deposit the entire amount by February 1, 1999. If it is $100 or less, you can either make a deposit or pay it with your Form 940–EZ by February 1. (If you deposit it by February 1, you may file Form 940–EZ by February 10, 1999.)

The deposit due dates are shown in the following chart:

If undeposited FUTA tax is over $100 on—	Deposit it by—
March 31	April 30
June 30	July 31
September 30	October 31
December 31	February 1

Note: *If any deposit due date falls on a Saturday, Sunday or legal holiday, you may deposit on the next business day.*

How to deposit. If you are not required to use EFTPS (see **Electronic deposit requirement** on page 1), use **Form 8109,** Federal Tax Deposit Coupon, when you make each tax deposit. The IRS will send you a book of deposit coupons when you apply for an employer identification number (EIN). Follow the instructions in the coupon book. If you do not have coupons, see section 11 in Circular E (Pub. 15).

Make your deposits with an authorized financial institution (e.g., a commercial bank that is qualified to accept Federal tax deposits) or the Federal Reserve bank for your area. To avoid a possible penalty, do not mail deposits directly to the IRS. Records of your deposits will be sent to the IRS for crediting to your business accounts.

Specific Instructions

You must complete lines A and B and Part I. If your FUTA tax (line 6) is over $100, you must also complete Part II. Please remember to sign the return.

Line A. Enter the amount of your state unemployment contributions. If your state has given you a 0% experience rate so there are no required contributions, enter "0% rate" in the space.

Line B(1). Enter the state where you pay state unemployment contributions. **If you pay to more than one state, you must file Form 940.**

Part I — Taxable Wages and FUTA Tax

Line 1 — Total payments. Enter the total payments you made during the calendar year for services of employees, even if the payments are not taxable for FUTA tax. Include salaries, wages, commissions, fees, bonuses, vacation allowances, amounts paid to temporary or part-time employees, and the value of goods, lodging, food, clothing, and noncash fringe benefits, contributions to a 401(k) plan, section 125 (cafeteria) plan benefits, and sick pay (including third party sick pay if liability transferred to employer). Also, include tips of $20 or more in a month

Page 3

reported to you by your employees. Enter the amount before any deductions.

How you make the payments is not important to determine if they are wages. Thus, you may pay wages for piecework or as a percentage of profits. You may pay wages hourly, daily, etc. You may pay wages in cash or some other way, such as goods, lodging, food, or clothing. For items other than cash, use the fair market value when paid.

Line 2 — Exempt payments. For FUTA purposes, "wages" and "employment" do not include every payment and every kind of service an employee may perform. In general, payments excluded from wages and payments for services excepted from employment are not subject to tax. **Do not** enter payments over $7,000 for each employee. Enter such amounts on line 3.

Enter payments such as the following on line 2 if you included them in total payments on line one.

1. Agricultural labor if you did not meet either 1 or 2 under *Agricultural employers* on page 2 and **all** payments to H-2(A) visa workers.

2. Benefit payments for sickness or injury under a worker's compensation law.

3. Household service if you did not pay total cash wages of $1,000 or more in any calendar quarter in 1997 or 1998.

4. Certain family employment. (See Cir. E (Pub. 15).)

5. Certain fishing activities. (See **Pub. 595,** Tax Highlights for Commercial Fishermen.)

6. Noncash payments for farmwork or household services in a private home. Only cash wages to these workers are taxable.

7. Value of certain meals and lodging. (See section 5 in Cir. E (Pub.15).)

8. Cost of group-term life insurance.

9. Payments attributable to the employee's contributions to a sick-pay plan.

10. Benefits excludable under a section 125 (cafeteria) plan.

11. Any other exempt service or pay.

For more information, see **Special Rules for Various Types of Services and Payments** in Circular E (Pub. 15).

Line 3 — Payments for services of more than $7,000. Enter the total amounts over $7,000 you paid each employee. For example, if you have 10 employees and paid each $8,000 during the year, enter $80,000 on line 1 and $10,000 on line 3. The $10,000 is the amount over $7,000 paid to each employee. **Do not** include any exempt payments from line 2 in figuring the $7,000.

Line 8 — Balance due. Make your check or money order payable to the "United States Treasury". However, if the amount on line 8 is under $1, you do not have to pay it.

Line 9 — Overpayment. If the amount on line 9 is under $1, we will send a refund or apply it to your next return only on written request.

Part II — Record of Quarterly Federal Unemployment Tax Liability

Complete this part only if your FUTA tax on line 6 is over $100. To figure your FUTA tax liability for each quarter, multiply by .008 that part of the first $7,000 of each employee's annual wages you paid during the quarter. Enter the result in the space for that quarter. Your total liability ("Total for year") must equal your total tax shown on line 6.

Record your liability based on when you pay wages, not on when you deposit the FUTA tax. For example, if you pay wages on March 29, your FUTA tax liability on those wages is $200, and you deposit the $200 on April 30, you would record that $200 in the first quarter, not in the second.

Privacy Act and Paperwork Reduction Act Notice. We ask for the information on this form to carry out the Internal Revenue laws of the United States. We need it to figure and collect the right amount of tax. Chapter 23, Federal Unemployment Tax Act , of Subtitle C, Employment Taxes, of the Internal Revenue Code imposes a tax on employers with respect to employees. This form is used to determine the amount of the tax that you owe. Section 6011 requires you to provide the requested information if you are liable for FUTA tax under section 3301. Section 6109 requires you to provide your employer identification number (EIN).

Routine uses of this information include giving it to the Department of Justice for civil and criminal litigation, and to cities, states, and the District of Columbia for use in administering their tax laws. If you fail to provide this information in a timely manner, you may be subject to penalties and interest.

You are not required to provide the information requested on a form that is subject to the Paperwork Reduction Act unless the form displays a valid OMB control number. Books or records relating to a form or its instructions must be retained as long as their contents may become material in the administration of any Internal Revenue law. Generally, tax returns and return information are confidential, as required by section 6103.

The time needed to complete and file this form will vary depending on individual circumstances. The estimated average time is: **Recordkeeping,** 6 hr., 23 min.; **Learning about the law or form,** 7 min.; and **Preparing and sending the form to the IRS,** 34 min.

If you have comments concerning the accuracy of these time estimates or suggestions for making this form simpler, we would be happy to hear from you. You can write to the Tax Forms Committee, Western Area Distribution Center, Rancho Cordova, CA 95743-0001. **DO NOT** send the form to this office. Instead, see **Where to file** on page 2.

Page 4

DIVESTITURE

APB OPINION NUMBER 29

According to APB Opinion Number 29, a gain or loss cannot be recorded on a corporate divestiture. However, footnote disclosure should be provided of the nature and provisions of the divestiture.

If there is an exchange of stock held by a parent in a subsidiary for stock of the parent company itself held by stockholders in the parent, there is a non-pro rata split-off of the business segment because a reorganization is recorded at fair value. However, if there is a split-off of a targeted company distributed on a proportionate basis to the one holding the applicable targeted stock, it should be recorded at historical cost provided the targeted stock did not arise in contemplation of the later split-off. If the contemplated situation did in fact exist, then the transaction is recorded at fair value. In a split-off, there is a distribution of shares being exchanged on a proportionate basis for the shares of the new entity. In a split-off, the transaction is in effect the acquisition of treasury stock. Retained earnings is not charged.

In a spin-off, there is a distribution of the segment's shares to the investor's shareholders without the holders surrendering their shares.

In some instances, a split-off or spin-off may be treated as a discontinued operation of a business segment.

In a split-up, there is a transfer of the operations of the original entity to at least two new entities.

APPENDIX A

FINANCIAL MANAGEMENT AND GOVERNMENT ORGANIZATIONS

FINANCIAL MANAGEMENT (AND RELATED) ASSOCIATIONS

American Association of Artificial Intelligence
445 Burgess Drive
Menlo Park, CA 94025
Phone: 415-328-3123
FAX: 415-321-4457

American Association of Association Executives
1575 Eye Street NW
Washington, DC 20005

American Bar Association
750 N. Lake Shore Drive
Chicago, IL 60611
Phone: 312-988-5000
FAX: 312-988-6281

American Economic Association
2014 Broadway
Suite 305
Nashville, TN 37203
Phone: 615-322-2595
FAX: 615-343-7590

American Institute of Certified Public Accountants
Harborside Financial Center
201 Plaza III
Jersey City, NJ 07311-3881
Phone: 800-862-4272; 212-596-6200; 201-938-3301
FAX: 212-596-6213; 201-938-3329

American Institute for Computer Sciences
2101 Magnolia Ave.
Suite 200
Birmingham, AL 35205
Phone: 800-729-AICS
FAX: 205-328-2229

American Management Association
135 West 50th Street
New York, NY 10020
Phone: 800-262-9699; 212-903-8216
FAX: 212-903-8168

American Production and Inventory Control Society
500 W. Annandale Road
Falls Church, VA 22046
Phone: 800-444-2742; 703-237-8344
FAX: 703-237-1071

American Statistical Association
1429 Duke Street
Alexandria, VA 22314
Phone: 703-684-1221
FAX: 703-684-2036

Applied Business Telecommunications
P.O. Box 5106
San Ramon, CA 94583
Phone: 800-829-3400; 405-743-0320

Association for Investment Management and Research (AIMR). (Formed by a merger of the **Financial Analysts Federation** and the **Institute of Chartered Financial Analysts**)
5 Boar's Head Lane
P.O. Box 3668
Charlottesville, VA 22903
Phone: 804-977-6600
FAX: 804-977-1103

Canadian Institute of Chartered Accountants
277 Wellington Street, West
Toronto, Ontario, M5V 3H2, Canada
Phone: 416-977-3222
FAX: 416-977-8585

Chartered Institute of Management Accountants
63 Portland Place
London W1N 4AB, England

The Conference Board
845 Third Avenue
New York, NY 10022
Phone: 212-759-0900
FAX: 212-980-7014

Conference Board of Canada
255 Smyth Road
Ottawa, Ontario K1H8M7, Canada
(Also refer to **Canadian Business Infoworld** on the World Wide Web:
http://csclub.uwaterloo.ca/u/nck-wan)

Financial Executives Institute
10 Madison Avenue
Morristown, NJ 07960
Phone: 800-336-0773; 201-989-4600
FAX: 201-898-4649

Financial Management Association
College of Business Administration
University of South Florida
4202 Fowler Avenue
Tampa, FL 33620
Phone: 813-974-2084
FAX: 813-974-3318

Institute of Internal Auditors
249 Maitland Avenue
Altamonte Springs, FL 32701
Phone: 407-830-7600
FAX: 813-974-3318

Institute of Management Accountants (formerly **National Association of Accountants**)
10 Paragon Drive
Montvale, NJ 07645
Phone: 800-638-4427; 201-573-9000

International Computer Training Association
Computer Learning Center
134 N. Peters Road
Knoxville, TN 37923
Phone: 800-354-3624

International Credit Association
243 North Lindbergh Blvd.
P.O. Box 27357
St. Louis, MO 63141-1757
Phone: 314-991-3030
FAX: 314-991-3029

National Association of Business Economists
1801 E. 9th Street
Suite 700
Cleveland, OH 44114
Phone: 202-463-6223
FAX: 202-463-6239

National Association of Credit Management
8815 Centre Park Drive
Suite 200
Columbia, MD 21045-2158
Phone: 410-740-5560
FAX: 410-740-5574

National Association for Female Executives
30 Irving Place
New York, NY 10003
Phone: 212-477-2200
FAX: 212-477-8215

National Society of Public Accountants
1010 North Fairfax Street
Alexandria, VA 22314-1574
Phone: 703-549-6400
FAX: 703-549-2984

National Tax Association
5310 E. Main Street
Columbus, OH 43213

New York Society of Security Analysts (NYSSA). (A local of the **Association for Investment Management and Research**)
1 World Trade Center
New York, NY 10048
Phone: 212-912-9249
FAX: 212-912-9310

North American Simulation and Gaming Association
c/o University of Wisconsin—La Crosse
203 Mitchell Hall
La Crosse, WI 54601
Phone: 608-785-8162

Risk and Insurance Management Society
655 Third Avenue
New York, NY 10017
Phone: 212-286-9292
FAX: 212-9865-9716

Society of Management Accountants of Canada
154 Main Street East
MPO Box 176
Hamilton, Ontario, Canada L8N 3C3
Phone: 905-524-4100

Tax Executives Institute
1001 Pennsylvania Avenue NW
Suite 320
Washington, DC 20004-2505
Phone: 202-638-5601
FAX: 202-638-5607

U.S. GOVERNMENT AGENCIES

Bureau of Economic Analysis
1441 L Street NW
Washington, DC 20230
Phone: 202-606-9900
FAX: 202-606-5310
World Wide Web: http://www.stat-usa.gov/BEN/Services/beahome.html

Department of Commerce
Fourteenth Street
Washington, DC 20230
Phone: 202-482-2000
World Wide Web Federal and Commerce Information Network:
http://www.fedworld.gov

Director for Budget, Planning, and Organization
Herbert Hoover Building
14th Street and Constitution
Avenue NW
Room 5820
Washington, DC 20230
Phone: 202-482-3490

Director for Financial Management
Herbert Hoover Building
14th Street and Constitution
Avenue NW
Room 6827
Washington, DC 20230
Phone: 202-482-1207
World Wide Web (Finance Net):
http://www.financenet.giv

Internal Revenue Service
1111 Constitution Avenue NW
Room 3000
Washington, DC 20224
Phone: 202-622-5000
World Wide Web:
http://ustreas.gov/basic/cover.html

International Economic Policy
Office of Financial Management
Herbert Hoover Building
14th Street and Constitution
Avenue NW
Room 3866
Washington, DC 20230
Phone: 202-482-3022
FAX: 202-377-5444

International Trade Administration
Office of Financial Management
Herbert Hoover Building
14th Street and Constitution
Avenue NW
Room 4112
Washington, DC 20230
Phone: 202-482-3809
FAX: 202-377-5933

National Technical Information Service
Fourteenth Street
Room 1067
Washington, DC 20230
Phone: 202-377-0365

Office of Business Liaison
Herbert Hoover Building
14th Street and Constitution
Avenue NW
Room 5026
Washington, DC 20230
Phone: 202-482-1360
FAX: 202-377-4054

Office of Business and Industrial Analysis
Herbert Hoover Building
14th Street and Constitution
Avenue NW
Room 4875
Washington, DC 20230
Phone: 202-482-0096

Office of Financial Management Service

Liberty Center Building
401 14th Street SW
Room 548
Washington, DC 20227
Phone: 202-874-0700

Office of the Chief Economist

Herbert Hoover Building
14th Street and Constitution
Avenue NW
Room 4868A
Washington, DC 20230
Phone: 202-482-4885

Office of the General Counsel

1500 Pennsylvania Avenue NW
Room 3000
Washington, DC 20220
Phone: 202-622-0287

Office of the Secretary of the Treasury

Main Treasury
1500 Pennsylvania Avenue NW
Room 3330
Washington, DC 20220
Phone: 202-622-1100

Securities and Exchange Commission

450 5th Street NW
Room 6010
Washington, DC 20549
Phone: 202-942-4150
FAX: 202-272-7050
World Wide Web (SEC Edgar):
http://www.sec.gov/edgarhp.html

Note: The Federal Web Locator is http://www.law.vill.edu/fed-agency/fedwebloc.html.

PROFESSIONAL JOURNALS

AAII Journal
American Association of Individual
Investors
525 N. Michigan Ave.
Chicago, IL 60611
Phone: 312-280-0170
FAX: 312-280-1625

Academy of Management Journal
P.O. Box 39
300 S. Union St.
Ada, OH 45810
Phone: 419-772-1953
FAX: 419-772-1954

Academy of Management Review
P.O. Drawer KZ
Mississippi State University
Mississippi State, MS 39762
Phone: 419-772-1953
FAX: 419-772-1954

Across the Board
The Conference Board, Inc.
845 Third Ave.
New York, NY 10022
Phone: 212-759-0900
FAX: 212-980-7014

American Business Law Journal
Prof. Gregory J. Naples
Department of Accounting
College of Business Administration
Marquette University
Milwaukee, WI 53233
Phone: 513-529-2945
FAX: 513-529-6992

American Economic Review
American Economic Association
2014 Broadway
Suite 305
Nashville, TN 37203
Phone: 615-322-2595
FAX: 615-343-7590

Antitrust Law & Economic Review
P.O. Box 3532
Vero Beach, FL 32964-9990

Applied Financial Economics
Chapman & Hall
One Penn Plaza
41st Floor
New York, NY 10019
Phone: 0171-865-0066
FAX: 0171-522-9623

Association Management
American Society of Association
Executives
1575 Eye St. NW
Washington, DC 20005
Phone: 202-626-2735
FAX: 202-408-9635

Bankers Magazine
Warren, Gorham & Lamont, Inc.
31 St. James Ave.
Boston, MA 02116
Phone: 800-950-1252

Barron's
Dow Jones & Co., Inc.
200 Burnett Rd.
Chicopee, MA 01020
Phone: 212-416-2700
800-628-9320
FAX: 212-808-7282

**Business & Professional Ethics
Journal**
P.O. Box 15017
Gainesville, FL 32604
Phone: 904-392-2084
FAX: 904-392-5577

Business and Society Review
25-13 Old Kings Hwy. N
Suite 107
Darien, CT 06820
Phone: 212-399-1088
FAX: 212-245-1973

Business Credit
National Association of Credit
Management
8815 Centre Park Drive
Suite 200
Columbia, MD 21045-2158
Phone: 410-740-5560
FAX: 410-740-5574

Business Economics
National Association of Business
Economists
1233 20th St. NW, Suite 505
Washington, DC 20036
Phone: 202-463-6223
FAX: 202-463-6239

Business Horizons
Graduate School of Business
Indiana University
Bloomington, IN 47405
Phone: 812-855-5507

JAI Press, Inc.
Subscription Dept.
55 Old Post Rd., No. 2
P.O. Box 1678
Greenwich, CT 06836-1678
Phone: 203-661-7602

Business Insurance
Crain Communications
740 N. Rush Street
Chicago, IL 60611
Phone: 312-649-5286
FAX: 312-280-3174

Business Quarterly
The University of Western Ontario
1393 Western Rd.
London, Ontario N6A 3K7, Canada
Phone: 519-661-3309
FAX: 519-661-3838

Business Week
P.O. Box 430
Hightstown, NJ 08520
Phone: 212-512-2000

CA Magazine
Canadian Institute of Chartered
Accountants
277 Wellington St. W
Ontario M5V 3H2, Canada
Phone: 416-977-3222
FAX: 416-204-3409

California Management Review
University of California at Berkeley
5549 Haas School of Business, #1900
Berkeley, CA 94720-7159
Phone: 510-642-7159
FAX: 510-642-1318
E-mail: cmr@haas.berkeley.edu

Canadian Business Review
Conference Board of Canada
255 Smyth Road
Ottawa, Ontario K1H8M7, Canada
World Wide Web: http://csciub.uwa-terloo.ca/u/nckwan

Canadian Business
CB Media Ltd.
70 The Esplanade
2nd Floor
Toronto, Ontario M5E 1R2, Canada
Phone: 416-364-4266

CFO
CFO Publishing Company
253 Summer St.
Boston, MA 02210
Phone: 212-779-4469
FAX: 212-779-4277

CMA
Society of Management
Accountants of Canada
154 Main St. East
MPO Box 176
Hamilton, Ontario, Canada L8N 3C3
Phone: 905-524-4100

Columbia Journal of World Business
Columbia University
Uris Hall
3022 Broadway, Room 810
New York, NY 10027-7004
Phone: 203-661-7602
FAX: 203-661-0792

Compensation & Benefits Management
Panel Publishers, Inc.
Aspen Distribution Center
7201 McKinney Cir.
Frederick, MD 21701
Phone: 212-354-4545

Compensation and Benefits Review
American Management Association
Subscription Services
Box 408
Saranac Lake, NY 12983
Phone: 800-262-9699
212-903-8216
FAX: 2120-903-8168

Computers in Accounting
Warren, Gorham & Lamont
31 St. James Avenue
Boston, MA 02116
Phone: 800-950-1252

Corporate Cashflow
Intertec Publishing
6151 Powers Ferry Road NW
Atlanta, GA 30339
Phone: 770-955-2500

Corporate Controller
Faulkner & Gray
11 Penn Plaza
New York, NY 10001
Phone: 800-535-8403
212-867-7060

Corporate Finance (London, England)
Euromoney Publications PLC
Nestor House
Playhouse Yard
London EC4V 5EX, England
Phone: 0171-779-8935
FAX: 0171-779-8541

Corporate Finance
CF-VH Associates
415 Madison Ave.
New York, NY 10017
Phone: 212-432-0045

Corporate Taxation
Faulkner & Gray
11 Penn Plaza
New York, NY 10001
Phone: 800-535-8403
212-967-7060

CPA Journal
The New York Society of CPAs
530 5th Ave.
New York, NY 10036-5101
Phone: 212-719-8351
FAX: 212-719-3364

Credit Union Magazine
5710 Mineval Point Road
Madison, WI 53705
Phone: 608-231-4079
FAX: 608-231-4370

Credit World
International Credit Association
243 North Lindbergh Blvd.
P.O. Box 27357
St. Louis, MO 63141-1757
Phone: 314-991-3030
FAX: 314-991-3029
E-mail: bmurray@lmb.com

Economic Review
Federal Reserve Bank of Kansas City
Kansas City, MO 64198
Phone: 216-579-3079
FAX: 216-579-2477

Economist
25 St. James Street
London SW1A 1HG, England
Phone: 44-171-830-7000
FAX: 44-171-839-2968

Employer Benefit Plan Review
Charles D. Spencer & Associates, Inc.
250 S. Wacker Dr.
Suite 600
Chicago, IL 60606-5834
Phone: 312-993-7900

Employee Benefits Journal
International Foundation of
Employee Benefit Plans
18700 W. Bluemound Rd.
P.O. Box 69
Brookfield, WI 53005
Phone: 414-786-6700
FAX: 414-786-2990

Executive Accountant
Association of Cost & Executive
Accountants
Tower House
141-149 Fonthill Rd.
London N4 3HF, England
Phone: 44-71-272-3925
FAX: 44-71-281-5723

Executive Director
1801 E. 9th St.
Suite 700
Cleveland, OH 44114

Financial & Accounting Systems
Warren, Gorham & Lamont
31 St. James Avenue
Boston, MA 02116
Phone: 800-950-1252

Financial Analysts Journal
The Associates for Investment
Management and Research
P.O. Box 3668
Charlottesville, VA 22903
Phone: 804-980-9775
FAX: 804-977-1103
E-mail: faj@aimr.com

Financial Executive

Financial Executives Institute
10 Madison Ave.
P.O. Box 1938
Morristown, NJ 07960-1938
Phone: 800-336-0773
FAX: 201-898-4649

Financial Management

Financial Management Association
College of Business Administration
University of South Florida
4202 Fowler Ave.
Tampa, FL 33620
Phone: 813-974-2084
FAX: 201-898-4649

Financial Markets, Institutions & Instruments

Blackwell Publishers
238 Main St.
Suite 501
Cambridge, MA 02142, or
108 Cowley Rd.
Oxford OX41JF UK
Phone: 800-216-2522
617-547-7110
FAX: 617-547-0789

Financial Planning

P.O. Box 3060 C
Southeastern, PA 19398
Phone: 212-765-5311
FAX: 212-765-6123

Financial Review

c/o Prof. M. Carnes, Jr., School of
Business
Georgia Southern College
L-B 8151
Statesboro, GA 30458
Phone: 912-681-5575
FAX: 912-244-3118

Financial World

Financial World Partners
1328 Broadway
New York, NY 10001
Phone: 212-594-5030
FAX: 212-629-1001

Forbes

60 Fifth Ave.
New York, NY 10011
Phone: 212-620-2200
800-888-9896

Fortune

P.O. Box 30604
Tampa, FL 33630-0604
Phone: 212-522-1212
800-621-8000

Harvard Business Review

Harvard Business School
Publishing Division
Soldiers Field
Boston, MA 02163
Phone: 800-988-0886
FAX: 617-495-6985

Industrial Management

Institute of Industrial Engineers
25 Technology Park-Atlanta
Norcross, GA 30092
Phone: 404-449-0460

Inc. Technology

Inc. Publishing Company
P.O. Box 54129
Boulder, CO 80322-4129
Phone: 800-234-0999

Industry Week

Penton Publishing Company
1100 Superior Ave.
Cleveland, OH 44114-2543
Phone: 216-696-7000
FAX: 216-696-7670

Internal Auditor
Institute of Internal Auditors
249 Maitland Avenue
Altamonte Springs, FL 32701
Phone: 407-830-7600
FAX: 407-831-5171

International Business
P.O. Box 5051
Brentwood, TN 37024-9736
Phone: 914-381-7700
FAX: 914-381-7713

International Economic Review
University of Pennsylvania
3718 Locust Walk
Philadelphia, PA 19104-6297
Phone: 215-898-5841
FAX: 215-573-2072

International Executive
John Wiley & Sons, Inc.
Susan Malawski, Director
Subscription Fulfillment and
Distribution
Subscriptions Dept.
605 Third Ave.
New York, NY 10158-0012
Phone: 212-850-6645

International Tax Journal
Panel Publishers, Inc.
Aspen Distribution Center
7201 McKinney Cir.
Frederick, MD 21701
Phone: 212-354-4545

Journal of Accountancy
American Institute of Certified
Public Accountants
Fulfillment Management
Harborside Financial Center
201 Plaza III
Jersey City, NJ 07311-3881
Phone: 201-938-3301
800-862-4272
FAX: 201-938-3329

Journal of Accounting, Auditing & Finance
Greenwood Publishing Group, Inc.
88 Post Rd. W
P.O. Box 5007
Westport, CT 06881
Phone: 800-225-5800
203-226-3571

Journal of Business & Economic Statistics
American Statistical Association
Subscriptions
1429 Duke St.
Alexandria, VA 22314-3402
Phone: 703-684-1221
FAX: 703-684-2036

Journal of Business Finance & Accounting
Blackwell Publishers
238 Main St.
Suite 501
Cambridge, MA 01242, or
108 Cowley Rd.
Oxford OX41JF UK
Phone: 800-216-2522
617-547-7110

Journal of Business Forecasting Methods and Systems
Graceway Publishing Co.
P.O. Box 159
Station C
Flushing, NY 11367
Phone: 718-463-3914
FAX: 718-544-9086

Journal of Business Strategy
Faulkner & Gray
11 Penn Plaza
New York, NY 10001
Phone: 800-535-8403
212-967-7000
FAX: 212-967-7155

Journal of Compensation & Benefits

Warren, Gorham & Lamont
31 St. James Avenue
Boston, MA 02116
Phone: 800-950-1252

Journal of Corporate Accounting and Finance

John Wiley and Sons, Inc.
Susan Malawski, Director
Subscription Fulfillment and Sales
605 Third Ave.
New York, NY 10158
Phone: 212-950-6000

Journal of Corporate Taxation

Warren, Gorham & Lamont
31 St. James Ave.
Boston, MA 02116
Phone: 800-950-1252

Journal of Cost Analysis

Society of Cost Estimating & Accounting
101 S. Whiting St., Suite 313
Alexandria, VA 22304
Phone: 703-751-8069
FAX: 703-461-7328

Journal of Cost Management (formerly Journal of Cost Management for the Manufacturing Industry)

Warren, Gorham & Lamont
31 St. James Ave.
Boston, MA 02116-4112
Phone: 800-950-1205
FAX: 617-423-2026

Journal of Economics and Business

Elsevier Publishing Co., Inc.
Journals Fulfillment Department
665 Ave. of the Americas
New York, NY 10017
Phone: 212-989-5800

Journal of Finance

New York University
Graduate School of Business
100 Trinity Place
New York, NY 10006

Journal of Financial and Quantitative Analysis

University of Washington
Graduate School of Business
Administration
Makenzie Hall, DJ-10
Seattle, WA 98195
FAX: 206-543-6872

Journal of Financial Economics

Elsevier Science S.A.
P.O. Box 564
CH-1001
Lausanne 1, Switzerland
Phone: 212-989-5800

Journal of Financial Planning

Institute of Certified Financial Planners
7600 E. Eastman Ave., Suite 301
Denver, CO 80231
Phone: 303-751-7600
FAX: 303-751-1037

Journal of Financial Research

Editor
Dept. of Finance
College of Business
Arizona State University
Tempe, AZ 85287-3906
Phone: 703-231-7699
FAX: 703-231-4706

Journal of Industrial Economics

Basil Blackwell Ltd.
108 Cowly Rd.
Oxford, OX4 1JF, England
Phone: 0865-791100
FAX: 0865-791347

Journal of International Financial Management and Accounting
Basil Blackwell Ltd.
108 Cowly Rd.
Oxford, OX4 1JF, England

Journal of International Taxation
Warren, Gorham & Lamont
31 St. James Ave.
Boston, MA 02116
Phone: 800-950-1252

Journal of Management
Graduate School of Business
Indiana University
10th & Fee Lane
Bloomington, IN 47405
Phone: 812-855-9209

JAI Press Inc.
Subscription Dept.
55 Old Post Rd., No. 2
P.O. Box 1678
Greenwich, CT 06836-1678

Journal of Money, Credit and Banking
Ohio State University Press
1070 Carmack Rd.
Columbus, OH 43210
Phone: 614-292-6930
E-mail:
mcgrothers@magnus.acs.ohio-state.edu

Journal of Portfolio Management
The Institutional Investor, Inc.
488 Madison Ave.
New York, NY 10022
Phone: 212-303-3300
FAX: 212-303-3527

Journal of Risk and Insurance
Dept. of Finance
College of Business

University of Central Florida
Orlando, FL 32816

Journal of Taxation
Warren, Gorham & Lamont
31 St. James Ave.
Boston, MA 02116
Phone: 800-950-1252

Journal of World Trade
P.O. Box 5134
1211 Geneva 11, Switzerland
Phone: 022-3103422
FAX: 022-3114592

Long Range Planning
Elsevier Science, Inc.
660 White Plains Rd.
Tarrytown, NY 10591-5153
Phone: 212-989-5800
914-524-9000
FAX: 914-333-2444

Management Accounting
Institute of Management
Accountants
10 Paragon Dr.
Montvale, NJ 07645-1760
Phone: 800-638-4427
201-573-9000
201-573-6269
FAX: 201-573-0639

Management Review
American Management
Association, Inc.
P.O. Box 408
Saranac Lake, NY 12983-0408
Phone: 800-644-2464
FAX: 212-903-8168

Management Today
Management Publications Ltd.
174 Hammersmith Road
London W671P, England
Phone: 0171-4134566

Managerial Auditing Journal
MCB University Press
60/62 Toller Lane
Bradford, West Yorkshire, England
BD89BY
Phone: 44-1274-777700

Mergers and Acquisitions
IDD Enterprises, L.P.
2 World Trade Center
18th Floor
New York, NY 10048
Phone: 212-432-0045
215-790-7000
FAX: 215-790-7005

Money
P.O. Box 30607
Tampa, FL 33630-0607
Phone: 800-633-9970

National Public Accountant
National Society of Public
Accountants
1010 N. Fairfax St.
Alexandria, VA 22314
Phone: 703-549-6400
FAX: 703-549-2984

National Tax Journal
National Tax Association-Tax
Institute of America
5310 Main St.
Columbus, OH 43213
Phone: 614-864-1221

Newsweek
251 West 57th Street
New York, NY 10019
Phone: 212-445-6000
800-631-1040

PC Magazine
Ziff-Davis Publishing Co.
P.O. Box 53131
Boulder, CO 80322-3131
Phone: 303-447-9330
800-289-0429

PC Week
Customer Service Department
P.O. Box 1770
Riverton, NJ 08077-7370
Phone: 609-461-2100

Pension Management
Argus Integrated Media
6151 Powers Ferry Road NW
Atlanta, GA 30339
Phone: 770-955-2500
FAX: 770-955-0400

Pensions & Investments
Circulation Dept.
965 E. Jefferson
Detroit, MI 48207
Phone: 212-210-0100
FAX: 212-210-0799

Planning Review
The Planning Forum
5500 College Corner Pike
P.O. Box 70
Oxford, OH 45056
Phone: 513-523-4185
FAX: 513-523-7539

Practical Accountant
Faulkner & Gray
11 Penn Plaza
New York, NY 10001
Phone: 800-535-8403
212-967-7060
FAX: 212-629-7885

Price Waterhouse Review
Price Waterhouse
1251 Avenue of the Americas
New York, NY 10020

Production and Inventory Management Journal
American Production and
Inventory Control Society
500 W. Annandale Rd.
Falls Church, VA 22046-4274
Phone: 800-444-2742
FAX: 703-237-1071

Public Finance
3 Robert Street
London, WCZN 6B4
Phone: 0171-895-8823
FAX: 0171-895-8825

Quarterly Review of Economics and Finance
JAI Press
P.O. Box 1678
55 Old Post Rd., No. 2
Greenwich, CT 06836-1678
Phone: 203-661-7602
FAX: 203-661-0792

Review of Financial Economics
JAI Press
55 Old Post Rd., No. 2
Greenwich, CT 06836-1678
Phone: 504-286-6240
FAX: 504-286-6094

Risk Management
Risk Management Society
Publishing
655 Third Ave.
New York, NY 10017
Phone: 212-286-9292
FAX: 212-986-9716

Sales & Marketing Management
335 Park Avenue South
New York, NY 10010
Phone: 212-592-6200

Simulation & Gaming
Sage Publications, Inc.
2455 Teller Rd.
Newbury Park, CA 91320
Phone: 805-499-0721

Sloan Management Review
P.O. Box 55255
Boulder, CO 80322-5255
Phone: 800-876-5764
617-253-7170
FAX: 617-253-5584

Small Business Controller
Warren, Gorham & Lamont
31 St. James Avenue
Boston, MA 02116
Phone: 800-950-1252
212-971-5000
FAX: 212-971-5113

Strategic Management Journal
John Wiley & Sons, Ltd.
Baffins Lane
Chichester, Sussex PO 19IUD,
England
Phone: 212-850-6000

Survey of Current Business
Superintendent of Documents
U.S. Government Printing Office
Washington, DC 20402
Phone: 202-606-9900
202-512-1800
FAX: 202-512-2250

Tax Advisor
AICPA
Harborside Financial Center
201 Plaza III
Jersey City, NJ 07311-3881
Phone: 800-862-4272
FAX: 201-938-3329

Tax Executive
Tax Executive Institute
1001 Pennsylvania Ave.
Washington, DC 20004-2505
Phone: 202-638-5601
FAX: 202-638-5607

Taxation for Accountants
Warren, Gorham & Lamont, Inc.
31 St. James Ave.
Boston, MA 02116
Phone: 800-950-1252

Taxes
Commerce Clearing House, Inc.
4025 W. Peterson Ave.
Chicago, IL 60646
Phone: 312-583-8500

World Economy
Blackwell Publishers
238 Main St.
Cambridge, MA 02142
Phone: 800-216-2522
617-547-7110

World
KPMG Peat Marwick
767 Fifth Ave.
New York, NY 10153

Worth
575 Lexington Avenue
New York, NY 10022
Phone: 212-751-4550

INDEX

Index   **485**

National Bureau of Economic
Research, **S325**
National capital markets, 901–2
National Council on Compensation
Insurance (NCCI) Inc., **S172**
National Environmental Policy Act
(NEPA), **S64**
National Institute of Standards and
Technology (NIST), **S23, S25**
National Labor Act, 704
National money markets, 901–2
National Public Accountant, **S467**
National Society of Public
Accountants, **S455**
National Tax Association, **S455**
National Tax Journal, **S467**
National Technical Information
Service, **S456**
Net operating loss deductions,
909
Net present value (NPV), 422–26
Net Prophet, **S267**
Network administrator, EDP
department, 34
Network security, **S20–S22**
Net working capital per share, 935
Neural networks, **S37–S39,** *See*
Artificial intelligence
New York Society of Security
Analysts (NYSSA), **S455**
New York Stock Exchange (NYSE),
reporting to, 31
Newsweek, **S467**
90-day Treasury bills, 719
Noise Control Act, **S65**
Noncontrollable costs, 216
Nondiscretionary projects, 432
Nonmanufacturing costs, 211
Nonprofit organizations:
  and capital budgeting, 437
  and cost-volume-revenue analysis,
    277–78
Nonstatistical sampling, 632–33
Nonvested stock, **S91**
Non-volume-related overhead costs,
  489–90
Normal capacity, 232
Normal selling price, accepting
  orders below, 289–90
North American Securities
  Administrators Association,
  S380
North American Simulation and
  Gaming Association, **S455**
Notes receivable, sample audit pro-
  gram for, 607–9

Occupational Safety and Health Act
  (OSHA), 703, **S46–S47**
Office of Business and Industrial
  Analysis, **S456**
Office of Business Liaison, **S456**
Office of Financial Management
  Service, **S457**
Office of the Chief Economist,
  S457

Office of the General Counsel, **S457**
Office of the Secretary of the
  Treasury, **S457**
One World, **S265**
Operating budget, 315–16
Operating exposure, 892, 896
Operating lease, 162
Operating leverage, 282
Operating method, leases, 165
Operating section, Statement of
  Cash Flows, 120–21
Operating (service) leases, 818
Operational auditing, 550
Operations, management analysis of,
  S301–S309
Opinion/recommendations, internal
  audit reports, 549
Opportunity costs, 217
Optimal budget, and linear pro-
  gramming, 512–17
Optimism Index, 717
Option contract, **S42**
Options Clearing Corporation
  (OCC), **S343**
Option Pro, **S359**
An Option Valuator/ An Option
  Writer, **S359**
Options, 775, **S340–S72,** *See*
  Financial derivatives
  analysis, **S359**
  premium, **S344**
  strategies, **S354–S58**
  writing, **S353**
Options and Arbitrage Software
  Package, **S359**
Optionvue IV, **S357, S359**
Option writing, **S353**
Options Clearing Corp. (OCC),
  S343
Oracle, **S265**
Ordinary repairs, fixed assets, 90
Organization costs, **S80–S81**
  amortization of, 909
Orion, **S262**
Oros EIS with Power Play, **S267**
Oros 3.0, **S267**
Out-of-pocket costs, 217
Out-of-the-money options, **S348–S49**
Outsourcing, **S173–S78**
Output controls, 36
Overhead costing, 485–90
  multiple-product situation, 486–90
    costing accuracy problems,
      488–89
    departmental rates, 488
    failure of volume-related cost
      drivers, 489–90
    plant-wide overhead rate,
      487–88
  single-product situation, 485–86
Overhead variances, 368–77
  fixed, 370–71
  total overhead, variances for,
    371–77
  variable, 369–70
Overseas Private Investment
  Corporation (OPIC), 901

Overstated liabilities, in balance
  sheet analysis, 654

Pabblo and Paccasso, **S170**
Pacioli 2000, **S260**
Par value method, treasury stock,
  109
Parent-subsidiary controlled group,
  S389–S90
Parol Evidence Rule, **S44**
Passwords, 36
  security, **S19–S20**
Patents, **S87**
Payback:
  advantages of, 419–20
  deficiencies of, 420
Payback period, 419–20
Payback reciprocal, 421
Pay-in-kind (PIK) preferred stock,
  194
Payroll modules, accounting soft-
  ware, 194
Payroll taxes, 923–28, **S425–S49**
  common paymaster provision,
    924–25
  disability insurance, 926–27
  electronic federal tax payment
    system, **S435**
  federal withholding taxes, 925,
    S425–S27
  independent contractor status, 924
  social security and Medicare taxes,
    923, **S425**
  tax deposits, 925–26, **S428–S34**
  unemployment insurance, 927–28,
    S435–S49
  worker's compensation, 926–27
PC Magazine, **S467**
PC Solutions, **S170**
PC Week, **S467**
Pecuniary externalities, **S334–S35**
Pedigree Software, **S264**
Pension Management, **S467**
Pension plans, 171–79, **S103–S106**
  annuity contracts, **S105–S106**
  curtailment in, 178
  defined benefit pension plan, 172,
    173–79, **S103–S104**
  disclosures, 177
  employees with more than one
    defined benefit plan,
    S103–S104
  minimum pension liability,
    175–77
  multiemployer, **S104**
  multiple employer, **S104–S105**
  trustee reporting for, 178–79
  defined contribution pension plan,
    172, 173
  Employee Retirement Income
    Security Act (ERISA), **S106**
  post-employment benefits,
    employer's accounting for,
    S106
  settlement in, 177–78
  termination in, 178

Index

Index   **491**